Lecture Notes in Artificial

Edited by J. G. Carbonell and J. Siekmann

Subseries of Lecture Notes in Computer Science

Danny Weyns   H. Van Dyke Parunak
Fabien Michel (Eds.)

Environments for Multi-Agent Systems III

Third International Workshop, E4MAS 2006
Hakodate, Japan, May 8, 2006
Selected Revised and Invited Papers

 Springer

Series Editors

Jaime G. Carbonell, Carnegie Mellon University, Pittsburgh, PA, USA
Jörg Siekmann, University of Saarland, Saarbrücken, Germany

Volume Editors

Danny Weyns
Katholieke Universiteit Leuven, Belgium
E-mail: Danny.Weyns@cs.kuleuven.be

H. Van Dyke Parunak
New Vectors LLC, Ann Arbor, USA
E-mail: Van.Parunak@newvectors.net

Fabien Michel
Université de Reims, France
E-mail: Fabien.Michel@univ-reims.fr

Library of Congress Control Number: 2007921671

CR Subject Classification (1998): I.2.11, I.2, C.2.4

LNCS Sublibrary: SL 7 – Artificial Intelligence

ISSN	0302-9743
ISBN-10	3-540-71102-3 Springer Berlin Heidelberg New York
ISBN-13	978-3-540-71102-5 Springer Berlin Heidelberg New York

Springer is a part of Springer Science+Business Media

springer.com

© Springer-Verlag Berlin Heidelberg 2007
Printed in Germany

Typesetting: Camera-ready by author, data conversion by Scientific Publishing Services, Chennai, India
Printed on acid-free paper   SPIN: 12025183   06/3142   5 4 3 2 1 0

Preface

Only three years have passed since the first volume on environment for multi-agent systems was published. In the meantime, the notion of environment has become an active subject of research in multiagent systems and has stimulated researchers of various types of multiagent systems to exploit new opportunities for their agent systems.

In the preface of the first volume, Parunak noted that the environment has been considered as a first-class member in the artificial life (AL) from the early days of this research line. During the three last years, an increasing number of multiagent system studies have successfully applied bio-inspired approaches where the environment plays a crucial role. Several papers in this volume generalize this idea to different kinds of agent systems, making it a multiagent system design principle: "taking away complexity from the agents' internal structure and putting it in the environment enables designers to manage complexity better." This principle has influenced designers of artificial societies that apply norms to regulate agents' interactions up to engineers that have developed real-world traffic control applications.

Interestingly, the environment is also the key aspect of innovative approaches that fruitfully reconcile the cognitive and the reactive point of views by having both kinds of agents cooperating through a *delegate multiagent system* software architecture. Also very interesting is the fact that classical environmental processes such as diffusion and evaporation are extended to process high-level information, introducing the notion of *cognitive stigmergy*.

At the first E4MAS workshop in New York 2004, participating researchers were mainly interested in comparing and sharing their visions on this both fundamental but still fuzzy concept of environment. Despite the fact that there was already a general agreement that environments were essential for multiagent systems, the very question "what is the very nature of an environment?" has not yet been fully answered.

The papers in this volume clearly illustrate how the environment can actively support the mediation of interactions among agents. The environment can be provided with different mechanisms and processes that enable agents to interact in original and unexpected ways, opening interesting research perspectives for the multiagent systems community. So, even if there still remain some differences on how researchers translate the concept of environment within their own agency perspective, the benefits of considering the environment as a concrete and active entity is becoming more and more obvious. The E4MAS series volumes are witnesses of this general awareness.

Including both selected and revised papers from the third E4MAS workshop as well as invited papers, this volume shows the use of the environment at different stages of the life cycle of multiagent systems. Without doubt, we are only at the beginning of exploiting the true potential that lies in the dynamics of the environment for multiagent systems. We hope that this volume is a stimulus for researchers to further explore this fascinating research line further.

Acknowledgements. We are grateful to the PC members for their critical review work. We also thank Alexander Helleboogh, Kurt Schelfthout, Tom De Wolf, Koen Mertens, Nelis Boucké, Robrecht Haesevoets, Bart Van Eylen and Tom Holvoet for their efforts for E4MAS. A special word of thanks to Tom De Wolf for managing the Web site.

December 2006   Fabien Michel

Organization

E4MAS 2006 was organized in conjunction with the Fifth International Joint Conference on Autonomous Agents and Multi-Agent Systems (AAMAS 2006), Hakodate, Japan, May 8, 2006.

Program Co-chairs

Danny Weyns — Katholieke Universiteit Leuven, Belgium
H. Van Dyke Parunak — NewVectors LLC, Ann Arbor, USA
Fabien Michel — Laboratoire d'Etudes et de Recherches Informatiques Reims, France

Program Committee

Rafael Bordini — University of Durham, UK
Sven Brueckner — NewVectors, LLC, Ann Arbor, USA
Yves Demazeau — Laboratoire Leibniz, IMAG, Grenoble, France
Marco Dorigo — Université Libre de Bruxelles, Belgium
Alexis Drogoul — Laboratoire d'Informatique de Paris 6, France
Jacques Ferber — Université de Montpellier II, LIRMM, France
Alexander Helleboogh — Katholieke Universiteit Leuven, Belgium
Tom Holvoet — Katholieke Universiteit Leuven, Belgium
Franziska Klügl — University of Würzburg, Germany
Marco Mamei — University of Modena and Reggio Emilia, Italy
Fabien Michel — Laboratoire d'Etudes et de Recherches Informatiques Reims, France
James Odell — Intelligent Automation, Inc., Ann Arbor, USA
Andrea Omicini — Università di Bologna, Italy
H. Van Dyke Parunak — NewVectors, LLC, Ann Arbor, USA
John Sauter — NewVectors, LLC, Ann Arbor, USA
Olivier Simonin — Université de Technologie de Belfort-Montbéliard, France
Karl Tuyls — Universiteit Maastricht, The Netherlands
Paul Valckenaers — Katholieke Universiteit Leuven, Belgium
Franco Zambonelli — University of Modena and Reggio Emilia, Italy

Website

http://www.cs.kuleuven.ac.be/~distrinet/events/e4mas/2006/

Table of Contents

Applications

A Reference Architecture for Situated Multiagent Systems

Danny Weyns and Tom Holvoet

DistriNet, Katholieke Universiteit Leuven
Celestijnenlaan 200 A, B-3001 Leuven, Belgium
{danny.weyns, tom.holvoet}@cs.kuleuven.be

Abstract. A reference architecture integrates a set of architectural patterns that have proven their value for a family of applications. Such family of applications is characterized by specific functionality and quality requirements. A reference architecture provides a blueprint for developing software architectures for applications that share that common base. As such, a reference architecture provides a means for large-scale reuse of architectural design.

This paper gives an overview of a reference architecture for situated multiagent systems we have developed in our research. We discuss various architectural views of the reference architecture. Per view, we zoom in on the main view packets, each of them containing a bundle of information of a part of the reference architecture. For each view packet we explain the rationale for the design choices that were made and we give built-in mechanisms that describe how the view packet can be exercised to build a concrete software architecture. We illustrate the use of the reference architecture with an excerpt of the software architecture of an industrial AGV transportation system.

1 Introduction

A reference architecture embodies a set of architectural best practices gathered from the design and development of a family of applications with similar characteristics and system requirements [28,6]. A reference architecture provides an asset base architects can draw from when developing software architectures for new systems that share the common base of the reference architecture. Applying the reference architecture to develop new software architectures will yield valuable input that can be used to update and refine the reference architecture. As such, a reference architecture provides a means for large-scale reuse of architectural design.

In this paper, we give an overview of the reference architecture for situated multiagent systems we have developed in our research. We start with an introductory section that explains the reference architecture rationale and sketches the background of the architecture. Next, we present the reference architecture. The architecture documentation consists of three views that describe the reference architecture from different perspectives. To illustrate the use of the reference

D. Weyns, H.V.D. Parunak, and F. Michel (Eds.): E4MAS 2006, LNAI 4389, pp. 1–40, 2007.
© Springer-Verlag Berlin Heidelberg 2007

architecture, we give an excerpt of the software architecture of an industrial AGV transportation system in which we have used the reference architecture for architectural design. The paper concludes with an overview of related work and conclusions.

2 Rationale and Background

In this section, we explain the reference architecture rationale. We summarize the main characteristics and requirements of the target application domain of the reference architecture and give a brief overview of the development process of the architecture. Finally, we explain how the reference architecture documentation is organized.

2.1 Reference Architecture Rationale

The general goal of the reference architecture is to support the architectural design of situated multiagent systems. Concrete motivations are:

- *Integration of mechanisms.* In our research, we have developed several advanced mechanisms of adaptivity for situated agents, including selective perception [48], advanced behavior-based action-selection mechanisms with roles and situated commitments [46,44], and protocol-based communication [47]. To build a concrete application these mechanisms have to work together. The reference architecture integrates the different mechanisms. It defines how the functionalities of the various mechanisms are allocated to software elements of agents and the environment and how these elements interact with one another.
- *Blueprint for architectural design.* The reference architecture generalizes common functions and structures from various experimental applications we have studied and built. This generalized architecture provides a reusable design artifact, it facilitates deriving new software architectures for systems that share the common base more reliably and cost effectively. On the one hand, the reference architecture defines constraints that incarnate the common base. On the other hand, the architecture defines variation mechanisms that provide the necessary variability to instantiate software architectures for new systems.
- *Reification of knowledge and expertise.* The reference architecture embodies the knowledge and expertise we have acquired during our research. It conscientiously documents the know-how obtained from this research. As such, the reference architecture offers a vehicle to study and learn the advanced perspective on situated multiagent systems we have developed.

2.2 Characteristics and Requirements of the Target Application Domain of the Reference Architecture

The reference architecture for situated multiagent systems supports the architectural design of a family of software systems with the following main characteristics and requirements:

- Stakeholders of the systems (users, project managers, architects, developers, maintenance engineers, etc.) have various—often conflicting—demands on the quality of the software. Important quality requirements are flexibility (adapt to variable operating conditions) and openness (cope with parts that come and go during execution).
- The software systems are subject to highly dynamic and changing operating conditions, such as dynamically changing workloads and variations in availability of resources and services. An important requirement of the software systems is to manage the dynamic and changing operating conditions autonomously.
- Global control is hard to achieve. Activity in the systems is inherently localized, i.e. global access to resources is difficult to achieve or even infeasible. The software systems are required to deal with the inherent locality of activity.

Example domains are mobile and ad-hoc networks, sensor networks, automated transportation and traffic control systems, and manufacturing control.

2.3   Development Process of the Reference Architecture

The reference architecture for situated multiagent systems is the result of an iterative research process of exploration and validation. During our research, we have studied and built various experimental applications that share the above specified characteristics in different degrees. We extensively used the Packet–World as a study case for investigation and experimentation. [40,42] investigate agents' actions in the Packet–World. [39] studies various forms of stigmergic coordination. [44] focuses on the adaptation of agent behavior over time. [32] yields valuable insights on the modelling of state of agents and the environment, selective perception, and protocol–based communication. Another application we have used in our research is a prototypical peer-to-peer file sharing system [48,20]. This application applies a pheromone–based approach for the coordination of agents that move around in a dynamic network searching for files. [38,8,31] study a field-based approach for task assignment to automatic guided vehicles that have to operate in a dynamic warehouse environment. Finally, [46] studies several experimental robotic applications. The particular focus of these robotic applications is on the integration of roles and situated commitments in behavior–based action selection mechanisms.

Besides these experimental applications, the development of the reference architecture is considerably based on experiences with an industrial logistic transportation system for warehouses [45,43,9].

In the course of building the various applications, we derived common functions and structures that provided architectural building blocks for the reference architecture. The reference architecture integrates the different agent and environment functionalities and maps these functionalities onto software elements and relationships between the elements. The software elements make up a system decomposition that cooperatively implement the functionalities. This system decomposition—the reference architecture—provides a blueprint for instantiating target systems that share the common base of the reference architecture.

2.4   Organization of the Reference Architecture Documentation

The architecture documentation describes the various architectural views of the reference architecture [13]. The documentation includes a module decomposition view and two component and connector views: shared data and communicating processes. Each view is organized as a set of view packets. A view packet is a small, relatively self-contained bundle of information of the reference architecture, or a part of the architecture. The documentation of a view starts with a brief explanation of the goal of the view and a general description of the view elements and relationships between the elements. Then the view packets of the view are presented. Each view packet consists of a primary presentation and additional supporting information. The primary presentation shows the elements and their relationships in the view packet. For the module decomposition view, the primary presentations are textual in the form of tables. The primary presentations of other views are graphical with a legend that explain the meaning of the symbols.

The supporting information explains the architectural elements in the view packet. Each view packet gives a description of the architectural elements with their specific properties. In addition to the explanation of the architectural elements, the supporting information describes variation mechanisms for the view packet and explains the architecture rationale of the view packet. Variation mechanisms describe how the view packet can be applied to build a software architecture for a concrete system. The architecture rationale explains the motivation for the design choices that were made for the view packet.

The documentation of the reference architecture presented in this paper is descriptive. Concepts and mechanisms are introduced briefly and illustrated with examples. The interested reader finds elaborated explanations in the added references. For a detailed formal specification of the various architectural elements, we refer to [37].

3   Module Decomposition View

The module decomposition view shows how the situated multiagent system is decomposed into manageable software units. The elements of the module decomposition view are *modules*. A module is an implementation unit of software that provides a coherent unit of functionality. The relationship between the modules is *is–part–of* that defines a part/whole relationship between a submodule and the aggregate module. Modules are recursively refined conveying more details in each decomposition step.

The basic criteria for module decomposition is the achievement of quality attributes. For example, changeable parts of a system are encapsulated in separate modules, supporting modifiability. Another example is the separation of functionality of a system that has higher performance requirements from other functionality. Such a decomposition allows to apply different tactics to achieve the required performance throughout the various parts of the system. However, other criteria can be drivers for a decomposition of modules as well. For example, in the reference architecture, a distinction is made between common modules that are used in all systems derived from the reference architecture, and variable modules that differ across systems. This decomposition results in a clear organization of the architecture, supporting efficient design and implementation of systems with the reference architecture.

Modules in the module decomposition view include a description of the interfaces of the modules that document how the modules are used in combination with other modules. The interface descriptions distinguish between provided and required interfaces. A provided interface specifies what functionality a module offers to other modules. A required interface specifies what functionality a module needs from other modules; it defines constrains of a module in terms of the services a module requires to provide its functionality.

The reference architecture provides three view packets of the module decomposition view. We start with the top-level decomposition of the situated multiagent system. Next, we show the primary decomposition of an agent. We conclude with the primary decomposition of the application environment.

3.1 Module Decomposition View Packet 1: Situated Multiagent System

Primary Presentation

System	Subsystem
Situated Multiagent System	Agent
	Application Environment

Elements and their Properties. A Situated Multiagent System is decomposed in two subsystems: Agent and Application Environment. We explain the functionalities of both modules in turn.

Agent is an autonomous problem solving entity in the system. An agent encapsulates its state and controls its behavior. The responsibility of an agent is to achieve its design objectives, i.e. to realize the application specific goals it is assigned. Agents are situated in an environment which they can perceive and in which they can act and interact with one another. Agents are able to adapt their behavior according to the changing circumstances in the environment. A situated agent is a cooperative entity. The overall application goals result from interaction among agents, rather than from sophisticated capabilities of individual agents.

A concrete multiagent system application typically consists of agents of different agent types. Agents of different agent types typically have different capabilities and are assigned different application goals.

The **Application Environment** is the part of the environment that has to be designed for a concrete multiagent system application. The application environment enables agents to share information and to coordinate their behavior. The core responsibilities of the application environment are:

- To provide access to external entities and resources.
- To enable agents to perceive and manipulate their neighborhood, and to interact with one another.
- To mediate the activities of agents. As a mediator, the environment not only enables perception, action and interaction, it also constrains them.

The application environment provides functionality to agents on top of the *deployment context*. The deployment context consists of the given hardware and software and external resources such as sensors and actuators, a printer, a network, a database, a web service, etc.

As an illustration, a peer-to-peer file sharing system is deployed on top of a deployment context that consists of a network of nodes with files and possibly other resources. The application environment enables agents to access the external resources, shielding low-level details. Additionally, the application environment may provide a coordination infrastructure that enables agents to coordinate their behavior. E.g., the application environment of a peer-to-peer file share system can offer a pheromone infrastructure to agents that they can use to dynamically form paths to locations of interest.

Thus, we consider the *environment* as consisting of two parts, the deployment context and the application environment. The internal structure of the deployment context is not considered in the reference architecture. For a distributed application, the deployment context consists of multiple processors deployed on different nodes that are connected through a network. Each node provides an application environment to the agents located at that node. Depending on the specific application requirements, different application environment types may be provided. For some applications, the same type of application environment subsystem is instantiated on each node. For other applications, specific types are instantiated on different nodes, e.g., when different types of agents are deployed on different nodes.

Interface Descriptions. Figure 1 gives an overview of the interfaces of the agent subsystem and the application environment subsystem.

The `Sense` interface enables an agent to sense the environment resulting in a representation, `Send` enables an agent to send messages to other agents, and `Influence` enables an agent to invoke influences in the environment. Influences are attempts of agents to modify the state of affairs in the environment. These interfaces are provided by the application environment.

The application environment requires the interface `Receive` to deliver messages to agents. Furthermore, the application environment requires the interface

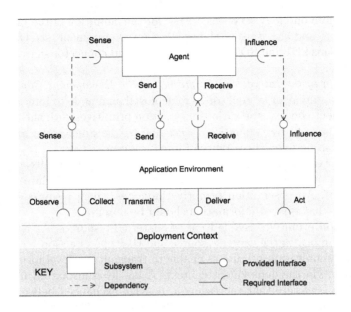

Fig. 1. Interfaces of agent, application environment, and deployment context

Observe from the deployment context to observe particular resources, Transmit to send messages to agents located on other nodes, and Act to modify the state of external resources (based on influences invoked by agents).

Finally, the deployment context requires the interface Collect to enable the collection of state from the application environment (requested by application environment instances in a distributed setting), and the interface Deliver to deliver the incoming messages to the agents.

Variation Mechanisms. There are four variation mechanisms for this view packet:

M1 *Definition of Agent Types.* Depending on the specific application requirements different agent types may be required. Agent types are characterized
by the capabilities of the agents reflected in different internal structures.
Variations on agent types are discussed in subsequent view packets and
views, see sections 3.2, 4.1, and 5.

M2 *Definition of Application Environment Types.* In a distributed setting, different application environment types may be required that are deployed on
different nodes. Application environment types differ in the functionality
they provide to the agents reflected in different internal structures. Variations in application environment types are discussed in subsequent view
packets and views, see sections 3.3, 4.2, and 5.

M3 *Definition of the Domain Ontology.* The ontology defines the terminology
for the application domain. Defining an ontology includes the specification
of the various domain concepts and the relationships between the concepts.

The domain ontology serves as a basis for the definition of the knowledge of the agents and the state of the application environment, see the variation mechanisms SD1 and SD2 of the component and connector shared data view in section 4.

M4 *Definition of the Interaction Primitives of the Deployment Context.* To enable the multiagent system software deployed on a node to interact with the deployment context, the various interaction primitives with the deployment context have to be concretized according to the application at hand. We distinguish between three types of interaction primitives.

(1) Observation primitives enable the multiagent system software deployed on a node to observe external resources and collect data from other nodes. An observation primitive indicates which resource is observed and what type of information should be observed.

(2) Action primitives enable to access external resources. An action primitive indicates the target resource and the type of action.

(3) Communication primitives enable to transmit low-level formatted messages via the deployment context. A low-level formatted message is a data structure that represents a message exchanged between a sender and one or more addressees and that is transmitted via the deployment context.

Design Rationale. The main principles that underly the decomposition of a situated multiagent system are:

- *Decentralized control.* In a situated multiagent system, control is divided among the agents situated in the application environment. Decentralized control is essential to cope with the inherent locality of activity, which is a characteristic of the target applications of the reference architecture, see section 2.2.

- *Self-management.* In a situated multiagent system self-management is essentially based on the ability of agents to adapt their behavior. Self-management enables a system to manage the dynamic and changing operating conditions autonomously, which is an important requirement of the target applications of the reference architecture, see section 2.2.

However, the decentralized architecture of a situated multiagent system implies a number of tradeoffs and limitations.

- Decentralized control typically requires more communication. The performance of the system may be affected by the communication links between agents.

- There is a trade-off between the performance of the system and its flexibility to handle disturbances. A system that is designed to cope with many disturbances generally needs redundancy, usually to the detriment of performance, and vice versa.

- Agents' decision making is based on local information only, which may lead to suboptimal system behavior.

These tradeoffs and limitations should be kept in mind throughout the design and development of a situated multiagent system. Special attention should be payed to communication which could impose a major bottleneck.

Concerns not Covered. We touch on a number of other concerns that are not covered by the reference architecture.

Crosscutting Concerns. Concerns such as security, monitoring, and logging usually crosscut several architecture modules. Crosscutting concerns in multiagent systems are hardly explored and are open research problems. An example of early research in this direction is [17]. That work applies an aspect-oriented software engineering approach, aiming to integrate crosscutting concerns in an application in a non-invasive manner. As most current research on aspect-oriented software development, the approach of [17] is mainly directed at the identification and specification of aspects at the programming level. Recently, the relationship between aspects and software architecture became subject of active research, see e.g. [4,35,14].

Human-Software Interaction. The reference architecture does not explicitly handle human-software interaction. Depending on the application domain, the role of humans in multiagent systems can be very diverse. In some applications humans can play the role of agents and interact directly—or via an intermediate wrapper—with the application environment. In other applications, humans can be part of the deployment context with which the multiagent system application interacts.

3.2   Module Decomposition View Packet 2: Agent

Primary Presentation

Subsystem	Module
Agent	Perception
	Decision Making
	Communication

Elements of the View. The Agent subsystem is decomposed in three modules: Perception, Decision Making and Communication. We discuss the responsibilities of each module in turn.

Perception is responsible for collecting runtime information from the environment. The perception module supports selective perception [48]. Selective perception enables an agent to direct its perception according to its current tasks. To direct its perception agents select a set of *foci* and *filters*. Foci allow the agent to sense the environment only for specific types of information. Sensing results in a *representation* of the sensed environment. A representation is a data structure that represents elements or resources in the environment. The perception module maps this representation to a *percept*, i.e. a description of the sensed environment in a form of data elements that can be used to update the agent's current knowledge. The selected set of filters further reduces the percept according to the criteria specified by the filters. While a focus enables an agent to observe the environment for a particular type of information, a filter enables the agent to direct its attention within the sensed information.

Decision Making is responsible for action selection. The action model of the reference architecture is based on the influence–reaction model introduced in [15]. This action model distinguishes between influences that are produced by agents and are attempts to modify the course of events in the environment, and reactions, which result in state changes in the environment. The responsibility of the decision making module is to select influences to realize the agent's tasks, and to invoke the influences in the environment [41].

To enable situated agents to set up collaborations, behavior-based action selection mechanisms are extended with the notions of *role* and *situated commitment* [46,33,32,47]. A role represents a coherent part of an agent's functionality in the context of an organization. A situated commitment is an engagement of an agent to give preference to the actions of a particular role in the commitment. Agents typically commit relative to one another in a collaboration, but an agent can also commit to itself, e.g. when a vital task must be completed. Roles and commitments have a well-known *name* that is part of the domain ontology and that is shared among the agents in the system. Sharing these names enable agents to set up collaborations via message exchange. We explain the coordination among decision making and communication in the design rationale of this view packet.

Communication is responsible for communicative interactions with other agents. Message exchange enables agents to share information and to set up collaborations. The communication module processes incoming messages, and produces outgoing messages according to well-defined communication protocols [47]. A communication protocol specifies a set of possible sequences of messages. We use the notion of a *conversation* to refer to an ongoing communicative interaction. A conversation is initiated by the initial message of a communication protocol. At each stage in the conversation there is a limited set of possible messages that can be exchanged. Terminal states determine when the conversation comes to an end.

The information exchanged via a message is encoded according to a shared *communication language*. The communication language defines the format of the messages, i.e. the subsequent fields the message is composed of. A message includes a field with a unique identifier of the ongoing conversation to which the message belong, fields with the identity of the sender and the identities of the addressees of the message, a field with the performative [5] of the message, and a field with the content of the message. Communicative interactions among agents are based on an *ontology* that defines a shared vocabulary of words that agents use in messages. The ontology enables agents to refer unambiguously to concepts and relationships between concepts in the domain when exchanging messages. The ontology used for communication is typically a part of the integral ontology of the application domain, see section 3.1.

Interface Descriptions. The interface descriptions specify how the modules of an agent are used with one another, see Fig. 2. The interfacing with the data repositories is discussed in section 4.1.

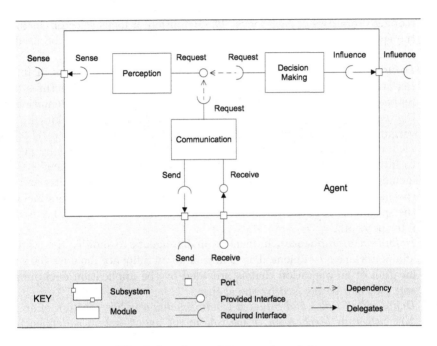

Fig. 2. Interfaces of the agent modules

The provided `Request` interface of the perception module enables decision making and communication to request a perception of the environment. To sense the environment according to their current needs, decision making and communication pass on a focus and filter selector to the perception module. Such a selector specifies a set of foci and filters that the perception module uses to sense the environment selectively [48].

The provided interface of agent, `Receive`, delegates for processing incoming messages to the provided `Receive` interface of the communication module. The ports decouple the internals of the agent subsystem from external elements.

The perception module's required `Sense` interface is delegated to the agent's required `Sense` interface. Sensing results in a representation of the environment according to the selected foci. Similarly, the `Send` interface of the communication module and the `Influence` interface of the decision making module are delegated to the required interfaces of agent with the same name.

Variation Mechanisms. This view packet provides the following variation mechanisms:

M5 *Omission of the Communication module.* For agents that do not communicate via message exchange, the communication module can be omitted. An example is an ant-like agent system in which the agents communicate via the manipulation of marks in the environment.

M6 *Definition of Foci and Focus Selectors.* Foci enable agents to sense the environment selectively. The definition of the foci in the agent system includes the specification of the kind of data each focus targets, together with the scoping properties of each focus. The definition of focus selectors includes the specification of the various combinations of foci that can be used to sense the environment.

M7 *Definition of Representations.* Sensing the environment results in representations. Representations are defined by means of data structures that represent elements and resources in the environment. The definition of representations must comply to the ontology defined for the domain, see variation mechanism M3 in section 3.1.

M8 *Definition of Filters and Filter Selectors.* Filters can be used by agents to filter perceived data. The definition of the filters in the agent system includes the specification of the kind of data each filter aims to filter and the specific properties of each filter. The definition of filter selectors includes the specification of the various combinations of filters that can be used to filter percepts.

M9 *Definition of Influences.* Influences enable agents to modify the state of affairs in the environment. The definition of an influence includes the specification of an operation that is provided by the application environment and that can be invoked by the agents.

M10 *Definition of Roles and Situated Commitments and Specification of an Action Selection Mechanism.* Each role in the agent system is defined by a unique name and a description of the semantics of the role in terms of the influences that can be selected in that role as well as the relationship of the role to other roles in the agent system. Each situated commitment in the agent system is defined by a unique name and a description of the semantics of the commitment in terms of roles defined in the agent system. Situated agents use a behavior-based action selection mechanism. Depending on the system requirements a particular action selection mechanism has to be defined. Roles and situated commitments have to be mapped onto the chosen action selection mechanism. [32] discusses an example where roles and situated commitments are mapped onto a free-flow decision making tree.

M11 *Definition of the Communication Language and the Ontology.* The communication language defines the format of messages. The definition of the communication language includes the specification of identities for agents and conversations, the specification of the various performatives of the language, and the format of the content of messages. The definition of the ontology for communication includes the specification of the vocabulary of words that represent the domain concepts used in messages and the relationships between the concepts. The ontology for communication is typically a part of the integral domain ontology, see variation mechanism M3 in section 3.1.

M12 *Definition of Communication Protocols.* The definition of a concrete communication protocol includes the specification of various steps of the protocol, i.e. the conditions and the effects for each step in the protocol [47]. An important aspect of this latter is the activation/deactivation of situated commitments. Statecharts [18,3] are one possible approach to specify a communication protocol.

Design Rationale. Each module in the decomposition encapsulates a particular functionality of the agent. By minimizing the overlap of functionality among modules, the architect can focus on one particular aspect of the agent's functionality. Allocating different functionalities of an agent to separate modules results in a clear design. It helps to accommodate change and to update one module without affecting the others, and it supports reusability.

Perception on Command. Selective perception enables an agent to focus its attention to the relevant aspects in the environment according to its current tasks. When selecting actions and communicating messages with other agents, decision making and communication typically request perceptions to update the agent's knowledge about the environment. By selecting an appropriate set of foci and filters, the agent directs its attention to the current aspects of its interest, and adapts it attention when the operating conditions change.

Coordination between Decision Making and Communication. The overall behavior of the agent is the result of the coordination of two modules: decision making and communication. Decision making is responsible for selecting suitable influences to act in the environment. Communication is responsible for the communicative interactions with other agents. Decision making and communication coordinate to complete the agent's tasks. For example, agents can send each other messages with requests for information that enable them to act more purposefully. Decision making and communication also coordinate during the progress of a collaboration. Collaborations are typically established via message exchange. Once a collaboration is achieved, the communication module activates a situated commitment. This commitment will affect the agent's decision making towards actions in the agent's role in the collaboration. This continues until the commitment is deactivated and the collaboration ends.

Ensuring that both decision making and communication behave in a coordinated way requires a careful design. On the other hand, the separation of functionality for coordination (via communication) from the functionality to perform actions to complete tasks has several advantages, including clear design, improved modifiability and reusability. Two particular advantages of separating communication from performing actions are: (1) it allows both functions to act in parallel, and (2) it allows both functions to act at a different pace. In many applications, sending messages and executing actions happen at different tempo. A typical example is robotics, but it applies to any application in which the time required for performing actions in the environment differs significantly from the time to communicate messages. Separation of communication from performing actions enables agents to reconsider the coordination of their behavior while they perform actions, improving adaptability and efficiency.

3.3 Module Decomposition View Packet 3: Application Environment

Primary Presentation

Subsystem	Module
Application Environment	Representation Generator
	Observation & Data Processing
	Interaction
	Low-Level Control
	Communication Mediation
	Communication Service
	Synchronization & Data Processing

Elements and their Properties. The Application Environment subsystem is decomposed in seven modules. We discuss the responsibilities of each of the modules in turn.

The **Representation Generator** provides the functionality to agents for perceiving the environment. When an agent senses the environment, the representation generator uses the current state of the application environment and possibly state collected from the deployment context to produce a representation for the agent. Agents' perception is subject to perception laws that provide a means to constrain perception. A perception law defines restrictions on what an agent can sense from the environment with a set of foci.

Observation & Data Processing provides the functionality to observe the deployment context and collect date from other nodes in a distributed setting. The observation & data processing module translates observation requests into observation primitives that can be used to collect the requested data from the deployment context. Data may be collected from external resources in the deployment context or from the application environment instances on other nodes in a distributed application. Rather than delivering raw data retrieved from the observation, the observation & data processing module can provide additional functions to pre-process data, examples are sorting and integration of observed data.

Interaction is responsible to deal with agents' influences in the environment. Agents' influences can be divided in two classes: influences that attempt to modify state of the application environment and influences that attempt to modify the state of resources of the deployment context. An example of the former is an agent that drops a digital pheromone in the environment. An example of the latter is an agent that writes data in an external data base. Agents' influences are subject to action laws. Action laws put restrictions on the influences invoked by the agents, representing domain specific constraints on agents' actions. For influences that relate to the application environment, the interaction module calculates the reaction of the influences resulting in an update of the state of the application environment. Influences related to the deployment context are passed to the Low-Level Control module.

Low-Level Control bridges the gap between influences used by agents and the corresponding action primitives of the deployment context. Low-level control converts the influences invoked by the agents into low-level action primitives in the deployment context. This decouples the interaction module from the details of the deployment context.

The **Communication Mediation** mediates the communicative interactions among agents. It is responsible for collecting messages; it provides the necessary infrastructure to buffer messages, and it delivers messages to the appropriate agents. Communication mediation regulates the exchange of messages between agents according a set of applicable communication laws. Communication laws impose constraints on the message stream or enforce domain–specific rules to the exchange of messages. Examples are a law that drops messages directed to agents outside the communication–range of the sender and a law that gives preferential treatment to high-priority messages. To actually transmit the messages, communication mediation makes use of the Communication Service module.

Communication Service provides that actual infrastructure to transmit messages. Communication service transfers message descriptions used by agents to communication primitives of the deployment context. For example, a FIPA ACL message [16] consists of a header with the message performative (inform, request, propose, etc.), followed by the subject of this performative, i.e. the content of the message that is described in a content language that is based on a shared ontology. Such message descriptions enable a designer to express the communicative interactions between agents independently of the applied communication technology. However, to actually transmit such messages, they have to be translated into low-level primitives of a communication infrastructure provided by the deployment context. Depending on the specific application requirements, the communication service may provide specific communication services to enable the exchange of messages in a distributed setting, such as white and yellow page services. An example infrastructure for distributed communication is Jade [7]. Specific middleware may provide support for communicative interaction in mobile and ad-hoc network environments, an example is discussed in [30].

Synchronization & Data Processing synchronizes state of the application environment with state of resources in the deployment context as well as state of the application environment on different nodes. State updates may relate to dynamics in the deployment context and dynamics of state in the application environment that happens independently of agents or the deployment context. An example of the former is the topology of a dynamic network which changes are reflected in a network abstraction maintained in the state of the application environment. An example of the latter is the evaporation of digital pheromones.

Middleware may provide support to collect data in a distributed setting. An example of middleware support for data collection in mobile and ad-hoc network environments is discussed in [29]. The synchronization & data processing module converts the resource data observed from the deployment context into a format that can be used to update the state of the application environment. Such conversion typically includes a processing or integration of collected resource data.

Interface Descriptions. The interface descriptions specify how the modules of the application environment are used with one another, see Fig. 3. The interfacing with data repositories of the application environment is discussed in section 4.2.

The Sense interface of the application environment delegates perception requests to the Sense interface of the perception generator. To observe resources in the deployment context, the perception generator's required interface CollectData depends on the CollectData interface that is provided by the observation & data processing module. The required interface Observe of observation & data processing is delegated to Observe interface of the application environment. The provided interface Collect of the application environment delegates requests for state of the application environment to the Collect interface of the observation & data processing module. The data that results from the observation of resources in the deployment context and possible state collected from other nodes is processed by the observation & data processing module and passed to the perception generator that generates a representation for the requesting agent.

For its functioning, the synchronization & data processing module requires the interface Observe. The processing of this interface is delegated to the Observe interface of the application environment. Synchronization & data processing provides the Collect interface to allow sharing of data among nodes in a distributed setting. This interface depends on the Collect interface provided by the application environment.

The Send interface of the application environment enables agents to send messages to other agents. The application environment delegates this interface to the

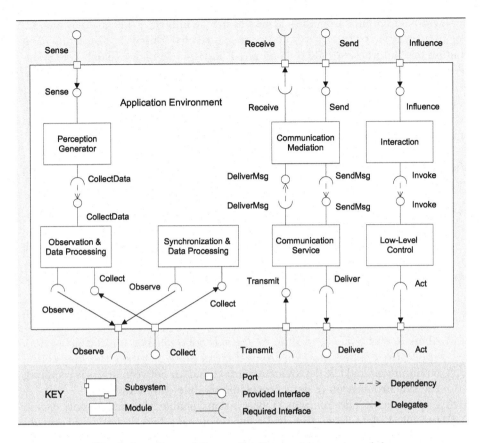

Fig. 3. Interfaces of the application environment modules

Send interface of communication mediation that mediates the communicative interaction. Communication mediation depends on the provided interface SendMSg of the communication service to convert messages into a low-level format and transmit them via the deployment context. For this latter, the communication service delegates to the Deliver interface of the application environment that depends on the message transfer infrastructure of the deployment context. The Transmit interface of the communication service delegates the transmission of messages to the Transmit interface of the application environment. The application environment provides the Deliver interface to deliver incoming messages. The Deliver interface of the application environment delegates incoming messages to the Deliver interface of the communication service. This latter converts the messages into an appropriate format for agents and depends on the DeliverMsg interface of communication mediation to deliver the messages. The Receive interface of communication mediation delegates the delivering of messages to the Receive interface of the application environment that passes on the messages to the addressees. The provided interface Influence of the application environment enables agents to invoke influences in the environment. For influences that attempt to modify the state of resources in the deployment context, the interaction module's required interface `Invoke` depends on the interface `Invoke` provided by the low-level control module. This latter interface provides the functionality to convert influences into low-level action primitives of the deployment context. The `Act` interface of the low-level control module delegates the actions to external resources to the `Act` interface of the application environment that invokes the actions in the deployment context.

Variation Mechanisms. This view packet provides the following variation mechanisms:

M13 *Omission of Observation, Synchronization, and Low-Level Control.* For applications that do not interact with external resources, the observation, synchronization, and low-level control modules can be omitted. For such applications, the environment is entirely virtual.

M14 *Omission of Communication Mediation and Communication Service.* For agent systems in which agents do not communicate via message exchange, the modules related to message exchange can be omitted, see also variation mechanism M5 in section 3.2.

M15 *Omission of Synchronization & Data Processing.* For multiagent system applications where no synchronization of state between the application environment and the deployment context and/or between nodes is required, the synchronization & data processing module can be omitted.

M16 *Definition of Observations.* Observations enable the multiagent system to collect data from the deployment context. The definition of an observation includes the specification of the kind of data to be observed in the deployment context together with additional properties of the observation.

The definition of the laws for perception, interaction, and communication is discussed in the shared data view, see section 4.2.

Design Rationale. The decomposition of the application environment can be considered in two dimensions: horizontally, i.e. a decomposition based on the distinct ways agents can access the environment; and vertically, i.e. a decomposition based on the distinction between the high-level interactions between agents and the application environment, and the low-level interactions between the application environment and the deployment context. The decomposition is schematically shown in Fig. 4.

The horizontal decomposition of the application environment consists of three columns that basically correspond to the various ways agents can access the environment: perception, communication, and action. An agent can *sense* the environment to obtain a *representation* of its vicinity, it can exchange *messages* with other agents, and an agent can invoke an *influence* in the environment attempting to modify the state of affairs in the environment.

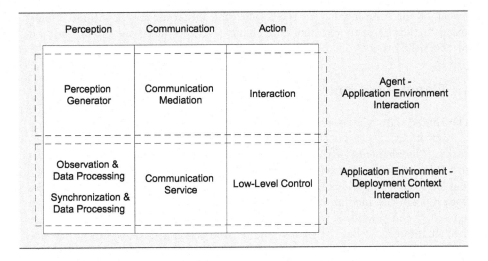

Fig. 4. Decomposition application environment

The vertical decomposition of the application environment consists of two rows. The top row deals with the access of agents to the application environment and includes representation generator, communication mediation, and interaction. The specification of activities and concepts in the top row is the same as those used by the agents. The top row defines the various laws that constrain the activity of agents in the environment. The bottom row deals with the interaction of the application environment with the deployment context and consists of observation and synchronization with data processing, communication service, and low-level control. The functionality related to the low-level interactions of the application environment includes: (1) support for the conversion of high-level activity related to agents into low-level interactions related to the deployment context and vice versa, and (2) support for pre-processing of resource data to transfer the data into a higher-level representation useful to agents, (3) interaction and synchronization among different nodes in a distributed setting.

The two-dimensional decomposition of the application environment yields a flexible modularization that can be tailored to a broad family of application domains. For instance, for applications that do not interact with an external deployment context, the bottom layer of the vertical decomposition can be omitted. For applications in which agents interact via marks in the environment but do not communicate via message exchange, the column in the horizontal decomposition that corresponds to message transfer (communication and communication service) can be omitted.

Each module of the application environment is located in a particular column and row and is assigned a particular functionality. Minimizing the overlap of functionality among modules, helps the architect to focus on one particular aspect of the functionality of the application environment. It supports reuse, and it further helps to accommodate change and to update one module without affecting the others.

4   Component and Connector Shared Data View

The shared data view shows how the situated multiagent system is structured as a set of data accessors that read and write data in various shared data repositories. The elements of the shared data view are *data accessors*, *repositories*, and the *connectors* between the two. Data accessors are runtime components that perform calculations that require data from one or more data repositories. Data repositories mediate the interactions among data accessors. A shared data repository can provide a trigger mechanism to signal data consumers of the arrival of interesting data. Besides reading and writing data, a repository may provide additional support, such as support for concurrency and persistency. The relationship of the shared data view is *attachment* that determines which data accessors are connected to which data repositories [13]. Data accessors are attached to connectors that are attached to a data store.

The reference architecture provides two view packets of the shared data view. First, we zoom in on the shared data view packet of agent, then we discuss the view packet of the application environment. The data accessors in this view are runtime instances of modules we have introduced in the module decomposition view. We use the same names for the runtime components and the modules (components' names are proceeded by a colon).

4.1   C & C Shared Data View Packet 1: Agent

Primary Presentation. The primary presentation is shown in Fig. 5.

Elements and their Properties. The data accessors of the Agent view packet are Perception, Decision Making and Communication. These data accessors are runtime instances of the corresponding modules described in section 3.2. The data accessors share the Current Knowledge repository.

The **Current Knowledge** repository contains data that is shared among the data accessors. Data stored in the current knowledge repository refers to state perceived in the environment, to state related to the agent's roles and situated commitments, and possibly other internal state that is shared among the data accessors. The communication and decision making components can read and write data from the repository. The perception component maintains the agent's knowledge of the surrounding environment. To update the agent's knowledge of the environment, both the communication and decision making components can trigger the perception component to sense the environment, see the module view of agent in section 3.2.

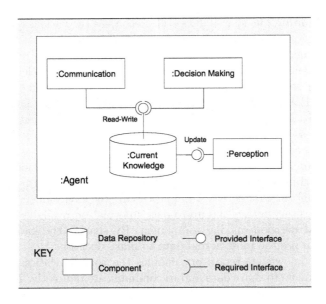

Fig. 5. Shared data view of an agent

Interface Descriptions. Fig. 5 shows the interconnections between the current knowledge repository and the internal components of the agent. These interconnections are called assembly connectors [3]. An assembly connector ties one component's provided interface with one or more components' required interfaces, and is drawn as a lollipop and socket symbols next to each other. Unless stated otherwise, we assume that the provided and required interfaces per assembly connector share the same name.

The current knowledge repository exposes two interfaces. The provided interface `Update` enables the perception component to update the agents knowledge according to the information derived from sensing the environment. The `Read-Write` interface enables the communication and decision making component to access and modify the agent's current knowledge.

Variation Mechanisms. This view packet provides four variation mechanisms:

SD1 *Definition of Current Knowledge.* Definition of current knowledge includes the definition of the state of the agent and the specification of the knowledge repository. The definition of the state of the agent has to comply to the ontology that is defined for the multiagent system application, see variation mechanism M3 in section 3.1. The specification of the knowledge repository includes various aspects such as the specification of a policy for concurrency, specification of possible event mechanisms to signal data consumers, support for persistency of data, and support for transactions. The concrete interpretation of these aspects depends on the specific requirements of the application at hand.

Design Rationale. The shared data style decouples the various components of an agent. Low coupling improves modifiability (changes in one element do not affect other elements or the changes have only a local effect) and reuse (elements are not dependent on too many other elements). Low coupled elements usually have clear and separate responsibilities, which makes the elements better to understand in isolation. Decoupled elements do not require detailed knowledge about the internal structures and operations of the other elements. Due to the concurrent access of the repository, the shared data style requires special efforts to synchronize data access.

Both communication and decision making delegate perception requests to the perception component. The perception component updates the agent knowledge with the information derived from perceiving the environment. The current knowledge repository makes the up-to-date information available for the communication and decision making component. By sharing the knowledge, both components can use the most actual data to make decisions.

The current knowledge repository enables the communication and decision making components to share data and to communicate indirectly. This approach allows both components to act in parallel and at a different pace, improving efficiency and adaptability (see also the design rationale of the module decomposition view of agent in section 3.2).

An alternative for the shared data style is a design where each component encapsulates its own state and provides interfaces through which other elements get access to particular information. However, since a lot of state is shared between the components of an agent (examples are the state that is derived from perceiving the environment and the state of situated commitments), such a design would increase dependencies among the components or imply the duplication of state in different components. Furthermore, such duplicated state must be kept synchronized among the components.

4.2   C & C Shared Data View Packet 2: Application Environment

Primary Presentation. The primary presentation is depicted in Fig. 6.

Elements and their Properties. The Application Environment consists of various data accessors that are attached to two repositories: State and Laws. The data accessors are runtime instances of the corresponding modules introduced in section 3.3.

The **State** repository contains data that is shared between the components of the application environment. Data stored in the state repository typically includes an abstraction of the deployment context together with additional state related to the application environment. Examples of state related to the deployment context are a representation of the local topology of a network, and data derived from a set of sensors. Examples of additional state are the representation of digital pheromones that are deployed on top of a network, and virtual marks situated on the map of the physical environment. The state repository may also

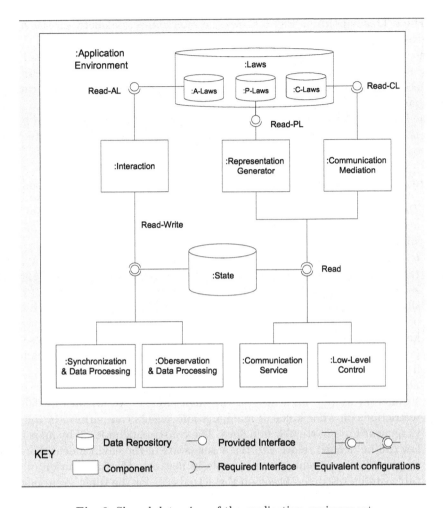

Fig. 6. Shared data view of the application environment

include agent-specific data, such as the agents' identities, the positions of the agents, and tags used for coordination purposes.

To perform their functionalities, interaction, synchronization & data processing, and observation & data processing can read and write state of the application environment. Representation generator, communication mediation and communication service, and low-level control only need to read state of the state repository to perform their functionalities.

The **Laws** repository contains the various laws that are defined for the application at hand. The laws repository is divided in three sub-repositories, one with the perception laws, one with the action laws, and one with communication laws. Each of these sub-repositories is attached to the component responsible for the corresponding functionality.

Interface Descriptions. Fig. 6 shows the interconnections between the state repositories and the internal components of the application environment.

The state repository exposes two interfaces. The provided interface `Read` enables attached components to read state of the repository. The `Read-Write` interface enables the attached components to access and modify the application environment's state.

The laws repository exposes three interfaces to read the various types of laws: `Read-AL`, `Read-PL`, and `Read-CL`. These provided interfaces enable the attached components to consult the respective types of laws.

Variation Mechanisms. This view packet provides one variation mechanism:

SD2 *Definition of State.* The definition of state includes the definition of the actual state of the application environment and the specification of the state repository. The state definition has to comply to the ontology that is defined for the application domain, see variation mechanism M3 in section 3.1. The specification of the state repository includes various aspects such as the specification of a policy for concurrency, specification of possible event mechanisms to signal data consumers, support for persistency of data, and support for transactions. As for the definition of the current knowledge repository of an agent, the concrete interpretation of these aspects depends on the specific requirements of the application domain at hand.

SD3 *Definition of Action Laws.* Action laws impose application specific constraints on agents' influences in the environment. An action law defines restrictions on what kinds of manipulations agents can perform in the environment for a particular influence. The constraints imposed by an action law can be defined relative to the actual state of the environment. For example, when an agent injects a tuple in network, the distribution of the tuple can be restricted based on the actual cost for the tuple to propagate along the various links of the network.

SD4 *Definition of Perception Laws.* Perception laws impose application specific constraints on agents' perception of the environment. Every perception law defines restrictions on what can be sensed from the current state of the environment for a particular focus. The constraints imposed by a perception law can be defined relative to the actual state of the environment. For example, restrictions on the observation of local nodes in a mobile network can be defined as a function of the actual distance to the nodes in the network.

SD5 *Definition of Communication Laws.* Communication laws impose application specific constraints on agents' communicative interactions in the environment. A communication law defines restrictions on the delivering of messages. The constraints imposed by a communication law can be defined relative to the actual state of the environment. For example, the delivering of a broadcast message in a network can be restricted to addressees that are located within a particular physical area around the sender.

Design Rationale. The motivations for applying the shared data style in the design of the application environment are similar as for the design of an agent. The shared data style results in low coupling between the various elements, improving modifiability and reuse.

The state repository enables the various components of the application environment to share state and to communicate indirectly. This avoids duplication of data and allows different components to act in parallel.

The laws repository encapsulates the various laws as first–class elements in the agent system. This approach avoids that laws are scattered over different components of the system. On the other hand, explicitly modelling laws may induce a important computational overhead. If performance is a high-ranked quality, laws may be hard coded in the various applicable modules.

5   Component and Connector Communicating Processes View

The communicating processes view shows the multiagent system as a set of concurrently executing units and their interactions. The elements of the communicating processes view are *concurrent units*, *repositories*, and *connectors*. Concurrent units are an abstraction for more concrete software elements such as task, process, and thread. Connectors enable data exchange between concurrent units and control of concurrent units such as start, stop, synchronization, etc. The relationship in this view is *attachment* that indicates which connectors are connected to which concurrent units and repositories [13].

The communicating processes view explains which portions of the system operate in parallel and is therefore an important artefact to understand how the system works and to analyze the performance of the system. Furthermore, the view is important to decide which components should be assigned to which processes. Actually, we present the communicating processes view as a number of core components and overlay them with a set of concurrently executing units and their interactions.

The reference architecture provides one view packet of the component and connector communicating view. This view packet shows the main processes involved in perception, interaction, and communication in the situated multiagent system.

5.1   C & C Communicating Processes View Packet 1: Perception, Interaction, and Communication

Primary Presentation. The primary presentation is shown in Fig. 7.

Elements and their Properties. This view packet shows the main processes and repositories of agent and the application environment. We make a distinction between *active processes* that run autonomously, and *reactive processes* that are triggered by other processes to perform a particular task.

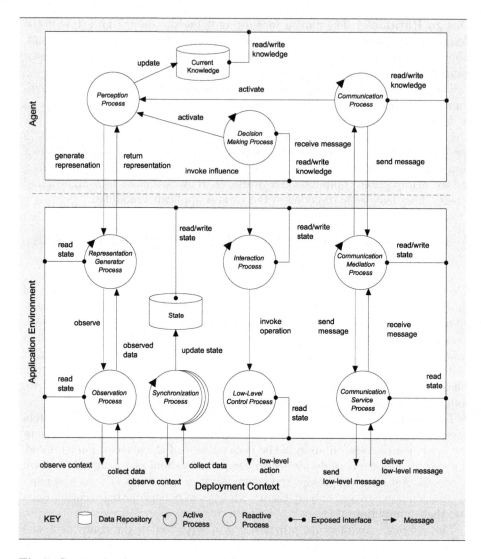

Fig. 7. Communicating processes view for perception, interaction, and communication

The discussion of the elements in this view packet is divided in four parts. Successively, we zoom in on the communicating processes of perception, interaction, and communication, and the synchronization processes of the application environment.

Perception. The Perception Process of agent is a reactive process that can be activated by the Decision Making Process and the Communication Process. Once activated, the perception process requests the Representation Generator

`Process` to generate a representation. The representation generator process collects the required state from the `State` repository of the application environment, and optionally it requests the `Observation Process` to collect additional data from the deployment context and possibly state of other nodes. State collection is subject to the perception laws. The observation process returns the observed data to the representation generator process, and subsequently the representation generator integrates the perceived state and generates a representation that is returned to the perception process of the agent. The perception process converts the representation to a percept that it uses to update the agent's `Current Knowledge`. Finally, the requesting process can read the updated state of the agent. The current knowledge repository can provide a notification mechanism to inform the decision making and communication process when a state update is completed.

Interaction. The `Decision Making Process` is an active process of agent that selects and invokes influences in the environment. The `Interaction Process` collects the concurrently invoked influences and converts them into operations. The execution of operations is subject to the action laws of the system. Operations that attempt to modify state of the application environment are executed by the interaction process, operations that attempt to modify state of the deployment context are forwarded to the `Low-Level Control Process`. This latter process converts the operations into low–level interactions in the deployment context.

Communication. The `Communication Process` is an active process that handles the communicative interactions of the agent. Newly composed messages are passed to the `Communication Mediation Process` that applies the communication laws and subsequently passes the messages to the `Communication Service Process`. This latter process converts the messages into low–level interactions that are transmitted via the deployment context. Furthermore, the `Communication Service Process` collects low–level messages from the deployment context, converts the messages into a format understandable for the agents, and forward the messages to the communication mediation process that delivers the messages to the communication process of the appropriate agent. Messages directed to agents that are located at the same host are directly transferred to the appropriate agents.

Synchronization Processes in the Application Environment. The `Synchronization Processes` are active processes that (1) monitor application specific parts of the deployment context and keep the corresponding state of the application environment up-to-date, (2) maintain application specific dynamics in the application environment, and (3) synchronize state among nodes according to the requirements of the application at hand.

Variation Mechanisms. There is one variation mechanism in this view packet.

CP1 *State Synchronization.* The parts of the deployment context for which a representation has to be maintained in the application environment have to be defined. The deployment context may provide a notification mechanism to inform synchronization processes about changes, or the processes may poll the deployment context according to specific time schemes. Besides, for each activity in the application environment that happens independently of agents, an active process has to be defined. Finally, processes to synchronize state among nodes must be defined. Appropriate middleware may be used to support the synchronization of state among nodes.

Design Rationale. Agents are provided with two active processes, one for decision making and one for communication. This approach allows these processes to run in parallel, improving efficiency. Communication among the processes happens indirectly via the current knowledge repository. The perception process is reactive, the agent only senses the environment when required for decision making and communicative interaction. As such, the perception process is only activated when necessary.

The application environment is provided with separate processes to collect and process perception requests, handle influences, and provide message transfer. The observation process is reactive, it collects data from the deployment context when requested by the representation generator. The low-level control process is also reactive, it provides its services on command of the interaction mediation process. The communication service is reactive process that handles the transmission of messages when new messages arrives. Finally, synchronization processes are active processes that act largely independent of other processes in the system. Synchronization processes monitor particular dynamics in the deployment context and keep the corresponding representations up-to-date in the state of the application environment; they maintain dynamics in the application environment that happen independent of agents, and synchronize state among nodes.

Active processes represent loci of continuous activity in the system. By letting active processes run in parallel, different activities in the system can be handled concurrently, improving efficiency. Reactive processes, on the other hand, are only activated and occupy resources when necessary.

6 Excerpt of a Software Architecture for an AGV Transportation System

We now illustrate how we have used the reference architecture for the architectural design of an automated transportation system for warehouse logistics that has been developed in a joint R&D project between the DistriNet research group and Egemin, a manufacturer of automating logistics services in warehouses and manufactories [45,2]. The transportation system uses automatic guided vehicles (AGVs) to transport loads through a warehouse. Typical applications include distributing incoming goods to various branches, and distributing manufactured products to storage locations. AGVs are battery-powered vehicles that can navigate through a warehouse following predefined paths on the factory floor.

The low-level control of the AGVs in terms of sensors and actuators such as staying on track on a path, turning, and determining the current position is handled by the AGV control software.

6.1   Multiagent System for the AGV Transportation System

In the project, we have applied a multiagent system approach for the development of the transportation system. The transportation system consists of two kinds of agents: transport agents and AGV agents. Transport agents represent tasks that need to be handled by an AGV and are located at a transport base, i.e. a stationary computer system. AGV agents are responsible for executing transports and are located in mobile vehicles. The communication infrastructure provides a wireless network that enables AGV agents at vehicles to communicate with each other and with transport agents on the transport base.

AGVs are situated in a physical environment, however this environment is very constrained: AGVs cannot manipulate the environment, except by picking and dropping loads. This restricts how AGV agents can exploit their environment. Therefore, a virtual environment was introduced for agents to inhabit. This virtual environment provides an interaction mediation level that agents can use as a medium to exchange information and coordinate their behavior. The virtual environment is necessarily distributed over the AGVs and the transport base, i.e. a local virtual environment is deployed on each AGV and the transport base. The local virtual environment corresponds to the application environment in the reference architecture. State on local virtual environments is merged opportunistically, as the need arises. The synchronization of the state of neighboring local virtual environments is supported by the ObjectPlaces middleware [29,30].

6.2   Collision Avoidance

As an illustration of the software architecture of the AGV transportation system, we take a closer look at collision avoidance. AGV agents avoid collisions by coordinating with other agents through the virtual environment. AGV agents mark the path they are going to drive in their environment using hulls. The hull of an AGV demarcates the physical area the AGV occupies in the virtual environment. A series of hulls then describes the physical area an AGV occupies along a certain path. If the area is not marked by other hulls (the AGVs own hulls do not intersect with others), the AGV can move along and actually drive over the reserved path. In case of a conflict, the virtual environment resolves the conflict taking into account the priorities of the transported loads to determine which AGV can move on. Afterwards, the AGV agent removes the markings in the virtual environment. Fig. 8 shows the primary presentation of the communicating processes view for collision avoidance. The communicating processes view presents the basic layers of the AGV control system and overlay them with the main processes and repositories involved in collision avoidance.

The top layer consists of the AGV agent that is responsible for controlling an AGV vehicle. The main functionalities of an AGV agent are: (1) obtaining

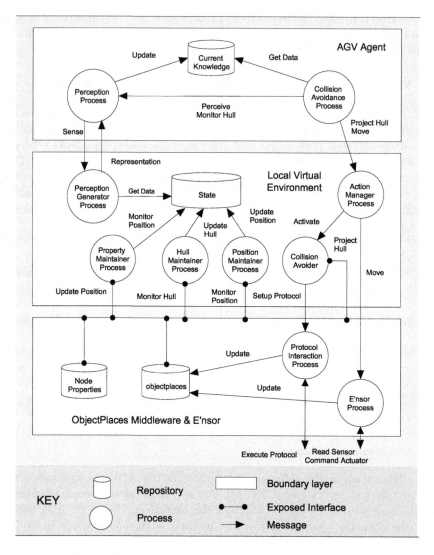

Fig. 8. Communicating processes for collision avoidance

transport tasks; (2) efficiently and safely handling jobs; (3) maintaining the AGV machine (charging battery, calibrating etc.).

The middle layer consists of the local virtual environment that is responsible for (1) representing and maintaining relevant state of the physical environment and the AGV vehicle; (2) representing additional state for coordination purposes; (3) synchronization of state with neighboring local virtual environments.

The bottom layer consists of the ObjectPlaces middleware and the E'nsor software. The ObjectPlaces middleware enables communication with software systems on other nodes, providing a means to synchronize the state of the local virtual environment with the state of local virtual environments on neighboring nodes. E'nsor is the low-level control software of the AGV vehicle. The E'nsor software provides an interface to command the AGV vehicle and to read out its status. The E'nsor interface defines instructions to move the vehicle over a particular distance and possibly execute an action at the end of the trajectory such as picking up a load. The physical execution of the commands is managed by E'nsor. As such, the AGV agent can control the movement and actions of the AGV at a fairly high-level of abstraction.

We now discuss the main architectural elements involved in collision avoidance in turn.

The **Perception Process** is part of the agent's perception component, and corresponds to the perception process in the reference architecture. If the perception process receives a request for perception, it requests the up-to-date data from the local virtual environment and updates the agent's current knowledge.

The **Perception Generator Process** is part of the representation generator and corresponds to the representation generator process in the reference architecture. This process is responsible for handling perception requests, it derives the requested data from the state repository of the local virtual environment according to the given foci. An observation & data processing process (as in the the reference architecture) is absent in the local virtual environment. State from the deployment context and other nodes that is needed by the AGV agent is maintained by dedicated synchronization processes.

Collision Avoidance Process is part of the AGV agent's decision making component and is a helper process of the decision making process. The collision avoidance process calculates the required hull projection for collision avoidance, based on the most up-to-date data, and projects the hull in local virtual environment. Once the hull is locked, the collision avoidance process invokes a move command in the local virtual environment.

The **Action Manager Process** is part of the interaction component and corresponds to the interaction process in the reference architecture. The action manager process collects the influences invoked in the local virtual environment and dispatches them to the applicable processes. For a hull projection, the action manager process passes the influence to the collision avoider process of the local virtual environment. A move influence is passed to the E'nsor process.

Objectplaces repository is a repository of data objects in the ObjectPlaces middleware that contains the hulls the AGV agent has requested.

NodeProperties is a data repository in the middleware in which relevant properties of the node are maintained, an example is the AGV's current position. Maintenance of node properties in the repository is handled by the **Property Maintainer Process**. This process is a an instance of a synchronization process of the local virtual environment. The data objects of the NodeProperties repository are used by the middleware to synchronize the state among local virtual environment on neighboring nodes. For example, the current position in the node properties repository is used by the ObjectPlaces middleware to determine whether the AGV is within collision range of other AGVs.

The **Collision Avoider** is a helper process of the action manager process that projects the requested hull in the objectplaces repository and initiates the collision avoidance protocol in the middleware.

The **Protocol Interaction Process** is a process of the ObjectPlaces middleware that is responsible for executing the mutual exclusion protocol for collision avoidance with the AGVs in collision range. This process maintains the state of the agent's hull in the objectplaces repository.

The **Hull Maintainer Process and Position Maintainer Process** are part of the synchronization component. These processes are application-specific instances of synchronization processes in the reference architecture. The hull maintainer process monitors the hull object in the objectplaces repository and keeps the state of the hull in the state repository of the local virtual environment consistent. The position maintainer process maintains in a similar way the actual position of the AGV vehicle.

Finally, the **E'nsor Process** is part of E'nsor and corresponds to a low-level control process in the reference architecture. The E'nsor process (1) periodically provides updates of the vehicles physical state (such as position and battery status), and (2) translates the high-level actions from the action manager process into low-level commands for the vehicle actuators.

7   Related Work

In this section, we discuss a number of representative reference architectures and reference models for multiagent systems.

7.1   PROSA: Reference Architecture for Manufacturing Systems

[49] defines a reference architecture as a set of coherent engineering and design principles used in a specific domain. PROSA—i.e. an acronym for Product–Resource–Order–Staff Architecture—defines a reference architecture for a family of coordination and control application, with manufacturing systems as the main domain. These systems are characterized by frequent changes and disturbances. PROSA aims to provide the required flexibility to cope with these dynamics.

The PROSA reference architecture [11,36] is built around three types of basic agents: resource agent, product agent, and order agent. A resource agent contains a production resource of the manufacturing system, and an information processing part that controls the resource. A product agent holds the know-how to make a product with sufficient quality, it contains up-to-date information on the product life cycle. Finally, an order agent represents a task in the manufacturing system, it is responsible for performing the assigned work correctly and on time. The agents exchange knowledge about the system, including process knowledge (i.e. how to perform a certain process on a certain resource), production knowledge (i.e. how to produce a certain product using certain resources), and process execution knowledge (i.e. information and methods regarding the progress of executing processes on resources). Staff agents are supplementary agents that can assist the basic agents in performing their work. Staff agents allow to incorporate centralized services (e.g, a planner or a scheduler). However, staff agents only give *advice* to basic agents, they do not introduce rigidity in the system.

The PROSA reference architecture uses object-oriented concepts to model the agents and their relationships. Aggregation is used to represent a cluster of agents that in turn can represent an agent at a higher level of abstraction. Specialization is used to differentiate between the different kinds of resource agents, order agents, and product agents specific for the manufacturing system at hand.

The target domain of PROSA is a sub-domain of the target domain of the reference architecture for situated multiagent systems. As such, the PROSA reference architecture is more specific and tuned to its target domain. The specification of the PROSA reference architecture is descriptive. PROSA specifies the responsibilities of the various agent types in the system and their relationships, but abstracts from the internals of the agents. As a result, the reference architecture is easy to understand. Yet, the informal specification allows for different interpretations. An example is the use of object-oriented concepts to specify relationships between agents. Although intuitive, in essence it is unclear what the precise semantics is of notions such as "aggregation" and "specialization" for agents. What are the constraints imposed by such a hierarchy with respect to the behavior of agents as autonomous and adaptive entities? Without a rigorous definition, such concepts inevitable leads to confusion and misunderstanding.

[21] presents an interesting extension of PROSA in which the environment is exploited to obtain BDI (Believe, Desire, Intention [27]) functionality for the various PROSA agents. To avoid the complexity of BDI-based models and the accompanying computational load, the agents delegate the creation and maintenance of complex models of the environment and other agents to the environment. The approach introduces the concept of "delegate multiagent system". A delegate multiagent system consists of light-weight agents which can be issued by the different PROSA agents. These ant-like agents can explore the environment, bring relevant information back to their responsible agent, and put the intentions of the responsible agent as information in the environment. This allows delegate multiagent systems of different agents to coordinate by aligning or adapting the information in the environment according to their own tasks. A similar idea was proposed by Bruecker in [10], and has recently further been elaborated by Parunak and Brueckner, see [26]. The use of the environment in the work of [21] is closely connected to our perspective on the role of the environment as an exploitable design abstraction. The main challenge is now to develop an architecture that integrates the BDI functionality provided by a

delegate multiagent system with the architecture of the cognitive agent that issues the delegate multiagent system in the environment.

7.2   Aspect-Oriented Agent Architecture

In [17], Garcia et al. observe that several agent concerns such as autonomy, learning, and mobility crosscut each other and the basic functionality of the agent. The authors state that existing approaches that apply well-known patterns to structure agent architectures—an example is the layered architecture of Kendall [22]—fail to cleanly separate the various concerns. This results in architectures that are difficult to understand, reuse, and maintain. To cope with the problem of crosscutting concerns, the authors propose an aspect-oriented approach to structure agent architectures.

The authors make a distinction between basic concerns of agent architectures, and additional concerns that are optional. Basic concerns are features that are incorporated by all agent architectures and include knowledge, interaction, adaptation, and autonomy. Examples of additional concerns are mobility, learning, and collaboration. An aspect-oriented agent architecture consists of a "kernel" that encapsulates the core functionality of the agent (essentially the agent's internal state), and a set of aspects [24]. Each aspect modularizes a particular concern of the agent (basic and additional concerns). The architectural elements of the aspect-oriented agent architecture provide two types of interfaces: regular and crosscutting interfaces. A crosscutting interface specifies when and how an architectural aspect affects other architectural elements. The authors claim that the proposed approach provides a clean separation between the agent's basic functionality and the crosscutting agent properties. The resulting architecture is easier to understand and maintain, and improves reuse.

State-of-the-art research in aspect-oriented software development is mainly directed at the specification of aspects at the programming level, and this is the same for the work of Garcia and his colleagues. The approach has been developed bottom up, resulting in specifications of aspects at the architectural level that mirror aspect-oriented implementation techniques. The notion of crosscutting interface is a typical example. Unfortunately, a precise semantics of "when and how an architectural aspect affects other architectural elements" is lacking.

The aspect-oriented agent architecture applies a different kind of modularization as we did in the reference architecture for situated multiagent systems. Whereas a situated agent in the reference architecture is decomposed in functional building blocks, Garcia and his colleagues take another perspective on the decomposition of agents. The main motivation for the aspect-oriented agent architecture is to separate different concerns of agents aiming to improve understandability and maintenance. Yet, it is unclear whether the interaction of the different concerns in the kernel (feature interaction [12]) will not lead to similar problems the approach initially aimed to resolve. Anyway, crosscutting concerns in multiagent systems are hardly explored and provide an interesting venue for future research.

7.3   Architectural Blueprint for Autonomic Computing

Autonomic Computing is an initiative started by IBM in 2001. Its ultimate aim is to create self-managing computer systems to overcome their growing complexity [23]. IBM has developed an architectural blueprint for autonomic computing [1]. This architectural blueprint specifies the fundamental concepts and the architectural building blocks used to construct autonomic systems.

The blueprint architecture organizes an autonomic computing system into five layers. The lowest layer contains the system components that are managed by the autonomic system. System components can be any type of resource, a server, a database, a network, etc. The next layer incorporates touchpoints, i.e. standard manageability interfaces for accessing and controlling the managed resources. Layer three constitutes of autonomic managers that provide the core functionality for self-management. An autonomic manager is an agent-like component that manages other software or hardware components using a control loop. The control loop of the autonomic manager includes functions to monitor, analyze, plan and execute. Layer four contains autonomic managers that compose other autonomic managers. These composition enables system-wide autonomic capabilities. The top layer provides a common system management interface that enables a system administrator to enter high-level policies to specify the autonomic behavior of the system. The layers can obtain and share knowledge via knowledge sources, such as a registry, a dictionary, and a database.

We now briefly discuss the architecture of an autonomic manager, the most elaborated part in the specification of the architectural blueprint. An autonomic manager automates some management function according to the behavior defined by a management interface. Self-managing capabilities are accomplished by taking an appropriate action based on one or more situations that the autonomic manager senses in the environment. Four architectural elements provide this control loop: (1) the monitor function provides the mechanisms that collect, aggregate, and filter data collected from a managed resource; (2) the analyze function provides the mechanisms that correlate and model observed situations; (3) the plan function provides the mechanisms that construct the actions needed to achieve the objectives of the manager; and (4) the execute function provides the mechanisms that control the execution of a plan with considerations for dynamic updates. These four parts work together to provide the management functions of the autonomic manager.

Although presented as architecture, to our opinion, the blueprint describes a reference model. The discussion mainly focusses on functionality and relationships between functional entities. The specification of the horizontal interaction among autonomic managers is lacking in the model. Moreover, the functionality for self-management must be completely provided by the autonomic managers. Obviously, this results in complex internal structures and causes high computational loads.

The concept of application environment in the reference architecture for situated multiagent systems provides an interesting opportunity to manage complexity, yet, it is not part of the IBM blueprint. The application environment could enable the coordination among autonomic managers and provide supporting services. Laws embedded in the application environment could provide a means to impose rules on the autonomic system that go beyond individual autonomic managers.

7.4   A Reference Model for Multiagent Systems

In [25], Modi et al. present a reference model for agent-based systems. The aim of the model is fourfold: (1) to establish a taxonomy of concepts and definitions needed to compare agent-based systems; (2) to identify functional elements that are common in agent-based systems; (3) to capture data flow dependencies among the functional elements; and (4) to specify assumptions and requirements regarding the dependencies among the elements.

The model is derived from the results of a thorough study of existing agent-based systems, including Cougaar [19], Jade [7], and Retsina [34]. The authors used reverse engineering techniques to perform an analysis of the software systems. Static analysis was used to study the source code of the software, and dynamic analysis to inspect the system during execution. Key functions identified are directory services, messaging, mobility, inter-operability services, etc.

Starting from this data a preliminary reference model was derived for agent-based systems. The authors describe the reference model by means of a layered view and a functional view. The layered view is comprised of agents and their supporting framework and infrastructure which provide services and operating context to the agents. The model defines framework, platform, and host layers, which mediate between agents and the external environment. The functional view presents a set of functional concepts of agent-based systems. Example functionalities are administration (instantiate agents, allocate resources to agents, terminate agents), security (prevent execution of undesirable actions by entities from within or outside the agent system), conflict management (facilitate and enable the management of interdependencies between agents activities), and messaging (enable information exchange between agents).

The reference model in an interesting effort towards maturing the domain. In particular, the reference model aims to be generic but does not make any recommendation about how to best engineer an agent-based system. Putting the focus on abstractions helps to resolve confusion in the domain and facilitates acquisition of agent technology in practice.

Yet, since the authors have investigated only systems in which agents communicate through message exchange, the resulting reference model is biased towards this kind of agent systems. The concept of environment as a means for information sharing and indirect coordination of agents is absent. On the other hand, it is questionable whether developing one common reference model for the broad family of agent-based system is desirable.

8   Conclusions

In this paper, we presented a reference architecture for situated multiagent systems. The general goal of the reference architecture is to support the architectural design of self-managing applications. Concrete contributions are: (1) the reference architecture defines how various mechanisms of adaptivity for situated multiagent systems are integrated in one architecture; (2) the reference architecture provides a blueprint for architectural design, it facilitates deriving new software architectures for systems that share its common base; and (3) the reference architecture reifies the knowledge and expertise we have acquired in our research, it offers a vehicle to study and learn the advanced perspective on situated multiagent systems we have developed in our research.

We presented the reference architecture by means of three views that describe the architecture from different perspectives. Views are presented as a number of view packets. A view packet focusses on a particular part of the reference architecture. We gave a primary presentation of each view packet and we explained the properties of the architectural elements. Besides, each view packet is provided with a number of variation mechanisms and a design rationale. Variation mechanisms describe how the view packet can be applied to build concrete software architectures. The design rationale explains the underlying design choices of the view packet and the quality attributes associated with the various view packets. [37] provides a detailed formal specification of the various architectural elements.

We illustrated how we have used the reference for the architectural design of an AGV transportation system. In particular, we showed how a set of abstractly defined processes in the reference architecture are instantiated to provide the functionality for collision avoidance.

The reference architecture serves as a blueprint for developing concrete software architectures. It integrates a set of architectural patterns architects can draw from during architectural design. However, the reference architecture is not a ready-made cookbook for architectural design. It offers a set of reusable architectural solutions to build software architectures for concrete applications. Yet, applying the reference architecture does not relieve the architect from difficult architectural issues, including the selection of supplementary architectural approaches to deal with specific system requirements. We consider the reference architecture as a *guidance* for architectural design that offers a reusable set of architectural assets for building software architectures for concrete applications. Yet, this set is not complete and needs to be complemented with additional architectural approaches.

References

1. IBM, An Architectural Blueprint for Autonomic Computing, (6/2006). www-03.ibm.com/autonomic/.
2. EMC^2: Egemin Modular Controls Concept, Project Supported by the Institute for the Promotion of Innovation Through Science and Technology in Flanders (IWTVlaanderen), (8/2006). http://emc2.egemin.com/.

3. The Unified Modeling Language, (8/2006). http://www.uml.org/.
4. C. Atkinson and T. Kuhne. Aspect-Oriented Development with Stratified Frameworks. *IEEE Software*, 20(1):81–89, 2003.
5. J. Austin. *How To Do Things With Words*. Oxford University Press, Oxford, UK, 1962.
6. L. Bass, P. Clements, and R. Kazman. *Software Architecture in Practice*. Addison Wesley Publishing Comp., 2003.
7. F. Bellifemine, A. Poggi, and G. Rimassa. Jade, A FIPA-compliant Agent Framework. In *4th International Conference on Practical Application of Intelligent Agents and Multi-Agent Technology*, London, UK, 1999.
8. N. Boucké, D. Weyns, T. Holvoet, and K. Mertens. Decentralized allocation of tasks with delayed commnencement. In *2nd European Workshop on Multi-Agent Systems, EUMAS*, Barcelona, Spain, 2004.
9. N. Boucké, D. Weyns, K. Schelfthout, and T. Holvoet. Applying the ATAM to an Architecture for Decentralized Contol of a AGV Transportation System. In *2nd International Conference on Quality of Software Architecture, QoSA*, Vasteras, Sweden, 2006. Springer.
10. S. Brueckner. *Return from the Ant, Synthetic Ecosystems for Manufacturing Control*. Ph.D Dissertation, Humboldt University, Berlin, Germany, 2000.
11. H. Van Brussel, J. Wyns, P. Valckenaers, L. Bongaerts, and P. Peeters. Reference Architecture for Holonic Manufacturing Systems: PROSA. *Jounal of Manufactoring Systems*, 37(3):255–274, 1998.
12. M. Calder, M. Kolberg, E. Magill, and S. Reiff-Marganiec. Feature Interaction: A Critical Review and Considered Forecast. *Computer Networks*, 41(1):115–141, 2003.
13. P. Clements, F. Bachmann, L. Bass, D. Garlan, J. Ivers, R. Little, R. Nord, and J. Stafford. *Documenting Software Architectures: Views and Beyond*. Addison Wesley Publishing Comp., 2002.
14. C. Cuesta, M. del Pilar Romay, P. de la Fuente, and M. Barrio-Solórzano. Architectural Aspects of Architectural Aspects. In *2nd European Wirkshop on Software Architecture, EWSA*, Lecture Notes in Computer Science, Vol. 3527. Springer, 2005.
15. J. Ferber and J. Muller. Influences and Reaction: a Model of Situated Multiagent Systems. *2nd International Conference on Multi-agent Systems, Japan, AAAI Press*, 1996.
16. FIPA. Foundation for Intelligent Physical Agents, FIPA Abstract Architecture Specification. http://www.fipa.org/repository/bysubject.html, (8/2006).
17. A. Garcia, U. Kulesza, and C. Lucena. Aspectizing Multi-Agent Systems: From Architecture to Implementation. In *Software Engineering for Multi-Agent Systems III, SELMAS 2004*, Lecture Notes in Computer Science, Vol. 3390. Springer, 2005.
18. D. Harel. Statecharts: A Visual Formalism for Complex Systems. *Science of Computer Programming*, 3(8):231–274, 1987.
19. A. Helsinger, R. Lazarus, W. Wright, and J. Zinky. Tools and Techniques for Performance Measurement of Large Distributed Multiagent Systems. In *2nd International Joint Conference on Autonomous Agents and Multiagent Systems, AAMAS*, Melbourne, Victoria, Australia. ACM, 2003.
20. A. Holvoet. Visualisation of a Peer-to-Peer Network. *Master Thesis, Katholieke Universiteit Leuven, Belgium*, 2004.
21. T. Holvoet and P. Valckenaers. Exploiting the Environment for Coordinating Agent Intentions. In *3th International Workshop on Environments for Multiagent Systems, E4MAS*, Hakodate, Japan, 2006.

22. E. Kendall and C. Jiang. Multiagent System Design Based on Object Oriented Patterns. *Journal of Object Oriented Programming*, 10(3):41–47, 1997.

23. J. Kephart and D. Chess. The Vision of Autonomic Computing. *IEEE Computer Magazine*, 36(1).

24. G. Kiczales, J. Lamping, A. Menhdhekar, C. Maeda, C. Lopes, J. Loingtier, and J. Irwin. Aspect-Oriented Programming. In *European Conference on Object-Oriented Programming*, Lecture Notes in Computer Science, Vol. 1241, Berlin, Heidelberg, New York, 1997. Springer-Verlag.

25. P. Modi, S. Mancoridis, W. Mongan, W. Regli, and I. Mayk. Towards a Reference Model for Agent-Based Systems. In *Industry Track of the 5th International Joint Conference on Autonomous Agents and Multiagent Systems*, Hakodate, Japan, 2006. ACM.

26. H. V. D. Parunak and S. Brueckner. Concurrent Modeling of Alternative Worlds with Polyagents. In *7th International Workshop on Multi-Agent-Based Simulation*, Hakodate, Japan, 2006.

27. A. Rao and M. Georgeff. BDI Agents: From Theory to Practice. In *1st International Conference on Multiagent Systems, 1995, Agents, San Francisco, California, USA*. The MIT Press, 1995.

28. P. Reed. Reference Architecture: The Best of Best Practices. *The Rational Edge*, 2002. www-128.ibm.com/developerworks/rational/library/2774.html.

29. K. Schelfthout and T. Holvoet. Views: Customizable abstractions for context-aware applications in MANETs. *Software Engineering for Large-Scale Multi-Agent Systems, St. Louis, USA*, 2005.

30. K. Schelfthout, D. Weyns, and T. Holvoet. Middleware that Enables Protocol-Based Coordination Applied in Automatic Guided Vehicle Control. *IEEE Distributed Systems Online*, 7(8), 2006.

31. W. Schols, T. Holvoet, N. Boucké, and D. Weyns. Gradient Field Based Transport Assignment in AGV Systems. In *CW-425, Technical Report*. Departement of Computer Science, Katholieke Universiteit Leuven, Belgium. http://www.cs.kuleuven.ac.be/publicaties/rapporten/CW/2005/.

32. E. Steegmans, D. Weyns, T. Holvoet, and Y. Berbers. A Design Process for Adaptive Behavior of Situated Agents. In *Agent-Oriented Software Engineering V, 5th International Workshop, AOSE, New York, NY, USA*, Lecture Notes in Computer Science, Vol. 3382. Springer, 2004.

33. E. Steegmans, D. Weyns, T. Holvoet, and Y. Berbers. Designing Roles for Situated Agents. In *5th International Workshop on Agent-Oriented Software Engineering*, New York, NY, USA, 2004.

34. K. Sycara, M. Paolucci, M. Van Velsen, and J. Giampapa. The RETSINA MAS Infrastructure. *Autonomous Agents and Multi-Agent Systems*, 7(1-2):29–48, 2003.

35. B. Tekinerdogan. ASAAM: Aspectual Software Architecture Analysis Method. In *4th Working Conference on Software Architecture, WICSA, Oslo, Norway*. IEEE Computer Society, 2004.

36. P. Valckenaers and H. Van Brussel. Holonic Manufacturing Execution Systems. *CIRP Annals-Manufacturing Technology*, 54(1):427–432, 2005.

37. D. Weyns. An Architecture-Centric Approach for Software Engineering with Situated Multiagent Systems. *Ph.D Dissertation: Katholieke Universiteit Leuven*, 2006.

38. D. Weyns, N. Boucké, and T. Holvoet. Gradient Field Based Transport Assignment in AGV Systems. In *5th International Joint Conference on Autonomous Agents and Multi-Agent Systems, AAMAS, Hakodate, Japan*, 2006.

39. D. Weyns, A. Helleboogh, and T. Holvoet. The Packet-World: a Test Bed for Investigating Situated Multi-Agent Systems. In *Software agent-based applications, platforms, and development kits*. Whitestein Series in Software Agent Technology, 2005.

40. D. Weyns and T. Holvoet. Model for Simultaneous Actions in Situated Multiagent Systems. In *Multiagent System Technologies, 1st German Conference, MATES 2003, Erfurt, Germany*, Lecture Notes in Computer Science, Vol. 2831. Springer Verlag, 2003.

41. D. Weyns and T. Holvoet. Formal Model for Situated Multi-Agent Systems. *Fundamenta Informaticae*, 63(1-2):125–158, 2004.

42. D. Weyns and T. Holvoet. Regional Synchronization for Situated Multi-agent Systems. In *3th International Central and Eastern European Conference on Multi-Agent Systems, Prague, Czech Republic*, Lecture Notes in Computer Science, Vol. 2691. Springer Verlag, 2004.

43. D. Weyns and T. Holvoet. Architectural Design of an Industrial AGV Transportation System with a Multiagent System Approach. In *Software Architecture Technology User Network Workshop, SATURN*, Pittsburg, USA, 2006. Software Engineering Institute, Carnegie Mellon University.

44. D. Weyns, K. Schelfthout, T. Holvoet, and O. Glorieux. Towards Adaptive Role Selection for Behavior-Based Agents. In *Adaptive Agents and Multi-Agent Systems II: Adaptation and Multi-Agent Learning*, Lecture Notes in Computer Science, Vol. 3394. Springer, 2005.

45. D. Weyns, K. Schelfthout, T. Holvoet, and T. Lefever. Decentralized control of E'GV transportation systems. In *4th Joint Conference on Autonomous Agents and Multiagent Systems, Industry Track*, Utrecht, The Netherlands, 2005. ACM Press, New York, NY, USA.

46. D. Weyns, E. Steegmans, and T. Holvoet. Integrating Free-Flow Architectures with Role Models Based on Statecharts. In *Software Engineering for Multi-Agent Systems III, SELMAS*, Lecture Notes in Computer Science, Vol. 3390. Springer, 2004.

47. D. Weyns, E. Steegmans, and T. Holvoet. Protocol Based Communication for Situated Multi-Agent Systems. In *3th Joint Conference on Autonomous Agents and Multi-Agent Systems*, New York, USA, 2004. IEEE Computer Society.

48. D. Weyns, E. Steegmans, and T. Holvoet. Towards Active Perception in Situated Multi-Agent Systems. *Applied Artificial Intelligence*, 18(9-10):867–883, 2004.

49. J. Wyns, H. Van Brussel, P. Valckenaers, and L. Bongaerts. Workstation Architecture in Holonic Manufacturing Systems. In *28th CIRP International Seminar on Manufacturing Systems*, Johannesburg, South Africa, 1996.

A Unified Model for Physical and Social Environments

José-Antonio Báez-Barranco, Tiberiu Stratulat, and Jacques Ferber

LIRMM, Univ. Montpellier 2, CNRS
161 rue Ada, 34392 Montpellier Cedex 5, France
{baez,stratulat,ferber}@lirmm.fr

Abstract. The AGRE model proposed by Ferber *et al.* is based on an interesting generalization of both physical and social environments. In this paper we revisit the AGRE model and extend it with richer social concepts such as powers, norms and a dependency relationship which is similar to the *count as* operator introduced by Searle to describe the construction of social reality. Our main contribution consists in the fact that we attribute to the environment the main role in describing and controlling (social) interaction.

1 Introduction

In the area of multi-agent systems (MAS), Castelfranchi claimed [1] that *social order*, which is a (social) metaphor for the problem of coordinating the agents or organizing the interactions among them while preserving their autonomy, could be obtained by using social concepts such as norms and social control. Norms are rules describing the expected ideal behavior of an agent or of a group of agents. Social control means that the agents themselves observe the behavior of the other agents, control if it is norm compliant and act consequently. Recently, many research works [2,3,4,5] proposed models that integrate social and organizational concepts in MAS and suggested tools to implement the social metaphor. However, most of them propose *ad-hoc* solutions of how social concepts are constructed and then manipulated. For instance, there is not always very clear if the social knowledge (e.g. the obligation to do an action, the power of doing an act, the membership to an institution, etc.) is shared among agents or is represented somehow externally and independently of them.

In previous works we also have studied how to integrate in MAS the organizational concepts of group and role [6] and proposed the AGRE model [7]. The AGRE model is based on the idea that the environment could be used to represent not only the physical part of the interaction but also its social aspect. The agents interact only with the environment which will react according to agent's influences [8] and to the rules of change defined at both physical and social levels of interaction.

In this paper we present the AGREEN model which is a revisited extension of the AGRE model. Our main goal is to provide a much simpler and unified way of representing (physical and social) environments. The originality of our proposal consists in the fact that it attributes to the environment the main role in describing and controlling (social) interaction. This is the major difference when compared with other related works that use social concepts [3,4,9].

D. Weyns, H.V.D. Parunak, and F. Michel (Eds.): E4MAS 2006, LNAI 4389, pp. 41–50, 2007.
© Springer-Verlag Berlin Heidelberg 2007

The AGREEN model is based on a clear separation between what an agent tries to do and the effects obtained as consequences of its acts on the environment. The architect of an agent concentrates only on describing the internal structure of the agent, that is, on the design of the decision making mechanism that allows the agent to decide what to do next. The architect of the system describes the environment as a set of rules governing the interaction, ignoring how the agents are built. The main benefit of this separation is that it guarantees the autonomy of the agents and the non-intrusive control of their behavior. The non-intrusive control is based also on a clear distinction between what an agent can do, as capabilities (or powers), and what an agent is supposed to do as deontic constraints (i.e. obligations, permissions, interdictions).

Another advantage obtained from the separation agent/environment is that the semantics of an action could be given according to two perspectives: internal (agent's point of view) and external (environment's point of view). The external semantics could be further refined according to its social or physical aspect. This is a step forward towards giving to agent communication languages a public perspective and a social semantics, as requested by the agent community [10].

In the rest of the article we revisit the AGRE model and propose the AGREEN model that enhances AGRE with social concepts such as capabilities (powers), norms and a dependency relationship which is similar to the *count as* operator introduced by Searle to describe the construction of social reality [11].

2   Social Reality and AGRE

In this section we describe some social concepts such as norms and social reality that were announced in the original paper of AGRE but which deserve more attention.

2.1   Social Reality

The work of Searle on the construction of social reality [11] is becoming very influencing on the research in agent based systems [2,3]. The main idea is that a *social institution*, even that it has no physical support, has its own (social) reality and is constructed by mutual convention among its members on how to interpret what happens in the physical reality. Searle makes the distinction between brute facts and institutional facts. A *brute fact* represents something (true) bellonging to the physical reality (i.e. a piece of paper with a ten euros sign marked on it). An *institutional fact* is a fact that is considered to be true by collective acceptance by the members of a group or comunity of agents (i.e. money such as ten euros). According to Searle an institution is defined in terms of two types of rules: constitutive and regulative. *Constitutive rules* show how to construct the social reality by giving an interpretation to brute facts or other social facts. They have the form "X counts as Y in context C". For instance, in the money institution a piece of paper with ten euros special printings on it counts as a ten-euro banknote. Jones and Sergot [2] give a formalization of *count as*, and present the concept of institutionalized power as being the (social) capability to act in an institution. *Regulative rules* describe ideal normative situations or behaviors from the point of view of an institution.

2.2   The AGRE Model

In [7], Ferber *et al.* propose an extension of the AGR model [6] and consider an organization as being a special kind of environment. Social actions are associated with an organization, i.e. playing a role, entering and leaving a group, communicating inside a group, etc. The main ideas presented in that work concern (i) the use of both social and physical environments to describe the interaction among agents; (ii) the concept of *space* which is a generalization of the concepts of physical area and social group, introduced to partition the environment; and (iii) the concept of *mode*, which is a generalization of the concepts of physical body and social role, used to describe the agent's capabilities to influence [8] physical and respectively social environments.

However, the AGRE model presents some inconveniences. First, the generalized concepts of space, mode and institution show very well the relationship that should exist between an agent and an environment, but they remain abstract and unused. Moreover, like in AGR, there is no explicit description of the expected behavior of the agents, i.e. a role is simply a label with no other semantics. Normally we should be able to associate to a role powers and deontic constraints such as obligations, permissions or interdictions. Finally, AGRE in its original form did not take into account the ideas on social reality by Searle. What is missing in AGRE is something similar to the *count as* relationship that links together physical and social environments or more generally any two environments.

3   The AGREEN Model

In this section we show how to improve and generalize the concepts introduced initially in AGRE. That is, we propose: (i) to use only the generalized concepts of space, mode and capability, (ii) to better explain the role of the environment from the point of view of behavior control, (iii) to give more details on the role of modes as capabilities to act in an environment, and (iv) to try to generalize the relationship existing between physical and social environments.

In Figure 1 we give a simplified description of the main relationships existing between a space, a mode and an agent. In order to interact to other agents an agent will influence a space through its mode which provides controlled capabilities to act in an environment. According to what an agent is able to do in a space the environment will react to its influences. The reaction of the environment is finally the result of a more complex interaction between various objects which have the role to encapsulate the environment's state and behavior.

3.1   Spaces

As in AGRE, we borrow concepts from the object-oriented programming paradigm to specify an environment. The role of a space is to keep the information about the state of a physical or social environment. A space is for agents a sort of interaction place. Its state can change as a consequence of their influences. A space is characterized by a name and a space type as as explained below. The state of a space is given by the state

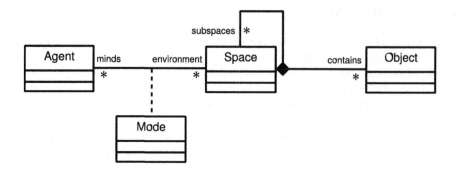

Fig. 1. Simplified UML representation of AGREEN

of the objects that compose it. The kinds of objects composing a space could be further divided in ordinary objects, modes and recursively other subspaces. In the following we will give definitions for all these concepts.

Definition 1 (Space). *A space S is a tuple $<Id_S, ST, O^*, M^*, S^*>$ where: Id_S is the space's Id that uniquely identifies it, ST is the current space type, and O^*, M^*, S^* represent the sets of objects, modes and respectively subspaces that compose a space.*

The type of a space is a concept similar to that of class in the object-oriented paradigm and contains the description of common properties and behaviors of identical instances, i.e. concrete spaces. A space type defines the structure of its instances, i.e. the way a space instance is composed of objects, modes, and other subspaces.

Definition 2 (SpaceType). *A space type ST is a tuple $<ATD_S^*, OT^*, MT^*, ST^*, DR^*, C_S^*>$ where ATD_S^* represents the set of attributes composing a space. An attribute could be an instance of a type taken from the sets OT^*, MT^* and ST^* which correspond to object types, mode types and respectively other space types. DR^* represents the set of explicit dependency rules that link an instance of ST to other spaces, and C_S^* is the set of environmental constraints for the environmental control.*

The set DR^* contains rules that determine how a space modifies its internal state according to some external changes produced by other spaces. A dependency rule between two spaces introduces constraints of various natures: causal (an internal event is the result of some external causes or events occurred in other spaces), logical (a local property is the logical consequence of some external properties), social (like *count as*). Note, for instance, that physical spaces have no social dependency rules.

3.2   Objects

Objects encapsulate the internal state of the environment and the laws that govern its change. An object exists at runtime and is characterized by a type and a state.

Definition 3 (Object). *An object O is a tuple $<Id_O, OT, AT_O^*>$ where: Id_O is the object's name that uniquely identifies it; OT is the object type; and AT_O^* is the set of attributes of the object.*

The type of object is similar to the class in object-oriented programming and contains the description of common properties and behaviors of identical instances, that is concrete objects. An object type describes the possible states of its instances and how they change under agents' influences.

Definition 4 (ObjectType). *An object type OT is a tuple $<ATD_O^*, M^*>$ where ATD_O^* is the set of attribute declarations and M^* is the set of methods defining how an object, instance of OT, changes its internal state.*

3.3 Modes

There are mainly two reasons to introduce the concept of mode: (i) to allow a space to individually attribute capabilities to agents; (ii) to allow a space to specify the expected behavior by using social deontic constraints. We propose to use the term *capability* to describe the unified concept of physical capability and social power. A capability is associated to a mode and a space, and defines the way an agent (called owner of the mode) is able to modify the space at runtime. A mode is characterized by a mode type and a set of attributes.

Definition 5 (Mode). *A mode M is a tuple $<Id_M, MT, A, AT_M^*, OPI^*>$ where: Id_M is the mode's name that uniquely identifies it, MT is the mode type, A is the owner's (agent) identifier, AT_M^* is a set of attributes, and OPI^* is a set of deontic constraints such as obligations, permissions and interdictions.*

Definition 6 (ModeType). *A mode type MT is a tuple $<ATD_M^*, P^*, C_M^*, N^*>$ where: ATD_M^* is the set of attribute declarations, P^* is the set of capabilities (or powers) that an instance of MT will offer to its owner, C_M^* is a set of conditions that should be fulfilled by an agent to obtain a mode in a space or to release it, and N^* is a set of norms that describe the conditions of apparition of deontic constraints that apply to a mode, instance of MT.*

The type of mode is similar to the class in object-oriented programming. It is an abstract description of the internal structure of its instances, the modes, and of the operations that could be executed on them to change their state. Since the notion of type is similar to that of class, we also introduce the concept of inheritance between two types. As in object-oriented software engineering, the inheritance is used to represent the *is-a* relationship or to reuse code.

In the definition of a mode type, the set C_M^* contains the conditions that should be verified on an agent at the creation of its mode or rechecked later to see if the agent still posses the necessary conditions to continue to interact with the environment.

The role of capability rules is to define what is possible for an agent to do in a space. When an agent influences the environment, the capability rule triggered by its mode is immediately executed by the environment. A capability rule also contains the preconditions on producing an influence on the environment. As shown before, a mode encapsulates the conditions that gives its owner the possibility to act in an environment. The capability rules are mainly employed to externally control the behavior of the agents inside a space through their modes, hence preserving their internal autonomy.

The role of norms is to implement the social control since they reflect the deontic aspect of interaction. They are of the following conditional form:

$$\textbf{if } Condition \textbf{ then } OPI(agent, \alpha)$$

where $OPI(agent, \alpha)$ describes deontic constraints such as the obligation, the permission or respectively the interdiction to do something or to arrive in a certain state of affairs α. If the $Condition$ part in a norm is $true$, the norm describes a permanent deontic constraint. We note that we do not consider general deontic constraints as in standard deontic logic, but directed deontic constraints on specific agents. Like capabilities, a deontic constraint is always connected to a mode.

As shown in the previous section, we only consider the context of social interactions. For instance, a physical mode (e.g. a body), is only a mode with an empty set of norms.

A norm could be used in various ways, for instance, as a simple container of normative information, eventually sanctioned by social penalties if violated and rewarded otherwise, or "regimented" by social mechanisms that force or block the execution of agent's actions in a space thanks to its modes. Since there is no common agreement on how to use norms in multi-agent systems, we leave open to an architect the choice of semantics and their implementation.

4   Example: Modeling Warbot

In this section we illustrate the concepts introduced in AGREEN by modeling Warbot [12], a video game where two teams of robots fight against each other to destroy the opponent's base.

In Warbot there are three physical types of robots:

- $Bases$, fixed robots which are able to perceive large areas and transform food in new agents,
- $RocketLaunchers$, mobile robots that have to bring food to the base and which are able to shoot other robots perceived in their neighborhood,
- $Explorers$, mobile robots specialized in searching for food but which move faster than $RocketLaunchers$.

Warbot is constructed following the idea of separating the minds of the agents from their bodies which are situated in an environment. That is, we consider that behind each robot there is an autonomous agent which decides for the robot what to do next. The environment (or the spaces) offers the agents the capabilities to interact. Thus, the interaction could be divided in four spaces: $arena$ which is used for the physical part of the game, $lions$ and $tigers$ which correspond to the organizational aspect of the game, and $game777$ which contains the score and the entire lifecycle of one play of the game. More exactly, the agents use robots to confront physically in $arena$ space, coordinate their attacks in $lions$ and $tigers$ spaces, and play one round Warbot games in $gameXXX$ spaces. A game play is finished if one of the bases has been destroyed in the $arena$ space.

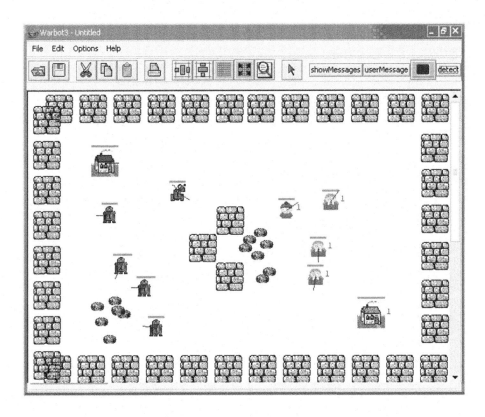

Fig. 2. Warbot, a robot video game

The space *arena* is defined as a two-dimensional physical space allowing physical robots to move, shoot, communicate in a certain range and pick up food. The space *arena* is an instance of *WarbotArena*, a space type which contains the definitions (see Figure 3 for some excerpts) of object types such as *Food*, *Obstacle* and *Missile*, and mode types such as *Robot*, *MobileRobot*, *RocketLauncher*, *Explorer*, *Base*. The *Robot* type is the super type of all the robot types and defines the capability of a robot to perceive and communicate in a certain range; *MobileRobot* inherits from *Robot* and adds the capability to move. Both *RocketLauncher* and *Explorer* inherit from *MobileRobot*. *Base* inherits directly from *Robot* and adds the capability to create new robots from food.

The spaces *lions* and *tigers* are spaces for social interaction between the members of the same team. Each team can have its own organizational structure and coordination rules, but for simplicity reasons we suppose that both teams are instances of the same space type *Team*. For instance, we can have that *Team* is composed by one *Leader* and many *Subordinate*s. All the modes in a space instance of *Team* have the capability to communicate. The *Leader* of a team contains in addition the capability (power)

```
SpaceType WarbotArena {                 SpaceType Team {
  ModeTypes = {                           ModeTypes = {
    ModeType Robot = {                       ModeType Leader {
      Attributes = {                            Capabilities = {
        int radius = 12;                          void order(Subordinate ag,
        int energy = 1000;                                    Request r) {...}
        int detectionRange = 130;                 boolean onDemand() {
      }                                             return plays(this.owner,
      Capabilities = {                                    MobileRobot,
        int getEnergy() {...}                             WarbotArena) &&
      }                                                   leader == null;
      Conditions = {                              }
        boolean onDemand() {...};             }
        boolean onRelease() {...};          }
        ...                               ModeType Subordinate { ...
      }                                     Norms = { {
    }                                         if ordered(Leader l, this,
    ModeType MobileRobot extends Robot            act)
      {                                         then obliged(this, act, l)},
      Attributes = {int speed;}                   ...
      Capabilities = {                      }
        void move () {...};       }
      }
      ...                               SpaceType WarbotPlay {
    }                                     ModeTypes = {
  }                                         ModeType Player { ...
  ObjectTypes = {                             Norms = { {
    ObjectType Food {...}                       forbidden (this, nextTo(this,
    ObjectType Obstacle {                                  base, 10)) }
      int x, y;                           ...
      int getX(); int getY();           Dependencies = {
    }                                     { WarbotArena,
  }                                           // count as
}                                             boolean nextTo(Player p, Base b,
                                                      int time) {...}
                                          }
                                        }
                                      }
```

Fig. 3. Types definitions for spaces, modes and objects

to give orders to a *Subordinate*. When a *Subordinate* receives an order it becomes obliged to obey the order. This rule is described by a norm defined in *Subordinate* mode type. Depending on the strategy of a team, the violation of such a norm could trigger various institutional actions, for instance, that affect the agent's trust level or socially isolate the agent from the rest of the team.

The space *game777* is an instance of *WarbotPlay*, a space type that defines the rules of the game. It contains, for instance, the conditions to start, pause or end a game, the conditions of a team to score one point or win a game, the penalties attributed to a team if some of its members don't obey the normative rules, such as a *Player* in a team should not stay next to a base more than a certain period of time. The constitutive rules of *WarbotPlay* depend mainly on what happens in an instance of *WarbotArena*.

In Figure 4 we show some possible content of a space at runtime.

```
arena = {                                    lions = {
   id = arena,                                  id = lions,
   spaceType = WarbotArena,                     spaceType = Team,
   subspaces = {},                              subspaces = {},
   modes = {                                    modes = {
      { id = base1,                                { id = boss,
        type = BaseRobot,                            type = Leader,
        owner = agbaseA,                             owner = ag332,
        attributes = {radius = 20, energy           attributes = {ordered(ex1,
            = 2000, ...},                                returnHome)},
        deontic constraints = {},                    deontic constraints = {},
      },                                           },
      { id = explorer1,                            { id = ex1,
        type = Explorer,                             type = Explorer,
        owner = rob33,                               owner = rob33,
        attributes = {..., x = 10, y =               attributes = {...},
            23, speed = 20, ...},                    deontic constraints = {obliged(
        deontic constraints = {}                         returnHome, boss)}
      },                                           },
      ...                                          ...
   },                                           },
   objects = {                                  objects = {...}
      { id = ob1,                             }
        type = Obstacle,
        attributes = {x = 20, y = 30}},
      },
      ...
   }
}
```

Fig. 4. Spaces at execution time

5   Conclusions

The AGREEN model described in this paper is a revisited extension of the AGRE
model. Its main goal is to provide a much simpler and unified way of representing
(physical and social) environments. The model is based on: (i) a clear separation between what an agent tries to do and the effects obtained as independent consequences
of its acts on the environments and (ii) a clear distinction between what an agent can
do, as capabilities, and what an agent is supposed to do, as deontic constraints.

Another message of this article is that, the institution, defined by Searle as a set of
constitutive rules of the form "X counts as Y in context C", is a concept general enough
to expressively describe mediated interaction and environment-based coordination. In
AGREEN, the space and its type, taken together, should be seen as the basic institutional unit. A space represents that part of the social reality constructed according to the
(constitutive) rules defined by its type. A space type actually corresponds to the context
C in Searle's terminology or to S in Jones and Sergot's formalization of *count as* operator (e.g. $X \Rightarrow_S Y$). It regroups all the constitutive rules relative to the same context C.
When modeling the interaction, the expressive power of institutional concepts comes
from the fact that we can divide the whole space of interactions in smaller parts and
consider them separately, in isolation or connected to others.

The unified institutional model proposed in this article, allows someone to uniformly describe various types of interaction. The difference between physical and social

interaction is that in the case of a physical space we don't have to specify deontic constraints and social dependency relationships. We note, however, that the social dependency relationship, which is similar to the *count as* operator, and the more general notion of dependency between any two spaces deserve both more attention and formal definitions. This will be subject of our future work.

Acknowledgements

This work has been supported by France Telecom R&D. We would like to thank Ludivine Crepin, Robert Demolombe, Vincent Louis, David Sadek and John Tranier for the fruitful discussions on various aspects described in this article, and the anonymous reviewers for their valuable suggestions.

References

1. Castelfranchi, C.: Engineering social order. In: ESAW'00. Volume 1972 of LNCS. (2000)
2. Jones, A.J.I., Sergot, M.: A formal characterisation of institutionalised power. Journal of the Interest Group in Pure and Applied Logics **4**(3) (1996) 429–445
3. Boella, G., van der Torre, L.: Structuring organizations by means of roles using the agent metaphor. In: WOA'04. (2004)
4. Vázquez-Salceda, J., Dignum, V., Dignum, F.: Organizing multiagent systems. Autonomous Agents and Multi-Agent Systems **11**(3) (2005) 307–360
5. Stratulat, T., Clérin-Debart, F., Enjalbert, P.: Norms and time in agent-based systems. In: Proceedings of the 8th International Conference on Artificial Intelligence and Law (ICAIL'01), St. Louis, Missouri, USA (2001)
6. Ferber, J., Gutknecht, O.: Alaadin: a meta-model for the analysis and design of organizations in multi-agent systems. In: ICMAS'98, IEEE Computer Society (1998) 128–135
7. Ferber, J., Michel, F., Báez-Barranco, J.A.: AGRE : Integrating environments with organizations. In: Environments for Multi-agent Systems. Volume 3374 of Lecture Notes in Computer Science., Springer (2005) 48–56
8. Ferber, J., Müller, J.P.: Influences and reaction : a model of situated multi-agent systems. In: Proceedings of the 2nd International Conference on Multi-agent Systems (ICMAS-96), The AAAI Press (1996) 72–79
9. Artikis, A., Pitt, J., Sergot, M.: Animated specifications of computational societies. In: AAMAS '02, New York, NY, USA, ACM Press (2002) 1053–1061
10. Singh, M.P.: Agent communication languages: Rethinking the principles. Computer **31**(12) (1998) 40–47
11. Searle, J.R.: The Construction of Social Reality. The Free Press (1995)
12. Warbot: A robot video game. http://www.warbot.org (2005)

Exploiting the Environment for Coordinating Agent Intentions

Tom Holvoet[1] and Paul Valckenaers[2]

[1] K.U.Leuven - Dept. Computer Science, DistriNet
Celestijnenlaan 200A, B-3001 Leuven, Belgium
Tom.Holvoet@cs.kuleuven.be
[2] K.U.Leuven - Dept. Mechanics, PMA
Celestijnenlaan 300B, B-3001 Leuven, Belgium
Paul.Valckenaers@mech.kuleuven.be

Abstract. One large and quite interesting family of MAS applications is characterized (1) by their large scale in terms of number of agents and physical distribution, (2) by their very dynamic nature and (3) by their complex functional and non-functional requirements. This family includes a.o. manufacturing control, traffic control and web service coordination. BDI-based agent architectures have proven their usefulness in building MASs for complex systems - their explicit attention for coping with dynamic environments is one obvious explanation for this. For the family of applications mentioned above, the complexity of the software for the individual agents using traditional BDI-approaches, however, is overwhelming.

In this paper, we present an innovative approach to BDI agents which alleviates agent complexity through so-called "delegate MASs", which use the environment and its resources to obtain BDI functionality. Delegate MASs consist of light-weight agents, which are issued either by resources for building and maintaining information on the environment, or by task agents in order to explore the options on behalf of the agents and to coordinate their intentions. We describe the approach, and validate it in a case study of manufacturing control. The evaluation in this case study shows the feasibility of the approach in coping with the large scale of the application and shows that the approach elegantly achieves flexibility in highly dynamic environments.

1 Introduction

The term "coordination and control applications" can be coined to refer to a large family of application which share a number of characteristics. First, in the applications, one can distinguish (1) an underlying physical or software environment, and (2) a software system that is connected to this environment. The underlying environment contains fixed entities or "resources" capable of performing particular operations, as well as mobile entities which can move in the environment. Second, the coordination and control software system is able to observe and direct the entities in the underlying environment. Third, the purpose of

D. Weyns, H.V.D. Parunak, and F. Michel (Eds.): E4MAS 2006, LNAI 4389, pp. 51–66, 2007.

the application is to execute "tasks". Executing a task requires moving through the environment and performing operations by using resources. The purpose of the software system is to manage the underlying environment by controlling entities that live in the environment, and coordinating the collective behavior of these entities. Fourth, the underlying system evolves several orders of magnitude slower than the coordination and control software. This allows the software to observe the environment and to plan ahead. Fifth, the environment itself is highly dynamic. Resources may crash, new resources may be added, connections between resources may be added, lost, or their characteristics (e.g. throughput, speed) may change. Members of this family of coordination and control applications include manufacturing control, traffic control and web service coordination, but also supply chain management and multi-modal logistics. As an example, in manufacturing control, the environment is the physical world equipped with resources such as machines and conveyor belts, and the tasks are the client orders for fabricating particular products. The software in manufacturing control is responsible for controlling the resources and for guiding the orders through the factory floor.

Centralistic software approaches tend to break when the underlying system is large scale in terms of physical distribution and number of entities. Based on the characteristics and requirements described above, a decentralized, multi-agent system approach is suitable for modeling and developing the software for these applications. Both the mobile entities (partially fabricated products, vehicles, client software) and the fixed entities or resources in the environment (machines or conveyor belts, roads and intersections, web services) are obvious candidates to be represented as agents - which we call task agents and resource agents respectively.

Research related to BDI-approaches [1,11] is particularly interesting and broad - we refer to just of few related topics here [12,8,6,2,3]. Building a realistic BDI agent involves many aspects, including - but not limited to:

- **knowledge engineering** information (beliefs) must be gathered from the environment and from the task and resources agents, and must be kept up-to-date according to some policy;
- **deliberation** based on the world model, the agent needs to decide what state of affairs it will intend to bring about;
- **means-ends reasoning** either through on-line planning or using plan libraries, a plan is devised to reach the intention;
- **direct communication** for many aspects, distributed communication protocols are necessary - most notably for coordinating the behavior of the task agents, but also to inform resources of agent intentions, exchange state with other task agents, and so on;
- **advanced concepts** including joint plans, joint intentions, learning may be quite useful.

Experience with BDI-agents in small-scale and toy applications, as discussed in a lot of literature contributions for over ten years, yield agents which were conceptually clean, yet these agents quickly become quite complex. For the application domains in coordination and control for large-scale systems in highly dynamic environments, the complexity of BDI-based models of agents and the expected computational effort is simply overwhelming.

Partially inspired by the recent trend to exploit the environment as a design abstraction for managing complexity in MAS [14], we propose a particular BDI-based approach that aims to avoid most of the internal agent complexity. Rather than creating and maintaining complex world and agent models themselves, the agents delegate this to the environment. In the approach, we introduce the concept of "delegate MASs" which are issued by the different agents. Delegate MASs consist of light-weight agents which perform particular activities on behalf of a task or resource agent. These light-weight agents can explore the environment and bring relevant information back to their responsible task agent, can evaluate optional paths, and can put the intentions of their task agent as information in the environment. This allows delegate MASs of different agents to coordinate by aligning or adapting the information in the environment according to their own tasks.

This paper is structured as follows. Section 2 describes the basic software architecture of our approach, which consists of task and resource agents and their environment. In Sect. 3, we refine this architecture by proposing how the agents deal with beliefs, desires and intentions through delegate MASs. As the contribution of this paper is on the approach rather than on the application domains, we restrict the examples and illustrations to manufacturing control. A concrete case study in manufacturing control is described in Sect. 4. Section 5 makes an evaluation and concluding remarks on the proposal, and points out directions for future work.

2   Basic Software Architecture for Coordination and Control Applications

We describe the basic components in the software architecture of our approach, i.e. task agents, resource agents, and the environment.

The environment. The environment of the targeted applications is a dynamic directed graph. The nodes in the graph represent the resources in the environment and the edges represent connections between different resources. The environment contains the mobile entities and allows these entities to move from resource to resource. A mobile entity that resides on a node in the graph can communicate with the resource on this node. When a mobile entity is on a particular node, the corresponding resource can perform an action on the task of this mobile entity.

The lower part of Fig. 1 shows an example of a simple factory of six resources, connected through unidirectional "left-to-right" connections.

Resource Agents. A resource agent represents a resource in the environment and contains an information processing part for controlling the resource. The resource agent lives in a virtual world that represents the underlying system,

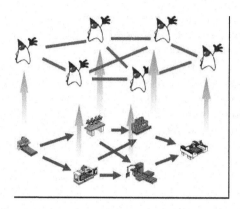

Fig. 1. A simple factory consisting of six resources, which are connected left to right

but which allows bidirectional communication for each connection (see upper part of Fig. 1). The resource itself offers processing capacity and functionality to the resource agent. In manufacturing control systems, a resource agent is an abstraction of the production means such as machines, conveyors, tool holders, material storage or even personnel.

A resource can abstractly be described as a set of capabilities. A capability specifies the operations that the resource is able to perform.

Resource agents need to be able to make schedules based on requests from task agents. Resource agents must also be able to answer "what-if questions": a task agent may ask a resource agent when and according to what quality standards a particular operation could be performed if the task would arrive at a future time. This allows task agents to evaluate the total time to completion and the expected quality of the finished task for a particular plan.

Task agents. A task agent represents and controls a task in the coordination and control application, and resides on a (physical or virtual) mobile entity in the environment. A task agent is responsible for performing its task by guiding its mobile unit through the environment, and communicating with resource agents in order to perform operations on the unit. A task has to be performed correctly and in time. Every task agent is aware of the goal of its task, and has available the schemes or plans that can be followed in order to reach this goal. For manufacturing control, the task agents represent (unfinished) client orders and are associated with the pallets with partially fabricated products. The production schemes describe possible sequences of operations on the product in order to obtain the final product. A task agent may represent customer orders, make-to-stock orders, prototype-making orders, orders to maintain and repair resources, etc.

Task agents are obvious candidates to be modeled as BDI agents. Task agents need to deal with the observations of the environment and its entities (beliefs), consider possible options on how to proceed (desires), choose a particular option (intention) and communicate this with the other task agents. This allows the agents to coordinate their behavior by accommodating their intentions.

Coordination is necessary as actions of one task agent may obviously influence the situation of the other task agents. If the situation in the environment is such that another option becomes substantially more favorable, the agent can reconsider and adopt a new intention.

Agent Interactions. Both resource and task agents control the entities in the environment, and obviously need to interact to achieve the goal of the application. A typical interaction amongst these agents goes as follows.

When a new "task" enters the system, a task agent is created and connected to the appropriate unit. The agent is aware of the initial state of the task and investigates possible next operations that can be performed. The agent searches and selects a combination of a next processing step and a suitable resource that has the capability to execute the step.

When the selected processing step is executed by the resource, the resource reports on the new state of the task. This may or may not be the expected outcome of the operation. Based on this state, the task agent investigates possible next steps based on the task schemes, and selects a combination of a processing step and a suitable resource again. This process is repeated until the task is finished.

3 Delegate Multi-Agent Systems for BDI Through the Environment

In the previous section, we identified the core abstractions and concepts for modeling a coordination and control application as a multi-agent system. In this section, we describe the functionality that is required for the task agents to be able to achieve their goals, and explain how we achieve this functionality through delegate MASs.

3.1 Required Functionality

Make feasibility information available. As routing tasks through the environment is an essential feature in coordination and control applications, the environment must provide a means to inspect *feasible paths*. A feasible path describes a sequences of resources that can be reached by following this path. Feasibility information reflects physical or topological constraints in the environment. If there is a path from one node H to a destination node D via node V, this must be observable as a feasible path.

Task agents need to explore relevant paths. Task agents need to explore the feasible paths that *correspond* to their task schemes. A feasible path corresponds to a task scheme if following this path routes the task agent along the resources that are necessary to reach its final goal. A task agent needs to consider all possible schemes (i.e. sequences of operations) which can bring the current task toward its goal, and match these plans with the feasibility information. The feasible paths that match a suitable scheme represent the different options that the task agent has to achieve its goal.

Exploring a path means to evaluate the path in a "what-if mode" in order to judge timing and quality if this path would be followed by the task agent.

Intentions. Based on the options that are available to a task agent and their evaluation in a what-if mode, the task agent chooses one path as its intention. Adopting an intention obviously has implications on the resource agents that will be visited as part of the intention. The task agent needs to communicate with those resource agents and inform them of when they will arrive and which operation the resource will need to perform. The resource agents need to book these reservations.

3.2   How: Delegate MASs

A typical approach would be to use direct communication protocols, knowledge engineering and means-ends reasoning to achieve this functionality. Here, we use delegate MASs for obtaining feasibility information, exploration and propagation of intentions toward the resource agents. To some degree, delegate MASs are inspired by food foraging in ant colonies. Food foraging ants execute a simple procedure. In absence of any signs in the environment, ants walk around randomly in search for food. When an ant discovers a food source, it drops a smelling substance - a pheromone - on its way back to the nest while carrying some of the food. This pheromone trail evaporates over time, and disappears if no other ant deposits fresh pheromone. Another ant in search for food will use pheromones in the environment as a source of information to direct its own behavior. Pheromones indicate possible routes to a food source, ants are urged by instinct to follow this trail to the food source. When the ant finds the food source, it will return with food, while depositing pheromone itself. When the ant discovers that the food source is exhausted, it starts a randomised search for food again. As the pheromone trail is no longer maintained, it disappears over time.

These simple behavior patterns result in an emergent behavior of the ant colony that is highly ordered and effective at foraging food while being robust against the uncertainty and the complexity of the environment. An important capability of this type of collective behavior is illustrated: global information - about where to find food in a remote location - is made available locally - in which direction must the ant move to get to this food. The following interesting principles are recognized: (1) make the environment part of the solution to handle a complex environment without being exposed to its complexity - ants are quite simple agents; (2) place relevant information as signs in the environment ensuring that locally available data informs about remote system properties; (3) limit the lifetime of this information (evaporation) and refresh the information as long as it remains valid - this allows the system to cope with changes and disturbances.

We exploit these principles in our approach and define three types of lightweight agents, which each represent a different delegate MAS and which share a common environment for indirect communication. To distinguish them from task and resource agents, we call the light-weight agents "ant agents" or ants further on. Delegate MASs consist of ant agents that reside in a virtual software environment which reflects the application environment, and in which ant agents can navigate. The responsibilities of the delegate MASs are restricted in that they are managed by the basic agents. Individual ant agents have a particular activity to perform autonomously, yet which information they distributem or how the information they gather is used, is the responsibility of the issuing basic agent.

Feasibility Ants. Feasibility ants form a delegate MAS that is issued by resource agents. Their purpose is to roam the environment and, at each node they pass, drop information on feasible paths that start from this node.

Resource agents which have not seen a feasibility ant passing by for a particular period will create new feasibility ants themselves at a certain frequency. The behavior of a feasibility ant is as follows.

A feasibility ant communicates with the resource agent at its current node, and asks for its capabilities. The ant observes the environment locally and finds out from which other nodes the current node can be reached. As the system environment is a directed graph, this means that the ant makes a list of all nodes that are predecessor of the current node. A clone of the feasibility ant is sent to each node in this list. The ants can be seen as moving upstream. When arrived at the new node, the ant asks the local resource agent for its capabilities, and merges this information with information of previous nodes. Now this ant knows that from this node, a sequence of operation that requires a capability from the current node followed by an operation that can be performed at its previous node is currently feasible. This information is dropped at the local information space of the current node, as a kind of road sign. Then the ant clones itself for every node upstream, and the process is repeated. A feasibility ant dies if there are no nodes upstream. Cycles can be dealt with by accumulating this information - as such the information may not only contain sequences but also iterations of resource capabilities. The information that is stored in local information spaces is time-stepped, and, if not refreshed by another feasibility agent in time, that information disappears. This is necessary to accommodate dynamic changes in the environment both on the topology and the resources in the topology.

This process can and must be fine-tuned for every application in order to avoid flooding. Hop limits, limited cloning budgets and probabilistic choices of upstream nodes are a few mechanisms that can be used, but which mechanisms are useful and effective depends on the concrete application.

Exploration Ants. Using the feasibility information available locally, a task agent is able to find out which paths are physically or virtually feasible for achieving the goal of its task. A task agent generates exploration ants at a certain frequency which explore feasible paths. These exploration ants are scouts that each explore a feasible route through the underlying system and evaluate this route. This evaluation typically concerns completion time and quality criteria on the final state of the task, but can also include a cost e.g. for the usage of fragile, expensive or critical resources. To make the evaluation, an exploration ant follows a path

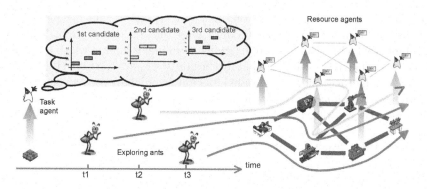

Fig. 2. Exploration ants, issued by a task agent, scout feasible paths by roaming the graph environment

through the environment, and interacts with the resource agents at the different nodes by asking the resource agent *what* the timing, quality or costs would be *if* a task in a particular state would arrive at a particular moment in time. The exploration ant collects this information, and then proceeds to the next node in the path, in which this behavior is repeated. When arrived at the end of the path, the exploration ant returns and reports back to its base, i.e. the task agent that created the exploration ant. Figure 2 illustrates this process for the simple factory shown in Fig. 1. The task agent on the left hand side creates three exploration ants for scouting feasible paths.

The information that a task agent gathers in this way from all its exploration ants is filtered out in order to withhold the paths that are valid options for the task at hand. An option is valid if, besides yielding the required goal, the goal is reached in due time and with an acceptable quality and cost.

The list of candidates get refreshed regularly as exploration ants are sent out regularly. Candidates that are not refreshed are removed over time, assuming that these candidates have become invalid or infeasible because of changes in the environment.

Intention Ants. Exploration as described above requires the resource agents to possess an adequate estimate of their future workload. To serve this purpose, task agents generate intention ants, which propagate the intention of task agents through the environment.

The process goes as follows. When a task agent has constructed a set of valid paths to follow, the task agent selects one candidate path to become its intention. The criteria used for this selection depends on the requirements of the task, and is application-specific. Then, the task agent creates intention ants, at a certain frequency, to inform the resource agents that are involved in this intended path.

The intention ants follow the selected path, and virtually execute the routing and processing of their selected candidate solution. On their virtual journey, the intention ants acquire travel, queuing, and processing times from the resource agents on their path. Any changes, which occurred since the exploration,

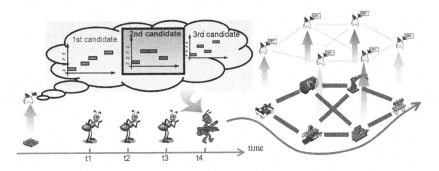

Fig. 3. Intention ants, issued by a task agent, communicate the intention of the task agent through the environment

immediately become visible when these resource agents provide the information. In contrast to the exploration ants, intention ants inform the resource agent that their order agent is likely to visit them at the estimated time and to perform a particular operation. In this way, intention agents make a (evaporating) booking on the resource, and the resource agent adjusts its load forecast (local schedule of the resource) to account for this visit. As a consequence, resource agents are able to predict their workload and performance more accurately to their visiting exploration and intention ants. Similar as exploration ants, intention ants report back to their task agent to inform the agent about the schedule and performance of the bookings.

Figure 3 illustrates this for our simple factory example. Based on the information that was gathered by the three exploration ants, the task ant decides that the path explored by the last exploration ant (which explored candidate path 2) fits the task requirements best. To confirm this and align this decision with the involved resource, an intention ant tries to walk the same path and make bookings on its way.

One important note to make is that, as a consequence of this process, the actual intention of a task agent, as it is distributed to the different resource agents, is only the path that the task agent intends to follow. This intention is then aligned with the schedules and performance of the involved resources. The task agent decides on the path to follow in an intention, the environment and its resources decide on the resulting schedule and performance, which may or may not correspond with the beliefs of the task agent based on the information from the exploration ants. As such, this process reliefs the task agent from massive communication using complex protocols to ensure e.g. a two phase commit for reserving all resources.

The intention information at the resource agent - the booking - evaporates. Task agents must create intention agents to refresh their intention at a frequency that is sufficiently high to maintain their bookings at the resources.

While refreshing, a task agent observes the evolution of the expected performance of its current intentions through the reports on the estimated performance that intention ants bring back. This performance estimate is compared to the estimates of the candidate solutions that are found and refreshed by the exploration agents. When the estimated performance of the current intention drops significantly below the estimated performance of other candidate solutions, the task agent may revise its intention. When the task of a task agent reaches the point where a decision needs to be executed, the task agent triggers the action in the underlying system in accordance with the intention.

Task and Resource Agents. Let us now list the responsibilities of task and resources agents. These lists should guide a developer of a coordination and control application to define a concrete software architecture for these agents.

A resource agent is responsible for (1) answering what-if questions from exploration ants, (2) making schedules based on requests for bookings by intention ants - the schedules must obviously respect resource constraints as well as follow a predefined policy for re-scheduling, e.g. when high-priority tasks make a booking, this may reject earlier reservations, (3) keep an up-to-date view on the resource that the resource agent is managing (e.g. observe operation quality and status), and (4) send out feasibility ants if no feasibility ants have contacted this resource agent for a while. These guidelines should suffice to produce a concrete architecture according to the requirements of a concrete application. The resource agent could execute each of these responsibilities in sequence, or one may opt to define concurrent execution of some of these responsibilities.

The responsibilities of the task agents are the following. First, a task agent must have knowledge about its task, about the initial state of the task, and about task schemes. Task schemes describe one or several plans to achieve the goal of the task, and given any intermediate state of the task, the task scheme should provide one or more sub-plans to fulfill the task. Second, a task agent must manage its beliefs. Beliefs on feasibility are readily available from the information space in the environment. Beliefs about explored paths are gathered by exploration ants. Third, this information needs to be filtered out, yielding valid paths - the agents desires. Fourth, based on the beliefs about the task and the options, a task agent then chooses or revises its intention. Fifth, at appropriate times and frequency, exploration ants as well as intention ants are sent out. Finally, a task agent is responsible for interacting with resource agents in order to perform operations on its task.

Again, these responsibilities are either executed as a sequence, or one may choose for concurrent execution of some of these responsibilities.

4   A Case Study in Manufacturing Control

We have applied the approach (in simulation) on several artificial toy examples, and on one realistic case. In a research and development project, in collaboration with an industrial partner, we investigated the approach for coordination and control of a factory that produces parts of weaving machines (see Fig. 4 for a screen shot of the factory in a simulation tool). The factory that is modeled in

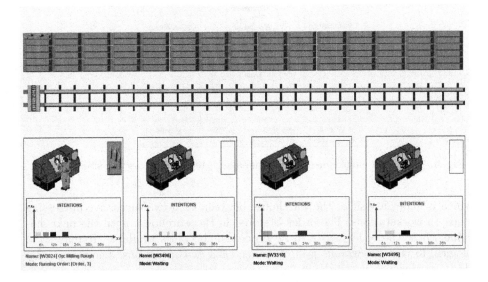

Fig. 4. A weaving machine factory - CNC machines and a warehouse, connected to a shared tram system

this case study has a particular topology, which consists of several workstations (machines, in the middle of the picture) and one warehouse (top of the picture), and a shared transportation unit (on the rails). The warehouse contains storage slots, which store containers with product parts. The warehouse is automated in that it is capable of managing these slots itself. Besides the machine workstations, an "input station" is responsible for entering new orders into the system, and one "output station" delivers finished product outside of the system. The transportation unit is a tram which can visit all workstations and the warehouse. This tram carries containers between the different workstations and between the workstations and the warehouse.

A schematic representation of this topology illustrates the directed graph of this environment, see Fig. 5. Conceptually, all workstations and the warehouse are bi-directionally connected to the tram resource.

A crucial requirement for the coordination and control software for this case is the optimization of usage of the transport system (the tram). During periods of heavy demand for transportation (rush hour), the tram is a bottleneck and causes workstations and operators to idle, which is expensive.

For this case, we conducted two sets of experiments. The experiments focus on the flexibility of the approach in dealing with unpredictable timings of machine operations. Experiments with changing topologies are promising results as well, but are not reported here.

In a first set of experiments, we applied a straightforward detailed design of our approach, in which the production schemes reflect current practice. The production schemes are simple deterministic lists of sequential processing steps,

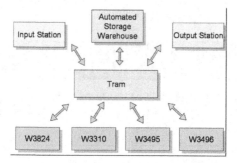

Fig. 5. The graph environment of the manufacturing control case - a star topology

which includes a visit to the warehouse between each two successive processing steps on workstations. The order is stored in the warehouse until the next machine where the order needs to be processed, becomes available. It may seem illogical to visit the warehouse in between each two operations. The reason why this is current practice is the inability of the current system to cope with flexibility for dealing with unpredictable timings of operations. When an operation is finished on one machine, and the workstation that is going to be used for the next step is available, a visit to the warehouse is unnecessary, and the order could be delivered immediately. If, however, because of variation in processing time, the workstation for the next operation is not available, even though it was predicted to be available at this time, the transport cannot be performed. The current industrial system (in reality) does not have up-to-date forecasts, and the effects of direct workstation-to-workstation transports on the system performance are therefore unclear and represent an unacceptable risk for the company.

The results obtained from this first set of experiments are quite satisfactory compared to the current characteristics of the system as it is operational today (numbers not available by non-disclosure). Results on the performance of the transport system and the bottleneck machines (W3824 and W3310) in the factory are reported in Table 1. The rightmost column displays aggregated results for all workstations.

In a second set of experiments, we aimed to test the effect of adding flexibility to the system by allowing more flexibility in the task schemes. In these experiments, visiting the warehouse is no longer mandatory but optional between each two processing steps. Besides this change in production schemes, the task agents and resource agents were identical to the first set of experiments. Our approach

Table 1. Results from the basic controller

	Tram	W3824	W3310	Total
avg. wait time	76	41	145	287
total wait time	4315	370	435	8928
max wait time	891	84	365	1587
utilization rate	8%	91%	89%	

Table 2. Results from the enhanced controller

	Tram	W3824	W3310	Total
avg. wait time	109	31	129	274
total wait time	4374	280	387	8488
max wait time	838	57	345	1587
utilization rate	6%	93%	90%	

can benefit from this extra flexibility in the task schemes as it relies on forecasts (intentions) that may be revised, e.g. in the case where processing a particular operation takes longer than predicted. Table 2 shows the results for these experiments. The main effect of this extra flexibility on the tram is a reduction of its load by 25% and the number of transports by 30%. This results in reduced waiting times for all workstation and especially for the bottleneck workstations. The utilization rate on the bottleneck workstations increases, implying that the overall throughput of the manufacturing system increases proportionally. This improvement is significant, even for small percentages, since it directly affects the financial return rate of the investments.

Further improvements are being investigated in this case. The excess capacity on the tram, outside rush hours, can be used to prepare the work during periods of high demand. The availability of an up-to-date prediction is essential for this enhancement since it both informs the system whether there is an opportunity to rearrange the storage and tells the system which rearrangement is likely to lower the workload during upcoming periods of high demand.

Related work on MAS for Coordination and Control. The research presented in this paper builds upon previous research on the PROSA reference architecture [13]. The PROSA architecture recognizes four types of agents, being Product agents, Resource agents, Order agents and Staff agents. Order agents represent specific client orders (comparable to our task agents), resource agents are similar to our resource agents, product agents represent a service which knows the product recipes (i.e. the possible sequences of operations that need to be performed on an order for producing the intended product), staff agents provide a service for the other agents by offering predefined pragmatic solutions for particular problems. The basic architecture of the approach presented here provides a cleaner conceptual model of the core agent types (product and staff agents are not considered as basic agent types, as they do not exhibit pro-active behavior but merely provide services to agents), and most of all allowed us to clearly relate the ant-based mechanisms to BDI-based architectures. This relation will foster this research in two ways. First, it is aimed to provide a more convincing case of our research to the community that is centered around BDI-based approaches. Second, it opens the pathway for studying our approach in terms of well-know and well-studied concepts (both core concepts as well as derivative concepts) in the field of BDI-based approaches.

The main contribution of a delegate MAS design is its ability to generate short-term forecasts; these forecasts account for recent updates on the state of the underlying system and the control system entities themselves. Moreover, feasibility ant agents propagate constraints in the underlying system to wherever they may be relevant.

In comparison, known scalable MAS coordination and control developments are myopic [4,9]. These approaches decide about task allocations when the preceding task is about to finish or is already finished. These systems use interaction protocols e.g. variations on the well-known contract net to implement decision-making mechanisms. A "utility function" in such interaction protocols needs to capture all future implications of the decisions. As a consequence, these designs have proven to be very successful in dynamic but homogeneous environments. For instance, [4] is capable of controlling a homogeneous collection of CNC machine tools (Computer Numerically Controlled machines)in a factory with a flexible transport system but fails to handle a mix of hard automation (low cost and very fast) with flexible but expensive CNC equipment and fails to handle transport systems that have limited flexibility (routing from resource A to resource B is not always feasible). In a delegate MAS, feasibility ant agents account for such heterogeneity and the forecasting functionality permits the coordination and control system to account early enough for the often erratic constraints in such production systems.

Early attempts to account for the complete sequence of production steps that are required to execute a task, suffer from combinatorial explosions. In such developments, resource agents, when they are unable to finish a task, recursively subcontract the remainder of this task to other resource agents before entering their bid [7]. Recently, advanced machine learning techniques have been applied to select candidate subcontractors and eliminate the combinatorial explosion [5]. However powerful, such solutions require software maintenance when the model of the underlying system changes (e.g. to account for storage and transportation) by an expert in such machine learning technology. Likewise, researchers have developed MAS control system that incorporate planning systems [10]. Again, changes to the model of the underlying system are likely require challenging maintenance efforts. In contrast, models in delegate MASs have a one-to-one correspondence to the corresponding entity in the real world; their is no modeling effort required to fit the coordination technology; delegate MAS designs stay close to reactive agent designs in that the world almost remains its own best model.

5   Evaluation and Conclusion

Developing a real-world coordination and control application will never be easy - the problem domains are too complex and the environment too dynamic for this. In this paper, we do not claim that other MAS approaches to these applications (e.g. classical BDI-based or other approaches), technically cannot be used to tackle these applications. Instead, we want (1) to emphasize the enormous complexity that is involved in the agent software for such realistic applications, and (2) to make a strong case that creative architectural alternatives are worth investigating. In the approach we propose, we stick to the basic philosophy of belief-desires-intention agents, but exploit the environment and delegate MASs, inspired by ant behavior, to realize beliefs, desires and intentions. This innovative approach yields quite interesting results for the targeted application domains, both in terms of the reduction of the agent software complexity and in overall performance in a highly dynamic environment.

The use of a delegate MAS allows the coordination and control system to handle changes and disturbances as "business-as-usual". Indeed, feasibility ants discover the (dis)appearance of resources during refresh. Likewise, lost connections and (re)connections are discovered during such refresh by feasibility ant agents. Furthermore, disturbances such as a rush order pushing reservations by other tasks backwards, or a temporary equipment malfunction causing similar shifts for reservations, are detected during refresh of both intentions and candidate solutions by respectively intention and exploration ants. Stale information, which refresh activities fail to update or remove, disappears through the evaporation mechanism within the time needed for a few refresh cycles.

One important difference between an approach using delegate MAS and traditional BDI approach for coordination and control systems is that a delegate MAS design extends Brooks concept of having the world as its own best model, while traditional BDI approaches rely on maintaining world models. The basic idea of having the "world as its own best model" only discusses the present state of the world. In contrast, the delegate MAS approach in this paper extends this idea toward the future state, using exploration and intention ants, while keeping modeling efforts acceptable. Indeed, resource agents only need to be knowledgeable and intelligent about their own small section of the world.

There is one caveat to the approach: the task agents must behave in a socially acceptable manner. This means that agents do not change their intentions too easily and too frequently. Otherwise, minor disturbances such as a short breakdown of a resource may create an avalanche of tasks that shift to alternative resources. The perceived improvement must be higher than a threshold value before the current intention is replaced by the more-promising alternative.

To avoid too many agents revising their intentions at the same time, possibly yielding thrashing behavior, task agents change their intentions probabilistically. As a result, only a small fraction of task agents may change their intentions, and the other agents are able to observe the consequences before changing their intentions as well. Adopting this mechanism ensures that task agents will gradually shift toward alternative routes when a disturbance occurs until a new equilibrium is reached.

To serve the purpose of this paper, the approach was described at a high-level of abstraction as a generic software architecture, and contained mainly hints and guidelines for designers of real coordination and control applications, and a report on experiments in one manufacturing control case. A detailed design of the approach specific for manufacturing control is available. Other detailed designs are likely to follow when adopting this approach in other concrete application domains.

References

1. M. E. Bratman. *Intentions, Plans, and Practical Reason.* Harvard, Cambridge, MA, USA, 1987.
2. L. Braubach, A. Pokahr, and W. Lamersdorf. Jadex: A bdi agent system combining middleware and reasoning. In M. K. R. Unland, M. Calisti, editor, *Software Agent-Based Applications, Platforms and Development Kits*, pages 143–168. Birkhuser-Verlag, Basel-Boston-Berlin, 9 2005. Book chapter.
3. L. Braubach, A. Pokahr, W. Lamersdorf, and D. Moldt. Goal representation for bdi agent systems. In R. H. Bordini, M. Dastani, J. Dix, and A. E. Fallah-Seghrouchni, editors, *Second International Workshop on Programming Multiagent Systems: Languages and Tools*, pages 9–20, 7 2004.
4. S. Bussmann, N. Jennings, and M. Wooldridge. *Multiagent systems for manufacturing control: A design methodology*, volume XIV of *Springer Series on Agent Technology*. Springer-Verlag, 2004.
5. B. Cs.Csji, L. Monostori, and B. Kdr. Reinforcement learning in a distributed market-based production control system, 2004.
6. F. Dignum, D. Morley, L. Sonenberg, and L. Cavedon. Towards socially sophisticated bdi agents. In *ICMAS*, pages 111–118. IEEE Computer Society, 2000.
7. A. Marcus, T. Vancza, and L. Monostori. A market approach to holonic manufacturing, 1996.
8. S. Parsons, O. Pettersson, A. Saffiotti, and M. Wooldridge. Intention reconsideration in theory and practice. In W. Horn, editor, *Proceedings of the Fourteenth European Conference on Artificial Intelligence (ECAI-2000)*. John Wiley & Sons, 2000.
9. H. Parunak, A. D. Baker, and S. J. Clark. The aaria agent architecture: From manufacturing requirements to agent-based system design. *Integrated Computer-Aided Engineering*, 8(1):45–58, 2001.
10. M. Pěchouček, A. Říha, J. Vokřínek, V. Mařík, and V. Pražma. Explantech: applying multi-agent systems in production planning. *International Journal of Production Research*, 40(15):3681–3692, 2002.
11. A. S. Rao and M. P. Georgeff. BDI-agents: from theory to practice. In *Proceedings of the First Intl. Conference on Multiagent Systems*, San Francisco, 1995.
12. J. Thangarajah, L. Padgham, and J. Harland. Representation and reasoning for goals in BDI agents. In M. J. Oudshoorn, editor, *Twenty-Fifth Australasian Computer Science Conference (ACSC2002)*, Melbourne, Australia, 2002. ACS.
13. H. Van Brussel, J. Wyns, P. Valckenaers, L. Bongaerts, and P. Peeters. Reference architecture for holonic manufacturing systems: Prosa. *Computers in Industry*, 37(3):255–276, 1998.
14. D. Weyns, H. V. D. Parunak, F. Michel, T. Holvoet, and J. Ferber. Environments for multiagent systems state-of-the-art and research challenges. In D. Weyns, H. V. D. Parunak, and F. Michel, editors, *E4MAS*, volume 3374 of *Lecture Notes in Computer Science*, pages 1–47. Springer, 2004.

CArtAgO: A Framework for Prototyping Artifact-Based Environments in MAS

Alessandro Ricci, Mirko Viroli, and Andrea Omicini

ALMA MATER STUDIORUM—Università di Bologna
via Venezia 52, 47023 Cesena, Italy
{a.ricci,mirko.viroli,andrea.omicini}@unibo.it

Abstract. This paper describes CArtAgO, a framework for developing artifact-based working environments for multiagent systems (MAS). The framework is based on the notion of *artifact*, as a basic abstraction to model and engineer objects, resources and tools designed to be used and manipulated by agents at run-time to support their working activities, in particular the cooperative ones. CArtAgO enables MAS engineers to design and develop suitable artifacts, and to extend existing agent platforms with the possibility to create artifact-based working environments, programming agents to exploit them. In this paper, first the abstract model and architecture of CArtAgO is described, then a first Java-based prototype technology is discussed.

1 Introduction

Artifacts have been recently proposed as first-class abstractions to model and engineer agent *working environments* in software MAS (multiagent systems) [1]. The background view, shared with other recent approaches in MAS literature— see [2,3] for a survey—, is that the environment plays a fundamental role in engineering of MAS. On the one hand, environment is a suitable locus for engineers to embed responsibilities, impacting on MAS design and development; on the other hand, it is a source of structures and services that agents can suitably use at run-time to support and improve their activities—both individual and social ones. The specific notion of *working environment* is intentionally analogous to the notion of human cooperative working environments, as they are studied by disciplines and theories in human science, such as Activity Theory and Distributed Cognition, and recently adopted also in the context of CSCW (Computer Supported Cooperative Work) and HCI (Human-Computer Interaction) [4,5]. There, a working environment—also referred as *field of work*—is such part of the environment explicitly designed to support and realise agent working activities. Typically, it is modelled as set of objects, tools, more generally "artifacts", which are constructed, shared, and either cooperatively (or competitively) used by humans, so as to mediate and sustain their activities.

Analogously to human society, such a perspective is likely to be fundamental also in the context of agent societies, in particular for designing and programming

D. Weyns, H.V.D. Parunak, and F. Michel (Eds.): E4MAS 2006, LNAI 4389, pp. 67–86, 2007.

complex software systems based on MAS. Given that MAS are growing increasingly complex, one may easily foresee that the next step in the evolution of cognitive MAS will require MAS models and architectures to deal with agents situated within suitable working environments. There, agents would autonomously construct, share, and co-operatively use different kinds of artifact—designed either by MAS designers or by the agents themselves—to perform MAS activities. It is worth noticing that such a perspective shares the aims and principles developed by the research work in Distributed Artificial Intelligence about theories of interaction, environments and the role of tools [6,7].

The artifact abstraction is at the heart of this conceptual framework—which can be referred as A&A (agents and artifacts)—and promotes a methodology for modelling and engineering working environments, by introducing new concepts and elements that impact on system design, development and run-time management. Artifacts can be generally conceived as passive, *function-oriented* computational entities, explicitly designed to provide some kind of *function*, and then to be *used* by agents to support their individual and collective (social) activities [1]. The notion of "function" here refers to the meaning that is generally used in human sciences such as sociology and anthropology, as well as in some recent work in AI [7], that is, the purpose for which the object has been designed for—for an artifact, to support agent activities.

This view directly impacts on the foundation of interaction and activity in agency: a MAS is conceived as an (open) set of agents that develop their activities by *(i)* computing, *(ii)* communicating with each other, and *(iii)* *using* and possibly constructing shared artifacts. Artifacts could be either the targets (outcome) of agent activities, or the *tools* that agents use as means to support such activities: as such, they are useful to reduce complexity of task execution. For instance, *coordination artifacts* [8] are artifacts providing coordination functionalities—such as blackboards, tuple spaces or workflow engines.

In this paper we introduce and discuss CArtAgO (Common "Artifacts for Agents" Open framework), a framework for prototyping MAS applications with artifact-based working environments. Essentially, CArtAgO provides *(i)* the API to define any useful kind of artifacts, *(ii)* the API to be exploited by agents (agent programmers) for interacting with working environments populated by artifacts—in particular to instantiate, use, manipulate artifacts—, and *(iii)* a run-time environment supporting the existence and dynamic management of working environments. CArtAgO does not introduce any specific model or architecture for agents and agent societies: the framework is meant to be integrated and used with existing agent platforms, possibly characterised by heterogeneous kinds of agent architectures. From a conceptual point of view, CArtAgO makes it possible to build MAS composed by heterogeneous agent societies, made of reactive and cognitive agents programmed with different agent languages or architectures, sharing the same working environments, and interacting through suitable mediating artifacts—besides communicating via ACL as usual.

The rest of the paper is organised as follows: first, we describe the abstract model and architecture of **CArtAgO** (Sect. 2), focusing in particular on the core of API introduced by the framework (Sect. 3); then, we describe a first concrete implementation prototype (Sect. 4) developed in Java, implementing the core part of the abstract model previously defined.

2   CArtAgO Abstract Model and Architecture

In this section we describe the basic elements and structure of **CArtAgO** working environments, by taking as a reference the abstract architecture schema described in [3] and depicted in Fig. 1, useful to understand **CArtAgO** with respect to the other approaches. Accordingly, the abstract architecture of **CArtAgO** (and of **CArtAgO** working environments) is composed by three main building blocks (see Fig. 2): *(i) agent bodies*—as the entities that make is possible to *situate* agents inside the working environment; *(ii) artifacts*—as the basic building blocks to structure the working environment; and *(iii) workspaces*—as the logical containers of artifacts, useful to define the topology of the working environment.

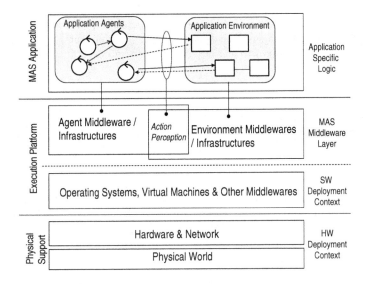

Fig. 1. Abstract representation of MAS layers with environment-based supports as depicted in [3]. Rectangles represent S/W and H/W tiers of the application at different levels. Agents are expressed as circles, environment abstractions as boxes. Arrows from agents to environment abstractions represent actions, dashed arrows in the opposite direction represent perceptions. Arrows between agents represent direct agent communications, while arrows between environment abstractions represent intra-environment interactions. Vertical lines represent the infrastructure supporting a concept at the MAS application level.

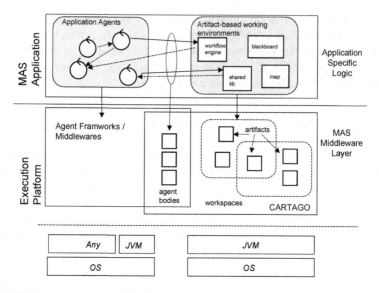

Fig. 2. MAS layers adopting CArtAgO support. Application environments are modelled in terms of artifact-based working environments. The CArtAgO middleware manage the life-cycle of working environments, composed by artifacts grouped in workspaces. Agent bodies are used to situate agents inside the working environments, executing actions upon artifact and perceiving artifacts observable state and events.

2.1 Agent Bodies

Agent bodies are what actually enable the coupling between an agent (mind) and a CArtAgO working environment. For each agent aiming at working inside a CArtAgO environment, an agent body is created. The agent body contains *effectors* to perform actions upon the working environment, and a dynamic set of *sensors* to collect stimuli from the working environment. The agent body is meant to be controlled by the agent, which actually plays the role of the "pilot" of the body. For the purpose, the agent body exposes a controlling interface that the agent mind could suitably exploit to interact with the environment.

By piloting their agent bodies, agents can interact with their working environment, executing *actions* provided for artifact construction, selection and usage, and perceiving *observable events* generated from such artifacts. Differently from the approach typically adopted in traditional agent architectures and more similarly to active perception [9], here perception is modelled as an intentional action referred as *sensing*. More precisely, environment observable events—generated by artifacts—are collected as stimuli by *sensors* which are part of the agent body. An agent can dynamically and flexibly link and unlink to its body different kinds of sensor, with different functionalities, such as buffering, filtering, ordering, and managing priorities. So, in CArtAgO sensing is the internal action that agents execute on their sensors to become aware (perceive) of the *stimuli* collected by the sensors. Stimuli typically concern observable events generated by artifacts.

2.2 Artifacts

Artifacts are the basic bricks managed by CArtAgO framework. Each artifact has a logic *name* specified by the artifact creator at instantiation-time, and an *id*, released by the framework, to univocally identify the artifact. The logic name is an agile way for agents to refer and speak about (shared) artifacts, while the id is required to identify artifacts when executing actions on them. The *full name* of an artifact includes also the name of the workspace(s) where it is logically located. Since an artifact can be located in multiple workspaces, the same artifact can be referenced by multiple full names.

Usage Interface & Observable Events. Analogously to artifacts in our society, the basic model which characterises the interaction between agents and artifacts is based on a notion of use and observation. Agents can use an artifact by triggering the execution of operations listed in the artifact *usage interface*. An operation is characterised by a name and a set of typed parameters. The execution of an operation typically causes the update of the internal state of an artifact, and possibly the generation of one or multiple *observable events*— including error conditions— that can be possibly collected by agents sensor as they are generated, and perceived by agents through explicit sensing actions.

The usage interface of an artifact can change according to artifact *observable state*, exposing different sets of operations according to the specific functioning state of the artifact. The notion of observable state is adopted to structure the functioning behaviour of an artifact in a set of labelled states, which can be recognised (observed) by the artifact users. For each artifact type a finite set of labelled observable states can be defined. For each concrete instance, the notion of current observable state is defined, and its value can change dynamically, during artifact functioning. Then, for each observable state a different usage interface can be defined. This feature makes it possible to structure the overall usage interface of an artifact, providing the right interface according to the functioning stage of the artifact. In other words, an artifact can expose different set of operations according to its observable state.

Dynamically, an agent can trigger the execution of an operation on an artifact if and only if the operation is (currently) part of the usage interface; if the operation does not belong to the usage interface, the agent action fails.

Function Description and Operating Instructions. In order to support a rational exploitation of artifacts by intelligent agents, each artifact is equipped with a *function description*, i.e. an explicit description of the functionalities it provides, and *operating instructions*, i.e. an explicit description of *how* to use the artifact to get its function—for instance in terms of the *usage protocols* that the artifact support. These descriptions are meant to be useful for cognitive agents that—by suitably inspecting and interpreting them—can *(i)* dynamically reason about which artifacts can be selected to support their activities, and *(ii)* get instructions to support activity execution, making it easier to set up plans and to reason about the expectation of using an artifacts. We consider such issues of foremost importance, at the core of the notion of computational environments designed to support the activities of agents—in particular cognitive / rational agents. Actually, research on these aspects—in particular on formal models and languages that can be used to specify function description and operating instructions, and their injection in existing agent reasoning architectures (such as BDI)—is still to be fully developed: we forward the interested reader to [10] for the first results.

In CArtAgO, we provide a minimal enabling support to such issues, by modelling function description and operating instructions as flat strings, specified by artifact designers and dynamically inspectable (observable) by agents through suitable actions. Currently, there is no predefined syntax and semantics for such information (see future work for comments on this point).

2.3 Workspaces

Artifacts are logically located within *workspaces*, which can be used to define the topology of the working environment. A workspace can be defined as an open set of artifacts and agents creating and using them: artifacts can be dynamically added to or removed from workspaces, agents can dynamically enter (join) or exit workspaces. The same artifact can belong to multiple workspaces.

In CArtAgO, each workspace is created by specifying a logic name and is univocally identified by an id. By defining a topology of the environment, workspaces make it possible to structure agents and artifacts organisation and interaction, in particular functioning as scopes for event generation and perception, and artifact access and use. On the one side, a necessary condition for an agent to use an artifact is that it must exist in a workspace where the agent is located. On the other side, events generated by the artifacts of a workspace can be observed only by agents belonging to the same workspace.

Intersection and nesting of workspaces are supported to make it possible to create articulated topologies. In particular, intersection is supported by allowing the same artifacts and agents to belong to different workspaces.

3 Core Primitives

After providing an overview of CArtAgO main components, in this section we describe the basic abstract set of core API provided by the framework on the one side to be used by agents (or agent programmers defining agent behaviour) to interact within working environments, and on the other side for defining artifact types, that is programming artifacts behaviour.

3.1 Agent Side

On the agent side, the API is represented by a set of primitives to control agent bodies and that eventually result in executing actions inside the working environment, making it possible basically to create and use artifacts, and perceive artifact observable state and events. Table 1 provides an abstract description of such primitives, grouped according to their functionalities:

Table 1. Actions available to agents to manage artifacts and workspaces

Artifact construction and disposal	`createArtifact(Name,Template,Config,{WsID}):ArID` `disposeArtifact(ArID)`

Artifact selection & use	`getArtifactID(Name,{WsID}):ArID`
	`execOp(ArID,OpName,{Args},{SensorID})`
	`sense({SensorID},{Pattern},{Timeout}):Perception`
	`focus(ArID,SensorID)`
	`unfocus(ArID,SensorID)`

Artifacts inspection	`getFD(ArID): FDDescr`
	`getOI(ArID): OIDescr`
	`getUID(ArID): UIDDescr`
	`getState(ArID): StateDescr`

Sensor management	`linkSensor(SensorType,SensorConfig): SensorID` `unlinkSensor({SensorID})`

Workspaces management	`getWsID(WsName):WsID`
	`createWS(WsName):WsID`
	`disposeWS(WsID)`
	`registerArtifact(ArID,WsID)`
	`deregisterArtifact(ArID,WsID)`
	`joinWS(WsID)`
	`exitWS(WsID)`

Artifacts construction & disposal — Basic primitives are provided to create (`createArtifact`) and dispose (`disposeArtifact`) artifacts dynamically. To create an artifact, a logic name must be specified, along with the `Template` that identifies the type of the artifact to be created, the initial configuration parameters needed for artifact creation and optionally the workspace where the artifact should be created. The action can fail if the template is unknown or the artifact instantiation is not completed due to some kind of problem (e.g. wrong initial configuration).

Artifact discovery & use — These primitives constitute the core of agent / artifact interactions, enabling an agent to use an artifact by executing operations and observing artifact state and events. To execute an operation, the action `execOp` is provided, specifying the artifact identifier, the operation name, the parameters, and (optionally) the specific sensor where to collect observable events generated by the artifact as a consequence of the operation execution. The action can fail either because the specified artifact is not available, or because the operation cannot be executed since it is not part of artifact usage interface. Action success means that the execution of the specified operation has been successfully triggered. The identifier of an existing artifact can be obtained by the `getArtifactID` primitive, specifying the artifact name and (possibly) its location (workspace).

After triggering the operation, an agent can observe related events through codesense primitives on the sensor specified in `execOp`. By executing sense actions, an agent is made aware of the stimuli that are dynamically collected by a sensor. In particular, the effect of the action is to fetch (remove) a stimulus from the sensor and to return it to the agent as a perception. The action fails if no stimuli are available. Different types of sensors can provide different semantics establishing the order in which events are fetched. A time parameter can be optionally provided to indicate the duration for the sensing action: if no events are available in the sensor within the specified time-frame, the action fails. By default, the time-frame is zero.

In order to support forms of *data-driven* (or, equivalently, *filter-driven*) sensing, a pattern parameter can be specified acting as a filter for fetching (selecting) the perception. Conceptually, the pattern defines a set of perceptions: a perception is fetched if and only if is included in the set. Typically, the pattern can be represented by a Boolean function, establishing—given a perception—if either it is part or not of such a set. It is worth noting that specifying a pattern in a sense action is different from creating sensors that filter stimuli as they are collected. An available stimulus which is not fetched by a sense action because not satisfying the pattern is not removed from the sensor and can be possibly fetched by subsequent sense actions.

Finally, primitives for continuous observation are provided: by executing a `focus` action, an agent becomes a permanent observer of the artifact whose identifier is specified as a parameter. As a permanent observer, all the observable events generated by the artifact are automatically collected by the sensor specified as second parameter, as they are generated; `unfocus` stops the observation.

Artifacts inspection — In order to support a *cognitive* use of artifacts, a basic set of primitive is provided to inspect the function description (`getFD`), the operating instructions (`getOI`), the usage interface (`getUID`), and the dynamic observable (exposed) state (`getState`) of the artifact.

Sensor management — Two basic primitives are provided to dynamically link and unlink sensors to the agent body: `linkSensor` links a sensor of the specified type and configuration to the body, returning the identifier to be used to refer the sensor; `unlinkSensor` unlinks a previously linked sensor.

Workspace manipulation — Finally, a basic set of primitives is provided to manipulate the logical topology of the environment, modelled through workspaces. Such primitives range from `joinWS` and `exitWS` to join and leave a workspace, to `getWsID` for getting a workspace identifier given its name, `createWS` for directly creating a new workspace and `disposeWS` for completely removing a workspace.

Since the same artifact can be part of multiple workspaces, some basic primitives are provided to register (`registerArtifact`) / de-register (`deregisterArtifact`) an artifact in / from a workspace, specifying the workspace id.

Most of these core services have been implemented in the prototype described in Sect. 4.

Table 2. Basic primitives for artifact programming

Observable event generation	`genEvent({OpID},EventType,{EventContent})` `genEventInWsp(EventType,{EventContent})`
Operation management	`getOpID: OpID`
Observable state management	`setObservableState(ObsStateName)` `getObservableState:ObsStateName`

3.2 Artifact Side

On the artifact side, CArtAgO provides a support to define new types of artifact, defining artifact structure and behaviour. The specific programming model adopted to implement in Java artifact types is described in detail in Sect. 4. Here we report the basic set of abstract primitives which can be exploited when defining artifact behaviour (see Table 2), useful essentially for generating observable events and switching artifact observable state.

Observable events can be generated as either related or not to the specific execution instance of an operation. For the purpose, each operation triggered on the artifact is labelled by a unique operation identifier (type `OpId` in the tables). Such an identifier can be explicitly retrieved by the **getOpId** primitive during the execution of the operation (as part of its execution body). Operation identifiers are meant to be manageable as normal data structures, for instance, creating list of operation identifiers and then generating events related to these operation when necessary, during artifact functioning, across operation executions (this aspect will be clarified by a concrete example described in Subsection 4.2).

An event can be then generated using the **genEvent** primitive by specifying the operation identifier to which the event must be related, as observable effect of this operation (and of the agent action that caused it). If no `OpId` is specified, the event is considered related to the current operation triggered. The effect of the execution of these primitives is the generation of an event which is eventually collected by the sensor (if specified) of the agent that triggered the operation and by all the agents that are observing—via focus—the artifact. To generate event unrelated to a specific operation execution, the primitive **getEventInWsp** is provided, which generates an event which is observed by all the agents focusing on the artifact.

Finally, a couple of primitives are provided to manage the current observable state of the artifact, in particular to set a new value with **setObservableState**, specifying a label identifying one of the possible set of observable states defined by the artifact type, and to retrieve current value with **getObservableState**.

Besides the events explicitly generated with the **genEvent** primitive, some other kinds of event are automatically generated by the framework and made observable to agents interacting with an artifact. In particular, an event is generated whenever the execution of an operation is completed, and whenever a new observable state is set (details about the specific types of these events are provided when describing in next section).

4   A First Prototype

A first prototype implementing most of the functionalities described in the previous section has been developed in Java and is available for download at the CArtAgO project web site[1]. Our objective was to set up a first framework for prototyping and experimenting applications engineered upon the A&A meta-model, and so designed in terms of set of agents—possibly with heterogeneous models and architectures—situated in the same working environment, designed in terms of specific kind of artifacts. The framework itself is not meant to define or constrain the specific agent architecture adopted to define the behaviour of the individual agents: conversely, the framework is meant to be integrated and exploited with external agent frameworks or platforms, in particular with those that adopt Java as underlying implementation language, extending them so as to support the creation and use of artifact-based environment according to the A&A perspective.

As an example, simpA (simple A&A programming environment) is a full-fledged agent-oriented framework for prototyping general-purpose applications based on CArtAgO. Basically, simpA provides a support for developing MAS based on agents with an *activity-oriented* architecture, with a native support for creating and using artifact-based working environment, engineered upon CArtAgO. The interested reader is invite to refer to the simpA web site[2].

Based upon CArtAgO and simpA, simpA-WS is a framework for prototyping service-oriented application—in particular Web Service-based—in terms of agents and artifacts. There, artifacts are used on the client side as interfaces for user application agents to flexibly access and use Web Services, on the service side as interfaces for service agents to get Web-service messages and requests to be processed, and to provide responses. More information can be found at the simpA-WS web site[3]. Working in the first real-world application examples, simpA-WS is currently being investigated as an agent-based technology for prototyping service-oriented applications in the context of logistics [4].

4.1   Prototype Overview

The framework is composed by four main parts:

API for setup working environments — The entry point class of the framework is the `Cartago` class (sketched in Fig. 3), which mainly provides static services to create or get the reference to existing working environments

---

[1] CArtAgO web site: http://www.alice.unibo.it/projects/cartago

[2] simpA web site: http://www.alice.unibo.it/projects/simpa

[3] simpA-WS web site: http://www.alice.unibo.it/projects/simpaws

[4] http://www.alice.unibo.it/projects/a4stil

```
public class Cartago {

    public static synchronized ICartagoEnvironment
        getInstance(String name){...}
    public static synchronized ICartagoEnvironment
        getInstance(String name, ICartagoLoggerManager logger){...}
    public static String getVersion(){...}
}
```

Fig. 3. Entry point class for the CArtAgO framework. The class can be used to instantiate and get the reference to working environment.

```
public interface ICartagoEnvironment {

    IAgentBody getAgentBody(String name) throws AgentBodyAlreadyPresentException;
    ArtifactId createArtifact(String name, Class template, ArtifactConfig param)
                                      throws ArtifactAlreadyPresentException,
                                             UnknownArtifactTemplateException,
                                             ArtifactConfigurationFailedException;
    ArtifactId createArtifact(String name, Class template)
                                      throws ArtifactAlreadyPresentException,
                                             UnknownArtifactTemplateException,
                                             ArtifactConfigurationFailedException;
    void registerLogger(ICartagoLogger logger);
    void unregisterLogger(ICartagoLogger logger);
}
```

Fig. 4. Interface for working environments, providing services for creating agent bodies, and for directly creating artifacts, useful to setup the initial configuration of the environment

identified by a logic name. Once created or retrieved the reference to a working environment, it is possible to use the services provided by its interface—ICartagoEnvironment, sketched in Fig. 4—to setup the environment possibly creating an initial set of artifacts (besides the ones created dynamically by agents), and to create agent bodies, for enabling agents participation to the environment.

API for controlling agent bodies — From the agent point of view, the participation and interaction within a working environment takes place through an agent body. The creation of an agent body is provided as the getAgentBody provided by a working environment. Such a creation is typically done during agent initialisation. Once its agent body is created inside the environment, the agent—here conceived as the agent "mind"—can control it by suitably exploiting the IAgentBody interface implemented by the agent body, containing the core set of API described in Subsection 3.1. A sketch of the IAgentBody interface is reported in Fig. 5. It is possible to recognise the primitives for creating and disposing artifacts, for executing operations, sensing perceptions, managing sensors, and so on.

API for defining artifact types — A core part of the framework is given by the support provided to define new kind of artifacts, programming their structure and behaviour. We adopted a programming model that favours rapid prototyping of artifacts, exploiting as much as possible the support

```
public interface IAgentBody {

    ArtifactId createArtifact(String name, Class template, ArtifactConfig param)
                        throws ArtifactAlreadyPresentException,
                               UnknownArtifactTemplateException,
                               ArtifactConfigurationFailedException;
    ArtifactId createArtifact(String name, Class template)
                        throws ArtifactAlreadyPresentException,
                               UnknownArtifactTemplateException,
                               ArtifactConfigurationFailedException;
    void disposeArtifact(ArtifactId id) throws UnknownArtifactException;
    ArtifactId getArtifactId(String name) throws UnknownArtifactException;

    OpId execOp(ArtifactId id, Op op) throws OperationException;
    OpId execOp(ArtifactId id, Op op, SensorId sid) throws OperationException;

    Perception sense(SensorId sensorId)
                    throws NoPerceptionException;
    Perception sense(SensorId sensorId, IPerceptionFilter p)
                    throws NoPerceptionException;
    Perception sense(SensorId sensorId, int dt)
                    throws InterruptedException, NoPerceptionException;
    Perception sense(SensorId sensorId, IPerceptionFilter p, int dt)
                    throws InterruptedException, NoPerceptionException;

    void focus(ArtifactId aid, SensorId sid) throws SensorNotLinkedException;
    void unfocus(ArtifactId aid);

    SensorId linkSensor(AbstractSensor s);
    void unlinkSensor(SensorId id) throws CartagoException;
}
```

Fig. 5. Interface to control an agent body, including methods for triggering the execution of agent actions for artifact creation (**createArtifact**), artifact disposal (**disposeArtifact**), artifact discovery (**getArtifactId**), for triggering the execution of operation (**execOp**), for sensing perceptions (**sense**), for continuously observing artifacts (**focus**, **unfocus**), and for managing sensors (**linkSensor**,**unlinkSensor**)

```
public abstract class Artifact {
    ...
    protected final ArtifactId getId(){...}

    protected final OpId getOpId(){...}
    protected final OpRequestDescriptor getOpRequestDescriptor(){...}

    protected final void genEvent(String type) {...}
    protected final void genEvent(String type, Object content) {...}
    protected final void genEvent(OpId id, String type)
                                    throws InvalidOpIdException {...}
    protected final void genEvent(OpId id, String type, Object content)
                                    throws InvalidOpIdException {...}

    protected final void genEventInWsp(String type, Object content) {...}

    protected final void setObservableState(String state)
                                        throws UnknownArtifactStateException {...}
    protected final String getObservableState(){...}
}
```

Fig. 6. Base abstract class to define new artifact types. The basic set of primitives useful for programming artifact observable behaviour (in particular to generate observable events, to set and retrieve the observable state) are implemented as protected methods of this class.

given by the Java object-oriented environment. Accordingly, an artifact type can be defined by extending the basic `Artifact` class provided in the API: at run-time, artifacts instances are instances of this class. A sketch of the base class is shown in Fig. 6: the core set of the primitives described in Subsection 3.2 are available as protected methods provided by the class.

The artifact internal state is defined in terms of instance fields of the class, and the behaviour of operations can be defined by suitable instance methods of the class. In particular an operation `Op(Params)` can be implemented by a method of the kind:

```
@OPERATION(State1,State2,...) void Op(Params){...}
```

The annotation `@OPERATION`[5] is used to explicitly state that what follows is not to be interpreted as a normal method (meant to be invoked by other objects) but rather as the body of an artifact operation. It is worth remarking that methods representing operations have no return argument—a return argument would be meaningless in CArtAgO abstract model, as well as in the A&A general meta-model.

Currently, the concurrency model adopted for artifacts prevents operation execution requests to be served sequentially, so that only one operation at a time can be in execution on an artifact. Such a choice is quite effective in avoiding basic problems related to concurrent use of artifacts by agents (and in particular concurrent updates of artifact internal state). At the same time, this choice limits quite strongly the concurrency in artifact use, so future work will be devoted to explore further this issue.

As depicted in Fig. 6 and described in Subsection 3.2, observable events can be generated in the body of an operation by a family of primitives of the kind `genEvent`, specifying the event type, optionally an event content and the operation identifier to which the event must be related (`OpId` parameter). Events are collected by agent body sensors as stimuli, and then perceived by agents through `sense` action. Fig. 6 also includes the primitives that can be used to set and retrieve the current observable state of the artifact (`setObservableState` and `getObservableState`, respectively).

The manual of the artifact, containing information about function description, the operating instructions, as well as the list of the observable states, can be explicitly declared through the `@ARTIFACT_MANUAL` annotation preceding the artifact class declaration. If no states are declared, a single *default* state is defined. Defined the list of the observable states, an artifact programmer can specify the shape of the usage interface in relationship to the artifact observable state. This is possible by explicitly stating in the annotation of an operation what are the observable states in which the operation is meant to be visible (specifying `@OPERATION({State1,State2,...})`). If an operation has no states declared, then the operation is meant to be visible in all the states.

As a simple example, Fig. 7 shows the definition of an artifact type called `MyArtifact` (on the left), and an example of artifact use by an agent (on

---

[5] Annotations have been introduced along with the 5.0 version of Java.

```
\begin{verbatim}                          ...
@ARTIFACT_MANUAL(                         ICartagoEnvironment env = Cartago.getInstance("...");
  states = {"stateA","stateB"},           IAgentBody myBody = env.getAgentBody("...");
  start_state = "stateA",
  oi = @OPERATING_INSTRUCTIONS("..."),    ArtifactId aid = myBody.getArtifactId("myArtifact");
  fd = @FUNCTION_DESCRIPTION("...")        SensorId sid = myBody.linkSensor(new DefaultSensor());
) public class MyArtifact extends Artifact {
                                          BasicFilter myFilter1 = new BasicFilter({"new_value"});
  private int count;                      BasicFilter myFilter2 =
  private int max;                                  new BasicFilter({"op_completed",
                                                                    "state_changed"});
  public CounterArtifact(int max){
    this.max = max;                       boolean state_changed = false;
    count = 0;                            while (!state_changed){
  }                                         try {
                                              myBody.execOp(aid,"op1",sid);
  @OPERATION({"stateA"}) void op1() {
    count++;                                 // operation triggered:
    genEvent("new_value",count);            // sensing for one second for new_value events...
    if (count >= max){                      Perception p = myBody.sense(sid,myFilter1,1000);
      setObservableState("stateB");         log("current value: "+p.getContent());
    }
  }                                         // observing next observable event,
  @OPERATION({"stateA","stateB"}) void op2() {   // which should be either
    genEvent("value",count);                // op_completed or state_changed
  }                                         Perception p = myBody.sense(sid,myFilter2,1000);
}
                                            String type = p.getType();
                                            if (type.equals("state_changed")){
                                              state_changed = true;
                                            }
                                          } catch (NoPerceptionException ex){
                                            // something wrong happened in the artifact
                                            // or simply artifact too slow in executing the op...
                                            break;
                                          } catch (OperationNotAvailableException ex){
                                            // inc was not part of artifact usage interface...
                                            break;
                                          }
                                        }
                                        ...
```

Fig. 7. *(Left)* Complete definition of the `MyArtifact` type; *(Right)* A code fragment showing an example of use of a `MyArtifact` artifact

the right). As declared in the artifact manual, artifacts of sfMyArtifact kind have two possible observable states, labelled as `stateA` and sfstateB, with the former functioning as starting state. In the `stateA` state, the usage interface includes both the `op1` and `op2` operations, while in the `stateB` state the usage interface includes only `op2`. The execution of the `op1` operation causes the update of an internal counter of the artifact, whose new value is made observable by generating a `new_value` event. When the internal counter reaches a maximum value (provided with artifact initialisation), the artifact changes its observable state from `stateA` to `stateB`. The execution of the `op2` operation simply makes the current value of the internal counter observable, by generating an event of the kind `value`. As far as the artifact use is concerned, in the fragment—after creating an agent body inside the working environment where the artifact is located—`op1` operation is executed repeatedly, logging each time the value perceived by observing events generated as a consequence of the operation execution, until a change of artifact state is observed. In the example, two filters—instances of the class `BasicFilter`, part of the utility class of CArtAgO—are used to select the perceptions. Using BasicFilter, a stimulus is selected if and only if its type description matches one of the descriptions provided as parameter of BasicFilter constructor (implemented as array of strings).

Run-time environment and related tools — This is the part actually responsible of the life-cycle management of working environments at run-time. Conceptually, it is the *virtual machine* where artifacts and agent bodies are instantiated and managed that is responsible of executing operations on artifacts and collecting and routing observable events generated by artifacts. Some tools are also made available in CArtAgO for on-line inspection of working environment state, in particular artifact state and behaviour, in terms operation executed and events generated.

4.2   A Complete Example: Hello Philosophers!

To illustrate a simple but complete example of MAS application exploiting artifact-based working environments, we consider the "Hello philosophers" example—listed among the basic examples in CArtAgO distribution—, which is used here analogously to the (in)famous "Hello world" example for traditional programming languages.

The example refers to the well-known problem introduced by Dijkstra in the context of concurrent programming to check the expressiveness of mechanisms and abstractions introduced to coordinate set of cooperating / competing computing agents. Briefly, the problem is about a set of N philosophers (typically 5) sharing N chopsticks for eating spaghetti, sitting at a round table (so each philosopher share her left and right chopsticks with a friend philosopher on the left and one on the right). The goal of each philosopher is to live a joyful life, interleaving thinking activity, for which they actually do not need any resources, to eating activity, for which they need to take and use both the chopsticks. The goal of the overall philosophers society is to share the chopsticks fruitfully, and coordinate the access to shared resources so as to avoid forms of deadlock or starvation of individual philosophers—e.g. when all philosophers have one chopstick each. The social constraint of the society is that a chopstick cannot be used simultaneously by more than one philosopher.

The problem can be solved indeed in many different ways. By adopting the A&A perspective, it is natural to model the philosophers as cooperative agents and the table—managing the set of chopsticks—as the coordination artifact that agents share and use to perform their (eating) activities. It is easy to encapsulate in the table artifact the enactment of the social policy that makes it possible to satisfy both mutual exclusion for the access on the individual chopsticks, and avoid deadlock situations.

Fig. 8 shows the complete application, with the table artifact implemented upon CArtAgO, the agent philosophers directly implemented as flat Java threads, without relying on a specific agent architecture.

The usage interface of the table artifact is composed by only two operations, getChops and releaseChops, which can be used respectively to get two chopsticks

```
import alice.cartago.*;                    import java.util.*;
import java.util.*;                        import alice.cartago.*;

public class Table extends Artifact {      public class Philosopher extends Thread {
  private boolean[] chops;                   private int lchop, rchop;
  private List<PendingReq> reqs;             private IAgentBody myBody;
                                             private String name;
  public Table(int nchops){
    chops = new boolean[nchops];            public Philosopher(String name, int c0, int c1,
    reqs = new LinkedList<PendingReq>();               String envName) throws Exception {
    for (int i = 0; i<chops.length; i++){     this.name=name;
      chops[i]=true;                          lchop = c0;
    }                                         rchop = c1;
  }                                           ICartagoEnvironment env = Cartago.getInstance(envName);
                                              myBody = env.getAgentBody(name);
  @OPERATION void getChops(int c0, c1){     }
    if (chops[c0] && chops[c1]){
      chops[c0] = chops[c1] = false;        public void run() {
      genEvent("chops_acquired");             try {
    } else {                                    ArtifactId tableId = myBody.getArtifactId("table");
      PendingReq req =                          SensorId sid = myBody.linkSensor(new DefaultSensor());
                new PendingReq(c0, c1, getOpId());  Op getOp = new Op("getChops",lchop, rchop);
      reqs.add(req);                            Op releaseOp = new Op("releaseChops",lchop, rchop);
    }                                           IPerceptionFilter myFilter =
  }                                                     new BasicFilter("chops_acquired");
                                                while (true){
  @OPERATION void releaseChops(int c0, int c1){   myBody.execOp(tableId,getOp,sid);
    chops[c0] = chops[c1] = true;               try {
    Iterator<PendingReq> it = reqs.listIterator();  myBody.sense(sid,myFilter,5000);
    while (it.hasNext()){                         eating();
      PendingReq r = it.next();                 } catch(NoPerceptionException ex) {
      if (chops[r.c0] && chops[r.c1]){           log("starved.");
        it.remove();                             break;
        chops[r.c0] = chops[r.c1] = false;     }
        try {                                   myBody.execOp(tableId,releaseOp);
          genEvent(r.reqId,"chops_acquired");   thinking();
        } catch (Exception ex){}              }
      }                                       } catch (Exception ex){
    }                                         }
  }                                         }

  private static class PendingReq {         private void eating(){...}
    public int c0,c1;                       private void thinking() {...}
    public OpId reqId;                       private void log(String msg){...}
    public PendingReq(int c0, int c1, OpId id){  }
      this.c0 = c0; this.c1 = c1; reqId = id;
    }
  }
}

public class HelloPhilosophers {
  public static void main(String[] args) throws Exception {
    String envName = "restaurant";
    ICartagoEnvironment env = Cartago.getInstance(envName);
    env.createArtifact("table",Table.class,new ArtifactConfig(5));
    for (int i = 0; i<5; i++){
      new Philosopher("philo-"+i,i, (i+1)%nphilo,envName).start();
    }
  }
}
```

Fig. 8. Dining philosophers interacting within through a CArtAgO working environment called **restaurant**. Philosophers agents are simply implemented upon flat Java threads, while the table is implemented as a **table** artifact of class **Table**.

from the table and to give them back. The inner machinery of the **table** artifact ensures mutual exclusion on the access on chopsticks (an artifact executes one operation at a time, analogously to monitors) and deadlock avoidance (by releasing the chopsticks only if both are available, enqueueing the pending requests). It is worth noting the way in which observable events are generated: if the chopsticks are available when an instance of **getChops** operation is triggered, then the event **chops_acquired** is immediately generated, through the **genEvent** primitive; otherwise, the pending request is enqueued and the event is generated as soon as the chopsticks become available with the execution of a `releaseChops` operation.

On the agent side, a philosopher gets an agent body during its initialisation, and then exploits it during its main activity—which is defined by the body of the method `run`. It is worth remarking that here we adopted such a simplistic implementation for agents just to make the description of CArtAgO usage and integration with agent platforms as simple and concise as possible. The same example using simpA agent framework can be found in simpA distribution. Agent main activity accounts for repeatedly alternate eating and thinking sub-activities, using the table artifact to get (and release) the chopsticks. In particular, to get the chopsticks the agent triggers the execution of the `getChops` operation on the table artifact, specifying a sensor (previously linked to its body) to collect stimuli related to this action. Then, it pro-actively observes the sensor for 5 seconds using the `sense` primitive, filtering stimuli that concern `chops_acquired` events. If no perception is sensed within 5 seconds, the philosopher starves and terminates. Otherwise, it performs its eating activity and then, after eating, it releases the chopsticks by executing a `releaseChops` operation on the `table` artifact, without specifying any sensor (since, in this simple implementation, it is not interested to observe the effects of such an action).

5   Related Works

The approach based on artifacts shares the same engineering aims introduced by Weyns and colleagues in [11], where they identify a general model and an architecture that can be (re-)used to engineer environments in MAS, despite of the specific application domain. The model presented by the authors is *concern-based*: the environment is modelled as a set of modules that represent different functional concerns of the environment. A similar focus, but in some sense less general, can be found also in the work of Platon and colleagues [12], where a general model for environments providing functionalities for *over-hearing* and *over-sensing* is presented. Our notion of artifact could be compared at a first glance with the notion of functional modules describe by Weyns and colleagues. The main difference is that artifacts are conceived to be first-class abstractions both for the engineers designing and programming agent environment *and for the agents using such an environment*: agents do not perceive the environment as a single entity providing a set of functionalities (which are internally engineered upon a set of modules), but directly create, share, use, manipulate, destroy artifacts, each designed to encapsulate some kind of function.

The model for perception and sensing described in the paper shares many points with the model—more general—discussed in [9], introducing the notion of *active perceptions*. Such a model decomposes perceptions into a succession of three functionalities: sensing, interpreting and filtering. First, sensing maps the state of the environment to a representation. The agent can select a set of *foci*, that enable the agent to sense specific type of data in the environment. The representation of the state is composed according to a set of *perception laws*, that can be used by designers to enforce specific constraints on perceptions. Then, agents interpret representations by means of *descriptions*, that are blueprints that map representation onto percepts, modelled as expressions that can be understood by the internal machinery of the agent. Finally, agents can select a set of *filters*, to restrict the perceived data according to specific context relevant selection criteria.

In our model, *sensors* and *sense* actions provide some of the functionalities discussed above. In particular, by following the meaning introduced by the authors, each sensor can be used as a specific focus: the idea is that an agent can dynamically create and link to their body different kind of sensors, with distinct features (such as buffering, filtering, etc), to partition the perceptions from the environment, in our case related to artifacts (even if the model can be extended to consider also perceptions directly related to other agents). Similar to perceptual laws discussed above, sensor activity can be constrained according to laws enforced by the organisational and physical context where the agent is situated: this aspect will be explored in future work, with the introduction of an explicit support for organisation modelling on top of workspaces (see Sect. 6). Pattern-driven sensing described in Sect. 3 could be framed as a simplified form of filtering as defined in active perceptions, with some points that concern also interpretation: patterns act as simple filters that agents can specify to fetch in a data-driven way the data collected by sensors, and require that an explicit description is adopted for describing the events or stimuli posted to sensors.

Finally, the artifact abstraction and CArtAgO framework draw on the research work on *tuple centres* as programmable tuple-based coordination media and TuCSoN coordination model [13]. Artifacts can be framed as a generalisation of the notion of tuple centre: more precisely, tuple centres can be conceived as a type of *coordination artifacts* [8], as artifacts designed to encapsulate programmable coordination services.

6 Concluding Remarks

In this paper we described CArtAgO, as a framework supporting the engineering of artifact-based working environment in MAS. First we described the abstract model and architecture of the framework, and then a first basic prototype technology implementing most of the core functionalities.

Among the issues not considered for lack of space—and that can be found in the artifact conceptual framework—we mention here: *(i)* artifact *composition*—support for linking together existing artifacts to dynamically compose complex artifacts, by defining and exploiting artifact *link interfaces*; *(ii)* artifact *management*—support for inspecting, controlling, testing artifact state and behaviour, by defining and exploiting artifacts *management interface*, besides usage interface. Among the issues not currently faced in CArtAgO, and that will be part of our future work, we mention here *distribution, security,* and *organisation*.

As far as distribution is concerned, currently in CArtAgO there is no explicit account for the way in which workspaces—and possibly also artifacts—can be distributed across multiple nodes of a networks. In current version, working environments are confined to a single CArtAgO virtual machine (node) and then agents can create and use artifacts that live in their local environment. Distribution is achieved by ad-hoc linking of artifacts, that is, by exploiting network connections that makes it possible the low-level communication among artifacts belonging to different workspaces and working environments. In future work we will focus on extending the framework towards a full-fledged *infrastructure*, providing a first-class support for such an aspect.

Security and organisation are related issues, and call for the introduction of an explicit support for organisation built on top of the basic CArtAgO abstractions, which would be effective also to model security aspects such as access control. By drawing on our previous research work about such aspects on TuCSoN infrastructure, in CArtAgO we plan to introduce a *role*-based model, inspired to RBAC (Role-Based Access Control) architectures [14], such as RBAC-MAS [15]. Such a model will be based on the notion of *workplace*. A workplace defines the set of roles and related organisational rules or *contracts* being in force in a workspace. The contracts defines, in particular, the norms and policies that rule agent access to the artifacts belonging to the workspace. For example, depending on the role(s) that an agent is playing inside the workplace, it may have or not the permission to use some artifacts or to execute some specific operations on some specific artifacts. So, workplaces would define an organisational layer—and, consequently, a security layer—on top of workspaces.

Besides the above three main points, future work will be devoted also: *(i)* to improve the development of the prototype, including all the missing features that are currently part of the abstract model—such as the support for workspaces—and future extensions—such as workplaces; *(ii)* to integrate existing services as kinds of artifact, in order to be easily re-used when engineering applications on top of CArtAgO: an example is given by artifacts wrapping TuCSoN tuple centres, providing agent coordination facilities; *(iii)* to define suitable formal models and ontology for describing function descriptions, operating instructions, and observable state description, possibly reusing existing research efforts on service description models and (standard) languages, such as OWL-S.

Finally, existing and ongoing research in environment for MAS will be important to improve the theoretical foundation of CArtAgO, concerning the notion of artifact and related concepts: for instance, the research work on active perceptions can be important to improve and extend the model of sensing currently adopted.

References

1. Ricci, A., Viroli, M., Omicini, A.: Programming MAS with artifacts. In Bordini, R.P., Dastani, M., Dix, J., El Fallah Seghrouchni, A., eds.: 3rd International Workshop "Programming Multi-Agent Systems" (PROMAS 2005), AAMAS 2005, Utrecht, The Netherlands (2005) 163–178
2. Weyns, D., Omicini, A., Odell, J.: Environment as a first-class abstraction in multi-agent systems. Autonomous Agents and Multi-Agent Systems **14** (2007) 49–60 Special Issue on Environments for Multi-agent Systems.

3. Viroli, M., Ricci, A., Holvoet, T., Shelfthout, K., Zambonelli, F.: Infrastructures for the environment of multiagent systems. Autonomous Agents and Multi-Agent Systems **14** (2007) 5–30 Special Issue on Environments for Multi-agent Systems.
4. Nardi, B.A.: Context and Consciousness: Activity Theory and Human-Computer Interaction. MIT Press (1996)
5. Kirsh, D.: Distributed cognition, coordination and environment design. In: European conference on Cognitive Science. (1999) 1–11
6. Agre, P.: Computational research on interaction and agency. Artificial Intelligence **72** (1995) 1–52
7. Amant, R.S., Wood, A.B.: Tool use for autonomous agents. In Veloso, M.M., Kambhampati, S., eds.: AAAI/IAAI'05 Conference, Pittsburgh, PA, USA, AAAI Press / The MIT Press (2005) 184–189
8. Omicini, A., Ricci, A., Viroli, M., Castelfranchi, C., Tummolini, L.: Coordination artifacts: Environment-based coordination for intelligent agents. In: AAMAS'04. Volume 1., New York, USA, ACM (2004) 286–293
9. Weyns, D., Steegmans, E., Holvoet, T.: Towards active perception in situated multiagent systems. Applied Artificial Intelligence **18** (2004) 867–883
10. Viroli, M., Ricci, A.: Instructions-based semantics of agent mediated interaction. In: AAMAS'04. Volume 1., New York, USA, ACM (2004) 286–293
11. Weyns, D., Holvoet, T.: Formal model for situated multiagent systems. Fundamenta Informaticae **63** (2004) 125–158
12. Platon, E., Honiden, S., Sabouret, N.: Oversensing with a softbody in the environment: Another dimension of observation. In Kaminka, G.A., Pynadath, D.V., Geib, C.W., eds.: Workshop "Modeling Others from Observation" (MOO 2005), IJCAI-05, Edinburgh, Scotland (2005)
13. Omicini, A., Zambonelli, F.: Coordination for Internet application development. Autonomous Agents and Multi-Agent Systems **2** (1999) 251–269
14. Sandhu, R., Coyne, E.J., Feinstein, H.L., Youman, C.E.: Role-based control models. IEEE Computer **29** (1996) 38–47
15. Omicini, A., Ricci, A., Viroli, M.: An algebraic approach for modelling organisation, roles and contexts in MAS. Applicable Algebra in Engineering, Communication and Computing **16** (2005) 151–178 Special Issue: Process Algebras and Multi-Agent Systems.

Environment as Active Support of Interaction

Julien Saunier[1], Flavien Balbo[1,2], and Fabien Badeig[1,2]

[1] LAMSADE, Université Paris-Dauphine
Place du Maréchal de Lattre de Tassigny, Paris Cedex 16
[2] INRETS/GRETIA, 2, Avenue du Général Malleret-Joinville, -F94114 Arcueil
{balbo,saunier,badeig}@lamsade.dauphine.fr

Abstract. Indirect interactions have been shown to be of interest in MultiAgent Systems (MAS), in the simulation area as well as in real applications. The environment is also emerging as a first-order abstraction. Intuitively, the environment being a common medium for the agents, it should be a suitable paradigm to provide an infrastructure for both direct and indirect interactions. However, it still lacks of a consensus on how the two relate to each other, and how the environment can support effectively notions as communication or awareness. We propose a general and operational model, Environment as Active Support of Interaction, that enables the agents to actively participate in the definition of their perceptions. Then, we show how the model provides a suitable framework for the regulation of the MAS interactions.

1   Introduction

The environment is emerging as a first-order abstraction in MultiAgent Systems (MAS) [19], thus opening many challenges in terms of modeling, methodology and engineering, but also of autonomy and awareness of the agents [15,16]. In these works, it has been shown that it is possible to take advantage of the environment in order to improve the interactions. It notably assumes providing both observability of the entities in this environment and the sharing of the interactions. This use of the environment extends the traditionnal means and models of interaction. Early work [1] featured the sharing of the communications via the environment. This modeling allows flexibility and shows low computation and communication costs [21]. The Environment as Active Support of Interaction (EASI) model extends these principles to cover other inter-agents interactions, and notably enables the agents to choose their perceptions.

An important part of the solicitations in real-life situations comes from other means than direct transmissions [5]. They are enabled by a particular state of the participants, the *awareness*, which has long been considered as the result of unwanted perceptions. We argue that the awareness is an active state, and not only the result of stimuli. Works in the fields of psychology and sociology have discussed whether or not there also has to be an active participation of the "perceiver". For example, Heath [10] says that awareness is both a state of availability to the environment and an ability to "filter relevant information

D. Weyns, H.V.D. Parunak, and F. Michel (Eds.): E4MAS 2006, LNAI 4389, pp. 87–105, 2007.
© Springer-Verlag Berlin Heidelberg 2007

which is of particular significance". Moreover, even at the physiological level, Warren [18] highlights that hearing combines a receptive activity with, right from the lowest level, decisions of action. Based on this, we propose a model that enables the agents to control their perceptions, and thus that enables awareness, by means of the environment. We describe the EASI model and its benefits in term of active perception in section 2. Then we exploit this formalization to allow the environment to regulate the MAS and achieve interactional awareness in section 3. Section 4 goes into the detail of an illustrative example, and we explore related works in section 5.

2   The EASI Model

In EASI, we model the environment as a common space of interaction, in order to enable the agents to choose their perceptions. The problem when all the interactions can be observed is to give to the agents an *efficient* way of finding the interesting ones, i.e. only those that are potentially needed. To find useful information within a very large data set, we have based our model on the symbolic data analysis (SDA). The goal of SDA is to discover data by modeling both qualitative and quantitative data grouped into symbolic objects. The SDA algebra is compatible with first-order logic and SQL, and can thus be implemented for instance via rule-based engines, Active Databases, etc. For multiagent systems, we consider that the environment contains symbolic descriptions of the elements that have a role in the interaction: agents, messages and objects. The objective is to enable the agents to use these descriptions in order to adapt the potential interactions to their needs.

Let us introduce basic SDA definitions [3]. A symbolic object is a triple $s = (a, R_s, d_s)$ where R_s is a set of comparison operators between descriptions ($R_s \subset R$ with R the set of operators), d_s is a set of descriptions ($d_s \subset D$, with D the set of descriptions) and a is a mapping from Ω (set of individuals, also called entities) in L ($L = \{true, false\}$ or $L = [0, 1]$). In this paper, we consider only the first case where L is boolean. An assertion is a special case of a symbolic object and is written as follows: $\forall w \in \Omega \ as(w) = \wedge_{i=1,...,p} [y_i(w) R_i d_i]$ where $y_i(w)$ is the value of the individual w for the symbolic variable y_i. When an assertion is asked of any particular entity $w \in \Omega$, it assumes a value true ($as(w) = true$) if that assertion holds for that entity, or false ($as(w) = false$) if not. A symbolic object is the intention definition of the entities according to a relation set between their own description and a description set d. The extension definition of a symbolic object (in this case an assertion) is noted $E(s) = \{w \in \Omega \mid as(w) = true\}$, it is the set of entities whose description matches the intention definition.

2.1   Interaction Model: Basic Definitions

Based on the SDA definitions, and considering the particular features of the MAS paradigm, we define the environment as a tuple of the sets that are necessary to its description.

Definition 1 (Environment of Interaction). $E = \langle \Omega, D, P, R, F \rangle$

- Ω is the set of entities.
- $P = \{P_i | i \in I\}$, P is the set of observable properties.
  $P_i : \Omega \rightarrow d_i \cup \{null, unknown\}$. P_i is a mapping from an entity to the value of its property i.
- $D = \prod_{i \in I} d_i$ with d_i the description domain of P_i.
- $R = \prod_{i \in I} R_i$ with R_i the set of comparison operators of P_i.
- F is the set of filters.

For SDA, the search for pertinent sets of entities is an objective, but in multi-agent systems they are generally given by the problem analysis. For instance, a particular type of agent is a subset of entities. More generally, the set of entities representing a MAS is $\Omega = A \cup O \cup IO$, where:

- A is the set of agents.
- O is the set of objects.
- IO is the set of interaction objects.

The basic component of our model is an entity. This abstraction level is necessary to model every kind of interaction: an entity is described by symbolic variables and a particular interaction involves a subset of entities that are identified through the required symbolic variables description. As a minimum, an interaction puts together an agent and an interaction object, and optionally other agents, interaction objects, or objects of the environment. The interaction objects are particular objects that convey information, for example messages and traces.

In this paper, the agents are communicative agents using interaction objects to interact. For each of these subsets of entities, a description, noted respectively D_{IO} and D_A, is given. If $I = 1 \ldots p$ is the set of indices of the symbolic variables, then $I_{IO} \subset I$ and $I_A \subset I$ are the subsets related to IO and A. The application description y from SDA is renamed P, which stands for observable Property. If an observable property is not defined for an entity, then its default value is $null$; if the property exists but does not have a value, its default value is $unknown$.

The entities sharing the same properties can be grouped together. A subset of entities is the extension of an assertion verifying the existence of a subset of P. Let d_e ($d_e \subset D$) be the description set of the subset e ($e \subset \Omega$), P_e ($P_e \subset P$) its application description, and I_e ($I_e \subset I$) the subset of indices, e is the extension of the assertion $as(w) = \wedge_{i \in I_e}[P_i(w) \neq null]$.

An *agent category* A_C is a subset of A. The agents that belong to a category share the same defined properties, and each agent is member of at least one category.

Definition 2 (Agent Category). *If a is an agent then $\exists A_C \subset A, a \in A_C$, $as(a) = \wedge_{i \in I_{A_C}}[P_i(a) \neq null]$.*

An agent category is a particular assertion defined by a set of mandatory non null P; however the value(s) of these properties may be different for each of the entities. The set of agents that belong to this category is the extension of the assertion, i.e. all the individuals in A for which these P are defined. The categories of agents are not a partition of A, so that an agent may belong to several categories.

In our model, only what is useful for interaction – from the viewpoint of the environment – is taken into account. This can be seen as the public part of the agents, which is independent from their private part (such as their knowledge or their internal architecture). This definition implies that, from the interaction viewpoint, the agents that have identical descriptions are similar: they can receive the same messages.

Following the agent category definition, an *interaction object category* is composed of interaction objects that exhibit the same observable properties.

Definition 3 (Interaction Object Category). *If io is an interaction object then $\exists IO_s \subset IO, io \in IO_s, as(io) = \wedge_{i \in I_{IO_s}}[P_i(io) \neq null]$.*

As for the agents, our model only takes into account what has to be observable within the environment. In EASI, there is no conceptual difference between each kind of interaction object (message, or object such as traces); they are defined only according to their description set. Thus, an interaction is defined in a generic way. For instance, a category of interaction objects may be an Agent Communication Language, in which case the category will be defined by the set of observable properties necessary to its mapping. For example, the set of observable properties defining the FIPA-ACL[1] message category is: *messagetype, sender, receiver, reply-to, content, language, encoding, ontology, protocol, conversation-id, reply-with, in-reply-to, reply-by.*

These general definitions are the framework to define the agents and interaction objects in EASI.

The observability of particular properties may be necessary to ensure some features, for example the semantics of the communication language(s). A *minimal property* is a property that is required for each entity.

Definition 4 (Minimal property of an entity). $p \in P$ *is a minimal property for the category E_C iff $\forall e_i \in E_C, p(e_i) \neq null$.*

The MAS designer may define minimal properties for a category of entities: each entity must have a non null description for these properties. For an operational use, we add a specific observable property, the agent identifier:
$\forall a \in A, P_{id}(a) \neq null$ with $P_{id} : A \to \mathbb{N}$.

This definition implies that P_{id} is a minimal property for an agent: the existence and observability of this property is mandatory for all the agents.

SDA is originally an analysis tool for complex data, it is powerful to describe the entities of the MAS both at design time and at run-time. The context of the MAS is made up of the observable properties of the entities. We use these

---

[1] http://www.fipa.org/specs/fipa00070/SC00070I.html

descriptions to manage dynamically the interaction infrastructure via filters. We have seen that in SDA an assertion puts together entities according to a description. To model an interaction, more than one kind of entity must be gathered, this is why a filter is a conjunction of assertions on these entities. A filter has to connect at least the description of an agent to the other components of the interaction. Thus, a *filter* is a conjunction of constraints on the descriptions of an agent and of a context that triggers (if satisfied) an action of this agent.

Definition 5 (Filter). *If* $a \in A$, $C \subset \Omega$, $C_{act} \subset C$, $f(a, C) = \wedge_{i \in I_{fa}} [P_i(a) \ R_i^{fa} \ d_i^{fa}] \wedge (\forall e \in C \wedge_{i \in I_{fe}} [P_i(e) \ R_i^{fe} \ d_i^{fe}])$, $holds(f(a, C)) \rightarrow action(a, C_{act})$.

In this definition a is the description of the agent(s) involved and $I_{fa} \subset I$ contains the indices of P that are used in f as selection criteria for the agent. $R_i^{fa} \subset R$ and $d_i^{fa} \subset D$ are respectively the operators and descriptions that define the conditions on the agent(s) description a. The notation is the same for the elements e of the filter context C. By context, we mean the other entities gathered by the filter. The observable state of an agent, the exchange of a message between agents, the presence of a particular object or the combination of these instances can be used to define a particular context. As with the assertions, the filters can take two values, *true* or *false*, which indicate whether the agent(s) that fulfill the description will be affected by the action associated to the filter – case *true*, the filter *holds* – or not – case *false* –. The nature of this action $action(a, C_{act})$ depends on the type of filter, and involves a subset of the entities belonging to the context.

In the case of interaction filters, the action when the filter holds is the perception of an interaction object. This is formalized by introducing the primitive $perceive(a, \{io\} \cup C_{act})$, which means the perception of the interaction object io and possibly of a part of the context C_{act} by the agent(s) described by a:

Definition 6 (Interaction Filter). *If* $a \in A$, $io \in IO$, $C \subset \Omega$, $C_{act} \subset C$, $f(a, \{io\} \cup C) = \wedge_{i \in I_{fa}} [P_i(a) \ R_i^{fa} \ d_i^{fa}] \wedge_{i \in I_{fio}} [P_i(io) \ R_i^{fio} \ d_i^{fio}] \wedge (\forall e \in C \wedge_{i \in I_{fe}} [P_i(e) \ R_i^{fe} \ d_i^{fe}])$, $holds(f(a, \{io\} \cup C)) \rightarrow perceive(a, \{io\} \cup C_{act})$.

In this definition, which is a special case of the previous one, an io transmission is imposed to define an interaction. An interaction filter is the conjunction of at least two assertions, the first is related to the receiver and the second is related to the io. C is still the context of the interaction and is optional, as the conditions on the io and a may be sufficient. In the following definitions, let F be the set of filters in the environment.

The use of filters enables the agents to choose the interaction objects they will perceive. The author of a filter – the entity that adds it in the environment – attaches a priority level to it. Practically, the priority is a numeral. It determines, according to the needs of the author, the order of the filters in the environment.

Definition 7 (Filter Priority). $\forall f \in F, \exists k \in IP, priority : F \rightarrow IP, f \mapsto k$ *where* IP *is an interval on* $\mathbb{N}$.

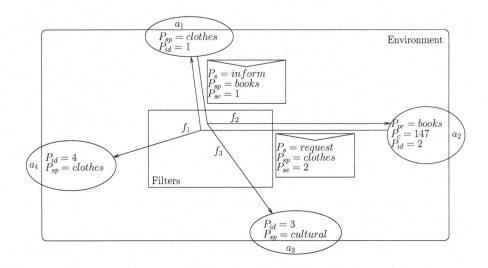

Fig. 1. Example 1: MarketPlace

These definitions are illustrated by an example of MarketPlace (Fig.1): sellers (specialized in a domain) and clients (looking for a set of products) communicate in order to find the best agreement. Each client has to buy virtual money, which is used to carry out the payments in a secure way. According to EASI, the following modeling is proposed: the set of entities is $\Omega = A \cup M_L$, with A the set of agents and M_L the set of messages defining an *ad hoc* langage. There are eight properties:

1. P_{id} (*id* for identifier): $A \rightarrow \mathbb{N}_A$ ($\mathbb{N}_A \subset \mathbb{N}$);
2. P_{sp} (*sp* for specialty): $A \rightarrow \{cultural, clothes, ...\}$;
3. P_{pr} (*pr* for products): $A \rightarrow \mathcal{P}(\{books, ...\})$ with $\mathcal{P}(E)$ the power set of E;
4. P_c (*c* for credit): $A \rightarrow \mathbb{N}$;
5. P_s (*s* for subject): $M_L \rightarrow \{request, accept, inform\}$;
6. P_r (*r* for receiver):$M_L \rightarrow \mathbb{N}_A$;
7. P_{se} (*se* for sender): $M_L \rightarrow \mathbb{N}_A$;
8. P_p (*p* for price): $A \rightarrow \mathbb{R}$.

The properties of the agents and messages respectively are $I_A = \{1...4\}$ and $I_{M_L} = \{2, 3, 5, 6, 7, 8\}$. Seller ($A_{Se}$) and Client ($A_{Cl}$) are the two categories of agents, respectively with $I_{Se} = \{1, 2\}$, and $I_{Cl} = \{1, 3, 4\}$. There are also two categories of messages: M_{Di} (*Di* for discount) is used by the sellers to send special offers on products, with $I_{Di} = \{3, 5, 7, 8\}$; and M_{Co} (*Co* for contract) is exchanged by sellers and clients to find an agreement, with $I_{Co} = \{2, 5, 6, 7\}$.

According to the Definition 6, the observable properties are numbered in the filters; we replace these numbers by explicit tags, e.g. P_2 by P_{sp}. The definitions of the filters are summarized in Fig. 2. f_1 is a multicast example: a client sends a request according to the specialty of a seller to negotiate the price of a product.

$$holds(f(a, \{m\} \cup C)) \rightarrow perceive(a, \{m\}) \; with$$
$$f_1(a, \{m\}) = [P_{sp}(a) = P_{sp}(m)] \wedge [P_s(m) = request]$$
$$f_2(a, \{m\} \cup C) = [P_s(m) = inform] \wedge [P_{pr}(m) \in P_{pr}(a)]$$
$$\wedge (\forall m_r \in E(A_m)[P_p(m) < P_p(m_r)]), \; C = E(A_m)$$
$$f_3(a, \{m\} \cup C) = [P_{sp}(a) = P_{sp}(a_r)] \wedge [P_{id}(a) \neq P_{id}(a_r)]$$
$$\wedge [P_s(m) = inform] \wedge [P_{se}(a) = P_{id}(a_r)], \; C = \{a_r\}$$

Fig. 2. Example 1: Filters

f_2 enables interactions based on the needs of the receiver(s): a client receives only the best special offer for the products it is looking for. The set of special offers is the extension $E(A_m) = \{m_o \in M_L | A_m(m_o) = true\}$ of the assertion $A_m(s) = [P_s(s) = inform] \wedge [P_{pr}(s) = P_{pr}(m)]\}$. Finally, f_3 is an example of overhearing: a seller receives every special offers proposed by other sellers $(a_r \in A)$ with the same specialty.

2.2   Information on the Interaction

The EASI formalization enables us to gather information on the interaction situation by defining significant sets of entities. The *perception domain* of a filter according to an agent and a message is an extension of the assertions composing a filter, i.e. the sets of agents and interaction objects concerned by this filter. The perception domain indicates whether or not the agents and the messages have the observable properties required by the filter definition, but it does not verify the properties values.

Definition 8 (Perception Domain of a Filter). *For a filter* $f(a, \{io\} \cup C)$:

- $E(f_a) = \{A_C \subset A | \forall a \in A_C \wedge_{i \in I_{f_a}} [P_i(a) \neq null]\}$
- $E(f_{io}) = \{IO_L \subset IO | \forall m \in IO_L \wedge_{i \in I_{f_{io}}} [P_i(io) \neq null]\}$

These sets contain the descriptions of entities that a filter gathers to produce an interaction and are used by the agents to compose their interactional domain. When $E(f_a) = null$ or $E(f_{io}) = null$, there is currently no agent (respectively interaction object) which corresponds to the descriptions. This means the filter is either badly conceived, or has expired. In the example, for f_1 we have $E(f_{1,io}) = M_{Co}$, the contract messages are dispatched thanks to this filter; and $E(f_{1,a}) = A_{Se}$, the seller agents are the potential receivers.

The *perception channels* of an Agent is the set of filters that concern this agent, i.e. the agent belongs to the perception domain of all and only these filters.

Axiom 1 (Perception Channels of an Agent). $\forall a \in A, perception_a = \{f \in F | a \in E(f_a)\}$.

For an agent a, $perception_a$ is composed of the filters added by the agent itself and for each of these filters, $E(f_a)$ and $E(f_{io})$ concern its needs as receiver. $perception_a$ also contains the filters added by other agents, but which concern a. In this case, $E(f_a)$ and $E(f_{io})$ represent the needs of the sender(s) using the filter. $perception_a$ is the "interface" to interact with an agent: the agent can perceive an interaction object only through one of these filters. This interface evolves according to the needs of the agent itself and to those of the agents wanting to interact with it. For $a_1 \in A_{Se}$ a seller agent, $perception_{a_1}$ is $\{f_1, f_3\}$: f_1 corresponds to the needs of the clients and f_2 to its needs as a seller.

The *percept* of an agent corresponds to the set of interaction objects the agent can perceive thanks to its perception channels. This set is defined as follows:

Axiom 2 (Percept of an Agent). $Percept_a = \{io \in IO | \exists f \in perception_a, io \in E(f_{io})\}$.

If $percept_a$ is empty then a is "deaf". It can be a choice; this agent has a task to perform and does not need to perceive interaction objects, and no other agent wants to interact with it. Because this set is dynamically updated, it may be a temporary choice. Nevertheless, this agent can send messages and therefore is not isolated from an interactional viewpoint. If $perception_a$ is not empty but $Percept_a$ is, it means that $perception_a$ does not match the "language" the other agents use: it uses observable properties that currently do not exist in any io description. For $M_{Co} = \{m_1\}$ and $M_{Di} = \{m_2\}$, we have $Percept_{a_1} = \{m_1, m_2\}$.

In the same way, EASI proposes to analyse the link between a message and the potential interactions: the *channels* of an interaction object is the set of filters it may be transmitted through.

Axiom 3 (Channels of an Interaction Object). $\forall io \in IO, channel_{io} = \{f \in F | io \in E(f_{io})\}$.

If $channel_{io}$ is empty, then no agent will perceive this interaction object, because there is no filter that matches it. In this case, the sender has either to create a new filter or to modify the message. The perception domain of a message corresponds to the set of its receivers. In our example, $channel_{m_2}$ is composed of f_1 and f_3.

Finally, the *perception domain* of an interaction object is the set of agents that could perceive this interaction object.

Axiom 4 (Perception Domain of an Interaction Object). $Receiver_{io} = \{a \in A | \exists f \in channel_{io}, a \in E(f_a)\}$.

If $channel_{io}$ is not empty and $Receiver_{io}$ is, it means that the description of the receiver is not correct and the filters in $channel_{io}$ have to be modified. In the exemple, we have $Receiver_{m_2} = \{a_1, a_2\}$ with $a_2 \in A_{Cl}$.

As the filter definition includes the context of the interaction as well as the description of other entities, these sets represent the potential interactions.

3   Environment and Rules

The EASI model has already been applied to real applications, for an Agent Traveler Information Server [21], and for the management of bus networks [2]. In these systems, we use the expert system technology to manage the activity of the environment. The mapping from EASI onto an expert system is straightforward:

the knowledge base represents the set of entities, the rule base represents the set of filters and the rule firing ensures the dynamicity.

The applications have been implemented with rule engines using the RETE algoritm [8]. In addition, EASI has been implemented within Madkit[2], a multiagent platform based on the Agent Group Role (AGR) model [7]. In Madkit, each message is delivered by the kernel that manages the groups, roles and identifiers of the agents. With our extension, an agent can communicate by two different means in the same MAS: 1) it sends and receives messages thanks to the kernel; 2) it puts in and perceives messages from the environment in which it participates.

The model we have described so far enables the agents to act on their own perception channels to match their needs. It is sufficient for cooperative agents, but the compliance to the potential rules of the environment is entrusted to the agents. This is not sufficient for heterogeneous systems. For instance, in the MarketPlace example, the seller a_1 can add the following filter:

$holds(f(a, \{m\}) \rightarrow perceive(a, \{m\})$ $with$

$f_4(a, \{m\}) = [P_s(m) = inform] \wedge [P_{pr}(m) \in P_{pr}(a)] \wedge [P_{id}(a_1) = P_{se}(m)].$

In this filter, a is a description, a_1 is an individual. It "forces" the clients to receive all a_1's special offers despite their initial filter(s), for example f_2 which triggered the perception of only the best special offer. In this section, we complete the model in order to deal with this issue.

3.1 Origin of a Filter

We consider that the filters dedicated to the management of the MAS belong to the environment. These filters are added either by a group of system agents, or by an environment internal mechanism. This leads us to split the filters in two categories, depending on their "author": the environment, or an agent. Thus, $F = F_E \cup F_A$, with F_E the set of filters added on behalf of the environment and F_A the set of filters added by the agents. The author of a filter will be noted as superscript, f^e for the environment and f^{a_x} for an agent a_x.

In this way, the environment can add percepts to the agents, which will receive messages that would not have been received otherwise. The filters are the rules of the environment, they define the interactional politics of the MAS, for example a standard transmission behavior for certain kinds of messages. The advantages of this approach are (i) to enable the existence of the rules inside the environment itself, and not external to it (by monitoring, for example), in order to regulate the MAS by controling in real-time the actions instead of doing it a posteriori and (ii) to unburden the agents of this task.

In order to provide an intuitive understanding of our model, we will build up a new example as the model goes along to illustrate how the filters can be used in this new context. We use the metaphor of a physical environment to instantiate the model. We focus our example on the message transmission rules, for cognitive agents. In this second example (Fig. 3), the agents – a_1 to a_4 – are situated on a two-dimensional grid. To begin with, we only consider distance

---

[2] www.madkit.org

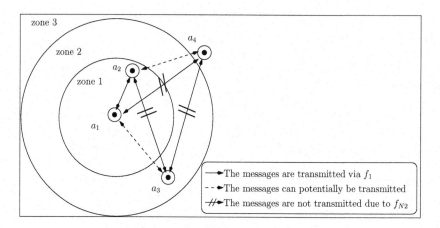

Fig. 3. Example 2. The circles represent the delimitation implied by the environment filters for the agent a_1.

as the determining criteria. The filter of the environment induces a partition of the space for each agent. The first filter manages proximity: the agents always perceive the messages that are sent by agents close to them, e.g. a_1 perceives the messages from a_2 as long as they stay at the same distance, and reversely a_2 perceives the messages from a_1. Let the agents have three observable properties, P_{id} for their identifier, P_x and P_y for their position on the grid. The messages have one observable property, P_{se} for their sender. d is the maximal distance at which a message is always perceived. The filter of the environment is:

$holds(f_1^e(a, \{m\} \cup C)) \rightarrow perceive(a, \{m\})$ with
$f_1^e(a_r, \{m\} \cup C) = [\sqrt{(P_x(a_r) - P_x(a_s))^2 + (P_y(a_r) - P_y(a_s))^2} < d] \wedge [P_{se}(m) = P_{id}(a_s)], C = \{a_s\}$.

3.2 Negative Filters and Priority

The filters put by the environment trigger the perception even if the agents do not want to perceive it. To support the opposite case – the environment blocks the perception –, we must be able to put *negative filters*, noted f_N, which means that when the filter holds, the concerned *io* is not perceived by the concerned agent(s):

Definition 9 (Negative Interaction Filter). *If* $a \in A$, $io \in IO$, $C \subset \Omega$,
$f_N(a, \{io\} \cup C) = \wedge_{i \in I_{fa}} [P_i(a) R_{fa} d_{fa}] \wedge_{i \in I_{fio}} [P_i(io) R_{fio} d_{fio}] \wedge (\forall e \in C \wedge_{i \in I_{fe}} [P_i(e) R_{fe} d_{fe}])$, $holds(f_N(a, \{io\} \cup C)) \rightarrow \neg perceive(a, C_{act})$.

Let us continue the example. The second filter of the environment will be a negative filter: an agent cannot receive a message sent from further than a specified distance: for example a_1 will not be able to receive any message from the agents in the zone 3. Let D be the distance from where on a message cannot be perceived. The corresponding filter of the environment is:

$holds(f_{N2}^e(a, \{m\} \cup C)) \rightarrow \neg perceive(a, \{m\})$ with
$f_{N2}(a_r, \{m\} \cup C) = [(P_x(a_r) - P_x(a_s))^2 + (P_y(a_r) - P_y(a_s))^2 > D^2] \wedge [P_{se}(m) = P_{id}(a_s)]$, $C = \{a_s\}$.

Whether or not the agents perceive the messages sent from the intermediate zone depends on their filters: the agents can add filters to focus their attention toward particular interactions of interest.

Both the agents and the environment can add negative filters. The environment, for its regulation task, has to be able to prevent the perception of interaction objects, e.g. for security reasons or to ensure a ban. For the agents, the negative filters enable them to control and limit voluntarily their perceptions. In real life situation, when someone has no particular task to accomplish, he is "actively" aware, which means he focusses his attention on what is going on around. If there is a conversation around, he will overhear it. Yet, if he becomes busy, he will focus straight on his current task, and thus reduce his perceptions on what he has to do; the conversations around will not be heard. We give the agents the same ability to act on their own percepts, not only in a positive way, by increasing their awareness, but also in a negative way, by limiting their perceptions according to their occupancy, will or needs. Removing their own filters is not sufficient, because they may still receive messages via filters belonging to the other agents.

We did not mention previously the relative priorities of the filters of the environment and of the agents, because the filters of the one could only add percepts to the others. Now that the effects of the filters can be contradictory, it is necessary to introduce different priorities according to both the author of the filters and the type of the filters. As we emphasize the regulation by the environment to ensure the compliance with the rules of the MAS, the filters added by the environment have to be stronger than those added by the agents: the priority of the environment filters is higher (Axiom 5), and the inference relation of a higher priority disables those of a lower priority for every agent/interaction object couple holding (Axiom 6):

Axiom 5 (Relative Priorities: Environment and Agents). $\forall f^e \in F_E$, $\forall f^a \in F_A, priority(f^e) > priority(f^a)$.

Axiom 6 (Conflict Resolution). $\forall f_x, f_y \in F, a \in A, io \in IO, C_x, C_y \subset \Omega$, $priority(f_x(a, io, C_x)) > priority(f_y(a, io, C_y))$, $holds(f_x(a, io, C_x)) \wedge holds(f_y(a, io, C_y)) \rightarrow \neg holds(f_y(a, io, C_y))$.

This means that for every agent/io couple, at most one interaction filter is triggered; and this filter is the one which has the highest priority.

To resolve the last ambiguous case, a conflict between two filters which have the same priority, we ensure that a negative filter is stronger than a positive one, i.e. the negative filter applies:

Axiom 7 (Precedence: Negative and Positive Filters). $\forall f_{Nx}, f_y \in F, a \in A, C_x, C_y \subset \Omega, priority(f_{Nx}(a, io, C_x)) = priority(f_y(a, io, C_y))$, $holds(f_{Nx}(a, io, C_x)) \wedge holds(f_y(a, io, C_y)) \rightarrow \neg holds(f_y(a, io, C_y))$.

(case)		(A)	(B)	(C)
	$\wedge$	$\nexists f^e(a,\{io\}) \in F_E$	$\exists f^e(a,\{io\}) \in F_E$	$\exists f^e_N(a,\{io\}) \in F_E$
(1)	$\nexists f^a(a,\{io\}) \in F_A$	$\times$	$perceive(a,\{io\})$	$\neg perceive(a,\{io\})$
(2)	$\exists f^a(a,\{io\}) \in F_A$	$perceive(a,\{io\})$	$perceive(a,\{io\})$	$\neg perceive(a,\{io\})$
(3)	$\exists f^a_N(a,\{io\}) \in F_A$	$\neg perceive(a,\{io\})$	$perceive(a,\{io\})$	$\neg perceive(a,\{io\})$

Fig. 4. In a particular context, the truth value of the perception of an interaction object io by the agent a is determined according to the filters of the environment and of the agents

With this new partition of the filters – between the environment and the agents – and the introduction of the negative filters, we must study the different cases of co-presence of conflicting filters in the environment. The perception (or not) of the interactions will be determined according to the priorities. The table in Fig. 4 sums up the different cases of absence and/or presence of filters added by the environment and the agents.

In the previous example, if a_1 wants to overhear a_3 and a_4, it will put the following filter:
$holds(f_3^{a_1}(a,\{m\})) \rightarrow perceive(a,\{m\})$ $with$
$f_3^{a_1}(a,\{m\}) = [P_{se}(m) = (P_{id}(a_3) \vee P_{id}(a_4))] \wedge [P_{id}(a) = P_{id}(a_1)]$

a_1 will receive the messages from a_3 (Fig. 4, case (A)(2)), but as long as f_{N2}^e holds, it will not receive the messages emitted by a_4 (case (C)(2)). If their position change and the distance between a_4 and a_1 becomes shorter than D, a_1 will begin to perceive its messages.

3.3   Undesirable Behavior

Finally, we study the case of conflicts between the agents. This may result from undesirable behavior, or from poor design of the filters. In the case where there is no filter issued by the environment (Fig. 4, case (A)), if the sole priority is the one of the environment on the agents, an agent can block every filter of the other agents by adding a negative filter generic enough to cover every agent and every message, or inversely "flood" them with messages. In order to tackle this problem, we introduce a particular kind of filter: the personal filters. The *personal filters* are the filters whose author is the only potential receiver.

Definition 10 (Personal Filter). f *is a personal filter iff* $\exists a_x \in A, \forall a \in A, f \in F_A, C \subset \Omega, f^{a_x}(a,C) = [P_{id}(a) = P_{id}(a_x)] \wedge (\forall e \in C \wedge_{i \in I_{fe}} [P_i(e) \ R_{fe} \ d_{fe}])$.

When an agent adds a filter for itself, it is a personal filter. More precisely, personal filters trigger the perception (or not perception) of an io only for its author. This is determined thanks to its identifier P_{id}. We note $F_{AP} \subset F_A$ the set of personal filters in the environment. In this way, we distinguish filters that implicate only their owner from filters that implicate – exclusively or not – other agents. In order to counter the threat of an agent putting filters to the detriment of other agents, the personal filters have a higher priority than the others:

Axiom 8 (Relative Priorities: Personal and Standard Filters).
$\forall f^{a_x} \in F_{AP}, f^{a_y} \in F_A \setminus F_{AP}, priority(f^{a_x}) > priority(f^{a_y}).$

This means that the agents personal filters overrule the filters they did not add personally in the environment, except of course for the rules of the environment. For example, if the agent a_4 does not want a_1 to perceive any messages, it will put a filter such as:
$holds(f^{a_4}_{N4}(a, \{m\})) \rightarrow \neg perceive(a, \{m\})$ with
$f^{a_4}_{N4}(a, \{m\}) = [P_{id}(a) = P_{id}(a_1)] \wedge [P_{sender}(m) \neq null].$

However, both the filters of the environment and the filters added by a_1 will overrule a_4's filter: a_1 will continue to receive the messages emitted nearby thanks to f^e_1, and it will also perceive the messages emitted by a_3 (and eventually a_4) thanks to $f^{a_1}_3$, which is a personal filter. That means that a_4 cannot block a_1 against its will.

This priority allows the agents to thwart other agents' misbehaviors, intentional or not. Thus, we can prevent an agent from blocking the standard behavior of our model. When the filters are added, the environment checks that the priority given to the filter by the agent is compliant with this order, by detecting whether the filter is personal or not. Depending on the politics of the MAS, the filters which are not compliant with their standard level of priority are either refused or corrected.

The priority levels of the different kinds of filters, according to their author and nature, allow the implementation of a "natural" order of precedence: all the agents must comply with the rules of the environment, then under these mandatory rules, they define their own interactions and perceptions, and finally they may perceive other solicitations. We emphasized in the introduction that the awareness is the result of external stimuli, which are not chosen, and of decisions of perceptions. In our model, the stimuli the agents undergo are those carried out through the filters of the environment, while it can decide to focus its attention by adding filters for itself.

In the following section, we introduce more complete examples of filters to show how it is possible to modulate the interaction rules according to the previous definitions and axioms.

4 Example

In the previous examples, we focused on communication and message exchanges. In this section, we provide an example of a situated multiagent system, where software agents use different kinds of interaction. The aim is not to describe the whole system, but to illustrate the flexibility introduced by the regulation of the MAS by the environment via the EASI model. Hence, we describe in detail only the interactional aspects of the MAS.

We consider a multiagent application with situated agents, i.e. localized agents that cooperate in a decentralized way. The agents are positionned on a two-dimensional grid. The characteristics of the observable properties of the entities are presented in detail in Fig. 5. We have one category of agents A, which

Notation	Meaning	Definition domain	$\in A$	$\in IO_M$	$\in IO_T$	$\in O_C$
P_{id}	identifier	$D_{identifierA} \subset \mathbb{N}$	X			
P_p	position	$([0 \ldots w], [0 \ldots h])$	X		X	X
P_c	capability	$\{lift, carry\}$	X			
P_b	busy	$\{true, false\}$	X			
P_s	subject	$\{request, accept, private\}$		X		
P_{se}	sender	$D_{identifierA}$		X		
P_r	receiver	$D_{identifierA} \cup unknown$		X		
P_d	direction	$\{N, NE, E, SE, S, SO, O, NO\}$			X	

Fig. 5. Summary table of the observable properties. $\in A$ is a short notation for $\forall a \in A, P \neq null$, which means that the agents belonging to A share this observable property. Similarly, IO_M and IO_T are the sets of interaction objects, with $IO_M, IO_T \subset IO$, and O_C is the set of crates, $O_C \subset O$. w and h are respectively the width and the height of the grid.

means all the agents share the same observable properties: their identifier, their position, their capability and whether they are busy or not. We define two types of interaction objects. The objects of the first type IO_M show their subject, their sender and their intended receiver; those of the second type IO_T show their position and a direction. There are also crates O_C in the environment, the only observable property of these objects is their position. The goal of the agents is to move all the crates to the edges of the grid. To move a crate, an agent with the *lift* capability and another with the *carry* capability have to coordinate together. The behavior of the agents is as follows: (1) it moves; (2) if a crate is found, the agent has to contact the nearest agent with the complementary capability (an agent has only one capability). This is achieved by sending a message with the requested capability and the object position to the nearby agents, which might answer by an "accept" message; (3) it is busy until the object has been moved to an edge of the grid.

The rules of perception of the environment for the messages $m \in IO_M$ are the following: spacially, d is the maximal range of perception of a message. This is enforced via the rule f_{N1}^e. The filters related to the perception are sumed up by order of priority in Fig. 6. In order to ease the simulation, the environment provides a default handling of the coordination messages: a message that has "request" for subject will be perceived by every agent that has the requested capability and that is not busy. There are two manners to create this behavior, either by adding f_3^e, which follows strictly the previous textual description, or by adding f_{N3}^e/ and f_3^e/, respectively forbidding an agent to receive messages when it is busy and adding the perception of the "request" messages to the agents that have the requested capability. The choice is significant, because although for this particular context, the resulting behavior will be the same, the second choice blocks all further possibility of message perception for the busy agents (Axioms 5 and 6). Hence, we choose the first alternative: the "request" messages are automatically handled, and by not specifying a negative filter, we allow them to be overheard.

	filter	pos	neg
Priority ↑	$f^e_{N1}(a, \{m\} \cup C) = [d(a,a_r) > d] \wedge [P_{id}(a_r) = P_{se}(m)]$, $C = \{a_1\}$		X
	$f^e_3(a, \{m\} \cup C) = [[P_c(a) \neq P_c(a_r)] \wedge [P_{id}(a_r) = P_{se}(m)]$ $\wedge [P_b(a) \neq false] \wedge [P_s(m) = \text{``request''}],\ C = \{a_r\}$	X	
	$f^e_{N3\prime}(a, \{m\}) = [P_b(a) = true]$		X
	$f^e_{3\prime}(a, \{m\} \cup C) = [P_c(a) \neq P_c(a_r)] \wedge [P_{id}(a_r) = P_{se}(m)]$ $\wedge [P_s(m) = \text{``request''}],\ C = \{a_r\}$	X	
	$f^e_4(a, \{m\}) = [P_{id}(a) = P_r(m)] \wedge [P_s(m) = \text{``accept''}]$	X	
	$f^e_5(a, \{m\}) = [P_{id}(a) = P_r(m)] \wedge [P_s(m) = \text{``private''}]$	X	
	$f^e_{N5}(a, \{m\}) = [P_{id}(a) \neq P_r(m)] \wedge [P_s(m) = \text{``private''}]$		X
	$f^e_{N6}(a, \{t\}) = [d(a,t) > 1]$		X
	$f^e_7(a, \{t\}) = [d(a,t) = 0] \wedge [P_b(a) = false]$	X	
	$f^{a_x}_8(a, \{m\}) = [P_{id}(a) = P_{id}(a_x)] \wedge [P_s(m) = \text{``request''}]$	X	
	$f^{a_x}_{N9}(a, \{m\}) = [P_{id}(a) = P_{id}(a_x)] \wedge [P_b(a) = true]$		X
	$f^{a_x}_{10}(a, \{t\}) = [P_{id}(a) = P_{id}(a_x)] \wedge_{\forall o \in O_C} [d(a,o) > d]$	X	

Fig. 6. Interaction filters, ordered by priority. "pos" means that it is a positive filter $(holds(f(a, \{io\} \cup C)) \rightarrow perceive(a, \{io\}))$, and "neg" a negative filter $(holds(f(a, \{io\} \cup C)) \rightarrow \neg perceive(a, \{io\}))$. $d(e_1, e_2)$ is the distance function between the entities e_1 and e_2, if $P_p(e_1), P_p(e_2) \neq null$.

The answer to this message is achieved by an "accept" message, which is "addressed" to the sender of the original request. Thus, the environment enables dyadic interaction for the "accept" messages thanks to the filter f^e_4. Let us note that thanks to f^e_{N1}, there is no need to specify the distance criteria in the other filters: since it has the highest priority, the other filters are momentarily disabled for every couple agent/io that complies with its conditions. Furthermore, the environment enables the agents to communicate "privately", i.e. their messages cannot be overheard by other agents. If the sender tags its message as "private", f^e_5 causes its perception by the specified receiver, and f^e_{N5} prevents the message from being perceived by other agents. Let us note that it is also possible to temporiraly add or remove the filters concerning a particular behavior, for instance the private messaging, and thus allowing the agents to send private messages only during specific periods.

Contrary to the messages, the interaction objects of the second type $(t \in IO_T)$ are localized and persistent, they are a kind of *trace*. If an agent finds several crates, it will carry one to an edge of the grid, and on its way it will put in the environment one trace every two squares, with the direction of the crates. The traces are not subjected to the other filters, because it does not have the requested observable properties (sender, subject...). Hence, we have to define their management. The agents can perceive the traces only if they are in an adjacent square, with $f^e_{N6}(a, t)$. The traces will automatically be perceived by each agent (not busy) passing on their position thanks to $f^e_7(a, t)$.

The basic interactional rules are enforced by the environment, so that the agents only have to add filters concerning specific behaviors, adapted to their strategies. For example, an agent a_x may try to overhear the request messages it should not perceive because it is busy, or it does not have the wanted capability, with $f_8^{a_x}$. We emphasized that we did leave the choice to the agent of whether it should perceive messages when it is busy or not. If its choice is that it should not, it can add the filter $f_{N9}^{a_x}$ to forbid it. Finally, the traces are useful for the agents if they are searching for crates. The corresponding filter is $f_{10}^{a_x}$: the agent a_x will perceive the nearby traces only if there is no crate in its direct range of perception. These filters are managed dynamically, hence enabling the agents to modify their interactional environment according to their needs.

This example shows how it is possible to design the rules of a both the MAS and the agents, and how this can be modified, either statically at design time, or dynamically at runtime. The designer only needs to foresee which properties could induce an effect on the behavior of the environment, and thus should be rendered observable.

5   Related Works

Some applications have substantiated the concept of awareness, and notably of overhearing. For instance, in the context of teams of autonomous agents the coherence of the team increases significantly thanks to the use of a protocol based on overhearing [12]. Overhearing has also been used in several works to monitor MASs, as in STEAM [11]. These systems highlight the usefulness of the concept of overhearing, but their implementation using massive broadcast or subscription limits their ability to be used. The built-up of awareness involves two phases, the effective sending and the filtering. In broadcast based implementations, the filtering is realized in every agent: each agent receives all the messages and has to filter them. With our method, the filtering is done before the actual sending of the messages.

Channelled multicast [4] proposes a focused broadcast, by means of dedicated channels of communication. However, because of a publish and suscribe system, it is still the sender which assumes the transmitting task. Furthermore, the more specialized and thus the more close to the needs of the agents the channels are, the more complex the system becomes. On the contrary, our model delegates to the environment the transmission and enables picking up the interesting interactions in the same environment. MIC* [9] is an agent formal environment which represents interactions as Interaction Objects (IO). These IOs, once produced, are separate from the agents and managed by the environment. They belong to Interaction Spaces (IS), in which they are propagated. The IS are composable, according to their physical and formal location. However, in MIC* the receivers are still passive in the choice of their communication, even though the environment does play a role in the perception of the IOs.

Distributed environments like Javaspaces[3] or LIME [13] are close to our system, as they allow the sharing of objects or tuples. For example, LIME proposes communication spaces that are dynamically shared according to their accessibility. These communication spaces are tuple spaces built on the tuples of each

---

[3] http://java.sun.com/products/jini/

agents and reconstructed at each reading. However, Javaspaces does not allow multiple template matching, and LIME does not assure the consistency of the tuple spaces. We can also mention TuCSon, which is based on programmable tuple-centres and enables to deal with coordination artifacts [16]. The artifacts are the closest to our approach. However, though the artifacts are interesting to manage indirect interactions via non-agent entities, it does not deal directly with the treatment of the messages.

The electronic institutions [6] propose run-time verification of the interaction protocols. This ensures a strict compliance with the specifications of the MAS. However, only the "control" part is taken into account, the infrastructure is not intended to also facilitate the interaction.

About the models, Weyns [20] proposes a complete framework for *active perception*. However, the subject is treated from the viewpoint of the agents, and not of the environment. This model does not include the problem of message management, when the objective of our work is to propose a model that unifies both the perception and the message management. Tummolini [17] defines the concept of *Behavioral Implicit Communication* (BIC), within the framework of cooperative systems for task achievement, as the set of every interaction that can be observed in an implicit way, i.e. information conveyed by actions or communications of the other agents. However, several properties are required to fulfill BICs: the observability of the actions and their results, the ability for the agents to infer the right information (and possibly an action), and the ability for the agents to anticipate the effects of their own actions on the other agents. This makes the framework difficult to use in real applications. Platon's model of overhearing [14] is the most generic to our knowledge, as it considers overhearing independently of the domain of the application. The introduction of the T-compound as design pattern permits a graphical representation of overhearing to model the interactions, based on existing works in the field of object computing. Platon has recently extended his model to over-sensing [15]. The agents have soft-bodies that have public states, which are verified (both in visibility and accessibility) by the environment. The modifications of the public states are spread throughout the environment. However, the model doesn't mention the case of the messages, and even if the agents are provided observability, the model does not address the question of the exploitation of the environment by the agents. In this sense, our works are complementary.

6   Conclusions and Future Directions

We have introduced EASI and drawn its main features, such as flexible management and regulation of the MAS interactions. Our model provides a common channel for the interactions, and the primitives that enable the agents to modulate their perceptions, both in positive and negative ways. It also provides a structure of regulation of the interactional politics of the MAS, by putting together environmental rules, personal choices and context-aware perception and transmission. To improve the regulation part of our model, we plan to explore the issue of the ownership and rights on filters and objects.

EASI can be used to support awareness, by enabling both external stimuli managed by the environment and an active control of its perceptions thanks to the filters. This implies an increase of potential perceptions of interactions, and we intend to take advantage of this modeling of awareness in order to work on opportunistic behaviors. The modeling presented in this paper may also lead to unexpected situations, which will have to be studied closely, as well as mechanisms to detect and prevent them. On the implementation side, the observability of the properties and the filtering process can present problems for large agent societies, which will have to be discussed.

By enabling the agents to choose their interactions and foci, we also extended their autonomy. The next step is to propose an ontology of the available interactions in the environment in order to propose to the agents entry-points to the systems. We also intend to study more closely the effects of EASI on the protocols, notably how an agent can take advantage of the information perceived and how it can compose its interactions in this framework.

References

1. F. Balbo. A model of environment, active support of the communication. In *American Association of Artificial Intelligence Conference, AAAI-99, Workshop on Reasoning in Context for AI Applications, AAAI Press*, pages 1–5, 1999.
2. F. Balbo and S. Pinson. Toward a multi-agent modelling approach for urban public transportation systems. In A. Omicini, P. Petta, and R. Tolksdorf, editors, *Engineering Societies in the Agent World II*, volume 2203 of *LNAI*, pages 160–174. Springer Verlag, 2001.
3. H. Bock and E. Diday. *Analysis of Symbolic Data. Exploratory Methods for Extracting Statistical Information from Complex Data*, volume 15. Springer Verlag, 2000.
4. P. Busetta, A. Donà, and M. Nori. Channeled multicast for group communications. In *AAMAS '02: Proceedings of the first international joint conference on Autonomous agents and multiagent systems*, pages 1280–1287, New York, NY, USA, 2002. ACM Press.
5. J. Dugdale, J. Pavard, and B. Soubie. A pragmatic development of a computer simulation of an emergency call center. In *Designing Cooperative Systems : The Use of Theories and Models, IOS Press*, pages 241–256, 2000.
6. M. Esteva, J. guez Aguilar, B. Rosell, and J. Arcos. Ameli: An agent-based middleware for electronic institutions. In R. Jennings, C. Sierra, L. Sonenberg, and M. Tambe, editors, *Proceedings of the 3rd International Joint Conference on Autonomous Agents and Multi-Agent Systems (AAMAS 2004)*, pages 236–243. ACM Press, 2004.
7. J. Ferber and O. Gutknecht. A meta-model for the analysis and design of organizations in multi-agent systems. In *ICMAS '98: Proceedings of the 3rd International Conference on Multi-Agent Systems*, pages 128–135, Washington, DC, USA, 1998. IEEE Computer Society.
8. C. L. Forgy. Rete : A fast algorithm for the many pattern/many object pattern match problem. *Artificial Intelligence*, 19:17–37, 1982.

9. A. Gouaïch, F. Michel, and Y. Guiraud. Mic*: a deployment environment for autonomous agents. In *Proceedings of Workshop on Environments for Multi-Agent Systems*, volume 3374 of *LNAI*, pages 109–126. Springer Verlag, 2005.

10. C. Heath, M. S. Svensson, J. Hindmarsh, P. Luff, and D. vom Lehn. Configuring awareness. *Comput. Supported Coop. Work*, 11(3):317–347, 2002.

11. G. Kaminka, C. Pynadath, and M. Tambe. Monitoring teams by overhearing: A mutli-agent plan-recognition approach. *Journal of Artificial Intelligence Research*, 17:83–135, 2002.

12. F. Legras and C. Tessier. Lotto: Group formation by overhearing in large teams. In *Advances in Agent Communication*, volume 2922 of *LNAI*, pages 254–270. Springer Verlag, 2004.

13. G. P. Picco and M. L. Buschini. Exploiting transiently shared tuple spaces for location transparent code mobility. In *COORDINATION '02: Proceedings of the 5th International Conference on Coordination Models and Languages*, pages 258–273, London, UK, 2002. Springer Verlag.

14. E. Platon, N. Sabouret, and S. Honiden. Overhearing and direct interactions: Point of view of an active environment, a preliminary study. In *Proceedings of Environment for Multi-Agent Systems, Workshop held at the Fourth Joint Conference in Autonomous Agents and Multi-Agent Systems*, pages 121–138, 2005.

15. E. Platon, N. Sabouret, and S. Honiden. Tag interactions in multiagent systems: Environment support. In *EUMAS*, pages 270–281, 2005.

16. A. Ricci, M. Viroli, and A. Omicini. Programming mas with artifacts. In *Proceedings of the 3rd International Workshop on Programming Multi-Agent Systems, ProMAS 05*, pages 163–178, July 2005.

17. L. Tummolini, C. Castelfranchi, A. Ricci, M. Viroli, and A. Omicini. "exhibitionists" and "voyeurs" do it better: A shared environment approach for flexible coordination with tacit messages. In *Proceedings of Workshop on Environments for Multi-Agent Systems*, volume 3374 of *LNAI*, pages 215–231. Springer Verlag, 2004.

18. R. Warren. *Auditory perception. A new analysis and synthesis.* Cambridge: Cambridge University Press, 1999.

19. D. Weyns, H. V. D. Parunak, F. Michel, T. Holvoet, and J. Ferber. Environments for multiagent systems, state-of-the-art and research challenges. *Lecture Notes in Computer Science Series*, 3374:2–52, 2005.

20. D. Weyns, E. Steegmans, and T. Holvoet. Towards active perception in situated multi-agent systems. *Special Issue of Journal on Applied Artificial Intelligence*, 18 (9-10):867–883, 2004.

21. M. Zargayouna, F. Balbo, and J. Saunier. Agent information server: a middleware for traveler information. In *6th International Workshop on Engineering Societies in the Agents World (ESAW'05)*, volume 3963 of *LNAI*, pages 3–16. Springer Verlag, 2005.

Environmental Support for Tag Interactions

Eric Platon[1,2], Nicolas Sabouret[2], and Shinichi Honiden[1]

[1] National Institute of Informatics, Sokendai, 2-1-2 Hitotsubashi, 101-8430 Tokyo
[2] Laboratoire d'Informatique de Paris 6, 104, Ave du Pdt Kennedy, 75016 Paris
{platon,honiden}@nii.ac.jp, nicolas.sabouret@lip6.fr

Abstract. Tag interactions are agent interactions that complement and differ from speech act communication models. Tags are public information that agents expose to others in the system to allow two types of interactions. Tag monitoring interactions let agents observe the tags of others actively. Tag fortuitous interactions make agents realize the tag of others with unrequested and application-dependent messages. In this paper we model tag interactions based on the agent *environment* and *computational bodies* to enact, maintain, and regulate their execution. We discuss the model and we identify further issues in the current state of the research. An example application is described in detail to show the potential of introducing tag interactions.

1 Introduction

In Multi-Agent Systems (MAS), interactions are usually message-passing between two agents, so that the main research activities deal with communication languages, interaction protocols, and their exploitation (e.g. negotiation, argumentation). However, systems capabilities appear limited in comparison to interaction opportunities in human agencies [1]. The potential for interaction diversity of software agents seems underexploited, although some situations can leverage interaction schemes with different semantics, such as indirect (e.g. stigmergy, see [2] for a survey), implicit [3], or opportunistic interactions [4]. Typically, one can conclude a friend is ill just due to her appearance, even though she *does not communicate* her state intentionally. How can we model such an interaction? To this end, we exploit the idea that human-beings do not only communicate through their languages, but also through their bodies. We call this type of interaction *tag interaction* and propose to endow software agents with an explicit computational body that exposes observable information labeled as tags.

The management of tag interaction based on a software body differs from message-passing techniques. The source agent is not always aware of the information it expresses and it cannot always be considered as the 'operational sender' (e.g. my ill friend). Similarly, agents that receive information via tag interaction do not always know they play the role of receivers (e.g. realizing my friend is ill). Consequently, tag interaction requires an active entity that allows and executes such situations by dealing with the software body. The scope of this entity must encompass all agents that can participate in tag interaction and we think a

D. Weyns, H.V.D. Parunak, and F. Michel (Eds.): E4MAS 2006, LNAI 4389, pp. 106–123, 2007.

natural candidate for this function is a *computational environment*. This paper describes how such an environment can support tag interaction with intuitive examples from social and natural sources, and a detailed example application for fault tolerance.

Section 2 details our terminology and demonstrates that an environment is a proper abstraction for tag interaction. Section 3 then exposes our formalization of the notion of tag interaction and environment. Section 4 exploits this formalization to describe environmental mechanisms. Section 5 exposes an example application devoted to an agent-based fault tolerant load balancing problem. Section 6 discusses the current state of our work, and section 7 presents future evolutions.

2   Tag Interaction and Environment

2.1   Software Agent for Tag Interaction

In the literature, an agent is an autonomous computational entity with interactive capabilities [5,6]. Our definition hereafter is related but separates explicitly the interactive nature of agents from their internals as shown on Fig. 1.

A software agent is an autonomous problem-solving entity endowed with an explicit boundary named *softbody* that exposes:

Sensors to receive information from the environment

Actuators to send information to the environment

A *public state* of the agent, observable in the environment

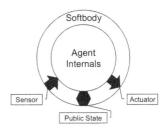

Fig. 1. A Software Agent

The problem-solving capabilities of the agent internals refer to the various existing agent architectures, like BDI [7] and KGP [8]. Internals are usually hidden from other agents, 'encapsulated' in a boundary that we name the *softbody* of software agents. This computational body features sensors and actuators for interactions with other agents and entities in the MAS [5].

In addition, the softbody exposes a *public state* of the agent. A public state contains information about the agent that can be sensed by others in the environment. Concretely, the public state is a list of variables named *tags* whose values reflect agent internals. The contents and types of information in the public state can be configured by the designer or dynamically by the system to define what can be observed about each agent. For example, we can infer in a discussion that someone may be lying when we observe her to blush, i.e. her public state exposes a change to a 'red skin color'. On the other hand, system designers might choose to prevent such an observation in a software auction system to avoid collusion means by body signals [9]. Public state content information can indeed influence agent reasoning processes and consequently their interactions.

The separation between the internals and the softbody is an architectural mean to preserve the autonomy of agents. Interactions are performed through the softbodies as interfaces, so that sending and reception of information are decoupled from internal process. Agents can decide autonomously in their internals how to process information, and which information to process or to ignore. External control is screened by the softbody, thus limited to the public state.

In the remainder of the paper, we will now refer to *software* agents simply as *agent* for readability concerns, although our model does not pretend to generalize to any kind of agent.

2.2   Tag Interaction

Definition. We define tag interaction as follows;

> Tag interaction is a set of mechanisms that models interactions based on the public state: (a) the expression of public state, (b) the sensing of public state, and (c) the monitoring and fortuitous propagation mechanisms.

Tag interaction mechanisms expose and sense public states with (a) and (b). We distinguish two types of propagation mechanisms to describe different situations in (c). *Tag monitoring interaction* is related to observation, when an agent collects information about others. This active inquiry mode is initiated by an agent and contrasts with the 'passive' reception mode of *tag fortuitous interaction*. This second type functions as a call-back mechanism: An agent receives information about the public states of other agents without explicitly requesting for it. For instance, one can feel a presence in a dark room through senses, even though we do not request this information in the first place. Fig. 2 depicts the two types of tag interaction.

Fig. 2. Left: Tag monitoring interaction. Right: Tag fortuitous interaction.

The left part of Fig. 2 shows the observing agent acting (e.g. looking at) so as to sense the public state of the observed agent. The right part shows that the public state of an observed agent is spread out to the sensor of any 'passing agent' (e.g. mobile). We argued in section 1 that these two situations need an active third-party entity to perform the information flows represented by the arrows of the two above figures, and a candidate is the environment.

Environmental Requirements. Observing an agent means the public state is 'readable', such as on the left of Fig. 2. But in usual agent approaches, reading actions are realized by contacting the observed agent that consequently becomes aware of this observation. In a discussion, we might however talk and simultaneously observe interlocutors to detect clues such as attitudes. Observation requires the observing agent to *receive* information, without requesting for it to the observed one. The environment is a third party that can provide mechanisms to perform this function.

Tag fortuitous interaction emphasizes the previous argument, since no agent triggers any information transfer, as on the right of Fig. 2 where the environment delivers public state information. A typical situation is when one fails to meet a friend. When the friend is eventually nearby, sensing her presence can be thought of as the fortuitous reception of a 'presence message event' delivered by the environment on change of the situation.

Finally, tag interaction requires an environment as a *regulating entity* [10]. The public state is a feature of the softbody that lets malicious agents fake attitudes or change the state of other arbitrarily if no regulation is enforced. As a general example, the public state 'position' should be modified consistently to avoid odd agent movements and collisions that should not occur in a simulation. The environment can enforce correctness of public states against system rules.

To summarize, tag interaction requires from the environment the following support, and our model aims at providing them.

- Enact monitoring interactions
- Enact fortuitous interactions
- Regulate interactions

This support needs to be provided transparently to avoid introducing into the agent any complexity related to the environment responsibilities. The model abstracts this issue by only specifying what are the environment responsibilities. Implementation issues lie at another level of analysis. The environment might be centralized or distributed depending on application requirements. This matter is further discussed in section 6.

2.3   Environment Model

Our definition of environment specializes a generic version [10], notably based on the work of Russell and Norvig [5], and Ferber [6]. It focuses on the salient characteristics of the environment for tag interaction.

The environment of a MAS is the entity where agents exist and that:

- Maintains the system topology
- Maintains mapping information of the agent population to the topology
- Performs tag interaction mechanisms
- Defines and enforces tag interaction rules

The environment is a stateful entity that defines and maintains a topology of the system, which can be spatial or abstract as in many simulations [11], network domains, file systems, or web-sites [12]. It can be either centralized or decentralized, depending on application requirements. The environment maintains information about agent situations in the system topology to manage information delivery and regulate their interactions. This information is only related to softbodies. That is, the environment does not need to deal with agent internals, since they are encapsulated into agents and an access by the environment to internals would violate the autonomy assumption. The environment also mediates tag interactions, which refers to public state evolution and change notification. Furthermore, the environment applies rules in the MAS to enforce certain public state values. Rules define ranges of possible values, so that system states remain consistent for the application. Rules also define how public state information is spread out in the system, for instance by defining a range of interaction [13,14]. These rules allow specifying change notification strategies to control the amount of tag information that is exchanged in the system (which can cause a significant cost variation as illustrated with the example application of section 5).

The definition meets the requirements we defined for tag interaction.

- Interaction mediation enacts an observation framework whereby the environment delivers observable events.
- Fortuitous events delivery is configurable by specific rules.
- Regulation is enforced by the rules while mediating interactions.

We notice that the environment has no deliberative capability and no decision power. The environment merely accomplishes its responsibilities in strict compliance with rules defined by design.

3   Formalization

3.1   Agent

Our formalization of an agent follows from the definition of section 2.1:

$$Agent = (\psi, \varphi, INF) \text{ , where } \varphi = (\mathcal{S}, \mathcal{A}, \mathcal{P}_s) \tag{1}$$

First in this formula, ψ is the internal state of the agent, and φ is the state of its softbody. A pair (ψ, φ) then represents a state of the agent. ψ ranges over the state space S_ψ, and φ ranges over S_φ. The softbody φ is further developed into a 3-tuple where $\mathcal{S}$ is the set of sensors of the agent, $\mathcal{A}$ the set of actuators, and $\mathcal{P}_s$ the *public state*, which can be a set of variables, e.g. in predicate logic.

The last element of the formalization is INF, a set of two reaction rules INF_ψ and INF_φ to determine the evolution of agent states (ψ, φ) on change of internals or softbody respectively. For any ψ and φ:

$$\frac{(\psi, \varphi) \ and \ \psi \to \psi'}{\varphi \to \varphi'} INF_\psi \tag{2}$$

$$\frac{(\psi, \varphi) \ and \ \varphi \to \varphi'}{\psi \to \psi'} INF_\varphi \tag{3}$$

The operational semantics of INF_ψ expresses the evolution of the state (ψ, φ) after the evolution from ψ to ψ'. The result of INF_ψ is the evolution of the softbody to reach φ'. The agent final state then becomes the pair (ψ', φ'). For instance, when an agent wants to open a door, it first *intends* (ψ evolution) and then *acts* (φ evolution) to complete its intention. INF_φ expresses similarly the evolution of internals due to the evolution of the softbody, e.g. input on sensors. INF operators explicate *how* internals and softbody are linked by a cause to consequence relation. *What* is modified along the evolution is application-dependent and relies on instances of the model.

3.2 Environment

Our formalization of the environment follows from the definition of section 2.3:

$$Environment = (\Omega, \Phi, TRANS) \tag{4}$$

A complete state of the environment is a pair (Ω, Φ). Ω is a 2-tuple, representing the environment internals:

$$\Omega = (\mathcal{T}opology, \mathcal{R}ules) \tag{5}$$

where $\mathcal{T}opology$ describes the structure (possibly dynamic) of the system, e.g. the ground in traffic simulations or the hyperlink network of a web-site [12]. Agents are situated in this topology to define their neighborhood. Management of tag interactions by the environment is performed according to this topology. $\mathcal{R}ules$ is the set of rules that define how the environment executes agent interactions.

Back to (4), $\Phi = \bigcup_i \varphi_i$ is the set of references to softbodies in the system. The environment exploits softbodies to serve the population of agents (e.g. information delivery) and to enforce system rules by imposing environmental regulation. The regulation lets agents control their softbodies in a range of acceptable states defined by environment rules over S_φ. A softbody is consequently *owned* and *controlled* by an agent, while the control is *regulated* by the environment.

We finally introduce $TRANS$, a set of reaction rules $TRANS_\Omega$ and $TRANS_\varphi$ to model the regulated interaction mechanisms of the environment with agent softbodies. For any Φ and Ω:

$$\frac{(\Omega, \Phi) \ and \ \Omega \to \Omega'}{\exists A \subset \Phi : \forall a \in A, \exists (\varphi^a, \varphi'^a) \in S_\varphi^2 : \varphi^a \to \varphi'^a} TRANS_\Omega \tag{6}$$

$$\frac{(\Omega, \Phi) \ and \ A \subset \Phi : \forall a \in A, \ \varphi^a \to \varphi'^a}{\Omega \to \Omega'} TRANS_\Phi \tag{7}$$

From an environment state (Ω, Φ) and an evolution of the internals Ω to Ω', $TRANS_\Omega$ causes the set of softbodies Φ to evolve, so that for softbodies in the subset $A = (a_1, ..., a_n) \in \Phi^n$, the transformation $TRANS_\Omega$ entails all φ_i to evolve to some φ_i' for each a_i. Similarly, $TRANS_\Phi$ models the converse transformation. The subset A depends on the $Topology$ and typically contains a 'neighborhood' of agents defined by application-dependent needs, such as an Euclidean or social (same taste, $etc.$) distance.

4   Environment Mechanisms for Tag Interaction

This section relies on the formalization to describe the mechanisms of the environment in tag interactions.

4.1   Agent Influence on the Environment

When an agent intends to execute an action (i.e. change own public state or observe) in the BDI sense [7], its internals evolve from ψ_{init} (intention selection) to ψ_{act} (intention attempt). The agent is initially in a state $(\psi_{init}, \varphi_{init})$, so that the change of internals causes the softbody to evolve due to the INF_ψ reaction rule. The softbody consequently evolves to φ_{act}:

$$\frac{(\psi_{init}, \varphi_{init}) \; and \; \psi_{init} \to \psi_{act}}{\varphi_{init} \to \varphi_{act}} INF_\psi \tag{8}$$

The modification of the softbody entails a reaction on the environment with the $TRANS_\Phi$ rule, from Ω_{init} to Ω_{check}:

$$\frac{(\Omega_{init}, \Phi) \; and \; \varphi_{init} \to \varphi_{act}}{\Omega_{init} \to \Omega_{check}} TRANS_\Phi \tag{9}$$

The environment then checks whether its new state is valid according to applicable rules. If so, it continues the action by propagation of the effect to other agents (see sections 4.2 and 4.3), and it completes the process by informing the source agent. A successful action entails Ω_{ok}. Success is observed with the softbody that becomes φ_{ok} under the application of $TRANS_\Omega$.

$$\frac{(\Omega_{check}, \Phi) \; and \; \Omega_{check} \to \Omega_{ok}}{\varphi_{act} \to \varphi_{ok}} TRANS_\Omega \tag{10}$$

Fig. 3 shows the case where a public state is turned from 'white' to 'black' successfully.

In case rules oppose the intention of the agent, the environment evolves from Ω_{check} to Ω_{nok} and counter-balances the agent attempt.

$$\frac{(\Omega_{check}, \Phi) \; and \; \Omega_{check} \to \Omega_{nok}}{\varphi_{act} \to \varphi_{fail}} TRANS_\Omega \tag{11}$$

Fig. 4 shows a case where the intention of the agent to turn its public state to black is not committed. Formula (11) follows formula (9) and cancels the action of the agent before its occurrence in the system (e.g. if one wants to push a wall, the body does not move). In the end, the softbody influences back the agent internals with INF_φ to 'report' the opposition of the environment. In both cases, the execution follows the sequence INF_ψ, $TRANS_\phi$, $TRANS_\Omega$, INF_φ.

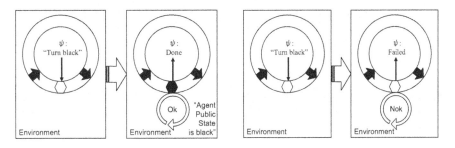

Fig. 3. Environment validates and commits the influence

Fig. 4. Environment prevents the influence

4.2   Environmental Effect on Agents

The environment acts on agents with the mechanisms described in the previous section. However, the effect of the environment on the public state cannot be overruled by agents in the first place, so that the sequence of reaction rules differs. With the same notations as before:

$$\frac{(\Omega_{init}, \Phi) \ and \ \Omega_{init} \rightarrow \Omega_{act}}{\varphi_{init} \rightarrow \varphi_{update}} TRANS_{\Omega} \tag{12}$$

The environment acts on the softbody that consequently evolves to φ_{update}, representing either a change of public state (Fig. 5) or an observation received on sensors. Then, the softbody informs its agent internals:

$$\frac{(\psi_{init}, \varphi_{init}) \ and \ \varphi_{init} \rightarrow \varphi_{update}}{\psi_{init} \rightarrow \psi_{update}} INF_{\varphi} \tag{13}$$

In this rule, the agent *cannot* compensate yet the effect on the public state. Such a situation is shown on Fig. 5. The public state of the agent turns from white to black state under environmental effect and the agent internals are informed. Agents can however react afterward in autonomy to either oppose or ignore the environmental effect. Typically, the agent can take subsequent actions to modify the environment, and such behaviors are governed by the same regulation sequence as in section 4.1. We can illustrate such situations with someone entering a river stream. The stream has an overwhelming strength at first and it carries

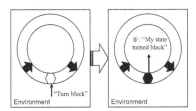

Fig. 5. Environmental effect on the agent public state

the swimmer downstream (assuming the public state contains the position of the agent). In reply, the swimmer can try to oppose the stream and may succeed in crossing it if the swimming abilities and strength are sufficient.

4.3 Public States Spread Management

Given an agent, three types of events imply a spread of the public state in the environment, namely modification of the public state by the agent, environmental dynamics, and modification attempts on the agent public state by other agents through the environment. Fig. 6 illustrates the case where an agent modifies its public state (left part). Validation of the modification by the environment (central part) is followed by the publication of the resulting state to agents in the neighborhood defined by the topology (right part). We describe hereafter how to process the public state spread management in the three aforementioned cases.

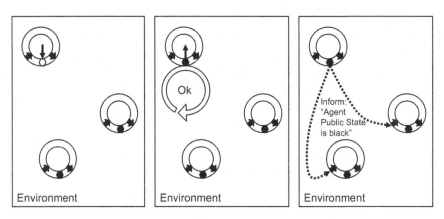

Fig. 6. Public State Management from left to right: the top-left agent modifies its public state; the environment validates the change; the change is spread to neighbors

Agent modification. Each agent controls its softbody and can modify the public state, under regulation by the environment. The procedure of modification is initially the same as the successful agent influence on the environment detailed in section 4.1. The sequential application of formulas (8) and (9) modifies the public state of the agent and validates it by the environment. Then, acknowledgment of the conformance of the new public state is performed with the publication of the modification in the neighborhood:

$$\frac{(\Omega_{check}, \Phi) \ and \ \Omega_{check} \rightarrow \Omega_{ok}}{\varphi^{a_\varphi}_{act} \rightarrow \varphi^{a_\varphi}_{ok}, \ \exists A \subset \Phi \setminus \{a_\varphi\}, \ \forall a \in A, \ \varphi^a \rightarrow \varphi^a_{news}} TRANS_\Omega \qquad (14)$$

The neighborhood A is included in the set of softbodies $\Phi \setminus \{a_\varphi\}$. Each softbody in A receives a notification on its sensors about the change '$\varphi_{act} \rightarrow \varphi_{ok}$' of a_φ (softbody of the agent that changed). Formula (14) is a generalization of formula (10) that only stated the successful completion of public state change without publication (case where the agent is alone in the system).

Environmental dynamics. Environmental dynamics apply to subsets of agents. Typically, Archimedes' Law applies to agents under water in a simulation, while a clock interrupt to represent time concerns all agents in the system. The application of environmental dynamics on public state follows the procedure of section 4.2. Each dynamics corresponds to an environmental rule set that targets a particular type of public state variable. If p in the public state of a softbody is the target of a rule, p is assigned a new value p' after application of the reaction operator $TRANS_\Omega$. Environment and softbody are consequently updated, and the new value p' is spread in the system. The corresponding formula is a generalization of formula (12) that modifies all softbodies, similarly to (14).

Attempts by other agents. When an agent intends to act on another agent to modify its public state (e.g. push an agent to change its position), the interaction is mediated by the environment. The procedure begins with a source agent that intends to act on the public state of a target agent. The intention leads to modifying the softbody with INF_ψ and it entails an effect on the environment with $TRANS_\Phi$. If the action is authorized in the system, the environment reaction is three-fold by applying the action to the target agent, publishing the action to other agents, and sending an acknowledgment to the source agent:

$$\frac{(\Omega_{check}, \Phi) \; and \; \Omega_{check} \to \Omega_{ok}}{\varphi^s_{act} \to \varphi^s_{ok}, \; \varphi^t \to \varphi^t_{changed}, \; \exists A \subset \Phi \setminus \{a^s, a^t\}, \; \forall a \in A, \; \varphi^a \to \varphi^a_{news}} TRANS_\Omega$$

The neighborhood A is included in $\Phi \setminus \{a^s, a^t\}$, where a^s is the softbody of the source agent and a^t the one of the target agent. In the end, each softbody informs its internals with INF_φ, so that agents are informed about the action. In particular, the target agent can react to this action.

5   Tag Interactions Applied to a Fault Tolerance Scenario

In this section, we describe an agent-based application with 'classical' and tag interaction approaches. The application is a load-balancing scenario that requires a fault tolerance mechanism to support the activity of the system. We detail the application, the two approaches, and a run of the system where fault tolerance is required in the case of 'agent death' [15].

5.1   The Load-Balancing Scenario and a Classical Approach

A client (e.g. the user) submits a set of tasks to the system. The role of the system is to perform the tasks and to report the results to the client. All tasks have same importance, they are independent, and they must all be completed. In other words, we suppose that tasks are not ordered and there is no time constraint to complete them. The base architecture of this scenario is a repository where clients submit their tasks and wait for the results. The repository is an indexed queue where tasks have three exclusive states, namely todo, doing, or done. The system must perform the tasks marked todo, signal tasks under process

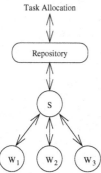

Task Allocation

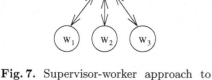

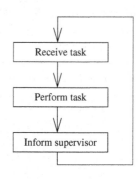

Fig. 7. Supervisor-worker approach to the load-balancing problem

Fig. 8. Internal state cycle of worker agents. The semantics of the arrow is the transition from one state to the other, once the associated action is completed.

with `doing` and the identifier of the processing unit, and mark completed tasks with `done` so that the client can take them. The index of the queue points to the next task marked with `todo`. The index approach is mainly introduced as a mean to simplify the task selection process and to ensure mutually exclusive access to tasks (necessary in the tag-based approach). Different elements that access the repository can only choose to perform the task pointed by the index (which is then atomically updated to the next task to be done).

A classical approach in MAS is a supply-chain where a supervisor agent delegates the tasks in the repository to worker agents, collects the results, and updates the task state. The delegation by the supervisor is the load-balancing mechanism of this approach: Tasks are allocated to available workers. The usual schema of this application is depicted in Fig. 7. Worker agents interact with the supervisor to receive tasks and return their results. Their internal state cycle is shown on Fig. 8. A typical run of the cycle is to receive a task, do it, and inform the supervisor about the result.

A typical problem in this application occurs when a worker fails. Without any specific mechanism to deal with this issue, the supervisor agent may wait indefinitely for the completion of the task, while the worker agent is 'dead', i.e. the underlying process anomalously stopped. One solution to this issue is to introduce timeouts. Each delegation of a task has a rendezvous timeout by which the worker agent must finish the task. Beyond the timeout, the supervisor considers the worker has encountered a problem and cannot complete the task. The task is then assigned to another worker.

Some problems of this approach are however the supervisor failure point and the limited flexibility. Distributed computing techniques exist to recover from supervisor failures (e.g. redundancy with the 'primary-backup' architecture [16]) but they maintain a centralization point that may cause performance drops in case of failures (replication cost, recovery time, etc.). Workers cannot interact directly to recover locally from some issues without the supervisor. The flexibility of a MAS approach can be improved relatively to these issues. Other issues such as the failure of the repository are not considered in this example.

5.2 Tag Interaction Approach

The reason for using tag interactions in the load-balancing scenario is to improve the flexibility of the application by a more balanced approach. Tag interactions allow removing one failure point such as the supervisor role by extending the capabilities of workers with adequate tags and sensing strategy.

Fig. 9 shows the system workers and their tags. Sensors and actuators on the softbody are simply message boxes to communicate in the environment and they are not represented for clarity reasons. Workers are endowed with two types of tags in their public state. Ref is a reference to the task the agent is executing. ECD (Expected Completion Date) indicates the time by which the worker declares to complete the task it is performing.

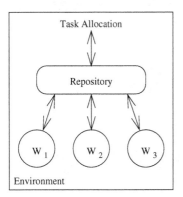
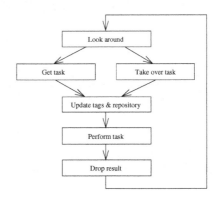

Fig. 9. Tag interaction approach to the load-balancing problem

Fig. 10. Internal state cycle of worker agents with tag interactions

The internal state machine of the workers is more complex due to the removal of the supervisor role. Fig. 10 shows a cycle with a disjunctive branch. Workers start by 'looking around' the tags on agents in their neighborhood and the state of the repository. If all ECD tags are future dates, the worker gets a new task from the repository. If an ECD tag is past and no other agent has signed up in the repository for the corresponding task, the worker takes over the task by reading the Ref tag[1] and updating the repository with its identifier. Alternatively, a task in execution by a neighbor (doing state) is selected if the neighbor is 'unreadable' (e.g. hardware error). The next step in the cycle is for the worker to update its own tags to let others know about its current state. The worker then performs the task and drops the result in the repository.

---

[1] We suppose every access to tags is mutually exclusive.

The environment is explicitly represented in this version of the system. Its role is restricted to the support of tag monitoring interactions. Other mechanisms are not used in this scenario (fortuitous interactions would require adapting and extending the worker cycle). The environment is decentralized over the machines that host the system. The different parts are synchronized dynamically with their adjacent parts in the environment topology similarly to [17]. Failure of parts of the environment only prevents workers in these parts to interact, while other workers can continue their tasks. Such environment can rely on a distributed event notifier adequately sophisticated to fulfill the requirements for tag monitoring interactions.

Notice that such a tag interaction process is arguably very costly if the environment is to publish any change to all workers in the system. This is the reason why the topology of the environment has to constrain the spread of change publication by the definition of the worker neighborhood. We chose to place, e.g., two agents in the neighborhood of each worker (we do not aim to study further the influence of this parameter at this stage of the work). The environment publishes the public state change of a worker to the two agents in its neighborhood, which significantly reduces the theoretical communication cost of these tag interactions from $O(n^2)$ to $O(n)$, where n is the number of workers.

5.3   System Run with Fault Tolerance

Tag interactions allow decentralizing the fault tolerance aspect of the application as can be observed in the following run of the application. Initially, the client places three tasks (t_1, t_2, t_3) in the repository and there are two workers in the system (w_1 and w_2). Fig. 11 represents a run where w_1 fails and w_2 exploits the tag information to recover the failure. Each interaction in this example follows the trace pattern INF_ψ, $TRANS_\phi$, $TRANS_\Omega$, INF_φ presented in section 4.1 (influence of agents on the environment).

The worker w_1 looks around for tags, but does not notice any problem (initial stage), so it gets t_1 and starts performing it with a public state (Ref, t_1) and (ECD, d_1), where d_1 is a date in the future. The second worker w_2 does the same and performs t_2 with the corresponding public state where $d_2 > d_1$. During the performance, w_1 fails and w_2 completes its current task. The worker w_2 starts a new cycle and looks around. As $d_2 > d_1$, w_2 can deduce that w_1 is dead, so that

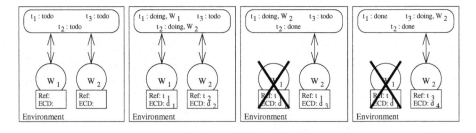

Fig. 11. Sequence of system states in the considered run

it takes over the task t_1, updates the identifier in the repository, and performs the task. In the last cycle, w_2 looks around and, as no problem exists in the neighborhood, it performs the last task t_3. The work request is then completed, despite one fault that has been automatically recovered.

6   Discussion

6.1   Applications

A criterion of an application that lends itself to tag interactions is *observation*. If observation is an essential characteristic of agents in an application, then tag interactions can be relevant. The load balancing scenario presented in section 5 shows how tag-based observation can contribute to the flexibility of software that relies on more classical schemes (e.g. the supervisor approach).

Applications that could leverage tag interaction are first simulations that need realistic interaction patterns encountered in nature. In particular, the environment plays an important role in simulations and the introduction of tag interaction can rely on extending existing work. Beyond simulation, tag interactions are useful in some electronic market types, where interaction opportunities are a critical factor. Auction systems (see [18] for a survey) and normative agencies such as Electronic Institutions [19] are active research areas that rely explicitly on direct interactions, and tag interaction can introduce more flexibility. We described an application to show such a flexibility, and tag interactions contribute positively to the system performance [20].

6.2   Present Issues

Various improvements can be applied to the current model of tag interaction. In previous work, agents could interact with others and objects [21]. Although the present paper focuses only on agents, the introduction of the softbody allows future work to exploit and generalize the approach to objects, where an object is assimilated to an 'empty softbody', i.e. without agent internals. In such a case, the public state would not reflect agent internals but an interface to handle the object, as with coordination artifacts [22] or the interface of web services. Another extension is to deal with simultaneous and concurrent events in the system, whereas we currently treat actions in sequence. In fact, these issues have been discussed for many years [6,23], and we leave them open for the moment. One consequence is that current implementations of our model feature a centralized component for the environment, whereas MAS would rather leverage distributed approaches. The model abstracts distribution issues for system design as it seems more convenient first to specify a solution by defining the responsibilities of the environment, and then to analyze an appropriate implementation. The work of Weyns et al. seems an appropriate base solution, where 'pieces' of environment are maintained and synchronized when required [17].

Finally, the issue of environment regulation deserves further studies on how to specify and implement rules. In particular, the issue of 'conservative rules' (in a physical sense) seems to be powerful means to control the system entropy.

6.3   Related Work

Castelfranchi described the Behavioral Implicit Communication (BIC) to explain why agents can communicate and coordinate by acting instead of using languages [24]. For example, an escaping prey 'communicates' its position to the predator only by moving, when it would prefer avoiding it. However, the prey is not explicitly the sender of messages about its position in the sense of usual Agent Communication Languages, i.e. it has no mental attitude of a sender. BIC explains this situation by identifying a *power of observation* that allows the observer to 'pull' messages. Even though the prey does not communicate its position, the predator fetches the information by observation. The environment has been related to BIC as the source whereby observers can get information about others. The further stage we aim at in this paper is to embed the observation of agents (the public state) in a concrete interaction model, which relies explicitly on the environment.

We propose to exploit embodiment in tag interaction among machines, and thus to allow software agents to use their body and information about others. Our proposal can be compared to the position of Kushmerick [1], with more emphasis on a model that can be engineered and the environment. Wrapper agents are similarly interfaces to legacy programs or they add some functionalities such as code mobility. Such wrappers differ from entities that reflect the state of the wrapped entity, so that we think they differ from the softbody. The KGP model of agency is implemented with a stateful body that features sensors and actuators [25,8]. The body collects sensed information to feed the agent knowledge base about the world. Such state is complementary but differs from our public state which exposes information about the agent itself to other agents in the system, thus offering a foundation for a tag-based reflexive architecture.

The public state is related to the 'tags' proposed by Holland in his theory of complex adaptive systems [26]. This theory has been exploited in the work of Hales in biologically-inspired systems [27]. The public state is another version of the tags. The essential difference with the work of Holland and Hales is that the public states is an attempt to use tags as an engineering element in the design of MAS.

Software environments have been considered in various work to mediate and control interactions. In particular, the coordination artifacts (CA) of Ricci et al. allow building such environments [28]. Engineering environments with CA populates MAS not only with agents, but also with artifacts that mediate interactions among agents. Although CA can provide an engineering approach to address tag interaction to some extent, we think CA cannot cover the notion of a body. The Agent Coordination Context of CA shares similar concepts with the softbody [29], but the ACC is an interface that is lent to agents during interactions, whereas the body belongs to the agent architecture. This difference is important in open systems, where designers want to build their own agents.

Tag interactions are related to tuple spaces and blackboard architectures, which are two notable technologies that are related to the environment [30,31,10]. Tag interactions differ however from these models since the notions of ownership of public state, topology, and regulation by the environment of the possible interactions are missing in tuple spaces and blackboards. In addition, tag interactions rely on dynamics of the environment to perform tag monitoring and fortuitous interactions. Tuple spaces and blackboards are usually passive entities that have no proper dynamics. One exception is however the 'tuple centers' introduced with the aforementioned CA.

Finally, tag interactions are related to the interaction models based on stigmergy, such as the pheromone and field infrastructures [13,2]. These interaction models are also supported by the environment. The main difference with tag interactions is that stigmergy relies on entities (pheromones, fields) that can evolve independently from agents, whereas tag interactions rely on the softbody that is part of agents. Once a pheromone is produced in the environment, its evolution is loosely coupled with the agent, e.g. a pheromone remains in the system, even though the agent is terminated. The softbody is instead strongly coupled to the agent and serves to expose relevant and up to date information.

7   Conclusion

In this paper, the environment in MAS is seen as a solution to support tag interaction. The environment provides an adequate abstraction to describe the mechanisms involved in tag interaction and to lead to an implementation framework. Also, tag interaction exemplifies a category of applications that requires an environment as first-class entity. We think that the connection between tag interaction and environment is an indication that future development of interaction theories should rely increasingly on the environment as a key element.

In future work, we aim at relating our model to distributed implementation schemes, since the current methodology leads to a monolithic model of the environment. Rules of the environment are also an important research direction with the definition of 'conservative rules'. Such rules may help in defining metrics of the system entropy to evaluate its coherence. Finally, the current mechanisms underlying tag interaction need to be modified to handle action simultaneity and concurrent interactions in the system, which should take advantage of other improvements in the modeling of tag interaction spaces.

References

1. Kushmerick, N.: Software agents and their bodies. Minds and Machines **7** (1997) 227–247
2. Parunak, H.V.D.: A survey of environments and mechanisms for human-human stigmergy. [32] 163–186
3. Tummolini, L., Castelfranchi, C., Ricci, A., Viroli, M., Omicini, A.: "Exhibitionists" and "Voyeurs" Do It Better: A Shared Environment for Flexible Coordination with Tacit Messages. In Weyns, D., Parunak, H.V.D., Michel, F., eds.: Environment for Multi–Agent Systems'04. Volume 3374 of Lecture Notes in Artificial Intelligence., Springer–Verlag (2005) 215–231

4. Balbo, F., Pinson, S.: Toward a Multi-agent Modelling Approach for Urban Public Transportation Systems. In Omicini, A., Petta, P., Tolksdorf, R., eds.: Engineering Societies in the Agent World'01. Volume 2203 of Lecture Notes in Artificial Intelligence., Springer–Verlag (2001) 160–174
5. Russell, S., Norvig, P.: Artificial Intelligence: A Modern Approach. Prentice Hall (Edition 2003)
6. Ferber, J.: Multi-Agent Systems: An Introduction to Distributed Artificial Intelligence. Addison-Wesley (1999)
7. Rao, A.S., Georgeff, M.P.: BDI Agents: From Theory to Practice. Technical report, Australian Artificial Intelligence Institute (1995)
8. Kakas, A.C., Mancarella, P., Sadri, F., Stathis, K., Toni, F.: The KGP model of agency. In de Mántaras, R.L., Saitta, L., eds.: ECAI, IOS Press (2004) 33–37
9. Rogers, A., Jennings, N.R.: Collusion in Agent–Based Systems. AgentLink News **17** (2005) 6–8
10. Weyns, D., Omicini, A., Odell, J.: Environment, First-Order Abstraction in Multiagent Systems. Autonomous Agents and Multi-Agent Systems **14, number 1** (2007) 5–30
11. Klügl, F., Fehler, M., Herrler, R.: About the Role of the Environment in Multiagent Simulations. In Weyns, D., Parunak, H.V.D., Michel, F., eds.: Environment for Multi–Agent Systems. Volume 3374 of Lecture Notes in Computer Science., Springer (2004) 127–149
12. Bandini, S., Manzoni, S., Vizzari, G.: Web Sites as Agents' Environments: General Framework and Applications. In Weyns, D., Parunak, H.V.D., Michel, F., eds.: Proceedings of Environment for Multi–Agent Systems at Autonomous Agents and Multi–Agent Systems'05. (2005)
13. Mamei, M., Zambonelli, F.: Motion Coordination in the Quake 3 Arena Environment: a Field-Based Approach. In Weyns, D., Parunak, H.V.D., Michel, F., eds.: Environment for Multi–Agent Systems'04. Volume 3374 of Lecture Notes in Artificial Intelligence., Springer (2005) 264–278
14. Platon, E., Sabouret, N., Honiden, S.: Oversensing with a softbody in the environment: Another dimension of observation. In Kaminka, G.A., Pynadath, D.V., Geib, C.W., eds.: Modeling Others from Observation. (2005)
15. Klein, M., Rodríguez-Aguilar, J.A., Dellarocas, C.: Using domain-independent exception handling services to enable robust open multi-agent systems: The case of agent death. Autonomous Agents and Multi-Agent Systems **7** (2003) 179–189
16. Tanenbaum, A.S.: Distributed Operating Systems. Prentice Hall (1994)
17. Weyns, D., Schelfthout, K., Holvoet, T., Lefever, T.: Decentralized Control of E'GV Transportation Systems. In Dignum, F., Kraus, S., Singh, M., eds.: Autonomous Agents and Multi–Agent Systems, ACM Press (2005) 67–74
18. Tsvetovatyy, M., Gini, M.L., Mobasher, B., Wieckowski, Z.: Magma: An agent based virtual market for electronic commerce. Applied Artificial Intelligence **11** (1997) 501–523
19. Esteva, M., Rodríguez-Aguilar, J.A., Sierra, C., Garcia, P., Arcos, J.L.: On the formal specifications of electronic institutions. In Dignum, F., Sierra, C., eds.: AgentLink. Volume 1991 of Lecture Notes in Computer Science., Springer (2001) 126–147
20. Platon, E.: Artificial intelligence in the environment: Smart environment for smarter agents in open e-markets. In: Proceedings of the Florida Artificial Intelligence Research Society, AAAI (2006)
21. Platon, E., Sabouret, N., Honiden, S.: Overhearing and direct interactions: Point of view of an active environment. [32] 121–138

22. Omicini, A., Ricci, A., Viroli, M., Castelfranchi, C., Tummolini, L.: Coordination Artifacts: Environment-based Coordination for Intelligent Agents. In: Autonomous Agents and Multi–Agent Systems, ACM Press (2004) 286–293

23. Weyns, D., Parunak, H.V.D., Michel, F., Holvoet, T., Ferber, J.: Environments for Multiagent Systems, State-of-the-Art and Research Challenges. In Weyns, D., Parunak, H.V.D., Michel, F., eds.: Environment for Multi–Agent Systems'04. Volume 3374 of Lecture Notes in Artificial Intelligence., Springer (2005) 1–47

24. Castelfranchi, C.: Silent Agents: From Observation to Tacit Communication. In Kaminka, G.A., Gmytrasiewicz, P., Pynadath, D., Bauer, M., eds.: Proceedings of Modeling Others from Observations. (2004)

25. Stathis, K., Kakas, A.C., Lu, W., Demetriou, N., Endriss, U., Bracciali, A.: PROSOCS: A platform for programming software agents in computational logic. In Müller, J.P., Petta, P., eds.: Proceedings of 'From Agents Theory to Agent Implementation'. (2004)

26. Holland, J.H.: Hidden Order: How Adaptation Builds Complexity. Addison Wesley (1996)

27. Hales, D.: Tag Based Co-operation in Artificial Societies. PhD thesis, University of Essex, England (2001)

28. Ricci, A., Viroli, M.: Coordination Artifacts: A Unifying Abstraction for Engineering Environment–Mediated Coordination in MAS. Informatica (2005)

29. Ricci, A., Viroli, M., Omicini, A.: Environment-based coordination through coordination artifacts. In Weyns, D., Parunak, H.V.D., Michel, F., eds.: Environment for Multi–Agent Systems'04. Volume 3374 of Lecture Notes in Artificial Intelligence., Springer–Verlag (2005) 190–214

30. Gelernter, D.: Generative communication in linda. ACM Transactions on Programming Languages and Systems **7** (1985) 80–112

31. Reddy, M., O'Hare, G.M.: Blackboard systems: A survey of their application. Artificial Intelligence Review **May** (1991)

32. Weyns, D., Parunak, H.V.D., Michel, F., eds.: Environments for Multi-Agent Systems II, Second International Workshop, E4MAS 2005, Utrecht, The Netherlands, July 25, 2005, Selected Revised and Invited Papers. In Weyns, D., Parunak, H.V.D., Michel, F., eds.: E4MAS. Volume 3830 of Lecture Notes in Computer Science., Springer (2006)

Cognitive Stigmergy: Towards a Framework Based on Agents and Artifacts

Alessandro Ricci, Andrea Omicini, Mirko Viroli, Luca Gardelli,
and Enrico Oliva

ALMA MATER STUDIORUM—Università di Bologna
via Venezia 52, 47023 Cesena, Italy
a.ricci@unibo.it, andrea.omicini@unibo.it, mirko.viroli@deis.unibo.it,
luca.gardelli@unibo.it, enrico.oliva@unibo.it

Abstract. *Stigmergy* has been adopted in MAS (multi-agent systems) and in other fields as a technique for realising forms of emergent co-ordination in societies composed by a large amount of ant-like, non-rational agents. In this paper we discuss a conceptual (and engineering) framework for exploring the use of stigmergy in the context of societies composed by cognitive / rational agents, as a means for supporting high-level, knowledge-based social activities.multi-agent We refer to this kind of stigmergy as *cognitive stigmergy*. Cognitive stigmergy is based on the use of *artifacts* as tools populating and structuring the agent working environment, and which agents perceive, share and rationally use for their individual goals. Artifacts are environment abstractions that me-diate agent interaction and enable emergent coordination: as such, they can be used to encapsulate and enact the stigmergic mechanisms and the shared knowledge upon which emergent coordination processes are based.

In this paper, we start exploring this scenario introducing an agent-based framework for cognitive stigmergy based on artifacts. After dis-cussing the main conceptual issues—the notion of cognitive stigmergy and the role of artifacts—, we sketch an abstract architecture for cogni-tive stigmergy, and outline its implementation upon the TuCSoN agent coordination infrastructure.

1 Introduction

In the last years, the study of *stigmergy* has influenced a number of different research fields, including MAS (multi-agent systems). In general, and in MAS research in particular, stigmergy is mostly used as the source of simple yet effec-tive coordination metaphors and mechanisms, to be exploited for building robust and reliable systems in unpredictable settings. The main source of inspiration is obviously represented by the studies on insects and ant societies [1], which have led to a basic meta-model based on (ant-like) *simple* and homogeneous *agents* possessing no relevant cognitive abilities. Such agents interact with each other through *local* modifications to the *environment*, eventually originating *global* structures and behaviours [2].

D. Weyns, H.V.D. Parunak, and F. Michel (Eds.): E4MAS 2006, LNAI 4389, pp. 124–140, 2007.

While this stream of research has produced a number of very interesting approaches in MAS (see [3,4] among the many others), it has also brought on two main biases: *(i)* the agent model is very simple—ant-like agents do not exploit any cognitive ability of theirs—and *(ii)* the environment model is often quite elementary, featuring pheromone-like signs/signals with simple mechanisms for diffusion, aggregation and evaporation—at most extended to force fields [5].

By contrast, a number of relevant works in the field of cognitive sciences put in evidence how stigmergy—as the social mechanism of coordination based on interaction through local modifications to a shared environment—is a fundamental coordination mechanism also e.g. in the context of human societies and organisations [6,7]. In this context:

- modifications to the environment are often amenable of an interpretation in the context of a shared, conventional system of signs;
- the interacting agents feature cognitive abilities that can be used in the stigmergy-based interaction;
- the environment is articulated, and typically composed of *artifacts*, which build up the social workspace, or field of work;
- artifacts can be suitably engineered in order to process information cognitively shared by agents.

Starting from this consideration, in this paper we start exploring what we call *cognitive stigmergy*, that is, the generalisation of stigmergic coordination to enable social activities of cognitive agents. We hence consider a wider notion of agency, which includes high-level knowledge representation capabilities, explicit representation of agent goals, inferential / planning / deliberation abilities, and so on. Our goal is to promote the idea that the general notion of stigmergy can suggest new models for interaction, coordination, and organization within MAS including cognitive agents.

Following the approaches in cognitive sciences, and Computer Supported Cooperative Work (CSCW) in particular [7], we stick to a meta-model featuring *artifacts*, which are instruments and tools that make up and constitute the agent environment, and which agents can select and use for their own purposes. Artifacts are environment abstractions [8] that are *(i)* the subject of cognitive agent activity, *(ii)* the enabler and rulers of agent interaction, and *(iii)* the natural *loci* for cognitive stigmergy processes.

The main aim of this line of research is to propose a reference conceptual framework for cognitive stigmergy, which can also serve as a basis for engineering practical experimentation in the field of MAS. We identify at least three different objectives:

- from a scientific-synthetic viewpoint, we aim at constructing a model for stigmergic coordination going beyond ant-like metaphors: agents are not only ants, and signs for stigmergy are not only pheromones. The cognitive abilities of agents, and the articulation of the environment through artifacts are the essential ingredients to move from stigmergy to cognitive stigmergy;

- from a scientific-analytic viewpoint, the proposed framework should be combined with agent-based and simulation technologies in order to provide predictive models for systems based on cognitive stigmergy, such as human organisations and societies;
- from an engineering viewpoint, we aim at devising out a framework for the construction of MAS stigmergic mechanisms to coordinate complex activities of any sort within articulated operating contexts. Coordinated MAS behaviour should then emerge as the result of both cognitive and non-cognitive activities by the agents, and by their local interaction mediated by suitably engineered artifacts.

In this paper, in particular, we focus on the first issue, and also sketch a possible approach to the third one. In particular, in Sect. 2 we recapitulate some of the multidisciplinary pillars that a theory of cognitive stigmergy should be based upon, then in Sect. 3 we first sketch our conceptual background. In Sect. 4 we provide some remarkable examples of artifacts for cognitive stigmergy, and finally, in Sect. 5, we shortly outline a possible methodological and technological framework for engineering MAS with cognitive stigmergy based on the TuCSoN infrastructure for MAS coordination, adopting tuple centres as artifacts. Conclusion and future work are provided in Sect. 6.

2 Trans-disciplinary Background

The notions of stigmergy, interaction through artifacts, and the many sorts of structures and behaviours that emerge in complex societies, are strictly interrelated concepts that have been the subjects of investigation in a multiplicity of heterogeneous research areas. Adopting a multi-disciplinary view is then rather mandatory—but in some sense quite usual in the field of MAS, given the generality and expressive power of abstractions like agent, society and environment.

Even more, a trans-disciplinary approach is potentially very fertile: taking examples and definitions of stigmergic coordination from both ethology and social sciences, bringing them to the MAS field, and building a general model for cognitive stigmergy, is a fascinating perspective indeed, which could induce novel interpretations and metaphors.

2.1 Definition and (Mis)Use of the Notion of Stigmergy

The original notion of *stigmergy* was introduced by Grassé in the late 50s while studying and trying to explain the behaviour of social insects. In its first formulation, stigmergy was defined as a "class of mechanisms that mediate animal-animal interactions which is fundamental for achieving emergent forms of coordinated behaviour at the society level". Originally, the concept of stigmergy was used to build up a coherent explanation of the so-called *coordination paradox* between the individual and the societal level: on the one hand, groups of social insects seem to be cooperating in an organised, coordinated way; on the other hand, each individual seems to be working as if it were alone, neither interacting with others nor involved in any collective behaviour [1]. The explanation to the coordination paradox provided by stigmergy is that insects interact *indirectly*: each insect (ants, bees, termites) affects the behaviour of other insects by indirect communication through the use of the environment, which is made of objects and artifacts such as material for the nest, or chemical traces.

From the original formulation of the notion of stigmergy, the key-role of the *environment* firstly emerges, which acts not merely as a passive landscape against which all the interactions occur, but rather as a mediator and a ruler of interactions. Secondly, stigmergic interaction is always *mediated*: it occurs locally to the interacting entity, and directly affects a portion of the environment. Finally, the environment is seen as confined / bounded to well-defined elements, such as a pheromone or a chunk of material for nest construction: so, objects, tools, instruments, and *artifacts* encapsulate the logic of local interaction, and are therefore prominent actors in the process of stigmergic coordination.

In the context of computer science, in general, and in the field of MAS, in particular, stigmergy has been widely used as a technique for complex problem solving, as well (more recently) as an approach to the design and development of systems [3,4]. This of course is mainly motivated by the need for system reliability and robustness in complex and unpredictable environments, which could in principle be addressed by mechanisms for self-organisation like stigmergy. On the other hand, however, ants and pheromones provide for a simple, easy-to-reproduce mechanism for stigmergy: as a consequence, stigmergy is often implicitly reduced to an ant-like phenomenon. This is not to say that ant-based mechanisms, models and technologies do not obtain significant outcomes: instead, a large number of remarkable results were indeed achieved in computer science [9], robotics [10], and MAS [11,12].

What is missing, we believe, is instead a wide and coherent view on stigmergy that while sticking to the general principles of the original Grassé's definition of stigmergy, would also account for the facts that *(i)* agents are possibly cognitive entities—agents are not always ant-like entities—, and *(ii)* environment is possibly more articulated than a mere pheromone container, but is rather composed of suitably engineered artifacts. This is exactly what we find in research from cognitive sciences.

2.2   Artifacts, Workspaces, and Stigmergic Coordination

Forms of indirect, mediated interaction are pervasive in complex systems, in particular in contexts where systems take the form of structured societies. In such contexts, in order to scale with activity complexity, sorts of *mediating artifacts* are shared and exploited to enable and ease interaction among the components. Mediating artifacts of different sorts can be easily identified in human society, which are designed and exploited to support coordination in social activities, and in particular in the context of cooperative work. Well-known examples are blackboards, form sheets, post-it notes, and archival tools. Mediation is well-focused by some theories such as Activity Theory [13] and Distributed Cognition [14] adopted in the context of CSCW and HCI (Human Computer Interaction), which explore how the environment can be shaped in terms of mediating artifacts and in order to better support cooperative work among individuals.

Among the most interesting references, the work by Susi [6] represents one of the most coherent efforts toward a theory of artifacts in social interactions, putting together HCI and cognitive sciences. From this work a picture clearly emerges where the activities within complex (human) organisations occur in the context of structured *workspaces*: workspaces are made of artifacts, which are subjects of the human cognitive activity, work as mediators of interaction, and encapsulate coordination functions. The notion of workspace (media spaces, virtual rooms, virtual workspaces in CSCW [7]) clearly exemplifies the idea of a non-trivial, non-passive, articulated environment—where artifacts represent the environment *articulation*. Also, artifacts are mostly a cognitive concept: intelligent activity is required to enact them, make them work, and understand their meaning as coordinating entities—as happens e.g. with triggers, placeholders or entry-points [6].

From a psychologist perspective, the work by Castelfranchi [15,16] points out another key issue: independently of the intentions motivating activities on artifacts (intention to communicate or not, for instance), any behaviour in a workspace is anyway amenable to an interpretation by the observers, which could bring meaningful information, and affect their subsequent behaviour. For instance, when Bianca takes one of the two glasses on the table to drink, she is not explicitly telling Bernie on the other side of the table "take the other glass"—she is just taking her glass plain and simple. However, Bernie is going to interpret Bianca's action on the shared workspace (the table with the glasses) as an implicit communication from her, and take the other glass anyway.

This is also quite apparent in some of the most well-known examples of shared knowledge-based human-oriented artifacts, such as platforms for cooperative work like Wiki (and the Wikipedia [17]), and even platforms for e-commerce (which are also huge sources of information) like Amazon [18]. For instance, one of the most obvious but effective ways of interaction in the Wikipedia is by annotating a page. When looked from an ant-like perspectives, this resembles the release of a pheromone on a shared environment articulated in pages: more (pheromones-)annotations "deposited" on the same page may "aggregate" to indicate a higher level of interest, then attract the interest of other (ants-)readers.

However, the cognitive nature of both page artifacts and annotations, along with the cognitive abilities of human agents, allows for less trivial forms of "stigmergic" processes. For instance, ranking a page based on its perceived utility enables more articulated forms of aggregation (like global average ranking), and may consequently lead to different evolution histories of the whole knowledge base.

Even mediated implicit communication is easy to be observed, for instance in Amazon. For instance, Lilo does not buy book A and then book B to say anything to anyone—just to read them both. However, logging and aggregating this sort of actions allow Amazon to say Stitch, who is buying book B, that "customers who bought this book also bought book A"—which quite often turns to be very informative in practise, and tends to influence both the individual and the overall behaviours. In other terms, individual cognitive actions (read a book presentation, decide to buy that book) in a local context (the view from the browser) upon a cognitive artifact (the purchase page) change the state of the environment (the Amazon portal) and then the behaviour of other individuals, such that in the overall the global behaviour of the system is affected.

Evidence of stigmergic processes involving cognitive features could not be clearer around us—in the scientific arena, as well as in our everyday life. The point is now how to use this evidence in MAS, so that both traditional results from the ant-biased interpretation of stigmergy and the cognitive interpretation drawn from CSCW, HCI, Activity Theory and cognitive sciences could be subsumed, coherently modelled, and then be used in order to build complex, robust and intelligent MAS.

3 Cognitive Stigmergy in MAS

Our objective in this work is the investigation of stigmergy principles in the context of cognitive MAS, i.e. societies of goal/task-oriented/driven agents interacting at the *cognitive level*. Such agents are therefore not necessarily simple and reactive ones, as in the ant case, but can typically be rational, heterogeneous, adaptive, and capable of learning. We adopt the term *cognitive stigmergy* to denote this approach, so as to remark the differences with respect to existing approaches to stigmergy in MAS, which are typically based on societies of agents whose capabilities and behaviour resemble those of insect-like entities.

As in the case of classic stigmergy, the environment is a central concept for cognitive stigmergy, as an enabler and mediator of the agent work and interaction. The general picture—reflecting a certain complexity in the corresponding engineering of applications—is given by a (possibly open) set of agents with their own specific tasks and goals, which perform their individual as well as social activities in the same working environment, sharing the same *field of work*. The interaction among the agents is indirect, uncoupled in time and space. From a modelling and engineering point of view, it is natural to model such a working environment as a first-class entity: agents are aware *(i)* of their field of work, *(ii)* of it being shared with other agents, and *(iii)* of its functionality, and of the opportunities to use it so as to achieve their objectives (*affordance* of the environment). Such opportunities are exploited by properly *using* the working environment, that is, by executing the operations that the environment makes available to agents and by observing its state.

As in the case of classic stigmergy, a main point here is that the environment is not a mere passive "container", but it embeds mechanisms and (reactive) processes that promote the emergence of local and global coordinated behaviours. Not only it has a state that can be observed and modified by agents, but also it encapsulates some laws that can be triggered by agent actions (or, by events such as a change in location, or the passing of time) and alter the environment state independently of agent intentions.

Under a cognitive perspective, the working environment in cognitive stigmergy can be framed as a set of shared stateful tools providing specific functionalities that are useful for agents performing their *individual* work. At the same time, such tools are designed to be collectively shared and used by agents, and are generally implemented so as to effectively and efficiently support their shared functionalities, thus largely impacting on the *social* level.

In the rest of this section, we focus on the answer to the following key question: how could this kind of working environment be modelled as a first-class entity in MAS? To this end, in the following we elaborate on the notion of *artifact* as a means to explicitly and directly design and build such a working environment.

3.1   Exploiting the Notion of Artifact

The notion of artifact (and the related conceptual framework) has been introduced recently in MAS as a first-class abstraction representing tools or objects (devices) that agents can either individually or collectively *use* to support their activities, and that can be designed to encapsulate and provide different kinds of functionalities or services [19,20]. If agents are meant to be first-class abstractions to model goal/task-oriented/driven pro-active entities, artifacts are those entities modelling systems (or parts of a system) that are better characterised as resources or tools *used* by agents for their own aims. In particular, and unlike agents, artifacts neither have internal goals, nor do they exhibit a pro-active behaviour; instead, they simply provide agents with some kind of functionality they could be suitably exploit, typically in the form of a service—in other words, while agents *communicate with* other agents, agents *use* artifacts.

According to the abstract model defined [19], artifacts in cognitive MAS can be characterised by (see Fig.1): a *function*, as its intended purpose, i.e. the purpose established by the designer / programmer / builder of the artifact— in other words the intended functionalities the artifact is meant to provide; a *usage interface*, as the set of the operations that agents can invoke to use the artifact and exploit its functionality; some kind of *operating instructions*, as a description of how to use the artifact to access its functionality; a *structure* and *behaviour*, concerning the internal aspects of the artifact, that is, how the artifact is structured and implemented in order to provide its function.

Unlike agents, artifacts are not meant to be autonomous or exhibit a proactive behaviour, neither are they expected to have social capabilities. Among the main properties that are useful according to the artifact purpose and nature, one could list [20]: *(i) inspectability* and *controllability*, i.e. the capability of observing and controlling artifact structure, state and behaviour at run-time, and of supporting their on-line management, in terms of diagnosing, debugging, testing; *(ii) malleability* (or, *forgeability*), i.e. the capability of changing / adapting artifact function at run-time (on-the-fly) according to new requirements or unpredictable events occurring in the open environment,[1] and *(iii) linkability*,

---

[1] Such adaptation is not meant to be realised autonomously by the artifacts themselves, but by MAS agents & engineers acting on the artifacts. Mechanisms for non-intentional self-adaptation of artifacts are not excluded a priori, but they are not directly related with malleability, and are not necessarily a desirable property of artifacts.

i.e. the capability of composing distinct artifacts at run-time as a form of composition, as a means to scale up with complexity of the function provided, and to support dynamic reuse. It is worth to be remarked that these artifact features are not agent features: typically, agents are not inspectable, do not provide means for malleability, do not provide operations for their change, and do not compose with each other through operational links.

Also, artifacts can have a *spatial extension*, i.e. given a MAS with a topology, the same artifact could cover different nodes: in other words, a single artifact can be both conceptually and physically distributed. For instance, a blackboard artifact can cover different Internet nodes, where agents may use it by exploiting a local interface. Technically, agents could be distributed, too—for instance, having the knowledge base in some node and the deliberation engine hosted by some other node: most often, an agent is situated within a specific location, at least by considering the agent models and architectures that are most diffused (an example is the FIPA model).

Given this notion of artifact, we can reformulate the context of cognitive stigmergy in terms of a set of agents sharing a set of artifacts representing their working environment. This set can be split along two different levels:

- a *domain level*, with artifacts that represent the target of the agent work, or an *objectification* of such a target.
- a *tool level*, with artifacts that represent the working tools which can help agents in doing their work.

Our objective is to instrument the tool level with a web of linked artifacts which can be used to improve the work of the collectivity of agents sharing the same working environment. At the systemic level, these artifacts are meant to be used both to improve the knowledge about the *practises* in using the artifacts at the domain level, and to possibly support *social construction* and *evolution / adaptation* of such artifacts, toward directions that are useful for the collectivity of agents in the overall. In order to support this functionality, the artifacts belonging to the tool level should encapsulate stigmergic mechanisms partially similar to the mechanisms found in ant-based systems and pheromone infrastructures: such mechanisms are described in Sect. 4.

3.2 Re-framing the Notion of Locality: Workspaces

In classic approaches to stigmergy the notion of topology (and related notion of locality) is mostly physical, defining from the viewpoint of agents—which are typically mobile—the portion of the environment which can be directly affected by their actions or can be perceived. In the case of cognitive stigmergy, this crucial notion could be formulated in a natural way with the notion of *workspace*, as the set of artifacts directly available (usable) for an agent. Workspaces can cross each other sharing agents and artifacts, can be nested, and so on: in synthesis they are a way to define the topology in a rigorous way.

Actually, the topology induced by this characterisation is more abstract and could be articulated along different dimensions. An important one is for instance organisation: the same artifacts could be accessible and usable in different ways according to the roles and permissions assigned to agents by the organisation they belong to.

It is worth noting that the nature and functionality of the artifacts could bring in situation where—to some extent—the principle of physical locality is violated. This is evident in our society, where artifacts (for humans) such as cell phones, televisions, or the Internet itself can be used to observe and interact in a direct way with entities—e.g. humans—located at completely different places of the world. Conceptually, the action of an agent executing an operation on an artifact of its workspace (its locality) can have "instant" effects on a completely different workspace. This happens because artifacts can be either shared among workspaces or linked together across workspaces.[2] Actually, the principle of locality still holds, since agents can only use the artifacts belonging to their workspaces.

3.3   From Pheromones to Annotations

In every stigmergic system, the effects of agent actions on the environment are understood as signs. Once created, signs persist independently of their creator and are observable by the other agents, and are subject of manipulation by the environment itself according to the laws which characterise the stigmergic processes—e.g. diffusion and evaporation. Differently from pheromones in the case of ant-based stigmergy, in the case of cognitive stigmergy signs typically hold a *symbolic* value, embodying information of some sort, with a formal or informal semantics, referring to some ontology. We refer to such a symbolic information in cognitive stigmergy as *annotations*.

Coming back to the two levels previously introduced, annotations are useful first of all for expressing some kind of comment or knowledge about the artifacts (and about the practise of use of artifacts) belonging to the domain level, which are targets of the agent work. Then, annotations are useful to objectify also comments or reflections that do not concern a specific artifact, but more generally a working practise, and could possibly refer to multiple artifacts. Finally, annotations can be used for expressing a comment on the annotations themselves, typically about their utility, effectiveness, and so on.

Knowledge provided by annotation is both explicit—the content of the annotation—and implicit—the "shape" and the context of the annotation, including for instance the possible intention of the agent or group of agents that created the annotation. The concept of shape for annotations could be considered as analogous to the concept of force in the case of speech acts: it modulates annotation content according to the information that could be of some use when reasoning on annotations.

Some of the artifacts defining working spaces in cognitive stigmergy are possibly devoted to the management of annotations, providing agents with operations

---

[2] One should remember that, from a physical point of view, an artifact could be distributed across multiple sites.

for creating and observing annotations, and embedding mechanisms for automatically manipulating annotations (with forms of aggregation, diffusion, selection, ordering) in order to implement the functionality required for cognitive stigmergy. Accordingly, we deal with two basic kinds of annotations:

- annotations explicitly and intentionally created by agents. These include, for instance, agent feedback (evaluation) about a specific artifact belonging to the domain level; agent feedback about a specific annotation on one such artifact; agent annotations about a set of artifacts, or a usage practise during a working session.
- annotations automatically created by the artifacts supporting their working activities. Examples include annotations reporting about how much an artifact has been used, how many agents exploited an artifact for their purposes, how many agents considered an annotation as useful for their purposes, which other artifacts have been used (and how) by agents using a given artifact.

4   Artifacts for Cognitive Stigmergy

Generally speaking, artifacts in cognitive stigmergy should first of all promote *awareness*, that is, making agents seamlessly aware of the work and practises of other agents, which could in turn be effective to drive or improve their own activities. Awareness is a key aspect to support emergent forms of coordination, where there is no pre-established plan defining exactly which are the dependencies and interactions among ongoing activities (involving agents and artifacts) and how to manage them—instead, such a plan emerges along with the activities themselves.

A simple but effective example of stigmergic mechanism promoting awareness can be found—for instance—in Amazon: a user consulting the page of a book is provided with a list of other books, bought by users that purchased the same book. This kind of mechanism in Wikipedia could be realised through a page annotation of the kind: "people consulting this page have also consulted pages X, Y, Z". In our framework, such a mechanism can be generalised by supporting the automatic creation of annotations on artifacts of the domain level, reporting information about which other artifacts have been used by agents using the same artifact.

In the remainder of this section we describe a basic set of artifacts which could constitute a simple example of an architecture supporting some form of awareness and other features characterising cognitive stigmergy. On the background of this architecture there is the notion of *working session*, as a temporal scope for an agent activities. An agent starts a working session with an objective in mind, which is supposed to persist for all the duration of the session. Knowing the (either explicit or implicit) objective of an agent during a working session is important to provide a context—in terms of the problem to be solved, the goal to be achieved, the task to be executed—to the annotations (evaluations, comments, ...) made by the agents, and to the practise of the agents using the artifact of the domain level. For instance, in Wikipedia, agent feedbacks about the utility of a page would be better understood and evaluated by taking into account the problem the agent is facing (i.e. what it is looking for).

4.1 Promoting Awareness: Dashboards, Logs, Diaries and Note-Boards

A first and necessary step toward awareness is to keep track of both the actions and the annotations made by individual agents during a working session. For this purpose, we identify three basic kinds of artifacts, corresponding to three different kinds of functionalities: dashboards, logs and diaries (see Fig.1):

- A *dashboard* provides the functionalities of a panel (interface) used to *focus* on a specific artifact (or a set of artifacts belonging to the domain level) to interact with the artifact and to take / observe / manage annotations. The concept of focus aims at representing the intention of using an artifact.
- A *log* is used to keep track of events, providing operation for their inspections and ordering.
- A *diary* is an artifact used to keep track of annotations intentionally made by an agent. The diary typically keeps the annotations organised by working sessions.

The dashboard is linked to the log so as to trace all the operations executed by the agent during a working session. Actually, the log of the operations executed by an agent is interesting also for analysing paths as sequences of executed operations, which can be important to identify and evaluate practises in using one or a set of artifacts belonging to the domain level. The stigmergic system could be instrumented so as to make agents aware of such practises and of the possibility to provide an evaluation, so as to augment the common awareness about good (and bad) practises.

Besides tracing individual agent actions and annotations, it is necessary to introduce artifacts that actually make it possible to effectively share annotations about specific artifacts of the domain level. For this purpose, the *note-board* artifact is introduced. A note-board is useful for keeping and managing all the annotations about a specific artifact (or set of artifacts) of the domain level. For instance, in the Wikipedia example we could have a note-board for each page (or group of pages) of the system.

A note-board is meant to contain both the annotations intentionally made by agents on the specific artifact, and the annotations automatically created by the artifact itself or by other artifacts by virtue of the stigmergic mechanisms and processes. A simple example can be an annotation reporting how many different kinds of agents used a specific artifact. Such a functionality can be obtained by properly combining the dashboard and note-board: for instance, each time a dashboard focuses for the first time on an artifact X, an annotation about this fact can be made on the note-board of artifact X. The note-board can then transform the set of such annotations in a single annotation (by means of *aggregation* mechanisms, described in next subsection), reporting the number of agents that used the artifact. Another

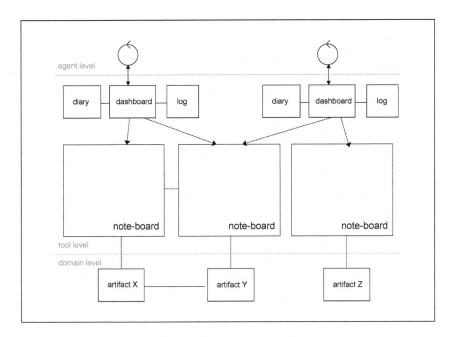

Fig. 1. An abstract representation of an architecture for cognitive stigmergy based on dashboard, log, diary and note-board artifacts

example could be an annotation reporting information about which other artifacts have been used by agents using this artifact. In this case, when the focus of an agent switches from an artifact X of the domain level to an artifact Y, a suitable annotation can be automatically created on the note-board of artifact X reporting the fact that an agent using artifact X has then used artifact Y, and on the note-board of artifact Y with the dual information.

The above examples suggest how the combined use of artifacts with relatively simple functionalities could be effective enough to improve agent awareness about their working practises. Functionalities provided by artifacts are instrumental to realise the forms of reinforcement and positive feedback that typically characterise stigmergic systems as dynamic non-linear systems: the more agents are aware of the usefulness of an artifact, the more they use it, augmenting the overall awareness about the utility of the artifact.

4.2   Some Basic Stigmergic Mechanisms

Analogously to the case of ant-based stigmergy, also in the context of cognitive stigmergy it is possible to identify some basic and recurrent mechanisms which can be embedded within artifacts in order to support stigmergic processes:

Diffusion — Diffusion is one of the basic mechanism in ant-based stigmergy. In the context of cognitive stigmergy, an analogous principle could be exploited to improve awareness, according to the simple rule that annotations that concern a specific artifact could be useful also for artifacts that are directly linked to that artifact according to some kind of relation explicitly established at the domain level. For instance, in the case of Wikipedia, annotations concerning a specific page could be useful also for pages that are directly linked to or directly link such a page.

Note-boards could be designed to suitably support diffusion capabilities: annotations intentionally made by agents about an artifact could be automatically propagated from the related note-board to all the note-boards of the linked artifacts. Then, among the information that gives shape to an annotation, a *diffusion level* could also be included, indicating whether the annotation has been made directly by an agent or it has been propagated from other artifacts. Different kinds of diffusion policies are possible: for instance, note-boards could support either diffusion of direct annotations only, or propagation of annotations, too, possibly specifying a sort of propagation radius in terms on maximum diffusion level.

Aggregation — In our framework, the aggregation mechanism accounts for automatically transforming a set of annotations—related by some criteria—into a single annotation, typically containing an explicit information describing the aggregation in the overall (for instance, a quantity). Note-boards have the fundamental role of aggregators of the annotations concerning a specific artifact of the domain level. For instance, note-boards could automatically aggregate annotations containing agents' feedback (evaluation) on an artifact or on an annotation made on the artifact.

Selection and Ordering — Annotations may have a different relevance according to the different kinds of criteria / dimensions, which can be either subjective or objective. Consequently, such annotations could be automatically ordered by artifacts managing them in order to reflect their relevance. An example of ordering criteria is freshness, measuring relevance of an annotation according to its age. Another one is pertinence, measuring the relevance of a propagated annotation according to its diffusion level, as defined previously. A selection mechanism accounts for keeping and making available only a limited set of annotations—typically the most relevant ones according to the selected criteria / dimensions. Selection is often combined with ordering. To some extent, selection and ordering mechanisms could be considered as a generalisation—in the context of cognitive stigmergy—of the evaporation mechanism, as found in ant-based system. Also *dissipation*—a frequent mechanism in stigmergy system—could be considered as a specific case of selection, where all annotations not selected according some criteria are forgotten.

Actually diffusion, aggregation, selection and ordering are general kinds of mechanisms which can be considered as useful for a wide range of artifacts. In the examples we mainly consider note-boards, however it is easy to identify their utility also in diaries, where annotations are typically organised (aggregated) according to working sessions, ordered according to temporal criteria, and possibly diffused to note-boards, in case they concern specific artifacts.

5   Building MAS with Cognitive Stigmergy

5.1   Toward an Agent Infrastructure for Cognitive Stigmergy

As mentioned in Sect. 1, the conceptual framework of cognitive stigmergy is meant to be useful both for modelling / simulating complex social systems—so as to analyse emergent social behaviours of societies evolving in some specific workspaces—and for engineering complex agent applications, aiming at achieving some sort of fruitful social behaviour in spite of the independent working activities of the individual agents and / or the absence of a global coordination plan to follow. In both cases, in particular for the latter one, it is of foremost importance to have models / infrastructures that make it possible to represent in the most direct and seamless way the main concepts of the framework, in particular artifacts of the kind discussed in the paper. Accordingly, such a middleware would provide a support for cognitive stigmergy as a service, which MAS applications could customise and exploit according to the need.

5.2   An Example: TuCSoN as a Middleware for Cognitive Stigmergy

As an example, TuCSoN[3] coordination infrastructure [21] can be used as a middleware to experiment cognitive stigmergy, since it provides on the one side a direct support for cognitive and generative communication, based on the generation and consumption of *tuples* as kind of annotations; on the other side, it provides a natural way to model artifacts as first-class abstractions, with the possibility to define their specific behaviour.

TuCSoN provides *tuple centres* as first-class abstractions that agents can use to support their communication and coordination. Technically, tuple centres are *programmable tuple spaces*—sort of reactive blackboards that agents access associatively by writing, reading, and consuming *tuples*—ordered collections of heterogeneous information chunks—via simple communication primitives (*out*, *rd*, *in*, *inp*, *rdp*) [22]. While the behaviour of a tuple space in response to communication events is fixed, the behaviour of a tuple centre can be tailored to the application needs by defining a set of specification tuples expressed in the ReSpecT language, which define how a tuple centre should react to incoming / outgoing communication events. Basically, ReSpecT primitives make it possible to manipulate the tuples inside the tuple centre and also to establish a link between the tuple centre with other tuple centres—for instance making it possible to insert tuples in other tuple centres directly via reactions. ReSpecT is Turing-equivalent [23], so in principle any kind of tuple manipulation is possible. From the topology point of view, tuple centres are collected in TuCSoN nodes, distributed over the network, organised into articulated domains. A node can contain any number of tuple centres, denoted by a specific name: the full name of a tuple centre consists in its local name plus the Internet address of the hosting TuCSoN node.

---

[3] The TuCSoN technology is available as an open source project at the TuCSoN web site http://tucson.sourceforge.net

Then, it is natural to use TuCSoN tuple centres as general-purpose artifacts that can be programmed according to the need, in order to provide specific functionalities. Annotations can be easily implemented as logic tuples. Interaction between agents and artifacts could be modelled on top of tuple centre basic communication primitives, by choosing a specific format for both tuples and tuple templates. Artifact behaviour could be implemented as a set of ReSpecT reactions implementing the basic stigmergic mechanisms discussed in the paper, by virtue of the Turing-equivalence of ReSpecT. In particular:

- aggregation mechanisms can be implemented as ReSpecT reactions consuming a specific set of tuples and producing a single tuple, according to some specific criteria;
- selection and ordering mechanisms can be implemented as reactions that create and maintain tuples containing a list of other tuples, imposing an order among them;
- both diffusion and artifact composition can be implemented by using the linkability property of tuple centres, with reactions that propagate tuples from a tuple centre to the others.

The basic set of artifacts identified in previous section—dashboards, diaries, logs and note-boards—can then be implemented as suitably programmed ReSpecT tuple centres. There is no space enough here to provide further details about design and implementation of such artifacts—which however are not overwhelmingly complex, indeed. Such details are likely to be discussed in a forthcoming work along with an evaluation of the system performance in supporting cognitive stigmergy.

6   Conclusion and Future Works

Stigmergy is a simple and powerful mechanism around which complex coordination patterns can be organised and built. Despite the generality of the original definition by Grassé [1], the full potential of stigmergy has yet to be developed in the area of MAS, as both a modelling and a constructive principle for complex agent-based systems.

In this paper, we proposed an extended interpretation of stigmergy, which we termed as *cognitive stigmergy*, which could on the one hand preserve the benefits of the ant-biased acceptation usually adopted in the MAS field, on the other hand promote the full exploitation of the cognitive abilities of agents and of the environment articulation in artifacts in the stigmergic process. After summarising our main sources of inspiration from a number of different research areas and technology contexts, we proposed a conceptual framework for cognitive stigmergy in MAS, and then sketched a possible engineering approach based on the TuCSoN infrastructure for agent coordination, using tuple centres as artifacts.

Future work will be devoted to further explore both the theoretical framework and the practical perspectives opened by this paper, focusing in particular on scenarios like e-learning systems, and implicit organisations based on over-hearing / over-sensing.

References

1. Grassé, P.P.: La reconstruction du nid et les coordinations inter-individuelles chez bellicositermes natalensis et cubitermes sp. la theorie de la stigmergie: essai d'interpretation des termites constructeurs. Insectes Sociaux **6** (1959) 41–83

2. Di Marzo Serugendo, G., Foukia, N., Hassas, S., Karageorgos, A., Kouadri Mostéfaoui, S., Rana, O.F., Ulieru, M., Valckenaers, P., Van Aart, C.: Self-organisation: Paradigms and applications. [24] 1–19

3. Parunak, H.V.D., Brueckner, S., Sauter, J.: Digital pheromone mechanisms for coordination of unmanned vehicles. In Castelfranchi, C., Johnson, W.L., eds.: 1st International Joint Conference on Autonomous Agents and Multiagent Systems (AAMAS 2002). Volume 1., Bologna, Italy, ACM (2002) 449–450

4. Valckenears, P., Van Brussel, H., Kollingbaum, M., Bochmann, O.: Multi-agent coordination and control using stigmergy applied to manufacturing control. In Luck, M., Mařík, V., Štěpánková, O., Trappl, R., eds.: Multi-Agent Systems and Applications. Volume 2086 of Lecture Notes in Computer Science., Springer (2001) 317–334 9th ECCAI Advanced Course ACAI 2001 and Agent Link's 3rd European Agent Systems Summer School (EASSS 2001), Prague, Czech Republic, 2-13 July 2001, Selected Tutorial Papers.

5. Mamei, M., Zambonelli, F., Leonardi, L.: Co-Fields: Towards a unifying approach to the engineering of swarm intelligent systems. In Petta, P., Tolksdorf, R., Zambonelli, F., eds.: Engineering Societies in the Agents World III. Volume 2577 of LNCS. Springer-Verlag (2003) 68–81

6. Susi, T., Ziemke, T.: Social cognition, artefacts, and stigmergy: A comparative analysis of theoretical frameworks for the understanding of artefact-mediated collaborative activity. Cognitive Systems Research **2**(4) (2001) 273–290

7. Schmidt, K., Wagner, I.: Ordering systems: Coordinative practices and artifacts in architectural design and planning. Computer Supported Cooperative Work **13**(5-6) (2004) 349–408

8. Viroli, M., Holvoet, T., Ricci, A., Schelfthout, K., Zambonelli, F.: Infrastructures for the environment of multiagent systems. Autonomous Agents and Multi-Agent Systems **14**(1) (2007) 49–60 Special Issue: Environment for Multi-Agent Systems.

9. Gambardella, L.M., Dorigo, M., Middendorf, M., Stützle, T.: Special section on ant colony optimization. IEEE Transactions on Evolutionary Computation **6**(4) (2002) 317–365

10. Holland, O., Melhuis, C.: Stigmergy, self-organization, and sorting in collective robotics. Artificial Life **5**(2) (1999) 173–202

11. Brueckner, S.A., Parunak, H.V.D.: Self-organizing MANET management. [24] 20–35

12. Mamei, M., Zambonelli, F.: Programming stigmergic coordination with the tota middleware. In: 4th ACM International Joint Conference on Autonomous Agents and Multiagent Systems, New York, USA, ACM (2005) 415–422

13. Nardi, B., ed.: Context and Consciousness: Activity Theory and Human Computer Interaction. MIT Press, Cambridge, MA (1996)

14. Hutchins, E.: Cognition in the Wild. MIT Press, Cambridge, MA (1995)

15. Castelfranchi, C.: When doing is saying: implicit communication before and without language and gestures. In: International Workshop "Evolving Communication: From Action to Language", Siena, Italy (2004) Communication.

16. Omicini, A., Ricci, A., Viroli, M., Castelfranchi, C., Tummolini, L.: Coordination artifacts: Environment-based coordination for intelligent agents. In Jennings, N.R., Sierra, C., Sonenberg, L., Tambe, M., eds.: 3rd international Joint Conference on Autonomous Agents and Multiagent Systems (AAMAS 2004). Volume 1., New York, USA, ACM (2004) 286–293

17. Wikipedia, The Free Encyclopedia: Home page. http://www.wikipedia.org (2006)

18. Amazon: Home page. http://www.amazon.com (2006)

19. Ricci, A., Viroli, M., Omicini, A.: Programming MAS with artifacts. In Bordini, R.P., Dastani, M., Dix, J., El Fallah Seghrouchni, A., eds.: Programming Multi-Agent Systems III. Volume 3862 of LNAI. Springer (2006) 206–221 3rd International Workshop (PROMAS 2005), AAMAS 2005, Utrecht, The Netherlands, 26 July 2005. Revised and Selected Papers.

20. Omicini, A., Ricci, A., Viroli, M.: *Agens Faber*: Toward a theory of artefacts for MAS. Electronic Notes in Theoretical Computer Sciences **150**(3) (2006) 21–36 1st International Workshop "Coordination and Organization" (CoOrg 2005), COORDINATION 2005, Namur, Belgium, 22 April 2005. Proceedings.

21. Omicini, A., Zambonelli, F.: Coordination for Internet application development. Autonomous Agents and Multi-Agent Systems **2**(3) (1999) 251–269

22. Omicini, A., Denti, E.: From tuple spaces to tuple centres. Science of Computer Programming **41**(3) (2001) 277–294

23. Denti, E., Natali, A., Omicini, A.: On the expressive power of a language for programming coordination media. In: 1998 ACM Symposium on Applied Computing (SAC'98), Atlanta, GA, USA, ACM (1998) 169–177 Special Track on Coordination Models, Languages and Applications.

24. Di Marzo Serugendo, G., Karageorgos, A., Rana, O.F., Zambonelli, F., eds.: Engineering Self-Organising Systems: Nature-Inspired Approaches to Software Engineering. In Di Marzo Serugendo, G., Karageorgos, A., Rana, O.F., Zambonelli, F., eds.: Engineering Self-Organising Systems: Nature-Inspired Approaches to Software Engineering. Volume 2977 of LNAI., Springer (2004)

Trace Signals: The Meanings of Stigmergy

Luca Tummolini and Cristiano Castelfranchi

Institute of Cognitive Sciences and Technologies (ISTC-CNR), Via San Martino della
Battaglia 44, 00185, Roma, Italy
{luca.tummolini, cristiano.castelfranchi}@istc.cnr.it

Abstract. When agents act is a common environment they leave traces. In this
paper we explore the importance of using such traces as signals (stigma). Trace
signals enable a flexible way to support indirect interaction between agents
without adopting dedicated communication channels and signals. Although the
kind of messages that can be exchanged with traces is limited, their importance
for decentralized and dynamic multi-agent systems is vast. A taxonomy of
trace-signals is provided and their role in different social interactions is
explored. Some of the benefits and limitations of this trace-based
communication are discussed.

Keywords: communication, stigmergy, multi-agent coordination, environment.

1 Introduction

Suppose you are at the movie theater looking for a seat. You suddenly notice a spot in
a very good row. Nobody is sat there at the moment; hence you decide to take it. You
move away a coat covering it, and you sit there.

Although this behavior is successful (you as an agent had a goal and you have
fulfilled it by easily removing an obstacle), this achievement is not without
consequences. In fact, if you had evaluated the situation more carefully, you could
have realized that the coat was also a *trace* of somebody else being there before you.
Taking this into consideration, your action could have been different.

The fact that such a scenario seems transparent to us is what makes it really
important. In this simple situation a sophisticated interaction is enabled by a simple
modification of the environment. Understanding what traces like these can "mean" is
necessary, we argue, to enable a very effective and flexible way to support interaction
and avoid possible conflicts between agents.

Moreover, with all probability, the coat was not there accidentally. Another agent
has left the coat on the seat on purpose, so that others even without seeing her
presence, but noticing her trace, could understand that the seat was already taken. A
trace as such is a *sign*. However if it is left to be noticed and understood by others, it
is also a *signal*. By leaving her coat there somebody intended to *inform* you about
something.

Although we are good at understanding the meaning of a trace in a context, we
don't necessarily recognize it as a *message*. In fact it is not necessary to understand
the communicative intention behind the trace to convey a meaning. However one that

D. Weyns, H.V.D. Parunak, and F. Michel (Eds.): E4MAS 2006, LNAI 4389, pp. 141–156, 2007.
© Springer-Verlag Berlin Heidelberg 2007

intends to exploit the potential of traces for improving interaction should carefully consider how the others react when seeing them.

The fact that similar trace signals seem to be everywhere tells us that we humans extensively rely upon this form of communication in our daily interactions.

Most probably, moreover, such communication is of the utmost importance also to support more conventional and structured forms of interactions like language and other institutions. In fact specialized means for communication can arise out of such simpler forms [5, 17] and interact with this non-specialized means to be effective (see below).

It is evident that leaving a coat on a seat to signal one's own presence, for example, interacts with operating conventions full of deontic consequences. When coming back one can even start fighting for one's seat. Given that she was expecting a certain behavior on your part, leaving a coat was also an implicit *prescription*. Can such normative reality develop spontaneously on top of mere interpersonal relations? Are implicit communication exchanges sufficient to support it?

Although this kind of normative consequences is only available to us, communicating with traces is not only a human fact.

Actually, the relevance of indirect interaction via environmental modifications has been first noticed in insect societies under the rubric of *stigmergy* [9]; in fact traces carrying messages are *stigma* in a strict sense: signals that are the product of previous modification of the environment by other agents. Stigmergic interaction overlaps with the use of traces for communication, and has been extensively studied in insect societies [1] and also used as a model for artificial ones [14].

However from our perspective, stigmergy, as it has been interpreted so far, has still been applied to a restricted number of phenomena without noticing its relevance in a very wide range of situations (from animal to human and artificial societies; from simple coordination to support for normative systems)[1]. The fact that current applications are still too heavily influenced by initial case studies[2] is probably due to a lack of a general theory of stigmergy.

In this paper we wish to convince the reader that agents, interacting in a traceable and observable environment[3], have the additional opportunity to exploit their own traces for communicating. We will first introduce our revised notion of stigmergy considered as a form of indirect communication (Section 2). On the basis of such framework, the use of traces as implicit signals will be clarified. A number of different messages that can be exchanged in this way will be discussed with the aim of offering a first taxonomy of trace-based messages (Section 3). Although the scope of what can be communicated behaviorally is limited, a descriptive and a directive use of traces will be disentangled (Section 4) and, from basic behavioral messages more complex ones will be introduced (Section 5). Finally, some of the benefits and limitations of this form of communication are examined.

Although in this explorative article we will extensively use examples from human societies, we contend that such general framework is useful also for engineers of

---

[1] For an exception see [16].

[2] See the impact of the pheromone metaphor in the vast majority of applications [2, 10,15].

[3] In [20] we have formally investigated these environmental requirements to support this form of communication.

artificial ones. If a long-term objective for artificial multi-agent systems is to have self-organizing and dynamic societies where the software agents are their own artificial engineers, we suspect that this form of communication will play a major and pivotal role.

2 Stigmergy Revisited

2.1 Communication Is Interaction

Influencing others by exploiting their capacity to understand signs seems to identify the simplest case of communication.

However, from this perspective, the notion of communication is still too broad. It would include all the cases in which we modify the environment to influence other agents. If you are sleeping and I open the windows and let the sunlight enter, I wake you up. If by seeing the sunlight you infer that it's time to wake up I didn't communicate this fact to you. In this scenario I have influenced you twice and that was my intention. I intended that you woke up and that you believed that it's time to wake up. To induce such belief I have relied on your capacity to read signs and understand them. Although I intended such results, the sunlight is not a signal that I have emitted.

Suppose differently that to wake you up, I have set the alarm clock with the aim of letting you know that it's time to wake up. When it starts ringing, you wake up and you realize that is the time to wake up. However you don't know and don't understand that the alarm clock has been set by somebody (that it is also a trace of somebody). Again, although in this situation setting the alarm clock *is* a trace, because you don't understand that a meaning can be inferred *from* a trace left by somebody (you don't see the sign *as* a trace), it seems that no communication happened and no signal have been transmitted.

Hence we argue that communication requires two minimal conditions: one for the addresser and one for the addressee.

The first condition is that the sign is emitted on purpose by the addresser to influence an addressee by informing her about something, hence the sign *is* a signal. The addresser should have either an informative intention or, at least, an informative function. Communication needs signals and not only unintentional signs.

The second condition, that so far has been ignored, is that such a signal is at least to be understood *as* a trace of somebody else by the addressee. The sign is to be recognized as the product of an agent such that the action of the addressee is in fact a reaction to another agent.

What is sufficient to consider an interaction between two agents as communication is that the addressee considers the signal produced by the addresser, at least, as a trace produced by another agent. Treating the sign also as a trace seems to be the minimal, but necessary, requirement.

If the addressee had to understand the sign as a signal, i.e. to grasp also the informative intention of the addresser, we couldn't consider as communication the exchange in the example of leaving the coat on the seat. As we have shown, for the communication to succeed, it was sufficient for you to understand the message ("an agent is here") without understanding it *as* a message ("this agent wants me to know that she is here").

Communication is a form of real interaction because is a process that can happen only between agents that understand a meaning through each other actions.

2.2 Indirect Communication

When looking for a room in an unknown building where a meeting is supposed to take place, it is useful to follow the ad-hoc signals that the organizers have hung on the entry wall. Usually such signals display an identification name (say the project acronym) and an arrow. You follow the direction pointed by the arrow. On your way, you also notice that other arrows signal the right direction when appropriate (i.e. when you have to decide which turn to make at the end of the stairs). Finally you find the room you were looking for.

It is evident that the organizers intended to communicate with you by sending a message. However, instead of directly transmitting the message by calling to give directions personally to everyone in advance, they have adopted a more effective strategy. They have modified in appropriate ways the environment, such that they can *indirectly* communicate with you (and with all the other participants). While in direct communication the environment is exploited as a channel to transmit the signal, in indirect communication the environment is just a support to record it, a memory. It is up to the agents to retrieve it and complete the transmission.

This form of indirect interaction (in this case communication) is very important because it is situated, cheap and exploits the environment also to abstract from irrelevant information.

Moreover such a standard example of human communication bears also a striking resemblance with the prototypical case of pheromone-based communication between animals. Ants, it is well-known [22], on their way to food, communicate by leaving pheromone signals that influence other ants. Very similarly, by attaching an arrow on a wall one can influence us when looking for directions. In both situations the interaction is indirect, and in both situations the agents exploit a signal that is there only to communicate (an explicit signal). The main difference is that the former signal is an evolved biological one, while the latter is a conventional signal that is intentionally produced. These two instances are cases of indirect communication based on the environment modification.

While such form of indirect communication is extremely important, what concerns us in this paper is a more specific case.

2.3 Implicit Signals and Behavioral Messages

In fact, although indirect in the same sense, the form of communication discussed in the introductory remarks is distinct from the above two cases because it exploits *implicit* signals.

Although agents can emit explicit signals (signs that have been shaped for influencing through informing; the arrows and the pheromone), often, as we have suggested in the introduction, they take advantage of implicit ones (signals that are only shaped for their practical goal but that can be nonetheless used for a communicative purpose).

It is important to stress that such signs are signals only implicitly. In fact the vehicle is not marked in a manifest way *as* a signal, as something that is for communication. Although the fact that being manifestly for communication needs further explanation [19], it can be argued that such explicitness at least entails that it cannot be denied that one is communicating because communication is the evident function of the sign. By using specialized or explicit signals we cannot deny that we are communicating because it is a tool designed or evolved for this function. It would be like denying the one is hammering, when one uses a hammer to drive a nail in.

Differently, when we exploit our usual practical actions to communicate we can deny that we are communicating. At least this entails that something more than communication is involved. In the end we are just after our practical goals knowing that somebody is observing us. The produced signs are used as signals but are not shaped to be signals.

This form of communication is behavioral in the sense that implicit signals deliver *behavioral messages* that are messages first of all about one's goal-directed behavior. Behavioral messages then are different from the messages with arbitrary meanings that can be exchanged with special conventionalized actions (explicit signals like a pointing gesture or a linguistic speech act) or with some external symbol specialized for communication (explicit signals like the arrows or the pheromones).

Hence we are interested in actions, and the traces that are left in the environment, that are explicitly shaped for a normal practical goal (like leaving the coat on the seat) and only implicitly used as signals to let somebody else understand something (i.e. such goal is additional to the practical one and does not need a special action to be achieved). Using a trace as an implicit signal then exploits the ability of others to understand something out of it[4].

2.4 A General Definition of Stigmergy

On the basis of the above considerations, it is now possible to clarify the notion of stigmergy. We define stigmergy as *the process of indirect communication of behavioral messages with implicit signals.*

We consider this interpretation of stigmergy as a generalization of current ones, and broadly compatible with them.

The classical notion as introduced by Grassé in 1959 [9] has emphasized the crucial consequences of indirect interaction. Agents modifying a common environment can create structures that feedback on their behaviors. A modified environment can mediate the interaction between the agents. Such local and indirect interaction enables even very simple organisms to create complex forms of coordination and organization at the collective level. Indirect interaction, or interaction through the environment, is necessary to understand self-organizing systems but self-organization is just a function of indirect interaction and not a defining feature.

---

[4] A sophisticated theory of the motivating results of an action is needed to provide a more complete analysis of weak and strong cases of this form of communication. Such richness however is not required for the aims of this paper. See Castelfranchi [5] for a more general discussion of the theory of behavioral implicit communication.

Without denying the extreme importance of this function, our aim is to show that this form of indirect interaction is usefully analyzed also as a form of communication: stigmergic interaction is a form of indirect communication where *the environment is used as a support to record messages.*

However this is still not enough. In fact, as we have shown, the great power of this form of communication is that it exploits the information that is embedded in usual practical actions and its traces without the need of specialized means of communication. Even though leaving explicit signals (signals that are shaped for communicating) in the environment can also support complex form of interaction, a more primitive but essential process exploits implicit signals.

In fact, if extracting information from others' behaviors is important for any social species and the environment can function as a sort of memory keeping track of this behavior in form of traces, then stigmergy is the process that takes advantage of this environmental property to support coordination.

Failing to notice that stigmergy is also a peculiar form of communication, we think, is one of the reasons that explain its still too limited impact. Focusing on the kind of messages that can be transmitted in this manner can illuminate the uses that stigmergic communication can have. And we are deeply convinced that the importance of stigmergy for animal, human and artificial societies is huge.

When traces are implicit signals, they are used to communicate something. This paper aims to specify more precisely what is this 'something' that can be implicitly exchanged between agents in a common environment.

3 One Trace, a Variety of Basic Behavioral Messages

If a trace is a long-term observable modification of the environment that is the outcome of an agent's action, then the kind of messages that a communicator can implicitly send are first of all strictly tied to herself and the action that has been thereby accomplished: the behavioral messages.

As in many standard accounts [21], an action is considered here as a goal-oriented modification (or forbearance from any modification) of the environment. For an action to happen, such a modification conceptually implies that (1) an agent (2) intends to do the action, and (3) in presence of the right opportunities (4) and with the right skills, (5) she modifies (or forbears from modifying) the environment (6) in order that (7) a certain result is realized.

In what follows we will provide a first taxonomy of trace messages organized around these seven core messages. We consider this variety of possibilities the *basic* behavioral messages on top of which more complex ones can be exchanged.

3.1 Informing About the Presence

The most basic message that a trace can deliver is a sign of the presence of another agent:

I inform you that: *"I'm here"*

At the core, in fact, the meaning of the trace signal used in the opening example, viz. the coat, is a sign about the presence of another agent already occupying the seat.

As every sign, also a trace like this can be used to fake a presence when this can be useful. Consider for example the habit of turning the lights on in one's house when one is going out. When a room is clearly visible from the outside, leaving a light on is a signal that is left for a possible intruder to mean that somebody is still at home. The light in itself has not a conventional meaning but the possible inferences that can be drawn by observing it are exploited to send a 'deceiving' message. Moreover, in this case, although the real goal of the practical action is informative, one does not want to be understood as communicating. This example is also useful to stress that sometimes it is not even desirable that the addressee understands that one is communicating. The light is intended to be understood as a simple trace and not as a trace intentionally emitted for some informative goal (the signal).

3.2 Informing About the Intention

From simple traces, it is possible to extract also information about one's intention to do a given action. Here the relevant meaning is:

I inform you that: *"I am committed to this action"*

A lot of social relationships require, beyond explicit words and declarations, the practical 'demonstration' of a given attitude or decision.

In particular demonstration of trust can be used to support trust relationships. As an example consider the phenomenon of trust dynamics studied by Castelfranchi and Falcone [6] where the fact that an agent trusts another one increases the latter trustworthiness (for example the trustee's care or persistence). Knowing this, the trusting agent intentionally exploits this process for example by leaving on the desk of a subordinate a very critical file. In this case the trace is an implicit signal of the intention to trust and is also necessary to create trust because it is a presupposition of the dynamic process. The (communicative) action of trusting and delegating impacts on the beliefs of the trusting agent that are the bases for the "reliance" decision producing the external action of delegating in the first place.

Differently, this kind of meaning highlights also the possibility of warning without words. Mafia's "warnings" fall for example in this category. The traces of burning, destroying, killing and even of hacking a secured server are stigma of true practical actions and the harm is a real one. However the basic aim of these behaviors (burning, killing, etc.) is informative. It is aimed at intimidating, terrifying via a specific meaning: "I'm willing to do this" and also "I'm powerful and ready to act" (see next basic message). This meaning is what really matter and what induces the addressee (that not necessarily is already the victim) to give up or to fear a given agent. The trace is a show down of intentions and power: a "message" to be "understood".

3.3 Informing About the Ability

One of the most frequent messages sent by a normal behavior is very obvious but at the same time incredibly relevant:

I inform you that: *"I'm able to do this"*

When learning to do something for example under the supervision of a teacher, each action is also a message to the teacher of one's own improvements and acquired abilities. Similarly, by leaving a trace of one's action that is observable by others one can convey this specific message.

The expression of one's ability by practical actions is crucial of course to select good partners in a way that can be costly to fake. Consider for example the fighting behaviors of animals competing for a female. Although the practical behavior is aimed to eliminate or induce the escape of a possible competitor, the fighting behavior when successful is also used as a signal of one's ability and power. In general, if showing, displaying, exhibiting and demonstrating are intentional actions (or evolved behaviors) then they are always also communicative actions.

Similarly, in many interactions a behavior is done or a trace is left also to increase trust and reputation. In fact, an agent knows that trust (for future interactions) depends on current behavior because the behavior will be read as a sign of competences and disposition (honesty, loyalty, persistence, etc.). Hence the agent can decide to give another one this impression and image for future interactions. But in fact, since the agent knows that the behavior is for the others a prognostic sign of one's own future behavior, with the current conduct it is also sent a message. If the agents need to choose each other as partners in teamwork activities, then the capacity to leave traces of one's own ability on purpose is a crucial message that can be used to speed up partner choices.

3.4 Informing About the Opportunity for Action

By leaving a trace, it is also possible to inform about obstacles and opportunities. In this case the meaning is:

I inform you that: *"These are the conditions for this action "*

Lines at the post office provide a lot of information to the newcomer. First of all, lines are signs informing about which are the active counters (the condition for action). Although this is not an intentional message sent by those who are queuing, however, it acquires a communicative function, on which the staff relies. In fact, when new electronic information devices are installed, it must be explicitly signaled which are the working counters.

The queue line also informs about the fact that the others are waiting to act; the condition for acting is there but not already available. Observable waiting is clearly a message that at least the other clients in the line intend the newcomer understand. In this case this message is sent on purpose just by maintaining an ordered line (this is why they are accurate in this). By understanding the message and start waiting, the newcomer too sends the same message again; the line self-organizes and maintains its emerging structure. Moreover, the physical shape of the line informs also on who is the last waiting person, back to whom the newcomer has to wait.

3.5 Informing About the Action Accomplishment

Another core and basic meaning of a trace is:

I inform you that: *"I have done this"*

This simple message is extremely important in interactions where, for example, a given behavior is expected by another agent. Consider for example, a child showing the mother that he is eating a given food, or a psychiatric patient showing to the nurse that he is drinking his drug. It is not the fact the one is able to eat or drink that is relevant here, but that, as expected, the eating and the drinking have been accomplished. It is this kind message is particularly important in the satisfaction of social commitments, expectations, and obligations.

Observable and perceivable traces of action accomplishment are also used for coordination. Suppose that you have to move a heavy table with another agent: it is natural in this case to use the table itself as a coordination device, and to exploit the physical sensations (that you know that the table will transmit to the other and that the other will take into account for adjusting his behavior) as messages. Feeling the direction and the acceleration that you impose to the table, the other will adjust her behaviors on this basis. If one on the contrary had to rely on verbal instructions the process would be extremely more demanding and probably impossible. The messages might not be precise or fast enough. Moreover they should be decoded and interpreted at the symbolic level before being translated into motor-commands blocking the coordinated flow in the activity.

3.6 Informing About the Goal

The next basic behavioral message is:

I inform you that: "I have this goal"

The notion of trace is general enough to cover also situations in which the agents' interaction is mediated by some external artifact (that of course is a part of the environment). Consider for example two soccer players that need to coordinate in order to pass the ball and score a goal. To let the other understand that one intends to perform a specific action among the various alternatives, often a soccer player starts acting on the expectation that the other will understand in which direction to go. By kicking the ball in one direction, the first player is communicating with the other team member what kind of plan is to be performed. In this case, the trace of the action is the ball going in a specific direction that is observable by the partner and again in this case the communication is supported by a modification of the environment.

3.7 Informing About the Result

The last basic behavioral message we are interested to point out is:

I inform you that: "This is the result"

Suppose for example that while cleaning the dishes, a glass is dropped and breaks into pieces. You decide not to remove the fragments in order to let your husband understand that, although he was convinced that they were unbreakable glasses, this glass being struck, it breaks. On this behavioral base, the husband can infer that actually the glasses are fragile. As it is clear from this example a trace can be an implicit signal not only when it is the result of an intentional action (as when you break something on purpose to send a message), but also a consequence of an intentional forbearance from acting (like in this case, when you abstain from cleaning).

4 Descriptive and Directive Traces

A minimal and very general classification of speech acts distinguishes at least *descriptive* from *directive* actions [13]. While descriptive actions are assertions about the state of the world, directives are regarded as the general class of requests for action.

Apart from direct reference to agency, what is common to all the above implicit signals is also that they are very simple descriptive acts. If it can be shown that implicit signals can also have a directive use, then a new class of possibility of interaction would available also with implicit communication.

4.1 Limiting What Implicit Signals Can 'Describe'

Even if implicit signals 'describe' something, the scope of what can be described in this way is limited by the limits of agency. As we suggested with the above examples, the state of the world described by a trace signal refers primarily only to the agent and her actions.

It seems however that some of the basic messages outlined above can do also something more. In fact, we have claimed, that a trace can also used to inform somebody else that an opportunity for action exists (fourth basic message) or that action has produced a certain result (seventh basic message). And these messages seem to involve a reference to something external to the agent herself pointing to the external environment. How is that possible?

Although a detailed analysis of this problem is beyond the scope of this paper, a brief justification is needed. We claim that an implicit signal can at least refer to two distinct environmental properties: its enabling property and its dispositional property.

A behavioral message can in fact refer to the external environment in relation to one's own action because it is also about the condition for or the opportunity to act. Although this message seems to refer to something beyond the agent, the environment is framed only relative to its possibility for action. This is the *enabling property* of the environment. In fact, if one observes an action or a trace without directly seeing the relevant details of the environment supporting the action, the existence of such enabling properties relevant to that action can be understood. The enabling property of the environment can be behaviorally communicated. Not only one can signal one's own ability to do an action (if you see me wet on the beach you can understand that "*I am able to swim*"), but also the fact that that environment enables that action ("Swimming can be done *here*", i.e. the water is not to so cold").

Secondly, one can also signal a property of the environment that is a consequence of interacting with it. For example, I can provoke in front of you a new acquaintance to intentionally let you understand that he is irascible. In this case, my trace (the fact that now he is angry because of my action) is intended to inform you about an aspect of the (social) environment. Or I can leave my wallet in a way that you and the other guy see it. Because I let him steal money from it, I intend to communicate to you that he has that disposition. The wallet left in these conditions triggering a consequence is used as an implicit signal a relevant aspect of this consequence. We consider this as the *dispositional property* of the environment (be it the social one like in these examples or the physical one like in the previous example of the broken glass) because the behavioral message communicates what happens to the environment, if one acts.

4.2 Directive Implicit Signals

It must not be forgotten that, although descriptive, the above behavioral messages are in any case aimed to influence the action of the addressees.

By informing the addressees of some aspect of one's own individual *self-regarding* action, the addresser intends to modify the action of other agents. On the other hand, by mentioning another agent as part of one's goal, an individual action can also be social or *other-regarding* [3]. To be precise, an implicit communicative action is social by definition: the communicating agent has the goal that the other is informed about something. But in all the examples the implicitly communicative actions exploit the fact that the observer is interpreting just the overt self-regarding aspect of the action.

However nothing prevents the addresser to exploit an overt social action to communicate something implicitly. A directive action (i.e. a request) then is just a peculiar way to influence another agent by way of signaling the *social* aspect of one's individual action.

Suppose in fact that an agent acts in order to facilitate (or hamper) the action of somebody else: i.e. by creating the opportunity for action. For example, a mother cooks a dinner and leaves it on the table observable to her son when he comes back home. Clearly, cooking is a practical action with a practical goal. In this case, the practical goal has also a social component because the mother is cooking for her son: her goal mentions another agent. The mother has the goal to change the environment in order to enable an action of somebody else. The result (the cooked food) then is a trace of a practical action that can be used, as every trace, to signal something.

If the son just understands the trace as the output of his mother self-regarding action, then she has informed him of the action result and he independently can use it.

Differently, if the observing agent is able to infer the social motivation behind the action, then the addresser can act precisely to inform the addressee about such social goal. Suppose for example that the mother wants her son to keep his diet, she can prepare light food on purpose and intentionally avoid cooking any caloric item like pasta. Here the intended behavioral message was about she wanting him to eat this food, hence an implicit request. If the son gets this information about her social goal, he has an additional reason for doing the action precisely because she has requested him to do so. Similarly, ashtrays on the tables of coffee shops are both descriptive and directive implicit signals. Instead of directly communicating to each costumer what to do when smoking, waiters exploit the environment to convey such meaning. The ashtray in fact is intentionally used both to inform about a possibility of action and about the waiters' goal that customer use it. Leaving ready to use ashtrays then is another case of stigmergic interaction[5].

Differently from descriptives, directive implicit messages aim to influence the other agents through *adoption* by informing of a social goal and by relying on the addressees' decision to pursue it as one's own [7]. This possibility paves the way for a set of new different kinds of implicit communicative acts: from requests, to commands and prescriptions.

---

[5] Understanding social goals then seems to enable communicative actions without the need of meta-communication (information about one's communicative intention).

5 From Basic to Complex Behavioral Messages

On the basis of this initial taxonomy we hope to have shown that implicit signals are vehicles of several useful messages. Such messages are diverse, can have different uses and can be enriched in many ways.

5.1 Informing About Reasons for Action

On the basis of the relevant basic message, a basic meaning can be elaborated on the basis of contextual and pragmatic inferences.

A trace of an accomplished action for example can support an inference about possible underlying reasons for doing the action. While buying a book, for our own pleasure, we in fact leave a strange trace in the environment: we modify the number of sold copies. This fact changes the position of the book in the bestsellers list, and this is also information (intentionally sent by the publisher or by the booksellers to the potential clients) that will be taken into account by other persons. From the fact that a number of agents have bought a specific book, potential new buyers can pragmatically infer that that book has been *evaluated* as a good one; hence the message is "this is a good book".

Although such an action just remains the practical action of buying a book with its practical intended effect for the buyers, it is also a piece of communicative behavior. In fact, even if the buyer does not intend in this case to inform anybody at all, in that market the behavior has acquired a parasitic communicative function that is exploited by making the trace observable. Moreover by aggregating various traces the message is even intensified in its meaning.

With a similar mechanism, vengeances and punishments are communicative acts too. They have the aim that the addressee understands that the harm is done on purpose and for a specific reason. Punishing in particular is intrinsically communicative given its 'teaching' aim. Punishment is not just a penalty; it is for the future, in order one learns, and thus in this case understanding the aim and the underlying reason is necessary for punishment to be effective.

5.2 Explicit and Implicit Messages Interact

In section 2, we have contended that ants leaving pheromone along their path to food are closer to the organizers attaching an arrow on a wall than to the lady leaving the coat on the seat to signal her presence. While in all these situations the agents are indirectly interacting by an appropriate modification in the environment (by leaving pheromone, a arrow or a coat), only the last one was a case of communication with trace signals. Both pheromone and arrows are explicit signals. We have also claimed that only traces of practical actions not specialized for communicating are real stigma. Hence, the suggested conclusion was that pheromone-based communication in itself is not stigmergic communication. This conclusion is of course disturbing because the concept of stigmergy was precisely introduced to explain this indirect form of interaction enabling ants to coordinate in a decentralized manner in the construction of a specific trail.

We argue that what is stigmergic in pheromone-based communication is not the explicit message left by dropping it in the environment but the one implicit in using it. There is an important implicit meaning in the action of using the pheromone that is about the reliability of the pheromone signal itself: "This signal is reliable". And the more the pheromone is used, the more the implicit message is generalized to the emergent collective product of the local interactions of the agents such that an emergent implicit signal is created like "This trail is good".

For an explicit signal to evolve and to stabilize in a population of agents in fact the main problem to be solved is precisely its *reliability* [11]. We suggest that, together with other possible mechanisms, implicit signals can be used to make explicit forms of communication more effective. In fact the aggregation of the practical actions of using one specific pheromone-signal instead of others carries information that is difficult to fake. The actions of following one trail are the real actions undertaken by the ants and can be used to fake only at a great cost for oneself.

We are not suggesting that implicit signals are better then explicit ones. However what we do claim is that dedicated communications channels should be designed to enable a combination with implicit communication processes in order to improve their robustness and effectiveness.

5.3 Different Messages with the Same Trace

Although for analytical purposes we have distinguished several distinct kinds of meanings that a trace-message can send, it is crucial to understand that different meanings can often co-exist at the same time in the same trace. A single trace in fact brings several messages/meanings in parallel to different addressees precisely because it does not adopt neither a dedicated channel nor a specialized explicit signal to carry these messages (with their relatively fixed conventional meanings) but exploits different interpretations of the behavior by different observers.

For example, the act of violating a norm can be a communicative act, either intentional or even functionally. Consider the aggressive behavior of an extremist protester. At the same time, the practical action of breaking the window of a bank communicates:

- to the authorities: "I intend to fight against you", "I do not respect your norms", "I do not fear you";
- to the peers and himself "I do not respect norms", "Violating is possible", "Do as I do. Follow me" "I'm reliable", "I'm one of you";
- and perhaps to the peers and himself: "Look how audacious I am, I'm skilled and strong";
- to the others pacific protesters: "you are cowards and integrated".

5.4 Tacit Agreements

Suppose you sit in a coffee shop with your friends but you don't intend to order anything. When the waiter arrives, you feel a sense of uneasiness. Alternatively, suppose that you resolve to order but the waiter refuses to serve you. In both situations the agents are violating some commitments they have taken. These agents have social commitments one to the other without having agreed about anything explicitly.

The importance of commitments like these in regulating interactions in widely recognized in multi-agents systems [8, 18]. However social commitments are always modeled as the output of explicit communication processes. Indeed this is not necessary. To establish a social commitment of an agent X to another agent Y two moves are essential [4]:

-    the move (usually by the commissive speech act of promising) of X creating his obligation and Y's right and expectation and
-    Y's move of consent, accepting X's action.

Both these actions must be communicated. Without such agreement (which creates a reciprocal – although asymmetric -commitment) no true social commitment of X to Y has been established. This process does not necessarily imply explicit communication between the agents. As in the above example, both X's committing act and Y's consent act can be (and frequently are) tacit.

One can characterize the principle of implicit committing as follows:

IF
there is mutual knowledge between X and Y about an expectation of Y about an action of X (where an expectation is a belief about a future state or action plus a goal about the same state or action) [12];
and
X intends to do that action also because he knows about Y's expectation;
and
X does not explicitly deny his intention, does not contradict Y's expectation;

THEN
X implicitly takes a social commitment to Y for that action; and
Y is entitled to consider X socially committed to her.

At the same time by relying on X and by letting X to believe so and believe that he is committed to Y, Y is implicitly accepting X's commitment, and agreeing about it (principle of implicit consent in social commitment).

Knowing about the waiter's expectation about you, your staying at the table is also a signal that you intend to order. Staying at the table in an observable way is a sign that is so interpreted by the waiter and you if you don't explicitly communicate the opposite you undertake an obligation to order. At the same time, because the waiter does not explicitly refuse your action, is implicitly accepting it and so he becomes committed to accept it when you place your order.

This mutual "understanding" among the agents is necessary and intended. Social commitments always requires communication but not necessarily explicit; on both side tacit communication can be enough and, as in the example, traces of one's presence can be used to deliver the messages.

6 Conclusion

In this paper we have sketched several arguments to support the relevance of using agents' traces as implicit signals of behavioral messages. We have provided a taxonomy of basic behavioral messages that can be indirectly communicated and we have individuated two possible uses of such communication: descriptive and directive. Finally we have also indicated some interesting directions in which simple behavioral messages can be enriched towards more complex meanings.

Stigmergy, the process of indirect communication of behavioral messages with implicit signals, is proposed as a powerful and flexible mechanism with the following characteristics:

- It is a form of communication that is situated and exploits the capacity of agents to understand each other actions and the environment. If one understands action of others in sensory-motor terms then communicating in this way facilitates situated interaction in the environment;
- However its situatedness is also its main limitation. Stigmergy is limited signal the here and now and to the this and that. To deliver more abstract and distant messages more symbolic means of communication are needed;
- Many messages can be delivered with a single trace. The relevance of the behavioral message that one is communicating is again a contextual problem.
- Although often broadcasting, stigmergy is mainly dyadic: I inform (all of) you about me and I inform (all of) you about my goal about (all of) you. Stigmergy can be used to describe something about the communicator and also to deliver directive communicative action towards the addressees;
- There is a primitive reference to the external world but only seen as an opportunity for action or about how it changes when acting. However properties of the environment in itself (i.e. the general topology) or that are not directly tied to the present action are not in its scope;
- Trace signals are more reliable because one has to really act and can be used to reinforce the reliability of cheap arbitrary signals (interaction with symbolic communication);
- More generally stigmergy can be exploited also by other coordination mechanisms like normative systems to facilitate the interaction process between the agents.

Our primary aim with this explorative paper was to convince the reader of the ubiquity and relevance of this phenomenon for many aspects of social life. This very same intention is also shared by Parunak in [16] who, however, does not distinguish explicit from implicit signals. We hope to have argued effectively for the relevance of studying implicit signals as a first level phenomenon. We cannot evaluate if we have met this objective, and so we at least intend to leave a trace about this attempt to signal an important direction of future research.

References

1. Camazine, S. Deneubourg, J., Franks, N.R., Sneyd, J., Theraulaz, G., Bonabeau, E.: Self-Organization in Biological Systems. Princeton University Press, Princeton, NJ (2001).
2. Bonabeau, E., Henaux, F., Guérin, S., Snyers, D., Kuntz, P., Theraulaz, G.: Routing in Telecommunications Networks with Ant-like Agents. In Second International Workshop on Intelligent Agents for Telecommunication Applications. Springer-Verlag (1998).

3. Castelfranchi, C.: Modelling Social Action for AI Agents. Artificial Intelligence, 103, 1-2, (1998) 157-182.
4. Castelfranchi, C.: Formalising the informal?: Dynamic social order, bottom-up social control, and spontaneous normative relations. Journal of Applied Logic, 1-2 (2003).
5. Castelfranchi C.: From Conversation to Interaction via Behavioral Communication. In S. Bagnara & G. Crampton Smith (Eds) Theories and Practice in Interaction Design, New Jersey (USA): Erlbaum, (2006) 157-179.
6. Castelfranchi, C., Falcone, R.: Trust Dynamics: How Trust Is Influenced by Direct Experiences and by Trust Itself. In Proceedings of the Autonomous Agents and Multiagent Systems Conference (AAMAS), (2004) 740-747
7. Conte, R., Castelfranchi, C.: Individual and Social Action. UCL Press, London (1995).
8. Fornara, N., Colombetti, M. A Commitment-based Approach to Agent Communication. Applied Artificial Intelligence, 18, 9-10, (2004) 853–866.
9. Grassé, P.P.: La Reconstruction du Nid et les Coordinations Inter-individuelles chez Bellicosoitermes Natalensis et Cubitermes. La Théorie de la Stigmergie: Essai d'Interprétation du Comportement des Termites Constructeurs. Insectes Sociaux, 6, (1959) 41-81.
10. Mamei, M., Zambonelli, F., Leonardi, L.: Co-Fields: A Physically Inspired Approach to Distributed Motion Coordination. IEEE Pervasive Computing, (2004).
11. Maynard-Smith, J., Harper, D.: Animal Signals. Harvard University Press, Cambridge, MA (2003).
12. Miceli M., Castelfranchi C.: The Mind and the Future: The (negative) Power of Expectations. Theory & Psychology, 12 (2002) 335-366.
13. Millikan, R.: Varieties of Meanings. MIT Press, Cambridge, MA (2004).
14. Parunak, V.: Go to the Ant: Engineering Principles from Natural Agent Systems. Annals of Operations Research, 75 (1997) 69–101.
15. Parunak, V., Brueckner, S., & Sauter, J.: Digital pheromones for coordination of unmanned vehicles. In Weyns, D., Parunak, V., Michel, F. (eds.) Environments for Multiagent Systems, First International Workshop (E4MAS 2004), Lecture Notes in Computer Science, Vol. 3374 Springer-Verlag (2005).
16. Parunak, V.: A Survey of Environments and Mechanisms for Human-Human Stigmergy. In Proceedings of the AAMAS workshop on Environment for Multi-Agent Systems (E4MAS 2005) Lecture Notes in Computer Science, Vol. 3830, Springer Verlag, (2005) 121-138.
17. Quinn, M.: Evolving Communication without Dedicated Communication Channels. In: Kelemen, J. and Sosik, P. (eds): Advances in Artificial Life: Sixth European Conference on Artificial Life, Lecture Notes in Computer Science, Vol. 2159. Springer-Verlag, (2001) 357-366.
18. Singh, M.: An Ontology for Commitments in Multiagent Systems: Toward a Unification of Normative. Artificial Intelligence and Law, 7 (1999) 97-113.
19. Sperber, D., Wilson, D.: Relevance; Communication and Cognition. Harvard University Press, Cambridge, MA (1986).
20. Tummolini, L., Castelfranchi, C., Omicini, A., Ricci, A., & Viroli, M.: "Exhibitionists" and "Voyeurs" do it Better: A shared environment for flexible coordination with tacit messages. In Weyns, D., Parunak, V., Michel, F. (eds.) Environments for Multiagent Systems, First International Workshop (E4MAS 2004), Lecture Notes in Computer Science, Vol. 3374 Springer-Verlag (2005).
21. Von Wright, G.H.: Norm and Action. Routledge and Kegan Paul, London (1963).
22. Wilson, E. O.: The Insect Societies. Belknap Press, Cambridge, MA (1971).

Regulation Function of the Environment in Agent-Based Simulation

Stefania Bandini and Giuseppe Vizzari

Department of Informatics, Systems and Communication
Università degli Studi di Milano–Bicocca
Via Bicocca degli Arcimboldi 8 20126 Milan - Italy
Tel.: +39 02 64487865; Fax: + 39 02 64487839
{bandini,vizzari}@disco.unimib.it

Abstract. The notion of environment as a first class abstraction in Multi–Agent Systems (MAS) has affirmed itself both as a necessary element of the related models and systems, and as useful source of concepts and mechanisms for their design and implementation. However, the functions and responsibilities that the environment should accomplish in different application contexts are still under debate in the agent research community. This paper is focused on agent-based simulation and in particular on the regulation function of the environment, which is a crucial factor supporting the enforcement of the required level of realism in the dynamics generated by the simulation system. In particular, the paper shows that the MAS based simulation context provides features that require a peculiar balance between agent autonomy and environment control on the overall system dynamics.

1 Introduction

The term environment was considered since the very first definitions of agent, agent-based system and Multi–Agent System (MAS). Nonetheless, only recent research efforts highlighted the fact that the environment for a MAS can be much more than external resources and a mere communication infrastructure, and it should be considered as a necessary element of MAS models and systems as well as an exploitable abstraction [1].

Even if several successful examples of agent-based models, systems and applications that effectively build on agent environment and related abstractions and mechanisms can be found (see, e.g., the proceedings of the first and second E4MAS workshop [2,3]), there is still an open debate on the functions and responsibilities that the environment should accomplish. While the fact that the support to agent interaction is delegated to a specific infrastructure and not to an agent is generally agreed upon, there are several aspects of agent interaction, especially in direct agent interaction approaches (e.g. management of social knowledge [4]), that are managed by particular agents whose only goal is to support other active entities in the overall system (i.e. middle agents). In this kind of approach, agent environment represents little more than a message passing infrastructure.

D. Weyns, H.V.D. Parunak, and F. Michel (Eds.): E4MAS 2006, LNAI 4389, pp. 157–169, 2007.

However, in specific situations one of the requirements on the overall system could provide properties to be enforced, even to the point of limiting agents' autonomy imposing rules and laws (e.g. to reify organizational abstractions regulating access to resources, or even security policies) on the overall system. In this kind of scenario, it can be more convenient (or even necessary) to extend the environmental responsibilities to manage all agents' actions that can have a direct influence on other entities in the system [5]. In other words, all actions that do not strictly pertain to the autonomously determined change of an agent's state should be carried out it the environment, and they should be actually checked against its rules and policies.

While system regulation and management are in general very relevant issues, especially in open multi–agent systems in which agents may be highly heterogeneous and (in general) not benevolent, these aspects are even more crucial in agent–based simulation systems. In fact, while a key aspect of an agent–based approach to modeling and simulation is the fact that the overall system dynamics are generated by means of the interaction of autonomous entities composing it, there can be specific aspects of the simulated systems that do not pertain to single agents but rather characterize the overall system. When simulating, for instance, the movement of autonomous entities roaming in a physical space, according to the desired precision on its representation and on the position of these entities, it could be necessary to enforce a non–interpenetration rule. The enforcement of this specific rule can be delegated to agent's behavioural specification (e.g. "do not move in a place that is already occupied by another agent or object"), only under the assumption of the existence of a notion of turn and a sequential activation of agents. In general, the enforcement and enactment of this kind of system rules cannot be delegated to agents, i.e. micro level entities, and it requires a controller at some higher level. In other words, system regulation is typically delegated to agents' environment.

On the other hand, the introduced example highlights one of the issues in defining and designing general models and mechanisms for MAS–based simulation, that is, a peculiar balance between agents' autonomy and environmental control. In fact, the presence of specific rules in the simulated reality may lead to totally different modeling approaches, and also on radically different notions of agents and their possibility to decide, not only on the choice of actions to be carried out but also on the moment in which they should be carried out. The idea that an agent is not provided with a thread of control of its own, and that it has to be triggered in order to carry out its own perceptions and actions is in contrast with most definitions of agent, but it is quite commonly adopted in MAS–based simulation approaches and systems.

This paper is going to discuss the regulation function delegated to the environment in the specific context of MAS–based simulation by focusing on the problem of agent activation. The following section will introduce motivations and peculiarities of this area of application, while Sect. 3 will discuss the role of environment in MAS–based simulation. Section 4 will then discuss the balance between agents' autonomy and environment control due to its regulation function, with specific reference to agents activation strategies. Conclusions and future developments will end the paper.

2   Agent-Based Simulation: Motivations and Peculiarities

Computer simulation represents a way to exploit a computational model to evaluate designs and plans without actually bringing them into existence in the real world (e.g. architectural designs, road networks and traffic lights), but also to evaluate theories and models of complex systems (e.g. biological or social systems) by envisioning the effect of the modeling choices, with the aim of gaining insight of their functioning. The use of these "synthetic environments" is sometimes necessary because the simulated system cannot actually be observed, since it is actually being designed or also for ethical or practical reasons.

Several situations are characterized by the presence of autonomous entities whose actions and interactions determine (in a non–trivial way) the evolution of the overall system. Agent-based models are particularly suited to represent these situations, and to support the study and analysis of topics like decentralized decision making, local-global interactions, self-organization, emergence, effects of heterogeneity in the simulated system. The interest in this relatively recent approach to modeling and simulation is demonstrated by the number of scientific events focused in this topic (see, to make some examples rooted in the computer science context, the Multi Agent Based Simulation workshop serie [6,7,8,9,10,11], and the Agent-Based Modeling and Simulation symposium [12]). Agent-based models have been adopted to simulate complex systems in very different contexts, ranging from social and economical simulation (see, e.g., [13]) to logistics optimization (see, e.g., [14]), from biological systems (see, e.g., [15])) to traffic (see, e.g., [16,17,18]) and crowd simulation (see, e.g., [19]).

This heterogeneity in the application domains also reflects the fact that, especially in this context of agent focused research, influences come from most different research areas. Several traffic and crowd agent models are deeply influenced by *physics*, and the related models provide agents that are modelled as particles subject to forces generated by the environment as well as by other agents (i.e. *active walker* models, such as [20]). Other approaches to crowd modeling and simulation build on experiences with *Cellular Automata* (CA) approaches (see, e.g., [21]) but provide a more clear separation between the environment and the entities that inhabit, act and interact in it (see, e.g., [22,23]). This line of research lead to the definition of models for situated MASs, a type of model that was also defined and successfully applied in the context of (reactive) robotics and control systems [24,25]. Models and simulators defined and developed in the context of social sciences [26] and economy [27] build on different theories (often non–classical ones) of *human behaviour* in order to gain further insight on it and help building and validating new theories.

The common standpoint of all these approaches is the fact that the analytical unit of the system is represented by the individual agent: the overall system dynamic is not defined in terms of a global function, but rather the result of individuals' actions and interactions. On the other hand, it must also be noted that in most of the introduced application domains, the environment plays a prominent role because:

- it deeply influences the behaviours of the simulated entities, in terms of perceptions and allowed actions for the agents;
- the aim of the simulation is to observe some aggregate level behaviour, that is actually observed in the environment.

Besides these common elements, the above introduced approaches often dramatically differ in the way agents are described, both in terms of properties and behaviour. A similar consideration can be done for their environment.

3   Environment in Agent-Based Simulation

Weyns et al. in [1] provide a definition of the notion of environment for MASs, and also discuss the core responsibilities that can be ascribed to it. In particular, in the specific context of simulation the environment is typically responsible for

- reflecting/reifying/managing the structure of the physical/social arrangement of the overall system;
- supporting agent perception and situated action (it must be noted that agent interaction should be considered a particular kind of action);
- maintain internal dynamics (e.g. spontaneous growth of resources, dissipation signals emitted by agents);
- define/enforce rules.

Agent–based models and simulators that are based on a physical approach generally consider agents as particles subject to and generating forces. The environment comprises laws regulating these influences and relevant elements of the simulated system that are not agents (e.g. point of reference that generate attraction/repulsion forces). It is the environment that determines the overall dynamics, combining the effects that influence each agent and applying them generally in discrete time steps. In this cycle, it captures all the above introduced responsibilities, and the role of agents is minimal (according to some definitions they should not be called agents at all), and running a simulation is essentially reduced to computing iteratively a set equations (see, e.g., [20,18]). In situated MAS approaches agents have a higher degree of autonomy and control over their actions, since they evaluate their perceptions and choose their actions according to their behavioural specification. The environment retains a very relevant role, since it provides agents with their perceptions that are generated according to the current structure of the system and to the arrangement of agents situated in it. Socioeconomic models and simulations provide various approaches to the representation of the simulated system, but are generally similar to situated MASs.

It is now necessary to make a clarification on how the notion of environment in the context of MAS–based simulation can be turned into a software architecture. Klügl et al. [28] argue that the notion of environment in multi-agent

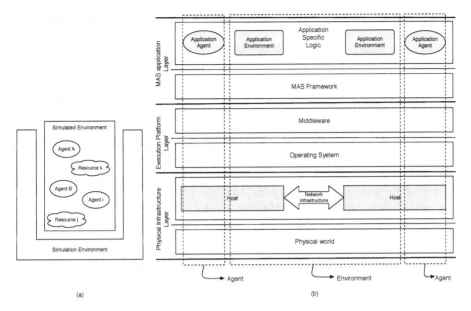

Fig. 1. A schema introduced in [28] to show differences and relationships between simulated and simulation environment (a), and a three layer deployment model for situated MAS introduced in [30] highlighting the crosscutting abstractions *agent* and *environment*(b)

simulation is actually made up of two conceptually different elements: the simulated environment and the simulation environment. The former is a part of the computational model that represents the reality or the abstraction that is the object of the simulation activity. The simulation environment, on the other hand, is a software infrastructure for executing the simulation. In this framework, to make an explicit decoupling between these levels is a prerequisite for good engineering practice. It must be noted that also a different work [29], non specifically developed in the context of agent-based simulation, provided a model for Deployment Environment, that is the specific part of the software infrastructure that manages the interactions among agents.

Another recent work is focused on clarifying the notion of MAS environment and describes a three layered model for situated MAS environments [30]. This work argues that environmental abstractions (as well as those related to agents) crosscut all the system levels, from application specific ones, to the execution platform, to the physical infrastructure. There are thus application specific aspects of agents' environment that must be supported by the software infrastructure supporting the execution of the MAS, and in particular the MAS framework. Figure 1 compares the two above described schemas.

The fact that the environment actually crosscuts all system levels in a deployment model represents a problem making difficult the separation between simulated environment and simulation infrastructure. In fact, the modeling choices can have a deep influence on the design of the underlying MAS framework and, vice versa, design choices on the simulation infrastructure make it suitable for some MAS and environment models but not usable for other ones. As a result, general MAS framework supporting simulation actually exist, but they cannot offer a specific form of support to the modeler, although they can offer basic mechanisms and abstractions.

SeSAm, for instance, offers a general simulation infrastructure but relies on plugins [28], for instance, for the definition of spatial features of the simulated environment with the associated basic functions supporting agent movement and perception in that kind of environment. With reference to Figure 1 (b), such a plugin would be associated to the Application Environment module, in the MAS application layer. However, these aspects represent just some of the features of the simulated environment, that can actually comprise rules and laws that extend their influence over the agents and the outcomes of their attempts to act in the environment.

4   Law Enforcement: Autonomy vs. Control

The specification of rules or laws for agents' environment represents a constraint to their actions. In order to verify the compliance of agents' actions to the aforementioned laws, the environment must be able to react to these actions, either accepting them and possibly changing the overall state of the system or rejecting them, applying some kind of policy to manage these exceptions. Such a policy could provide the fact that the environment informs the agent of the rejection of the previously chosen action (possibly indicating the reason of the rejection) and asks the agent to select another one. Another policy could simply cause the agent not to act, skipping the "action turn". The way agents are activated and their actions are managed, in other words what Weyns et al. call *model for action* [31], has of course a deep impact on the possibility of expressing laws of the environment. A seminal work analyzing this aspect of the dynamics of a MAS is the *influence and reaction model* by Ferber and Müller [32]; more recent works by Weyns and Holvoet elaborate on the previous model [33], introducing introducing regional synchronization of actions.

The following subsection will adopt an abstract sample situation, i.e. a model of agents moving in a discrete environment, to elaborate this topic in the specific context of simulation.

4.1   Agent Movement and Conflicts

Let us now consider a model for the representation of entities situated and moving in a physical space. The model provides a discrete abstraction of this environment, and in particular a lattice such that each cell can be occupied by at most one entity; moving entities are modelled as agents, and are only characterized by their position (a pair $\langle x, y \rangle$ representing its row and column in the lattice). This requirement maps to a specific law for the environment, that provides the fact that at most one agent can be situated in a cell at a given moment. To control the compliance of agents' actions to this law, agents must communicate

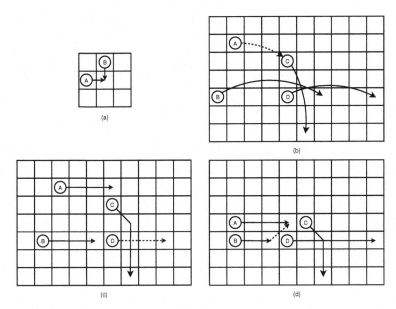

Fig. 2. Different kind of conflicts on agent movement in a discrete environment: in (a), agents A and B wish to move towards the same cell; in (b) agent A would like to move to an occupied cell, and this is forbidden by the "hop or stop" policy; in (c) agent D is blocked since its movement is crossed by the path of agent C, and this violates the "no crossing path" policy; in (d) a similar pair of actions is allowed, since the "sub–steps" policy is adopted and there are no conflicting sub–steps

their chosen movements to the environment, that will decide if the action can be accepted (and consequently change its structure) or it should be rejected. In the terminology adopted in [5], agents' movements can be considered as organization events, and the environment must be able to analyze and respond to these events. Finally, let us suppose that the system evolves through discrete time steps: there is a notion of turn and every agent can perform an action per turn.

Figure 2 (a) shows a sample situation in which one of the actions (respectively chosen by agent A and B must be rejected and prevented by the environment, since it would lead to an inconsistent state. The same Fig. but in (b), depicts a different situation, in which agents' actions are not single movements from a cell to an adjacent one (i.e. one that is part of Von Neumann neighborhood), but several subsequent movements of this kind, starting from the current position. This kind of situation is due to the fact that the modeled entities can be characterized by a different maximum velocity (i.e. number of single movements per turn). However, according to the order of activation of agents, there is a possible conflict between the movement of agent C and agent D. In fact, they can potentially require to occupy the same cell at the same time.

This kind of conflict has been analyzed in [34] in the context of crowd modeling and simulation with a CA approach, but those considerations are also relevant to a situated MAS approach. Some relevant possible policies for the management of this kind of conflict are the following:

- *"hop or stop"*: a movement action issued by an agent should be accepted if it does not lead to an inconsistent state, i.e. if it does not provide the presence of two agents in the same cell. If such a conflict arises, one of the conflicting actions is refused and the associated agent simply does not act; Figure 2 (b) presents a sample application of this kind of policy: the action of agent A is rejected, while other agents are allowed to perform their moves;
- *"no crossing paths"*: a movement action should be accepted unless at least one cell of the related path is also included in a path associated to another agent. Even in this case, if such conflict arises, one of the conflicting actions must be refused, and the related agent does not act. Figure 2 (c) presents a sample application of this strategy; in particular, the action of agent D is not allowed, since the associated path would cross the path of agent C;
- *"sub–steps"*: actions are divided into atomic steps (i.e. single movements from a cell to an adjacent one), and they are examined at this level. Those providing paths that do not present sub–steps conflicting with those of other agents' actions will be accepted, other ones will be ended before generating an inconsistent situation (i.e. not necessarily all the action is discarded). Figure 2 (d) shows a sample application of this kind of policy, that allows crossing paths, as long as the associated movements don't violate the non interpenetration law, but agent B cannot perform its whole action because the last sub–step would violate this law.

It must be noted that the choice on the particular policy for the management of conflicts on agent movement plays a relevant role in determining the level of realism of the dynamics generated by the simulation.

However, it must also be noted that the fact that a notion of turn exists, and that each agent performs a single action per turn, does not represent a precise specification of the model operation. In fact, there may be different ways of regulating the activation of agents inside a given turn, and specific choices about this point could simplify or even prevent the management of conflicts.

4.2   Strategies for Agent Activation

A schema summarizing the possible strategies for agent activation is shown in Fig. 3.

The traditional definitions and conceptions of the term agent stress the fact that an agent must be provided with a thread of control of its own, and this case is represented by the concurrent activation strategy. Agent, when this strategy is adopted, do not necessarily need an external triggering stimulus, but can be activated endogenously. In general, there is no notion of turn or any form of control on fairness or ordering of agents' actions. However, in the context of simulation, for sake of realism, fairness (or, more generally, a degree of control on how frequently agents effectively act), and in general in order to obtain results that can be analyzed and compared to actual data for sake of calibration and

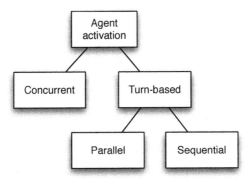

Fig. 3. A diagram showing the hierarchy of possible agent activation strategies

validation the notion of turn is a necessary feature of the simulation model. When a concurrent agent activation strategy is adopted, the notion of turn must then be introduced as a special case of agent coordination by using the environment itself as a medium for coordination [35]. Figure 4 shows a sample interaction among agents and the environment, in a concurrent agent activation strategy. In particular, Agent-2 acts first (carrying out the internal action 1); in order to assure fairness, it signals the environment that it has carried out an action. Agent-1 then emits a signal (e.g. a pheromone or a computational field) that the environment suitably diffuses in its spatial structure. Since there is no constraint on agent activation, Agent-2 decides to act and tries to emit a signal, before other agents (e.g. Agent-n) were able to carry an action for that turn. The environment will not carry out this action (and might even block the execution of Agent-2), until all agents executed one action for that turn. Supposing that Agent-n is the last one acting in the current turn (trying to move in the spatial structure of the environment, action n): as a consequence to this action, the environment will advance the turn (operation n.2), manage the necessary internal processes (e.g. pheromone evaporation), and it will eventually manage the second signal emission of Agent-2. The need of enforcing fairness among agents and causing them to act according to a notion of turn, obviously limits the parallelism of agents execution.

It is thus quite common the adoption of a turn–based agent activation strategy, in which agents are activated by an external trigger generated by the environment. Agents can carry out one or more actions per turn, according to a given criterion (e.g. agents are characterized by a speed that determines the number of actions they can perform each turn). However, there are many ways to activate agents in order to support their perception, the choice of the actions to be performed, and finally to effectively compute the effects of their actions. Agents could perceive the same situation, decide their actions and then act in a conceptually *parallel* way, such as in a CA. On the other hand, agents may be *sequentially* selected (according to a predefined or randomly generated order) to select their action, that can be carried out immediately in/by the environment.

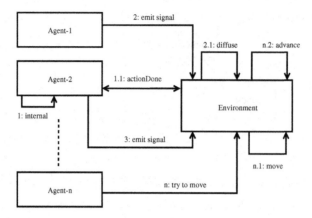

Fig. 4. An example of interaction among agents and the environment in a concurrent activation strategy

With reference to the example introduced in Sect. 4.1, it can be noted that a parallel agent activation could be suitably adopted for "hop by hop" or "no crossing path" policies, since they treat movement actions as atomic (even if they are made up of a set of basic single movements from a cell to an adjacent one) and the policy provides to cause one of the conflicting agents to skip its turn. To manage these policies with this agent activation strategy would mean to check for violations before modifying the state of the system and choose (according to a predefined priority or randomly) which actions to reject in order to solve conflicts.

The "sub–step" policy would be more difficult to manage in this way, since it is focused on fragments of action. Adopting a sequential agent activation strategy the turn is implicitly fragmented in a number of slots n equal to the number of agents actions. However, the turn could be subdivided into a higher number of slots $n = \sum_{a \in A} v_a$ where A is the set of agents and v_a is the velocity of agent a. It would be now possible to select and activate an agent and carry out a sub–step, checking that no conflict is generated, in order to enforce the "sub–step policy". Moreover, if agents were triggered every sub–step in order to choose a basic movement action, instead of selecting once their whole path for the turn, it would be possible to delegate them this check (i.e. include in their behavioral specification the fact that occupied cells must not the selected as destinations), preventing conflicts.

There is thus a deep relationship between the adopted agent activation strategy and the way environmental laws can be expressed and enforced. Moreover the choice on agent activation strategy can also determine to which extent agents can contribute in law enforcement (by respecting the rules, from a local point of view).

5   Conclusions and Future Developments

This paper has discussed the regulation function of the environment in the context of MAS based simulation. In particular, after presenting a brief of overview of this specific context of application in the agent research area, and after having discussed the role of the environment in this kind of application, the paper focused on the peculiar balance between agent autonomy and environmental control on agents' actions, and even on agents' activation, that is necessary to assure the desired level of realism in most simulation contexts. In particular, a specific example (i.e. the modeling of agents situated and moving in a physical space) was adopted to show the relevance of the choice of an agent activation strategy on the possibility of enforcing the laws of the environment.

The adoption of an agent-based approach to modeling and simulation is still relatively young, especially compared to other approaches such as those inspired by physics and those based on CA. Agent-based approaches can provide a be more expressive and less constrained framework to represent and manage complex systems, and relevant results were already obtained, but further work is necessary to be able to formally define models and mechanisms that can be used to design general MAS–based simulation system. Foundational works like [33] and [36] represent the first steps in this direction, that also provides a set of methodological and design challenges.

References

1. Weyns, D., Omicini, A., Odell, J.: Environment as a First Class Abstraction in Multiagent Systems. Autonomous Agents Multi-Agent Systems **14** (2007) 5–30
2. Weyns, D., Michel, F., Parunak, H.V.D., eds.: Environments for Multi-Agent Systems, First International Workshop (E4MAS 2004). Volume 3374 of Lecture Notes in Artificial Intelligence., Springer–Verlag (2005)
3. Weyns, D., Michel, F., Parunak, H.V.D., eds.: Environments for Multi-Agent Systems, Second International Workshop (E4MAS 2005). Volume 3830 of Lecture Notes in Artificial Intelligence., Springer–Verlag (2006)
4. Mařík, V., Pěchouček, M., Štěphanková, O.: Social Knowledge in Multi-Agent Systems. In: Multi-Agent Systems and Applications. Volume 2086 of Lecture Notes in Artificial Intelligence., Springer–Verlag (2001) 211–245
5. Schumacher, M., Ossowski, S.: The Governing Environment. In Weyns, D., Parunak, H.V.D., Michel, F., eds.: Environments for Multi-Agent Systems II, Second International Workshop, E4MAS 2005, Utrecht, The Netherlands, July 25, 2005, Selected Revised and Invited Papers. Volume 3830 of Lecture Notes in Computer Science., Springer–Verlag (2006) 88–104
6. Sichman, J.S., Conte, R., Gilbert, N., eds.: Multi-Agent Systems and Agent-Based Simulation, First International Workshop, MABS '98, Paris, France, July 4-6, 1998, Proceedings. In Sichman, J.S., Conte, R., Gilbert, N., eds.: MABS. Volume 1534 of Lecture Notes in Computer Science., Springer–Verlag (1998)
7. Moss, S., Davidsson, P., eds.: Multi-Agent-Based Simulation, Second International Workshop, MABS 2000, Boston, MA, USA, July, 2000, Revised and Additional Papers. Volume 1979 of Lecture Notes in Computer Science., Springer–Verlag (2001)
8. Sichman, J.S., Bousquet, F., Davidsson, P., eds.: Multi-Agent-Based Simulation, Third International Workshop, MABS 2002, Bologna, Italy, July 15-16, 2002, Revised Papers. In Sichman, J.S., Bousquet, F., Davidsson, P., eds.: MABS. Volume 2581 of Lecture Notes in Computer Science., Springer–Verlag (2003)

9. Hales, D., Edmonds, B., Norling, E., Rouchier, J., eds.: Multi-Agent-Based Simulation III, 4th International Workshop, MABS 2003, Melbourne, Australia, July 14th, 2003, Revised Papers. In Hales, D., Edmonds, B., Norling, E., Rouchier, J., eds.: MABS. Volume 2927 of Lecture Notes in Computer Science., Springer–Verlag (2003)

10. Davidsson, P., Logan, B., Takadama, K., eds.: Multi-Agent and Multi-Agent-Based Simulation, Joint Workshop MABS 2004, New York, NY, USA, July 19, 2004, Revised Selected Papers. In Davidsson, P., Logan, B., Takadama, K., eds.: MABS. Volume 3415 of Lecture Notes in Computer Science., Springer–Verlag (2005)

11. Sichman, J.S., Antunes, L., eds.: Multi-Agent-Based Simulation VI, International Workshop, MABS 2005, Utrecht, The Netherlands, July 25, 2005, Revised and Invited Papers. In Sichman, J.S., Antunes, L., eds.: MABS. Volume 3891 of Lecture Notes in Computer Science., Springer (2006)

12. Bandini, S., Petta, P., Vizzari, G., eds.: International Symposium on Agent Based Modeling and Simulation (ABModSim 2006). Cybernetics and Systems 2006, Austrian Society for Cybernetic Studies – 18th European Meeting on Cybernetics and Systems Research (EMCSR 2006).

13. Dosi, G., Fagiolo, G., Roventini, A.: An Evolutionary Model of Endogenous Business Cycles. Computational Economics **27** (2006) 3–34

14. Weyns, D., Boucké, N., Holvoet, T.: Gradient Field-Based Task Assignment in an AGV Transportation System. In: AAMAS '06: Proceedings of the fifth international joint conference on Autonomous agents and multiagent systems, ACM Press (2006) 842–849

15. Bandini, S., Celada, F., Manzoni, S., Puzone, R., Vizzari, G.: Modelling the Immune System with Situated Agents. In Apolloni, B., Marinaro, M., Nicosia, G., Tagliaferri, R., eds.: Proceedings of WIRN/NAIS 2005. Volume 3931 of Lecture Notes in Computer Science., Springer-Verlag (2006) 231–243

16. Bazzan, A.L.C., Wahle, J., Klügl, F.: Agents in Traffic Modelling - from Reactive to Social Behaviour. In Burgard, W., Christaller, T., Cremers, A.B., eds.: KI-99: Advances in Artificial Intelligence, 23rd Annual German Conference on Artificial Intelligence, Bonn, Germany, September 13-15, 1999, Proceedings. Volume 1701 of Lecture Notes in Computer Science., Springer–Verlar (1999) 303–306

17. Wahle, J., Schreckenberg, M.: A Multi-Agent System for On-Line Simulations Based on Real-World traffic data. In: Annual Hawaii International Conference on System Sciences (HICSS-34), IEEE Computer Society (2001)

18. Balmer, M., Nagel, K.: Shape Morphing of Intersection Layouts Using Curb Side Oriented Driver Simulation. In van Leeuwen, J.P., Timmermans, H.J., eds.: Innovations in Design & Decision Support Systems in Architecture and Urban Planning, Springer–Verlag (2006) 167–183

19. Batty, M.: Agent Based Pedestrian Modeling (editorial). Environment and Planning B: Planning and Design **28** (2001) 321–326

20. Helbing, D., Schweitzer, F., Keltsch, J., Molnár, P.: Active Walker Model for the Formation of Human and Animal Trail Systems. Physical Review E **56** (1997) 2527–2539

21. Schadschneider, A., Kirchner, A., Nishinari, K.: CA Approach to Collective Phenomena in Pedestrian Dynamics. In Bandini, S., Chopard, B., Tomassini, M., eds.: Cellular Automata, 5th International Conference on Cellular Automata for Research and Industry, ACRI 2002. Volume 2493 of Lecture Notes in Computer Science., Springer (2002) 239–248

22. Bandini, S., Manzoni, S., Vizzari, G.: Situated Cellular Agents: a Model to Simulate Crowding Dynamics. IEICE Transactions on Information and Systems: Special Issues on Cellular Automata **E87-D** (2004) 669–676

23. Henein, C.M., White, T.: Agent-Based Modelling of Forces in Crowds. In Davidsson, P., Logan, B., Takadama, K., eds.: Multi-Agent and Multi-Agent-Based Simulation, Joint Workshop MABS 2004, New York, NY, USA, July 19, 2004, Revised Selected Papers. Volume 3415 of Lecture Notes in Computer Science., Springer–Verlag (2005) 173–184

24. Weyns, D., Holvoet, T.: From Reactive Robots to Situated Multi–Agent Systems: a Historical Perspective on the Role of Environment in Multi–Agent Systems. In Dikenelli, O., Gleizes, M.P., Ricci, A., eds.: Engineering Societies in the Agents World VI, 6th International Workshop, ESAW 2005. Volume 3963 of Lecture Notes in Computer Science., Springer-Verlag (2006) 63–88

25. Weyns, D., Schelfthout, K., Holvoet, T., Lefever, T.: Decentralized Control of E'GV Transportation Systems. In: AAMAS Industrial Applications, ACM Press (2005) 67–74

26. Gilbert, N., Troitzsch, K.G.: Simulation for the Social Scientist (second edition). Open University Press (2005)

27. Pyka, A., Fagiolo, G.:   Agent-Based Modelling: A Methodology for Neo-Schumpeterian Economics. In: The Elgar Companion to Neo-Schumpeterian Economics. Edward Elgar (in press)

28. Klügl, F., Fehler, M., Herrler, R.: About the Role of the Environment in Multi-Agent Simulations. In Weyns, D., Parunak, H.V.D., Michel, F., eds.: Environments for Multi-Agent Systems, First International Workshop, E4MAS 2004, New York, NY, USA, July 19, 2004, Revised Selected Papers. Volume 3374. (2005) 127–149

29. Gouaich, A., Michel, F., Guiraud, Y.: MIC*: a Deployment Environment for Autonomous Agents. In: Environments for Multi-Agent Systems, First International Workshop (E4MAS 2004). Volume 3374 of Lecture Notes in Computer Science., Springer–Verlag (2005) 109–126

30. Weyns, D., Vizzari, G., Holvoet, T.: Environments for Situated Multi-Agent Systems: Beyond Infrastructure. In Weyns, D., Parunak, H.V.D., Michel, F., eds.: Environments for Multi-Agent Systems II, Second International Workshop, E4MAS 2005, Utrecht, The Netherlands, July 25, 2005, Selected Revised and Invited Papers. Volume 3830 of Lecture Notes in Computer Science., Springer–Verlag (2006) 1–17

31. Weyns, D., Parunak, H.V.D., Michel, F., Holvoet, T., Ferber, J.: Environments for Multiagent Systems State-of-the-Art and Research Challenges. In: Environments for Multi-Agent Systems, First International Workshop (E4MAS 2004). Volume 3374 of Lecture Notes in Computer Science., Springer–Verlag (2005) 1–47

32. Ferber, J., Müller, J.P.: Influences and Reaction: a Model of Situated Multiagent Systems. In: Proceedings of the 2th International Conference on Multi-agent Systems, AAAI Press (1996) 72–79

33. Weyns, D., Holvoet, T.: A Formal Model for Situated Multi-Agent Systems. Fundamenta Informticae **63** (2004) 125–158

34. Klüpfel, H.: A Cellular Automaton Model for Crowd Movement and Egress Simulation. PhD thesis, University Duisburg-Essen (2003)

35. Bandini, S., Manzoni, S., Vizzari, G.: Situated Agents Interaction: Coordinated Change of State for Adjacent Agents. In Malyshkin, V.E., ed.: Parallel Computing Technologies, 8th International Conference, PaCT 2005. Volume 3606 of Lecture Notes in Computer Science., Springer–Verlag (2005) 114–128

36. Helleboogh, A., Vizzari, G., Uhrmacher, A., Michel, F.: Modeling Dynamic Environments in Multi-Agent Simulation. Autonomous Agents and Multi-Agent Systems **14** (2007) 87–116

Establishing Global Properties of Multi-Agent Systems Via Local Laws

Wenxuan Zhang, Constantin Serban, and Naftaly Minsky

Department of Computer Science,
Rutgers University, Piscataway, NJ 08854, USA
{wzhang,serban,minsky}@cs.rutgers.edu

Abstract. This paper is part of a long term research program on multi-agent systems (MASs), based on the proposition that the interactions among the members of a large and heterogeneous system of autonomous agents need to be governed by a global and strictly enforced *law*; and that such laws need to be *local*, so that they can be complied with at the locus of each agent—without having any direct information of the coincidental state of other members of the MAS. Such concept of law has been realized under our LGI coordination and control mechanism.

This paper shows how local laws over a MAS can be used to establish global and *aggregate* system properties in a scalable manner; where by "aggregate properties" we mean properties defined over the coincidental interactions among several, possibly many, members of a given multi-agent system.

1 Introduction

This paper is part of a long term research program on multi-agent systems (MASs), based on the proposition that the interactions among the members of a large and heterogeneous system of autonomous agents—whether software agents or people—need to be governed by a global, overarching, *law*; and on the proposition that such a law needs to be enforced, and the enforcement should be done in a decentralized manner, for scalability.

As we have shown in [1], decentralized enforcement of a law of a distributed MAS requires the law to be formulated in a *local* manner, so that it can be complied with at the locus of each agent—without having any direct information of the coincidental state of other members of the MAS. Given that the law of a MAS is to be uniformly enforced over all the members of the MAS, it obviously has global consequences, despite its local nature. This is analogous to the local (differential) laws of physics, which have global consequences such as conservation of energy.

But can a local law be used to establish *aggregate* system properties, defined over the coincidental interactions among several, possibly many, members of a given multi-agent system. This is the question addressed in this paper.

D. Weyns, H.V.D. Parunak, and F. Michel (Eds.): E4MAS 2006, LNAI 4389, pp. 170–183, 2007.

Theoretically, the answer to this question is affirmative. In fact, we have shown in [2] that the local formulation of laws does not reduce their expressive power. But this result has been derived via a construction that adds an extra agent to a given MAS, which is employed as a centralized *reference monitor* that mediates all interactions between the members of the MAS, and can thus enforce arbitrary aggregate properties. Unfortunately, while formally local, the resulting law would not be scalable, defeating the purpose of localization. This makes the theoretical proved generality of local laws less than satisfying.

This paper is a more practical study of the effective expressive power of local laws. We will demonstrate here that at least some—and we believe many, if not most—aggregate properties of a MAS can be implemented via strictly local laws, involving only a minor degree of centralization, whose effect on the scalability of law enforcement is negligible.

We couch our discussion of this issue in terms of the coordination and control mechanism for multi-agent systems called *law-governed interaction* (LGI), which has been designed according to the above stated propositions. This mechanism has been introduced in 1991 [1], implemented experimentally in 1995 [3]; and after several extensions, such as in [2], it has been released for public use in [4].

The rest of this paper is organized as follows. We start in Sect. 2 with a motivating example of a policy that involves aggregate properties. In Sect. 3 we provide an overview of the LGI mechanism. In Sect. 4 we show how the aggregate properties of our example can be established by means of an LGI law. This is followed with brief discussion of related works in Sect. 5, and with conclusion in Sect. 6.

2   An Example

Consider a large distributed enterprise E, which spans a large geographical area. Suppose that the management of this enterprise decided to provide its employees with the ability to conduct confidential and orderly discussions among themselves, free from any danger of intervention or eavesdropping by the management. For this purpose, a policy called CD (for "confidential discussion") has been defined, which is to govern all such discussion groups, to be called CD-communities. The policy CD is stated informally below:

1. *Only employees of enterprise E who do not belong to management are permitted to be members of a CD-community.*
2. *The members of a given CD-community address each other via their self-chosen aliases, and members cannot infer the eName of its peers, or their LGI-addresses, from their aliases.*
3. *The alias chosen by a member of a CD-community must be unique, in the following senses: (a) no two community members can have the same alias; and (b) each employee can choose just one alias, preventing a single employee from participating under two different aliases.*
4. *Each community member should have access to the entire membership of his community (that is, to the entire list of aliases) at any given moment in time.*

Points 1 of this policy ensures that people not employed by the given enterprise, or people employed by the enterprise as managers, cannot participate in any CD-community, nor can they eavesdrop on any discussion within such a community. Note that this point involves a subtle sensitivity to the environment in which this community operates, sensitivity of the general kind advocated in [5] (we will support this particular sensitivity by means of digital certification). Point 2 ensures anonymity of the participants in any given CD-community, and thus personal confidentiality. Finally, Points 3 and 4, ensure a reasonable order in the discussion conducted by the members of a given CD-community. (All told, this is a minimalistic policy, which, as we shall see later, can be used as a basis over which more sophisticated policies can be defined).

Note that this is a global policy, with some inherently aggregate provisions, such as Point 3 of this policy that requires uniqueness of member aliases, and Point 4 which requires access of each member to the total community membership. This policy can be easily enforced via a central regulator that mediates all exchange of messages between members of an CD-community. But we will show that it can be done in a virtually decentralized, and thus scalable, manner, by specifying policy CD via a local LGI law.

Finally, we point out that that this is not just a toy example, as it deals with issues that appear frequently in multi-agent systems. Some broader perspectives over this example are discussed in Sect. 4.1.

3   An Overview of LGI

Law-Governed Interaction (LGI) is a message-exchange mechanism that allows an open and heterogeneous group of distributed *actors* to engage in a mode of interaction *governed* by an explicitly specified and strictly enforced policy, called the "law" of this group. By "actor" we mean an arbitrary process, whose structure and behavior is left unspecified. An actor engaged in an LGI-regulated interaction, under a law $\mathcal{L}$, is called an $\mathcal{L}$-*agent* (or simply an "agent," when the identity of the law does not matter); the messages exchanged under a given law $\mathcal{L}$ are called $\mathcal{L}$-messages; and the group of agents interacting via $\mathcal{L}$-messages is called an $\mathcal{L}$-community. LGI turns a set of disparate actors, which may not know or trust each other, into a *community* of agents that can rely on each other to comply with the given law $\mathcal{L}$. This is done via a distributed collection of generic components called *private controllers*, one per $\mathcal{L}$-agent, which need to be *trusted* to mediate all interactions between these agents, subject to a specified law $\mathcal{L}$ (as illustrated in Figure 1).

A prototype of LGI was released in October 2005 [4]; this section provides only a very brief overview of LGI. For more information, the reader is referred to the LGI tutorial and manual, available through the above mentioned website, and to a host of published papers.

The Concept of Law Under LGI. LGI laws are formulated in terms of three elements, called: *regulated events*, *control-state*, and *primitive operations*—which are defined in the context of each agent operating under LGI. Only an abstract description of these elements is provided here.

Regulated Events (or, simply, *events*) constitute the *domain* of LGI laws. They are the local events that may occur at an individual agent (called the *home* of the event at hand), whose disposition is governed by the law under which this agent operates. All regulated events are related to inter-agent interactions. They include *arrived* events, which represent the arrival at the home agent of a message from the outside; and *sent* events, which represent the attempt by the home agent to send a message. There are additional regulated events whose relevance to interaction is less direct. One of them is the *adopted* event, which represents the *birth* of an LGI agent—more specifically, this event represents the point in time when an actor adopts a given law $\mathcal{L}$ to operate under, thus becoming an $\mathcal{L}$-agent.

Control-State (or, simply, *state*) of a given LGI agent represents a function of the history of its interaction with other LGI agents. This function, mapping history of interaction to a state, is defined by a specific law. For example, if the number of messages already sent by a agent is somehow relevant to the law under which it operates, then this law would have to mandate maintaining this number as part of its state. That is, the semantics of the control-state is not universal, but is defined by a specific law.

Primitive Operations (or, simply, *operations*) are the actions that can be mandated by a law, to be carried out in response to the occurrence of a given regulated event. These operations can be classified into two groups. First, there are *communication-operations* that affect message exchange between the home-actor and others. These include the *forward* operation that forwards a message to another agent, and the *deliver* operation that allows the home-actor to actually receive a message that arrived on its behalf. Second, there are the *state-operations* that affect the state of the home-agent. These, and other operations to be introduced later, are called "primitive" because they are meant to be carried out *if and only if* they are mandated by the law.

The role of a law $\mathcal{L}$ under LGI is to decide what should be done if a given event e occurs at an agent x operating under this law, when the control-state of x is s. This decision, which is called the *ruling of the law*, can be represented by the sequence of primitive operations mandated by the law, to be carried out, atomically, at x. More formally, the concept of law can be defined as follows:

Let E be the set of all possible regulated-events, let S be the set of all possible states, and let O be the set of all primitive operations, then a law $\mathcal{L}$ is a function:

$$\mathcal{L} : E \times S \to O^* \tag{1}$$

In other words, *the law maps every possible (event, state) pair into a sequence of primitive operations, which constitute the* ruling *of the law.*

Several observation about this definition are in order: First, this definition does not specify any mechanism for enforcing LGI-laws, and does not even require enforcement. Indeed, the concept of law under LGI, like the concept of social law, is quite meaningful even if one leaves it up to individual agents to comply with it voluntarily. In our case such compliance means, in particular, that every agent subject to a law $\mathcal{L}$ carries out the ruling of this law for every regulated event that occurs in it. However, LGI does provide an enforcement mechanism for its laws.

Second, the above definition of the concept of law is *abstract*, in that it does not depend on the language used for specifying the function that constitutes a given law. This level of abstraction is useful for two reasons. First, it allows one to understand the basic properties of LGI, independently of the complexities of the language used for specifying its laws. Second, this abstraction provides LGI with a useful flexibility regarding the language actually used for specifying laws. In particular, it allows LGI to support multiple *law-languages*, while maintaining essentially the same semantics. Indeed, the current implementation of LGI supports two law-languages, based, respectively, on Prolog and on Java. In this paper, however, we will use an informal pseudo-code for describing laws, to be introduced later.

Finally, note that, as stated in the introduction, the law as defined above is *local*, so that it can be complied with at the locus of each agent—without having any direct information of the coincidental state of other members of the MAS. This is because all the elements over which the law is defined—namely, the events, the operations and the state—are all defined locally at each agent.

An Informal Language for Specifying Laws. In this paper laws will be described via a pseudo-code consisting of *event-condition-action* rules, which is similar to the formal Prolog-based law language of LGI.

The *event-condition-action* rules that constitute the pseudo-code have the form:

```
UPON e IF c DO [o],
```

where e is an event; c is an optional condition, defined over the event itself, and over the state of the home-agent; and [o], the action, is a list of one or more primitive operations, which constitute the ruling of the law.

The Decentralized Law-Enforcement of LGI. The enforcement of a given law over the community is carried out by a distributed set $\{T_x | x \in C\}$ of *controllers*, one for each member of community C. Structurally, all these controllers are generic, with the same law-enforcer $\mathcal{E}$, and all must be trusted to interpret correctly any law they might operate under. When serving members of community C_L, however, they all carry the *same law* $\mathcal{L}$. And each controller T_x associated with an agent x of this community carries only the *local control-state* CSx of x, while every $\mathcal{L}$-message exchanged between a pair of agents x and y passes through a pair of controllers, T_x and T_y (see Fig 1).

Due to the local nature of LGI laws, each controller T_x can handle events that occur at its client x strictly locally, with no explicit dependency on anything that might be happening with other members in the community. It should also be

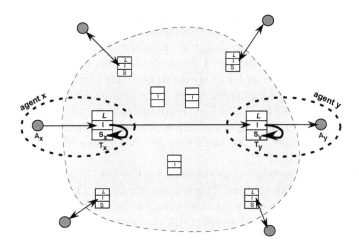

Fig. 1. Interaction via LGI: Actors are depicted by circles, interacting across the Internet (lightly shaded cloud) via their private controllers (boxes) operating under law L. Agents are depicted by dashed ovals that enclose (actor, controller) pairs. Thin arrows represent messages, and thick arrows represent modification of state.

pointed out that controller T_x handles the events at x strictly sequentially, in the order of their occurrence, and atomically. Finally we point out that the law-enforcement mechanism ensures that a message received under law L has been sent under the same law; i.e., that it is not possible to forge $\mathcal{L}$-messages. As described in [6], this is assured by the following: (a) The exchange of $\mathcal{L}$-messages is mediated by correctly implemented controllers, certified by a CA specified by law $\mathcal{L}$; (b) these controllers are interpreting the *same law* $\mathcal{L}$, identified by a one-way hash H of law $\mathcal{L}$; and (c) $\mathcal{L}$-messages are transmitted over crypto-graphically secured channels between such controllers. Consequently, how each member x gets the text of law $\mathcal{L}$ is irrelevant to the assurance that all members of C_L operate under the same law.

The creation of LGI-agents, and their naming. Given a controller T, an actor A may generate a new $\mathcal{L}$-agent by sending what is called an *adoption* message to T, thus adopting it for operating its controller, under a specified law $\mathcal{L}$. In response, T would create a new controller, subject to law $\mathcal{L}$, identifying it by a local name n (unique among the names given to the other private controllers already operating on T).

This new controller, and the agent it represents, are henceforth known by the name ``n@dName(T)'' where dName(T) is the domain-name of the controller $T$, such as ``ramses.rutgers.edu''. This name—for example joe@ramses.rutgers. edu—is the *LGI address* of the newly formed agent, to be used by other agents for communicating with it.

The Hierarchical Organization of Laws. LGI provides for laws to be organized into hierarchies, a facility designed for the modularization of complex laws, and to support such things as coalitions of institutions, and complex organizations such as enterprises. A hierarchy, or tree, of laws $t(\mathcal{L}_0)$, is rooted in some law $\mathcal{L}_0$. Each law in $t(\mathcal{L}_0)$ is said to be (transitively) subordinate to its parent, and (transitively) superior to its descendants. Given a pair of laws $\mathcal{N}$ and $\mathcal{M}$ in $t(\mathcal{L}_0)$, we write $\mathcal{N} \prec \mathcal{M}$ if $\mathcal{N}$ is subordinate to $\mathcal{M}$.

Semantically, the most important aspect of this hierarchy is that if $\mathcal{N} \prec \mathcal{M}$ then $\mathcal{N}$ *conforms* to $\mathcal{M}$, in the sense that law $\mathcal{N}$ satisfies all the stipulation of its superior law $\mathcal{M}$.

LGI provides a very efficient mechanism, outlined in [7], for constructing such law-trees, in a top-down manner. This is done as follows. The root $\mathcal{L}_0$ of a hierarchy is a normal LGI law, except that we create it to be *open* for refinements, by: (a) allowing it to consult a collection of rules designed to refine it—called a *delta*; and (b) taking the advice returned by this delta into account, when computing its ruling. The refinement of law $\mathcal{L}$ via the delta produces a regular LGI law $\mathcal{L}'$. $\mathcal{L}'$ could be closed to further refinements—which produces a hierarchy of depth two; or $\mathcal{L}'$ could further consult other deltas at a lower level, thus producing a cascade of refinements, and a hierarchy of arbitrary depth. In brief, each law $\mathcal{L}'$ in a hierarchy $t(\mathcal{L}_0)$ is created by *refining* a law $\mathcal{L}$, the parent of $\mathcal{L}'$, via a *delta* $\bar{\mathcal{L}}'$, a collection of rules[1].

4   A Virtually Decentralized Implementation of the CD Policy

We describe here a law $\mathcal{L}_{CD}$ that implements the informally stated policy CD introduced in Sect. 2. For simplicity, this law is written in our pseudo-code language. This law is also overly simplistic, in that it does not handle exceptions, which is important to do when dealing with message passing, and for which LGI provides ample tools, and it is missing certain minor details, as we point out later. However, a completed version of this law, written in our executable Java-based law-language, is published via http://www.moses.rutgers.edu/lcd1/Lcd.java1.

The $\mathcal{L}_{CD}$ law is written under the assumption that the enterprise E in question employs a certification authority (CA), called eCA, which issues identity-certificates to its employees. Each such certificate is supposed to authenticate an employee, identifying his official name in the enterprise, called his $eName$, which we assume to be unique; and specifying the position of this employee in the enterprise, such as whether he or she is a manager.

We start with a brief overview of the structure and behavior of the community operating under $\mathcal{L}_{CD}$. First, this community contains a distinguished agent called the *secretary*, denoted by S, which serves both as the registrar of the community, and its name-server. The secretary maintains in its control-state (CS) a set of

---

[1] This is somewhat analogous to inheritance of classes, except of the strict constraint of conformance between a superior law and its subordinates.

member profiles, each represented by a triple $\langle N, A, L \rangle$, where N is the eName of an employee, A is the alias by which this member is to be known to others in this community, and L is the LGI-address used for communication by the underlying LGI mechanism. The aggregation of these profiles in the CS of S would allow law $\mathcal{L}_{CD}$ to ensure the uniqueness required by Point 3 of our policy.

The other members of this community communicate with the secretary S, mostly for two purposes: (a) to register with it, thus becoming an *active* member of the community; and (b) to get from S the *ID* of other community members, where the *ID* is a pair $\langle A, L \rangle$, which is the member-profile of that member, as maintained by S , without its *eName*. Each community member maintains in its control-state a set (cache) of such IDs, called the *acquaintance list* (or *aList*) of this agent. This cache maps aliases, used for explicit addressing of members under this law, into the the LGI-addresses used by the underlying LGI mechanism. We will see later how the aList is populated, but as long as one communicates with members whose alias exists in one's aList, the communication is direct, and does not involve the secretary.

We will now discuss the operations of the *CD*-community in greater details, showing how it is governed by law $\mathcal{L}_{CD}$. This discussion is organized into a sequence of short paragraphs dealing with different aspects of this community, such as: joining the community, interacting with peer agents, and leaving the community. But we start with law $\mathcal{L}_{CD}$ itself.

Law $\mathcal{L}_{CD}$ that Governs Confidential Discussion Communities. Like all LGI laws, law $\mathcal{L}_{CD}$, displayed in Figure 2, consists of two parts: the *preamble*, and the *body*. The preamble is a small set of declarative clauses, which specify such things as: the name of the law ("CD," in this case); the language in which the law is written (not specified here, but could be either Prolog or Java); one or more trusted CAs, identified by their name under this law, and by their public keys (this is done for "eCA," in this case); and some aliases, used to simplify notations[2] (in this case, the alias "secretary" for the LGI-address of the agent that serves this role).

The body of the law is its algorithmic part. In this paper, the body is described by a sequence of numbered, and informally stated, event-condition-action rules, as defined in Sect. 3. Each of these rules is followed by a comment, in italic. These rules are executed by the controller associated with each agent, whenever a regulated event occurs at this agent; these rules are executed sequentially, from top to bottom. The rules of this particular law are discussed in some detail below.

Joining the CD community. Two steps are required for an employee e to join a *CD*-community, and be able to communicate with its other members. The first step would create a new $\mathcal{L}_{CD}$-agent whose control-state contains the authenticated eName of its actor, provided that this actor is a normal employee of enterprise E, and not a manager. But this new agent is *inactive*, as it cannot communicate with other members of the *CD*-community, except the secretary S.

---

[2] Note that the keyword "alias" here is not the "alias" used elsewhere in the paper.

Preambles:
law(CD)   *The name of the law*
authority(eCA, keyHash(hash–of–key–of–eCA))   *The CA trusted by the enterprise*
alias(secretary, secretary@rutgers.edu)   *The address of the secretary*

R1. UPON adopted(issuer, subject, attributes([entName:eName;position:position]))
         IF (issuer = eCA) and (position =/= manager) DO [myEName = eName]
         ELSE self–destruct
         END IF
The home agent must be authenticated upon adoption in order to join the community.

R2. UPON sent(source, join(eName,alias), secretary)
         IF (myEName = eName) DO [forward]
The home agent applies to be an active member,
by sending a message including its eName and a proposed alias to the secretary.

R3. UPON arrived(secretary, activate(alias), dest)
         DO [deliver; active = true; myAlias = alias]
The home agent is activated to be an active member.

R4. UPON sent(source, getID(alias), secretary)
         IF (active = true) DO [forward]
The home agent looks up the ID of another agent, by its alias.

R5. UPON arrived(secretary, id(alias, LGIAddress), dest)
         IF (active = true) DO [save id(alias,LGIAddress) in aList]
The home agent gets the ID from the secretary, and saves it in the local aList.

R6. UPON sent(source, M, destAlias)
         IF (active = true)
             destLGIAddress = getAddressFromAList(destAlias)
             IF (destLGIAddress is not null)
                 enhancedMessage = msg(source(myAlias), dest(destAlias), M)
                 DO[forward(source, enhancedMessage, destLGIAddress)]
             END IF
         END IF
When an actor attempts to send a message to another agent,
the controller would forward the message only if the home agent is an active member,
and it would piggyback the aliases of both the sender and the receiver on the message.

R7. UPON arrived(source, msg(source(sourceAlias),dest(destAlias),M), dest)
         IF (active = true) and (myAlias = destAlias)
             DO[deliver(sourceAlias,M,destAlias)]
             IF (the ID of the source agent is not in aList)
                 update aList
             END IF
         ELSE
             return an exception message to the source agent
         END IF
When the message arrives at the home agent, the controller would deliver the message
only if the home agent is an active member, and is the intended destination;
it would update the local aList if the ID of the source agent is not included.

R8. UPON sent(source, quit(eName), secretary)
         IF (myEName = eName) and (active = true) DO [forward; quit]
The home agent leaves the community.

Fig. 2. A fragment of $\mathcal{L}_{CD}$

The second step, if successful, would activate the agent in question, by providing it with an official *alias*, and allowing it to communicate with its peers.

The first step is to select an LGI-controller, and have it adopt law $\mathcal{L}_{CD}$—thus creating a new $\mathcal{L}_{CD}$-agent, which we call here x. The first event in the life of the new agent is the *adopted* event, handled by Rule R1 of $\mathcal{L}_{CD}$. This rule requires the adoption message sent by e to its controller to contain a certificate signed by eCA, and this certificate is required to contain two attributes: `position` and `entName`.

Now, if the value of the `position` attribute in the submitted certificate is not `manager` then the value of the `entName` attribute is assigned to the `myEName` variable of the CS of x. But if the position attribute of the certificate indicates that this employee is a manager, then Rule R1 will cause an exception message to be sent to employee e (not shown in Figure 2), and the newly formed LGI-agent would self destruct. This is in conformance with Point 1 of the CD policy, which allows only non-management employees to participate in this community.

At this point the newly created agent x is *inactive*, in the sense that it cannot do anything but send a message `join(eName,alias)` to the secretary S—which is the second step of joining an $\mathcal{L}_{CD}$-community. The event of sending the `join` message is handled by Rule R2 of $\mathcal{L}_{CD}$, which ensures that the first argument of this message is identical to the variable `myEName`, and is thus the authenticated *eName* of the employee in question.

Note that the rules of law $\mathcal{L}_{CD}$ that deal with the arrival of messages (such as `join`) at S, and with the responses of S to such messages, are not shown in Fig. 2, for simplicity[3] But the effect of sending the `join` message to S is as follows: when this message arrives at S, S would check that both the `eName` and the `alias` are unique in the CD community. Note that these condition—required by Point 3 of the CD policy—are checked with respect to the set of member-profiles, of all active community members, maintained by the secretary. If this condition is satisfied, S would send the message `activate(alias)` to x.

When a message `activate(alias)`, sent by S, arrives at x, it would be handled by Rule R3. This rule would save the value of `alias` in a variable `myAlias` in the CS of x; and it would set a variable `active` in the CS of x to be *true*. This would make x a fully active member of the CD-community, as we shall see below.

Populating the Acquaintance List (aList). As has already been pointed out, for a member x to be able to send a message to another member y, it needs to have its *ID* $\langle alias, LGIaddress \rangle$ in its *aList*, which serves the role of an addressing cache. This cache is populated in two ways:

First, by requesting, and obtaining, an *ID*, or a whole set of them, from the secretary. As depicted in Fig. 3, an active member x can send S a message `getID(y)`, where `y` is an alias of the member whose *ID* is being requested. The sending of this message is handled by Rule R4, which forwards it to S, provided that x is an active member. The secretary will reply by sending x the requested

---

[3] Note again that the complete law $\mathcal{L}_{CD}$ is published through
http://www.moses.rutgers.edu/lcd1/Lcd.java1

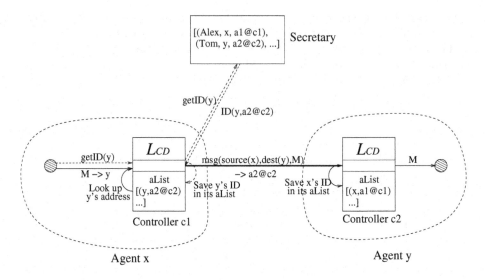

Fig. 3. Communication between two active members

ID, if any. When this reply arrives at *x*, it would be handled by Rule R5, which would store the new *ID* in the CS of *x*. In a similar fashion *x* can ask for the set of IDs of all current members of the community (but this capability is not shown in Figure 2).

The second way for the *ID* of *y* to be added to the *aList* of *x*, is for *y* to send any message to *x*. We will see how this is done next.

Communication Between the Members of a CD-Community. Exchange of messages among members of the *CD*-community are regulated by Rules R6 and R7. By R6, a message M sent to `destAlias` would not be forwarded to anybody if (a) if the sender is not an active member, or (b) if the sender does not have an *ID* ⟨*destAlias*, *L*⟩ in its *aList*. However, if both of these conditions are not satisfied; that is, if the sender is an active member, and if it does have the right *ID*, then the following message would be forwarded to the LGI-address L associated with the `destAlias`:

`msg(source(myAlias),dest(destAlias),M).`

Note that this message carries the aliases of the sender and of the target, along with the original message M—it is called an "enhanced message".

By Rule R7, when the enhanced message arrives at its target *y* the message M carried by it is delivered to its actor only if (a) *y* is an active agent, and if (b) *y* is the agent identified by the `destAlias` carried in the enhanced message. Also, if the *aList* of *y* does not contain the *ID* of the sender, then this *ID* will be added to it. However, if either of these conditions is not satisfied, then an appropriate exception message would be sent to the sender. We will not elaborate here on the various possible reasons for the above to conditions to fail. But one of them is that an employee may change the LGI-address from which it operates. More about this possibility below.

Migration of Agents. An important advantage of symbolic addressing via aliases, is that it abstracts out the actual IP-address from which one operates. This allows an employee to migrate, from one computer (and controller) to another, without requiring any change in how he is addressed by others. But, such migration requires the member profile maintained by the secretary to be updated. This is done as follows:

After an agent moves from one controller to another, its actor must submit its certificate again, to the new controller. If the certificate is valid, the agent would be authenticated as an enterprise employee and the controller would be able to obtain its eName. Then the agent would inform S about the address changing, by sending a message updateAddress(myEName). S would be able to locate the ID of the agent by the eName and thus update its LGI address. Also, S would reply a message to the agent, in order to activate it to be an active member, and to provide the alias it registered before.

Quitting the CD Community. An active member may remove itself from the CD community at will. It does this by sending a message quit(eName) to S, who will identify this member by its eName, then remove it from the list of active members.

By Rule **R8**, when sending the message, the law ensures that (1) eName has been bound to the variable myEName, the certified eName of the home agent, and (2) the value of the variable active is true, which means the home agent is an active member of the CD community. The home agent will quit the community by executing the quit operation, after the message is sent.

4.1   Broader Perspectives

Law $\mathcal{L}_{CD}$ is only a special case of a class of laws that can be used in a wide range of applications. We will mention here two types of such applications, both of which employ the hierarchical organization of laws provided by LGI, and briefly discussed in Sect. 3.

Confidential Discussion Groups Operating under Different Rules of Engagement. Elaborating on the motivation given in Sect. 2 for the CD policy, suppose that different groups of employees in enterprise E would like to operate under different kinds of rules of engagement, while conforming to the CD policy mandated by the enterprise. One group may want to restrict its members to a specific department, another group may want to establish a version of the Robert's Rules of Order suitable for electronic discussion, and a third group may want to support some kind of secure voting protocol.

This can be done by changing law $\mathcal{L}_{CD}$ into an equivalent law $\mathcal{L}_{CD}$' that admits refinements. The above mentioned refinements can then be defined as subordinate laws to $\mathcal{L}_{CD}$', which would thus be guaranteed to conform to the enterprise mandated CD policy. The mechanism for creating such refinements is beyond the scope of this paper, but the interested reader can find the necessary details in [7].

Symbolic Addressing. The symbolic addressing via aliases provided by law $\mathcal{L}_{CD}$ could be useful in general, and not just in the context of an enterprise. This is because the LGI-addressing is dependent on the absolute IP-address of the the controller being used by a given actor, and is difficult to maintain invariant of the location of the actors itself, which may be mobile. One can provide for symbolic addressing, by removing from $\mathcal{L}_{CD}'$ the part that requires authentication via certificate signed by a specified CA, but allowing it to be further refined, as discussed above. This would allow the creation of arbitrary laws that conform to the symbolic addressing capability of $\mathcal{L}_{CD}'$.

5   Related Work

The LGI coordination and control mechanism for multi-agent systems has been introduced in 1991 [1]. In the years following this work, several authors considered the role of laws in multi-agent systems. Some of these, like [8]and [9], view a law of a MAS as purely a specification device, without any enforcement mechanism. Others, such as [10], [11] and [12], did consider enforcement, but not in a decentralized manner. Moreover, none of these authors used local laws, which we consider essential to any coordination and control mechanism for multi-agent systems.

The literature regarding name services, which is the subject of the specific example used in this paper, is very rich. Suffice it to mention the most prominent name service, in current Internet infrastructure, the Domain Name System (DNS) [13]. But most of the standard name services, including DNS, do not provide any control over the community it serves, which is the main advantage of our approach to this issue.

6   Conclusion

The main objective of this paper has been to demonstrate that a regulatory mechanism for agent-based systems, which is based on strictly local laws, can be used to establish globally aggregate system properties with only minor effect on scalability.

In conclusion, we note that although this paper has bean couched in term of the LGI mechanism that enforces laws, its implication are not limited to LGI. Indeed, as we have pointed out, the concept of LGI law can be used for multi-agent systems, even if one leaves it up to individual agents to comply with the given law voluntarily. Since voluntary compliance also requires the law to be local, the ability of such laws to establish aggregate properties is important in this context as well.

References

1. Minsky, N.H.: The imposition of protocols over open distributed systems. IEEE Transactions on Software Engineering (February 1991)
2. Minsky, N.H., Ungureanu, V.: Law-governed interaction: a coordination and control mechanism for heterogeneous distributed systems. TOSEM, ACM Transactions on Software Engineering and Methodology 9(3) (July 2000) 273–305 (available from http://www.cs.rutgers.edu/~minsky/pubs.html).
3. Minsky, N.H., Leichter, J.: Law-governed Linda as a coordination model. In Ciancarini, P., Nierstrasz, O., Yonezawa, A., eds.: Object-Based Models and Languages for Concurrent Systems. Number 924 in Lecture Notes in Computer Science. Springer-Verlag (1995) 125–146
4. Serban, C., Minsky, N.H.: The lgi web-site (includes the implementation of lgi, and its manual). Technical report, Rutgers University (June 2005) (available at http://www.moses.rutgers.edu).
5. Weyns, D., Omicini, A., Odell, J.: Environment as a first class abstraction in multiagent systems. Journal on Autonomous Agents and Multiagent Systems 14(1) (January 2007)
6. Minsky, N.H.: Law Governed Interaction (LGI): A Distributed Coordination and Control Mechanism (An Introduction, and a Reference Manual). (June 2005) (available at http://www.moses.rutgers.edu/documentation/manual.pdf).
7. Ao, X., Minsky, N.H.: Flexible regulation of distributed coalitions. In: LNCS 2808: the Proc. of the European Symposium on Research in Computer Security (ESORICS) 2003. (October 2003) (available from http://www.cs.rutgers.edu/~minsky/pubs.html).
8. Shoham, Y., Tennenholz, M.: On the synthesis of useful social laws for artificial agents societies. In: Proceedings of AAAI-92. (1992)
9. Zambonelli, F., Jennings, N.R., Wooldridge, M.: Developing multiagent systems: the gaia methodology. ACM Transactions on Software Engineering and Methodology (TOSEM) (July 2003)
10. Esteva, M., de la Cruz, D., Sierra, C.: Islander: an electronic institutions editor. In: Proceedings of Conference on Autonomous Agents and Multi-Agent Systems (AAMAS). (2002)
11. Gatti, A., Lucena, C., Brio, J.: On fault tolerance in law-governed multi-agent systems. In: Proc. of ICSE'05, 4th Int. Workshop on Soft. Eng. for Large-Scale Multi-Agent Systems, ACM (July 2006)
12. Artikis, A., Sergot, M., Pitt, J.: Specifying norm-governed computational societies. Technical report, Department of Computing, Imperial College of Science Technology and Medicine, London (2006)
13. Mockapetris, P.: Domain names - concepts and facilities. (available at ftp://ftp.is.co.za/rfc/rfc1034.txt) (Nov. 1987)

E4MAS Through Electronic Institutions

Josep Lluís Arcos, Pablo Noriega, Juan A. Rodríguez-Aguilar,
and Carles Sierra

IIIA, Artificial Intelligence Research Institute
CSIC, Spanish National Research Council
08193 Bellaterra, Spain
{arcos,pablo,jar,sierra}@iiia.csic.es

Abstract. Today, the concept of an environment for multi-agent systems is in its pioneering phase. Consequently, the development of supporting software technologies is still rather primitive and environment technologies reflecting a specific world-of-interest to the agent systems are yet to be developed in full. In contrast, environment technologies that focus on the agent system itself have been in the agenda of MAS research from its very start. Electronic institutions are prominent in this respect for they have been conceived as a type of restricted MAS environment and have had an engineering technology developed around them. In this paper we explore how the restrictions currently imposed by electronic institutions may be overcome when they are seen as a part of a larger environment where agents act. In particular, we focus on *situating* electronic institutions by connecting them to a world-of-interest and how this process can facilitate full-fledged environment engineering.

1   Introduction

It has become increasingly clear that the applicability of agent technologies requires not only appropriate software agents but also taking into account the environment where those agents interact. In fact, in many cases the design and implementation of the environment is the crucial aspect of an application. The motivation for such focus is readily seen when the purpose of the MAS is to specify the conventions that structure or organize the interactions of participants –as when defining an electronic marketplace or what economist do with mechanism design— when one intends to use MAS technologies either to model social phenomena —as, for example, traffic behaviour— or when testing or experimenting with the uses just mentioned.

In this paper we are concerned with a particular type of environment, electronic institutions (e-Institutions), that can be used for all these purposes. We claim that e-Institutions are well-suited for applications involving "open" multi agent systems and we have three main developments around the idea of e-Institutions that allow us to sustain that claim. First a conceptual model that makes explicit the type of multi-agent systems that may be implemented as EI, second a language to specify arbitrary e-Institutions and, third, the tools

D. Weyns, H.V.D. Parunak, and F. Michel (Eds.): E4MAS 2006, LNAI 4389, pp. 184–202, 2007.
© Springer-Verlag Berlin Heidelberg 2007

to implement and run e-Institutions specified with that language. This paper presents these three developments and explores how they may be put to work in order to design and use artificial environments where human or software agents may interact according to an explicit set of conventions. The paper, however, is not limited to discussing e-Institutions. It goes a step further and explores the possibility of operationalising the environment where the e-Institution exists and the relation between the institution and that world. Although we have discussed some empirical aspects of establishing the links between an e-Institution and the world (cf. [10]) and presented some details on how the linking was implemented in specific examples ([20,19]), in this paper we want to focus on two aspects that we have not discussed in print before: on the one hand we will explain how we can use environment technologies to "situate" an e-Institution within its "world-of-interest", and on the other hand we will present the tools and means to build simulation environments for situated e-Institutions.

For these purposes the rest of the paper is structured as follows: First we present our three main developments on e-Institutions, namely, Sect. 2 discusses our conceptual model, Sect. 3 the way of specifying e-Institutions and, in Sect. 4, the way we make such e-Institutions operate. We then present, in Sect. 5, our ideas on situating e-Institutions in a world-of-interest, how those environments may be characterized and simulated (Sect. 6). We close the paper contrasting our proposal with some of the notions about environments discussed elsewhere in this volume.

2   A Conceptual Model for Electronic Institutions

Loosely speaking, e-Institutions are computational realizations of traditional institutions (cf. North [12] pp. 3 ss.); that is, coordination artifacts that establish an environment where agents interact according to stated conventions, and in such a way that interactions within the (electronic) institution would *count as* interactions in the actual world, as Fig. 1 illustrates.

The notion of e-Institution may be expressed more precisely by stating a conceptual model of e-Institutions that gives ground for their computational implementation. In order to make the conceptual model operational we hold the following assumptions:

1. *Agent neutrality.* Participating entities are agents, in the accepted sense of being persistent, identifiable, communication-capable humans or software programs. We do not assume anything about the rationality, capabilities or intentions but we do assume they are able to communicate with other agents.
2. *Dialogical Stance.* All interactions are construable as speech acts. We therefore assume that there is a shared language whose semantic and pragmatic content is somehow fixed by the institution and adopted by the participants.
3. *Agent-mediated commitment making.* We assume that when participants communicate with other agents they are able and entitled to establish and fulfill commitments, and eventually abide by their consequences.

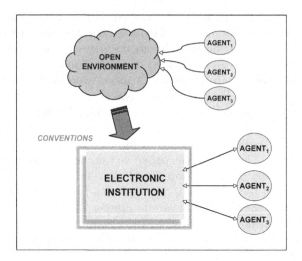

Fig. 1. e-Institutions create a virtual environment where interactions among agents in the real world correspond with illocutions exchanged by agents within the restricted environment. Legitimate illocutions —uttered within the institution— change the state of the institution and count as actions in the world.

4. *Institutional commitments.* Only illocutions uttered by participating agents have effect on the shared environment. The institution is the trustee of the intended conditions for illocution utterance and effects, hence of the commitments established through agent interactions within the institution.
5. *Repetitive Interactions.* We assume that it makes sense to institute interaction conventions when there are interactions that happen not once but many times following a regular pattern. Furthermore, we assume that such patterns of interaction apply not to specific individuals but to any agent that performs a given role during those interactions. We further assume that those repetitive interactions may be organized into some hierarchical system composed by sets of speech acts and relations among these sets.

These assumptions reflect our intuition about what institutions are and how we intend to implement them. Thus, because of assumption 1, we deal with a sort of open multi agent systems, i.e., those that are populated by independent, heterogeneous, self-interested agents whose ownership and accountability may be other than the environment's. As a matter of fact we want the e-Institutions to be an interface that separates the internal behaviour of agents from their external interactions.[1] Assumptions 2, 3 and 4 make our lives simple by reducing the world to what happens inside the e-Institution and restricting to structured conversations (speech acts and scene transitions) all that may happen there.

---

[1] Note that e-Institutions will be MAS that are open in as much as they admit agents of unknown origin and internals, but once these agents are inside the EI the behaviour of the agents is constrained —and to that extent— "closed" by the e-Institution.

Finally, assumption 5 is there to allow us to "structure" interactions into a network of regulated activities whose conventions apply to individuals performing a role. Although —as we shall see in Sect. 5— we may want to relax these assumptions in order to get a handle on some extra features, the conceptual model we are able to build from the five assumptions is practical and general enough to deal with a large class of MAS environments.

The model we propose ([9,21,5]) makes it possible to specify an e-Institution through the following components:

- A *dialogical* framework that defines ontology, social structure and language conventions.
- A *deontological component* that establishes the pragmatics of admissible illocutory actions. This is a set of norms that constrains possible illocutionary exchanges and manages the obligations established within the institution.

e-Institution is currently operationalized as EI_0. In particular, its deontological component is specified with two constructs:

- A *performative structure* that includes a network of scenes linked by transitions between scenes. Scenes are role-based interaction protocols specified as finite state machines, arcs labelled by illocutions and nodes corresponding to an institutional state. Transitions describe the role–flow policies between scenes.
- *Rules of behavior* that establish role-based conventions regulating commitments. These are expressed as pre and post-conditions of the illocutions that are admissible in the performative structure of the *e-Institution*.

Thus a typical e-commerce application like public procurement or auctioning may be implemented as an e-Institution that incarnates the conventions that regulate the (verbal) exchanges between buyers and sellers, supervisors, banks, etc. In such type of applications, the overall activity; for example, contracting the construction of a school house can be thought of as a play that is organized as a *performative structure* by network of sub-activities or *scenes*: call for bids, selection of best offer, contract agreement, etc.

The dialogical framework makes explicit those elements that the institution "speaks about" (chairs, doors, checks, contract, roles (supervisor, auctioneer, buyer,...), time, etc.) their intended semantics and the other conventions needed to express those illocutions that will be legitimate in the institution. Each scene describes an interaction protocol that states what can be said by whom and under what circumstances, for instance that before a supplier is entitled to make a bid for building a school house, it has to prove that it is a certified construction company. The high-level layout of the performative structure indicates scenes and transitions between scenes. These transitions state the conditions that agents must fulfill in order to move from one scene to another. Those conditions may involve synchronizations, changing roles, unfolding the actions of the same agent inside more than one scene (i.e., spawning *alteroids*) and other analogous situations, hence the depiction of the performative structure may be a rather complex picture, as shown for example in Fig. 3.

From an agent's point of view, two major benefits stem from the use of this conceptual model of e-Institutions for modelling environments. On the one hand, *e-Institutions help reduce the frame problem for agents*. As noted above, e-Institutions establish conventions on behavior, language, and protocols that force agents to behave in particular and restrictive ways. In a sense, the environment is given structure, so that the agents have an easy comprehension of its working laws. Think for instance on how auctions or parliaments work: buyers or MPs know when they can talk, what consequences their acts will have, and what actions are possible at each moment in time. These restrictions facilitate the programming of agents, since by restricting the set of actions that agents have to consider at each moment in time one can address the frame problem by limiting the set of options that agents have to think about.

In the next two sections we will show how this conceptual model gives rise to actual e-Institutions through the tools that we have built to specify and generate e-Institutions, and a middleware that activates the corresponding runtime e-Institutions to be enacted by actual agents.

3   Specifying Electronic Institutions

To specify an EI we need to deal expressly with three components mentioned before: dialogical framework, scenes and performative structures. We have a tool, ISLANDER [6], that allows us to make a graphical specification of those components and produces an XML file with the specification. That specification may then be used to build the actual e-Institution or by agent designers to build agents that conform to the institutional conventions.

3.1   Dialogical Framework

The dialogical framework is specified by enumerating all the roles that intervene in the institution, all the constants that may appear in an illocution and all the illocutionary particles that may be used. The right hand side of Fig. 2 enumerates the illocutions used in a Vickrey auction These involve two roles (auctioneer and buyer), some verbs (startauction, offer ,...), some variables (good, price,...) a function (all), the illocutory particles inform and request and a "silence" particle (in expression 5). Illocutions, as shown in the same figure, may also involve variables that may or may not be bound to a given value; that is indicated by the "!" sign, meaning that the variable is bound to the last instance or "?", unbound.

In EI_0 dialogical frameworks capture only simple social structures by the specification of roles and the relationships among them, if any. These relationships may be involved in the description of scenes and transitions. For example a role "dancer" in a ball room institution may be specialized into "female" and "male" dancers and some scene transitions may allow any "dancer" to pass, while the receiving scene may require only one of the two special types in a given illocution. In EI_0 only static separation of roles is permitted, that is, an agent may change subsumed roles during a transition but not inside a scene.

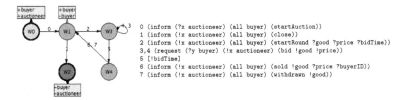

Fig. 2. An ISLANDER specification of a Vickrey bidding protocol. The left part shows the transition network whose arcs are labeled by the illocutory expressions on the right.

3.2 Scenes

Scenes are specified as transition networks with one initial state, one or more final states. Additionally, one or more entry states for each role and one or more exit states for each role. Illocutions connect states as a way of indicating that illocutions are the actions that happen inside the institution and that only what is said –if and when it is a legal illocution– changes the "state" of the institution as a whole.

For example, Fig. 2 depicts an ISLANDER specification of the VIckrey protocol for auctioning. In the left part of the figure, w0 is the initial state and w2 the end state. Boxes indicate that agents enacting a given role (**auctioneer** or **buyer**) may enter (+) or leave (-) certain states. Arcs are labeled by the illocutory expressions listed on the right part of the figure. Thus, for example, expression 4 states that an agent (y) acting as a buyer requests the agent (x) who acts as the auctioneer to accept a bid for the good being offered.

When specifying a scene in ISLANDER, each illocution may have preconditions and postconditions associated, so that the effects of illocutory actions — commitments— are properly governed by the institution and may be observed by participants. In practice, these conditions correspond to the rules of behaviour that individual agents are bound to obey. Scenes may also have some global conditions associated, like the minimal number of participants needed for the scene to be enacted or the average clearing price in a double auction.

In addition to well-formedness, ISLANDER takes care of some syntactic scene consistency checks thus preventing the most frequent miss-specifications such as incomplete dialogical frameworks, spurious roles, lack of acess and exit states, etc.

3.3 Performative Structure

In its most abstract conception, the performative structure (PS) captures the conventions that regulate the flow of commitments in an institution. In more concrete terms, the PS describes the way agents may engage in different activities. Therefore the PS is made up by scenes and the transitions that connect those scenes. Recall that scenes already had a scene protocol AND incoming and outgoing states for the roles involved; well, scene transitions are used to control how an agent, performing a given role, may pass from a proper exit state in one scene to a proper entry state in another scene.

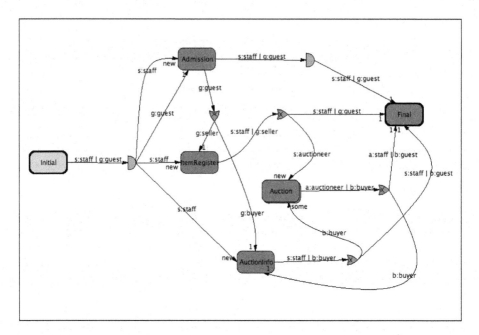

Fig. 3. An ISLANDER specification of the Performative Structure of an institution for simultaneous auctions. Boxes represent scenes and directed arcs inter-connect scenes through transition gates (of two types in this example: exclusive —crescents— and inclusive –half-circles– OR). Arcs are labeled by agent-variables and the roles these are to play. Moreover, arcs entering a scene are also labeled with a legend that indicate if transient agents may enter one scene, or one or more scenes of that type, or if a staff member may create new scenes of that type.

The management of transitions is rich in EI_0 because we want to be able to implement institutions where agents may be in two places at the same time (bidding in two auction houses that open the same hours), that institutional staff open scenes whenever needed, or that a given scene becomes closed once every participant has left. ISLANDER is able to express all these functionalities and the designer needs only point and click to enable them in a PS.

For example the performative structure depicted in Fig. 3 defines the relationships between the usual activities during the enactment of an auction. In this case —in addition to the initial and final scenes that are necessary in all e-Institutions— there are four basic scenes: Admission, ItemRegister, Auctioninfo, Auction, all depicted as boxes. Scenes are connected with directed arcs that come out of a scene, reach a transition (crescent-like figures) and then leave a transition into another scene. Staff members are present in all scenes, and therefore all scenes have in-arrows and out-arrows labeled with a staff or auctioneer (one kind of staff member). Likewise guests may either be buyers or sellers and although they enter the Admission scene as guest , they leave it either as seller (into the ItemRegister scene) or as buyer (into auctioninfo). Because this separation of roles is strict, the transition between the `Admission` scene and the other two is an "exclusive" transition, while the transition between the `Admission` and `Final` scenes is a direct (inclusive or) transition through which all `staff` and `guest` agents may go through. Since, by design, in this institution there may be simultaneous auctions taking place in different rooms and the same agent may be present in more than one room, the performative structure shows a transition from the `ItemRegister` scene that allows a staff member to become an `auctioneer` and open `new Auction` scenes, and a `buyer` may leave the `Auctioninfo` scene and enter one or more `Auction` scenes or proceed directly to `Final`.

4 Running Electronic Institutions

How can we implement and run an ISLANDER specified EI?

Implementation can be seen as a three-stage process that includes reinterpreting the conceptual model so that it may become operational through agents and an actual, functioning, computational realization of the particular e-Institution specified using ISLANDER. For the deployment of the actual e-Institution and its activation we rely on the software we have developed and is describe below.

The implementation process is the following:

1. Translate our specification model into the corresponding execution model as follows:
   - e-Institutions are populated at run-time by heterogenous, self-interested agents.
   - Agents interact within scenes via speech acts.
   - Agents move from scene (activity) to scene (activity).
   - The execution of an institution can be regarded as the execution of its different scenes (activities).
2. Deploy two types of internal (or institutional). First, we will need staff agents that are intended to perform all the actions that institutional staff is entitled and enabled to perform; second, we will attach to each external agent an institutional "governor" that controls all the information flow between the (external) agent and the institution and is thus able to enforce the institutional conventions that the external agent is bound to observe in addition to insulating the institutional environment from potential misbehaviour of the external agent (see Fig. 4).
3. Insert an "institutional environment" between the agents and their (communicative) interactions to fulfill three essential functions: i) mediation, ii) coordination and enforcement, and iii) information management.

We have assembled an "Electronic Institution Development Environment", EIDE [1] that includes all the software tools needed for deploying an ISLANDER-specified e-Institution.

The core of EIDE is an institutional engine, AMELI ([6]), that generates a run-time middleware for the agents that participate in the enactment of a given institution. The middleware is deployed to *guarantee* the correct evolution of

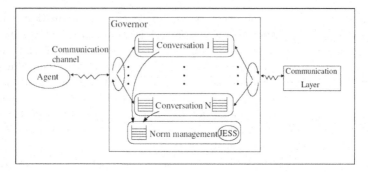

Fig. 4. Governors wrap around external agents and control information flows between these and the e-Institution. Governors keep track of the institutional state and update it when a valid illocution passes through them from an agent to the institution or back.

each scene to *warrant* legal movements between scenes and to *control* the obligations or commitments that participating agents acquire and fulfil and, finally, the middleware *handles* the information agents need within the institution. The AMELI generated middleware *mediates* between agents in order to facilitate agent communication within scenes. Broadly speaking, AMELI achieves those functions because, on the one hand it generates the staff agents and the institutional *governors* that mediate all communications with external agents and, on the other hand, handles all the institutional communication traffic by wrapping illocutions as messages that are handled by a standard agent-communication layer (e.g., JADE) as illustrated in Fig. 5.

Another EIDE tool, aBuilder, takes an ISLANDER specification and produces for each role that may be played in the institution an "agent skeleton". Those skeletons comply with all the conventions of the specified institution, in particular with its dialogical framework and the performative structure, and are compatible with the governors that are automatically produced at run time by the AMELI middleware. Hence, external agents may be built form scratch —based on the XML specification of the e-Institution— but they may also be readily built —on top of the aBuilder skeletons— by programming the decision means associated with illocutions and having the skeleton take care of navigation and communication within the e-Institution. The aBuilder tool is convenient for prototyping agents and (as will be seen in Sect. 6) to use agent skeletons to produce parametrized agents for modeling and testing institutions. In addition to AMELI and aBuilder, two more tools are part of EIDE: A simulation tool, SimDei, is used for animation and analysis of ISLANDER specifications and a Monitorig tool provides a graphical depiction of all the events that happen during the enactment of an e-Institution.

5   Situating Electronic Institutions

Today, the concept of an environment for multi-agent systems is in its pioneering phase. Consequently, the development of supporting software technologies

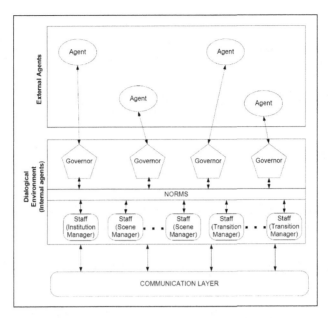

Fig. 5. An agent middleware for e-Institutions (AMELI) lays between participating agents and an agent communication infrastructure (e.g. JADE) composed of internal agents of two types: governors and staff agents

is in an early stage. Existing applications typically incorporate ad hoc implementations while analysis reveals how they may benefit from a more mature environment technology – e.g. from its time and resource management services. Environment technologies reflecting a specific world-of-interest (WoI) – e.g. a transport or manufacturing system – to the agent systems are yet to be developed in full [27]. In contrast, the environment technology that focuses on the agent system itself is being addressed by research already. e-Institutions are prominent in this respect [1].

Research into e-Institutions has been pioneering MAS environments for several years [11]. As shown in preceding sections, e-Institutions do not address the environment services and functionalities. Instead, as stated in Sect. 2, the research has focused on the norms and laws that apply to the agent society in a given *dialogical* environment. Thus, E-Institutions are a technology to enforce, monitor and encourage these norms and laws. Typically, they constrain the trajectories in the environment to the set of trajectories that are considered desirable, safe, acceptable, and/or manageable. Thus, the technology makes the agents in their agent society behave according to the needs and requirements of their environment.

And yet, is this enough? The answer is "not quite". Notice that, as pointed out above, MAS applications are usually concerned with some external WoI in addition to the agent society issues. The WoI is application-specific and refers to the part of the world that is relevant to the MAS application. For instance,

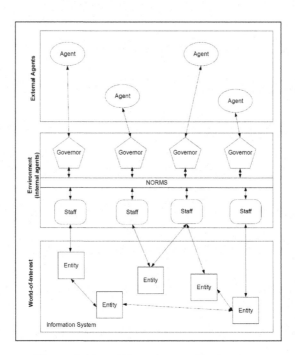

Fig. 6. Linking EIs with a world-of-interest

for a climate control application, the WoI comprises rooms, doors, heaters, etc. Therefore, it is necessary to extend the notion of e-Institution in order to link it with the notion of WoI. In this manner, participating agents will be able to *sense* and *act over* the WoI. Notice though that external agents cannot directly sense and act over the WoI. Instead, and likewise all interactions of external agents in the realm of an e-Institution, sensing and acting over the WoI is also *mediated* by the e-Institution wherein they interact. To summarise, what we propose is: (i) to directly *situate*[2] e-Institutions; and (ii) to indirectly (via mediation) situate external agents.

Figure 6 depicts how an e-Institution controls the interactions between the external agents and the WoI. The E-Institution is regarded as part of the environment and is still realised, as already shown in Fig. 5, by a collection of so-called staff agents. External agents only interact through the environment via dialogical actions that are filtered in or out by their governors. Thus, external agents can only sense and act over the entities in the WoI through their governors. Figure 7 details how to plug an entity into AMELI so that agents can subsequently sense/act over it. AMELI requires the implementation of a Java interface, the so-called `EInstitutionService`, per entity to incorporate into the platform all methods to operate on a given entity. Thereafter,

---

[2] We understand by *situatedness* the property of an AI program being located in an environment that it senses. Via its actions, the program can select its input, as well as change its environment.

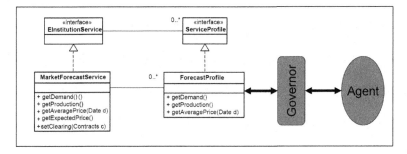

Fig. 7. Linking EIs with a world-of-interest

different interfaces to acces the service can be incorporated into AMELI as implementations of the `ServiceProfile` interface. These service profiles can be regarded as different views to the service. In Fig. 7, we provide a service example based on the electricity market in [23]. The service `MarketForecast` offers several forecast methods —expected demand (`getDemand`), expected energy production (`getProduction`), expected Kw price (`getExpectedPrice`)— as well as a method to retrieve past market price on a particular date (`getPrice(Date d)`), set the contract information corresponding to a market cleared by the market operator (`setClearing(Contracts c)`) to be employed by subsequent forecasts. The `ForecastProfile` profile only allows external agents to obtain information about past market prices on particular dates, and the expcted energy demand and production. The motivation to consider different profiles is that the very same e-Institution may require that external agents have different views to the very same service depending on their roles. For instance, profile `ForecastProfile` can be further split so that only consumers can access the production forecast, whereas only producers can access the demand forecast.

The flexibility of the notion of e-Institution comes from its clear separation of concerns between the internal behavior of agents and their external interactions (environment modeling). The environment modeling outlined in Sect. 3 and 4 does change once the situatedness of e-Institutions is taken into account. Hence, from the perspective of an agent, its environment is modeled as the result of composing the following elements:

- *A number of agents* (usually called staff agents) that model/expand their human counterparts in the real world or that simply behave according to an internal model.
- *A number of norms* that restrict the behaviour of agents preventing them to behave in unacceptable/impossible ways. In this respect norms can be thought as physical laws or as social conventions that shape/constraint the evolution of interactions that may or may not take into account the WoI. For instance, in an electricity market the market operator may either oblige each power station to supply its spare production if the produced power is less or equal than the market demand, or it may prohibit energy producers to operate on the network when the operator detects thermal overloads.

– *An explicit agreement on language and ontology.* Since illocutionary acts are the only actions permitted within an e-Institution, it fits well with the MAS configurations where real entities are represented/expanded by an agent that, in the case of e-Institutions, will be using illocutions as its action repertoire. Notice that the very same language is used for sensing/acting over the WoI.
– *An explicit set of activities.* Scenes represent tasks solved by groups of agents and are nodes within the performative structure that models the flow of agents. Actions within scenes are further fixed as a protocol that will only permit certain dialogues among the agents. Agents are restricted (by social conventions or physical laws) in what they can do at a particular moment in time. Such restrictions may now take into account the WoI. Furthermore, an agent's actions within a scene may now have consequences as: (i) changes to an agent's institutional state (e.g. a consumer agent may have its credit diminished after winning an auction); (ii) changes to the institutional state (e.g. the average market price does change after a market clearing occurs); and (iii) actions over the WoI (e.g. the thermal load of an electricity network changes after an energy producer agent delivers its supply to the network).

On the other hand, the fact that external agents have governors as their unique means of sensing and acting over the environment makes agents *neutral* to the WoI. In other words, external agents are unaware of *how* entities in the WoI are sensed by the e-Institution wherein they take part. And thus, changes to the services connecting entities to AMELI have no impact whatsoever on the inner architecture of external agents.

6   Environment Simulation

At this point we are ready to engineer E4MAS based on the notion of situated e-Institution. Nonetheless, as environment engineers, we must wonder whether our MAS application is to behave as expected. Checking the properties of an e-Institution is a highly intricate and computationally expensive task, as illustrated by [29,28,8,7]. Such checking becomes even more complicated when adding a WoI composed not only of *static* entities (e.g. a database), but also of *dynamic* entities endowed with varying behaviours (e.g. a heater, a weather forecast service). Hence, it would be desirable for environment engineers to count on dynamic verification tools that help them analyse the dynamic behaviour of their MAS applications. At this aim, in what follows we detail the tools we have developed to simulate environments created as situated e-Institutions.

We regard an environment simulation as the result of coordinating an e-Institution simulation and a WoI simulation as illustrated by Fig. 8. As to simulating an e-Institution we employ an extended version of SimDei (formerly introduced in [1]). SimDei allows to run discrete event simulations of AMELI along the lines of multi-agent simulations produced with the aid of libraries like Repast [16]. As to WoI simulations, we must choose the modelling simulation tool (e.g. Simile [24], Simulink [25], EJS [4])that best fits the WoI features; for instance, the entity connected through the service depicted in Fig. 7 must be

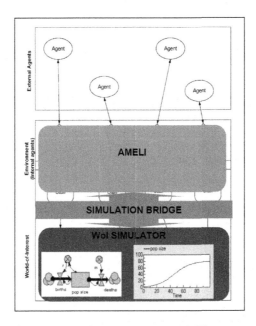

Fig. 8. Simulating situated EIs

modelled and simulated by some system dynamics simulator. Finally, it is necessary to glue the e-Institution simulation with the WoI simulation so that agents
in an e-Institution can sense and act upon the simulated WoI. This motivates
the introduction of the *simulation bridge* (see Fig. 8), a software component
whose main purpose is: (i) to synchronise both simulators; (ii) to forward WoI
variables' values to SimDei; and (iii) to translate actions within the simulated
e-Institution into WoI actions. Notice that the implementation of the simulation
bridge depends on the particular simulator we choose to simulate the WoI. At
present, we do offer implementations of the simulation bridge to connect SimDei
simulations to either Simulink [25] or EJS [4] simulations.

In order for the environment simulation to properly work, environment engineers are required to design simulations according to the simulation design
workflow depicted in Fig. 9. Such workflow requires that an environment engineer performs the following tasks:

- [1] **Islander specification** of an e-Institution as explained in Sect. 3.
- [2] **WoI model** describing the dynamics of the entities in the WoI.
- [3] **Agent skelentons' specification** with the aid of aBuilder [1], the software tool for agent development included in EIDE that supports the graphical specification of agent skeletons based on Islander specifications.
- [4] **SimDei configuration.** It is composed of: (i) parameters to generate
  populations of agents based on agent skeletons; and (ii) the observation variables, namely the objects to probe in the simulation along with the functions
  to employ to combine their observed values.

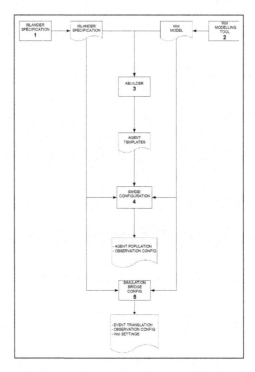

Fig. 9. The simulation design workflow

- **[5] Simulation bridge configuration.** It is composed of: (i) inital settings for the entities in the WoI; (ii) entities to probe in the WoI; and (iii) translation rules from institutional actions into WoI actions.

We believe that the generation of agent populations deserves special attention. The software tool aBuilder supports the specification of *parametrised* agent skeletons. Thus, an agent's action can be parametrised in two ways: (i) by defining whether an action is carried out or not as a parameter; (ii) by defining (some of) the actual values of each action as parameters. SimDei can exploit parametrised agent skeletons to generate agent populations by setting the number of agents to create from a given skelenton along with the means to set up values for their parameters. Figure 10 illustrates how to generate a population of buyer agents from the `Buyer` skeleton for an electricity market. SimDei will randomly generate between 50 and 100 buyer agents that shall assess the values of their `price` and `kw` parameters using two different Normal distributions.

After the design stage, at run time, SimDei, the chosen WoI simulator, and the simulation bridge are concurrently launched. SimDei starts by generating agent populations using agent skeletons created with aBuilder. Thereafter, SimDei feeds AMELI with an Islander specification to run it in simulation mode. SimDei also employs AMELI's monitoring tool to display the observed variables. The simulation bridge synchronises SimDei with the WoI simulator using its

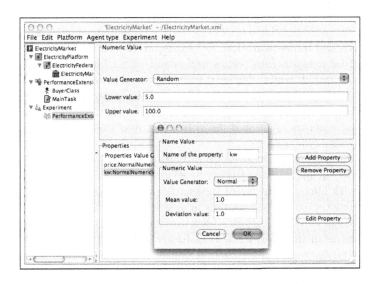

Fig. 10. Generating agent populations with SimDei

translation rules to reflect agents' actions over the WoI and observing the entities
to probe in order to convey the values of variables to SimDei.

We argue that several benefits stem from our approach to environment simulation. Firstly, SimDei promotes multi-agent simulation from the programming
level to the graphical specification level along the lines of graphical simulation tools (e.g. PowerSim [15], Arena [2], Simulink [25] or Simile [24]) unlike
multi-agent simulation tools like Repast [16] or Swarm [26]. Secondly, we observe that it is unusual that multi-agent simulation libraries do offer organisa-
tional/institutional patterns that provide higher levels of abstraction to programmers, and if so (like [16]) they are quite limited. SimDei handles institutional
patterns at the simulation level unlike state-of-the-art multi-agent simulation
tools like [16,26]. Thirdly, a wide range of modelling and simulation tools can
be employed together with SimDei whenever the appropriate simulation bridge
is available. Notice that in order to plug a simulation bridge to an e-Institution
simulation it must implement a generic API defined by SimDei. Lastly, notice
that external agents within an e-Institution are neutral to the simulation tool
employed for the WoI since all their sensing and acting is mediated by the
e-Institution.

7   Discussion

A review of the other papers in this volume gives us ground to contrast some
strengths and weaknesses of e-Institutions for engineering E4MAS.

First of all, we are confident that the approach of e-Institutions is appropriate for E4MAS whenever the intended MAS requires social structure and

regulation, as is the case for the approaches reported in [3,14]. In both instances e-Institutions would provide a set of alternative modeling constructs for an alternative design and implementation. For example, the notions of *space* and *mode* in [3] could be mapped into scenes and social roles. The notions of *rules* and *reaction rules* in [14] could also be readily captured in our framework. Namely, *reaction rules* regulating agent softbodies may be expressed as *norms* and as *postconditions* of agents' actions —within scenes— that change agents' institutional states, whereas *rules* may be translated into the specification of scenes and transitions.

Second, although e-Institutions do provide the means to enact a social structure, they do not include any means to structure the WoI. Thus, in particular, our framework offers no means of structuring the entities of the WoI according to a particular topology. Nevertheless, it is still possible to structure the WoI indirectly through an e-Institution: scenes provide locality by regulating the access to some entities in the WoI, while transitions between scenes model the change of locality –for example, in an auction house, the bidding scene *takes place* inside a bidding-hall and buyers *move* from there to a delivery hall (scene). In other words, by relating scenes with entities in the WoI we locally situate these. Therefore, a performative structure can be regarded as a way of building a *social* topology on top of a WoI.

Third, the approach in [22] based on the filtering of perceptions raises a very important issue concerning the regulation of perception in an e-Institution. So far, the focus of our framework has been to regulate agents' actions with the purpose of assessing whether they are institutionally valid or not. Thus, although e-Institutions offer a language to specify such regulations along with a software platorm, AMELI, to implement them, we do not provide the same degree of functionality to regulate perceptions, yet.

Fourth, we would like to point out that the work on artifacts [13,17] is the approach closer to e-Institutions. And yet, there are two significant differences among these approaches: (i) e-Institutions are tailored to a particular –even if large– family of applications while artifacts are claimed to be more generic; (ii) e-Institutions are a well established and proven technology that includes a formal foundation, and advanced engineering and tool support. For artifacts, these features are still in a preliminary phase.

Finally, we are decidedly in favour of: (i) designing reference architectures that provide a blueprint for developing software architectures for MAS along the lines of [30]; and (ii) building development tools to engineer computational environments along the lines of CArtAgO [18] and EIDE [1]. We regard both activities as complementary because we are aware that although —as discussed in [27]— a development tool like EIDE can help develop a wide range of MAS configurations, at least for the time being it is hard to envision a general purpose development tool for computational environments.

It is our belief that the approaches to E4MAS reported in this volume outline several promising paths to future research, we would like to issue a call for further joint developments.

Acknowledgements

The authors would like to thank our anonymous reviewers for their very pertinent commens. This work has been supported by projects IEA (TIN2006-15662-C02-01), OK (IST-4-027253-STP), eREP(EC-FP6-CIT5-28575) and 2006 5 OI 099.

References

1. Josep Lluis Arcos, Marc Esteva, Pablo Noriega, Juan A. Rodríguez-Aguilar, and Carles Sierra. Environment engineering for multiagent systems. *Engineering Applications of Artificial Intelligence*, 18(1):191–204, January 2005.
2. Arena. http://www.arenasimulation.com/.
3. José-Antonio Báez-Barranco, Tiberiu Stratulat, and Jacques Ferber. A unified model for physical and social environments. In Weyns et al. [31]. To appear.
4. Ejs, easy java simulations. http://www.um.es/fem/Ejs.
5. M. Esteva. *Electronic Institutions: from specification to development. PhD Thesis Universitat Politècnica de Catalunya (UPC), 2003.* Number 19 in IIIA Monograph Series. IIIA, 2003.
6. Marc Esteva, Juan A. Rodríguez-Aguilar, Bruno Rosell, and Josep L. Arcos. Ameli: An agent-based middleware for electronic institutions. In *Third International Joint Conference on Autonomous Agents and Multi-agent Systems (AAMAS'04)*, New York, USA, July 19-23 2004.
7. Marc Esteva, Wamberto Vasconcelos, Carles Sierra, and Juan Antonio Rodríguez-Aguilar. Norm consistency in electronic institutions. In *Proceedings of the XVII Brazilian Symposium on Artificial Intelligence (SBIA'04)*, number 3171 in Lecture Notes in Artificial Intelligence, pages 494–505. 2004.
8. Ismail Khalil-Ibrahim, Gabriele Kotsis, and Reinhard Kronsteiner. Substitution rules for the verification of norm-compliance in electronic institutions. In *Proceedings of the 13th IEEE International Workshops on Enabling Technologies: Infrastructure for Collaborative Enterprises (WET ICE04)*, pages 21–26. IEEE Computer Society, 2004.
9. P. Noriega. *Agent-Mediated Auctions: The Fishmarket Metaphor. PhD Thesis Universitat Autònoma de Barcelona (UAB), 1997.* Number 8 in IIIA Monograph Series. IIIA, 1999.
10. Pablo Noriega. Fencing the open fields, empirical concerns on electronic institutions (invited paper). In Olivier Boissier, Julian Padget, Virginia Dignum, Gabriela Lindemann, Eric Matson, Sascha Ossowski, Jaime Simao Sichman, and Javier Vázquez-Salceda, editors, *Coordination, Organizations, Institutions, and Norms in Multi-Agent Systems AAMAS 2005 International Workshops on Agents, Norms and Institutions for Regulated Multi-Agent Systems, ANIREM 2005, and Organizations in Multi-Agent Systems, OOOP 2005, Utrecht, The Netherlands, July 25-26, 2005, Revised Selected Papers*, volume 3913 of *Lecture notes in computer science*, pages 81–98. Springer, 2006.
11. Pablo Noriega and Carles Sierra. Electronic institutions: Future trends and challenges. In Matthias Klusch, Sascha Ossowski, and Onn Shehory, editors, *Proceedings of the 6th International Workshop on Cooperative Information Agents VI*, volume 2446 of *Lecture Notes in Computer Science*, pages 14–17. Springer Verlag, 2002.
12. Douglass C. North. *Institutions, Institutional change and economic performance.* Cambridge Universisy press, 40 west 20th Street, New York, NY 10011-4211, USA, 1990.

13. Andrea Omicini, Alessandro Ricci, Mirko Viroli, Cristiano Castelfranchi, and Luca Tummolini. Coordination artifacts: Environment-based coordination for intelligent agents. In *AAMAS*, pages 286–293. IEEE Computer Society, 2004.
14. Eric Platon, Nicolas Sabouret, and Shinichi Honiden. Tag interactions in multi-agent systems: Environment support. In Weyns et al. [31]. To appear.
15. Powersim. http://www.powersim.com.
16. Repast. http://repast.sourceforge.net.
17. Alessandro Ricci, Andrea Omicini, Mirko Viroli, Luca Gardelli, and Enrico Oliva. Cognitive stigmergy: A framework based on agents and artifacts. In Weyns et al. [31]. To appear.
18. Alessandro Ricci, Mirko Viroli, and Andrea Omicini. Cartago: An infrastructure for engineering computational environments in MAS. In Weyns et al. [31]. To appear.
19. Armando Robles, Pablo Noriega, Michael Luck, and Francisco Cantú. Using mas technologies for intelligent organizations: a report of bottom-up results. In Carlos Alberto Gelbukh, Alexander ; Reyes-Garcia, editor, *MICAI 2006: Advances in Artificial Intelligence. 5th Mexican International Conference on Artificial Intelligence, Apizaco, Mexico, November 13-17, 2006. Proceedings*, volume 4293 of *Lecture notes in computer science. Lecture notes on Artificial Intelligence*, pages 1116–1127. Springer, 2006.
20. Armando Robles, Pablo Noriega, Marco Julio Robles, Héctor Hernández, Víctor Soto, and Edgar González. A hotel information system implementation using mas technology. In *Proceedings of the Fifth International Joint Conference on Autonomous Agents and Multiagent Systems (AAMAS06 May 8-12 2006, Hakodate, Japan)*, pages 1542–1548. ACM, 2006.
21. J. A. Rodriguez-Aguilar. *On the Design and Construction of Agent-mediated Electronic Institutions, PhD Thesis, Universitat Autònoma de Barcelona (2001), 2001*. Number 14 in IIIA Monograph Series. IIIA, 2003.
22. Julien Saunier, Flavien Balbo, and Fabien Badeig. Environment as active support of interaction. In Weyns et al. [31]. To appear.
23. Carles Sierra, Jordi Sabater, Jaume Agustí, and Pere Garcia. *Methodologies and Software Engineering for Agent Sytems*, chapter The Sadde Methodology, pages 195–214. Kluwer Academic Press, 2004.
24. Simile. http://simulistics.com.
25. Simulink. http://www.mathworks.com/products/simulink/.
26. Swarm. http://www.swarm.org.
27. Paul Valckenaers, John Sauters, Carles Sierra, and Juan Antonio Rodríguez-Aguilar. Applications and environments for multi-agent systems. *Autonomous Agents and Multi-agent Systems*, 14(1):61–85, February 2007.
28. Wamberto Vasconcelos. Norm verification and analysis of electronic institutions. In Joao Leite, Andrea Omicini, Paolo Torroni, and Pinar Yolum, editors, *Declarative Agent Languages and Technologies II: Second International Workshop, DALT*, volume 3476 of *Lecture Notes in Computer Science*, pages 166–182. Springer-Verlag, 2005.
29. F. Viganò. A framework for model checking institutions. In *Proceedings of the ECAI Workshop on Model checking and Artificial Intelligence (MOCHART IV)*, 2006. To appear. Available from: www.istituti.usilu.net/viganof.
30. Danny Weyns and Tom Holvoet. A reference architecture for situated multiagent systems. In Weyns et al. [31]. To appear.
31. Danny Weyns, H. Van Dyke Parunak, and Fabien Michel, editors. *Environments for Multi-Agent Systems III*. Springer Verlag, 2007. To appear.

Spatially Distributed Normative Infrastructure

Fabio Y. Okuyama[1], Rafael H. Bordini[2], and Antônio Carlos da Rocha Costa[3]

[1] Programa de Pós-Graduação em Computação
Universidade Federal do Rio Grande do Sul (UFRGS)
Porto Alegre–RS, Brazil
okuyama@inf.ufrgs.br
[2] Department of Computer Science – University of Durham
Durham DH1 3LE, U.K.
R.Bordini@durham.ac.uk
[3] Escola de Informática – Universidade Católica de Pelotas (UCPel)
Pelotas–RS, Brazil
rocha@atlas.ucpel.tche.br

Abstract. In previous work, we introduced an approach to describe and simulate environments for situated multi-agent systems, based on a language called ELMS. Here, we present extensions to our approach which provide the means to allow normative information to be distributed in environments shared by multiple agents. Organisational structures for multi-agent systems are usually defined independently of any spatial or temporal structure. Therefore, when the multi-agent system is situated in a spatial environment, there is usually a conceptual gap between the definition of the system's organisational structures and the definition of the environment. Spatially distributing the normative information over the environment is a natural way to simplify the definition of organisational structures and the development of large-scale multi-agent systems. By distributing the normative information in different spatial locations, we allow agents to directly access the relevant information needed in each environmental context. The extensions to our approach for multi-agent environments allow for the definition of spatially distributed normative objects and the means to distribute and handle such objects in a shared environment.

1 Introduction

The environment is an important part of Multi-Agent Systems (MAS) [18], even more so for systems of situated agents. Multi-agent systems are usually designed as a set of agents, the environment where they interact, social structures, and the possible interactions among these components.

In previous work, we presented a language that allows MAS designers to describe, at high level, environments for situated multi-agent systems [12,1]. The language is called ELMS, and was created to be part of a platform for the development of (social) simulations based on multi-agent systems. In this paper, we present extensions that complement the environment description with structures which, by allowing the distribution of normative information over the environment, give support to connecting the environment and organisational structures.

D. Weyns, H.V.D. Parunak, and F. Michel (Eds.): E4MAS 2006, LNAI 4389, pp. 203–220, 2007.
© Springer-Verlag Berlin Heidelberg 2007

In particular, we present here a set of concepts for a spatially distributed infrastructure formed by *normative objects*, *normative places*, and *norm supervisors*. This infrastructure in our view facilitates the modelling and simulation of various real-world situation, which might be useful for testing approaches to achieve improved coordination in large-scale multi-agent systems. The notions of normative objects and normative places were originally introduced in [11], and we here build upon those initial ideas.

To understand the notion of *normative object*, consider the posters one typically sees in public places such as libraries or bars saying "Please be quiet" or "No smoking in this area". Human societies often resort to this mechanism for decentralising the burden of regulating social behaviour; people then adopt such norms whenever they have visual access to such posters. This should be equally efficient for computational systems because it avoids the need for having all the norms hard-wired in the agents or the need to providing a complete, exhaustive representation of all social norms in a single public structure, known to all agents, as it is usually the case in approaches to agent organisations.

Normative places are zones where normative objects are applicable. As an example, consider a research group whose *researcher* agents do their research both in a laboratory and in a library. In the laboratory, the interactions among researchers, staff, and with the environment are specific to the spatial scene of the laboratory space. The information about how to behave in a library is defined specifically for the library spatial location, where the researchers will also assume the role of *library users*. Normative information relevant for each such site (and each place at each site) can be posted to the agents with the help of normative objects. The *norm supervisor* agents are a special class of agents that monitor the agents' compliance to norms within the MAS. The norm supervisor agents may be *system agents*[1] specifically designed for such function or autonomous agents with such functionality enabled.

In summary, the extensions we introduce here support situated norms and leaves the necessary room for the inclusion of group structures that are spatially situated within a (simulated) physical environment. This is done using two means: first, *normative objects*, which are objects that can contain normative information; and second, a normative principle for *situated norms*, conceived as a special form of conditional rule, where an explicit condition on an agent's perception of a normative object appears: 'When playing the relevant role and being physically situated within the confines referred to by a situated norm $\mathcal{N}$ expressed in a normative object previously perceived, the agent is expected to reason about following norm $\mathcal{N}$; otherwise, it is excused from reasoning about it'. Also, normative objects may be directed towards a specific role in a given organisation. We can therefore model things such as a sign saying that students are not allowed beyond the library desk, while members of staff have permission to go through.

In the next section, we briefly present our platform and the various component languages we use to model multi-agent systems. In Section 3, we briefly review how an environment should be modelled using our approach. In Section 4, we present the normative extensions which are the main focus of this paper. We then illustrate our

---

[1] By "system agents" we mean agents that are part of the internal controlling structures put in place by the system designer.

approach with an example in Section 6; the example is based on the scenario presented in [3]. We discuss related work in Section 7, then conclude the paper.

2   The MAS-SOC Platform

One of the main goals of the MAS-SOC simulation platform (**M**ulti-**A**gent **S**imulations for the **SOC**ial Sciences) is to provide a framework for the creation of agent-based simulations which do not require too much experience in programming from users, yet allowing the use of state-of-the-art agent technologies. In particular, it should allow for the design and implementation of simulations with *cognitive* agents.

In our approach, an agent's individual reasoning is specified in an extended version of AgentSpeak [14], as interpreted by *Jason* [2], an Open Source agent platform based on Java (available at `http://jason.sf.net`). The extensions allow, among other things, for speech-act based agent communication, and there is ongoing work to allow for ontologies as part of an AgentSpeak agent's belief base.

The environments where agents are situated are specified in ELMS, a language we have designed for the description of multi-agent environments [12]. For more details on MAS-SOC, refer to [1]. We here concentrate on the ELMS extensions to describe social norms that apply to specific places within an environment, and to relate an organisational structure and the relevant normative aspects to the spatial structures defined within the physical environment.

3   Modelling Physical Environments

As presented in [12], we developed a language to describe environments and the means to execute the simulated environment. Agents in a multi-agent system interact with the environment where they are situated and interact with each other, typically through the shared environment. Therefore, the environment has an important role in a multi-agent system, whether the environment is the Internet, the real world, or some simulated environment.

We understand as environment modelling, the modelling of external aspects that an agent needs as input to its reasoning and for deciding on its course of action. In a multi-agent scenario, how one agent perceives another is an important issue. Thus, modelling explicitly the agent's "body" should also be included in environment modelling. Further, it is necessary to model explicitly the physical actions and perception capabilities that the agents are allowed to perform in a given environment.

The language we designed for modelling environments is called ELMS (**E**nvironment **D**escription **L**anguage for **M**ulti-Agent **S**imulation). Below we briefly review how a physical environment is described using this language.

To define an environment using ELMS, the following classes of constructs are used:

Agent Body: the agent's characteristics that are perceptible to other agents. Agent "bodies" are defined by a set of properties that characterise it and are perceptible to other agents. Such properties are represented as *string*, *integer*, *float*, and *boolean* values. Each "body" is associated with a set of actions that the agent is allowed to perform and of environment properties that the agent can perceive.

Agent Sensorial Capabilities (Perceptions): each sensorial capability is used to specify which environment properties will be perceptible to each agent that have a "body" with such capacity. It determines the environmental properties that will be sent to the agent and the specific circumstances where they are possible (e.g. an agent may be able to see in a radius of 2 cells, but only if there is nothing obstructing its vision).

Agent Effective Capacities (Actions): each effective capacity determines the environment changes that can be effected by an agent that has a "body" with such capacities. These changes are defined as assignments of values to the attributes of environments[2]. The production (instantiation) of previously defined resources (objects), and the consumption (deletion) of existing instances may also be part of an action description. Also, the conditions under which an action can be performed should be specified.

Physical Environment Objects and Resources: the objects and resources that are present in the environment. Although objects and resources can be conceptually different, both are represented by the same structure in ELMS. Agents interact with objects through the actions performed in the environment. Object structures are defined by a set of properties that are relevant to the modelling and could be perceived by agents. In the same way as the "bodies" of agents, the properties of resources are represented by *string*, *integer*, *float*, and *boolean* values.

Object Reactions: the objects can "react", under specific circumstances, responding to actions performed by the agents in the environment. Such reactions are given as the assignment of values to properties, the creation of previously defined object instances, and the deletion of existing object instances.

Space Structure (Grid): the space is (optionally) divided into cells forming a grid that represents the spatial structure of the environment. When a grid is used, it can be defined in 2 or 3 dimensions. As for resources, each cell can have reactions associated with them. Although the specified set of reactions apply to all of the cells, this does not mean that all cells will behave equally, since they may be in different states (i.e., each cell has independent attributes, thus having different contents and, clearly, different positions, which can all affect the particular reactions).

3.1 Notes on Environment Descriptions

Perceptions: agents do not normally have complete access to the environment. Perception of the environment will not normally give complete and accurate information about the whole environment and the other agents in it. However, since such restriction is not imposed by the ELMS model itself, designers can choose to create fully accessible environments if this is appropriate for a particular application.

Actions: it helps maintaining the coherence of the environment if agent actions are defined so as to be "atomic". As the choice of (courses of) action is meant to be part of the agent's *mind*, something that is more naturally seen as a whole series of actions should not be implemented as one action available to agents at the environment level.

---

[2] Note that properties of agent bodies are also properties of the environment.

Reactions: all object reactions triggered by some change in the environment are executed in a single simulation cycle. This is different from agent actions, as each agent can execute only one action per cycle.

Additionally to the constructs mentioned above, the following operational constructs are used in our approach to model the simulated physical environment.

Constructors: Each agent and resource may need to be initialised at the moment of its instantiation. This is defined by a list of initial value assignment to its attributes.

Observables: A list of environment properties whose values are to be displayed/logged; these are the specific properties of a simulation that the user wants to observe/analyse.

The simulation of the environment itself is done by a process that controls the access and changes made to the data structure that represents the environment (in fact, only that process can access the data structure); the process is called the *environment controller*. The data structure that represents the environment is generated by the ELMS interpreter for a specification in ELMS given as input. In each simulation cycle, the environment controller sends to all agents currently taking part in the simulation the percepts to which they have access (as specified in ELMS). Recall that ELMS environments are designed for cognitive agents, so perception is transmitted to the agents' practical reasoning (which in MAS-SOC typically run under *Jason* as separate processes) in messages as a list of ground logical facts. After sending perception, the controller process waits for the actions that the agents have chosen to perform in that simulation cycle and then execute the action in the environment, which means to perform the changes, as specified in the ELMS actions, in the environment data structures. Finally, the environment sends the updated perceptions to the agents, starting a new cycle.

4   Normative Infrastructure

Typically, environments will have some objects aimed at informing agents about norms, give some advice, or warn about potential dangers. For example, a poster fixed on a wall in a library asking for "silence" is an object in the environment, but also informs about a norm that should be respected within that space. Another example are traffic signs, which give advice about directions or regulate priorities in crossings. The existence of such signs, which we call *normative objects*, implies the existence of a regulating code in such context, and such code is formed by what we call *situated norms*.

In the examples above, the norms are only meant to be followed within certain boundaries of space or time, and lose their effect completely if those space and time restrictions are not met, which is the initial motivation for situated norms. Another important advantage of modelling some norms as situated norms is the fact that the spatial context where the norm is to be followed is immediately determined. Thus, the norm can be "pre-compiled" to its situated form, making it easier for the agents to operationalise the norm, and also facilitating the verification of norm compliance.

In this section we present the extensions to ELMS that are meant to provide an infrastructure allowing the distribution of normative information within an environment. Such infrastructure is aimed at being a connection point between the environment and organisational structures, improving significantly the possibilities of our simulation platform.

4.1   Normative Places

As described in previous sections, we have developed a language to describe environments for situated multi-agent systems. The description, based on the concepts of agent bodies, objects, and an optional grid, did not offer the means to define the notion of a "place", i.e., a set of cells where a set of connected activities are done or where groups or agent settings are related; we refer to them as *normative places*. They are effectively used to represent the physical spaces where organisations take place; that is, a normative place is the spatial scope of a particular organisation, and consequently the norms related to the activities of such organisation.

A *normative place* is defined simply by its name and the set of cells that are part of it. A *normative place* may have intersection with other normative places, or may even be contained by another. For example a "school" may be seen as a normative place with a large set of cells where some cells refer to a normative place "classroom" and others to the "library". The *normative place* definition allows for the definition of the spatial location where certain norms are valid and relevant, as it will be seen in the next section.

In order to ease the definition of repetitive normative place structures, types of normative places can be defined and then instantiated in specific positions of the grid. Examples of such definitions (in ELMS's XML format) are as follows.

```
<NORMATIVE-PLACE-TYPE NAME="library"/>

<NORMATIVE-PLACE-TYPE NAME="classroom"/>

<PLACE NAME="lib1" NORMATIVE-PLACE-TYPE="library">
     <CELL X="0" Y="0"/>
     <CELL X="0" Y="1"/>
</PLACE>

<PLACE NAME="cr1" NORMATIVE-PLACE-TYPE="classroom">
     <CELL X="2" Y="0">
</PLACE>
```

4.2   Normative Objects

Normative objects are "readable" by agents under specific individual conditions; that is, an agent can read a specific rule if it has a specific ability to perceive that type of object. In the most typical case, the condition is simply being physically close to the object.

Such objects can be defined before the simulation starts, or can be created dynamically during the simulation. Each normative object can be placed in a collection of cells of the spatial grid of the environment. Such cells represent the *normative place*, determining the first condition for the normative object being perceived: it is only in that normative place that the content of the normative object can be accessed and is relevant. If such collection of cells is not given, the normative object will only be perceived by agents under specific conditions. The conditions under which the normative objects can be perceived are defined by the simulation designer using the usual ELMS constructs for defining conditions.

The normative information in a normative object is *read* by an agent through its sensing/perception abilities. It contains the norm itself and also meta-information (e.g., which agent or institution created the norm). Normative objects can be defined before the simulation starts in a "norms definition file" or during the simulation, in both cases by the definition of the following properties:

Type: the type of the normative information contained in the object; it determines the level of importance (e.g. a warning, an obligation, a direction);

Issued by: where the power underlying the norm comes from (e.g., an agent, a group, an institution).

Norm: a string that represents the normative information; this should be in the format of AgentSpeak predicates in the case of MAS-SOC environments, or whatever format the targeted agents will be able to understand.

Placement: the set of normative spaces where the normative information applies. If omitted, the object is assumed to be accessible from anywhere, but normally under conditions determined by the designer (see the next item). This also determines the space where the normative information applies.

Condition: conditions under which the normative information can be perceived. The conditions can be associated with groups, roles, abilities, and current physical placement and orientation of agents and objects.

Id: identification string for eventual deletion/edition of the normative object.

We now briefly describe how the agents will receive normative information from normative objects. Whenever the agent position is such that access to the normative object is granted, and the *Condition* is satisfied, the agent will receive percepts of the form:

rule([PLACE],[GROUP],[ISSUED BY],[NORM])
For example: rule(home, family, parents, obligation(child,play(TOY),tidy(TOY)))

The example above can be read as: "This is a rule to be followed by members of the *family* group, issued by the *parents*, with application at the normative place *home* (see below), that says: if the action $play(TOY)$ is done by an agent of role *child*, then it is an obligation of that agent to do $tidy(TOY)$ as well". A rule like that would not normally be posted on a sign in a family home, but it illustrates the more general idea of situated norms as norms that apply within given environmental locations.

It is worth noting that the norm-abiding behaviour is not related just to the existence of a normative object at some place. Beyond the existence of such object, it is necessary for the agent to perceive the normative object, and autonomous agents will also reason about whether to follow or not the norm stated by the normative object, after perceiving it.

4.3   Pre-compilation of Norms

The *normative objects* are not meant to be only means to spread general norms. The norms informed through the normative objects are supposed to be contextualised (as determined by the simulation designer), incorporating information which is specific to the normative place where it is relevant.

Since the spatial context of the norm is limited and determined by the normative places, a generic norm can then be "pre-compiled" with such information, so that it becomes less abstract. This process is meant to make it easier to operationalise the norm, since the norm is "ready to use" and it is in the spatial context where it is relevant. Other advantages of having less abstract norms are that the verification of norm compliance is facilitated and that they can reduce the misinterpretations that could happen with abstract, non-contextualised norms.

For example a norm that says "Be kind to the elderly", may be quite hard to operationalise and verify, in general. However, in a fixed spatial context such as a bus or train, with the norm contextualised as "Give up your seat for the elderly", or in a street crossing, with the norm contextualised as "Help elderly people to cross the street", the norm would be much more easily interpreted by the agents, and similarly much more easily verified by any norm compliance checking mechanism.

4.4   Norm Supervisors

Since the agents are free to reason about abiding or not to a norm stated in a normative object, besides having in general limited perception capabilities with respect to normative objects, there is also a need to monitor the behaviour of those agents. In order to be able to act as a norm supervisor, an agent may need extra information and perhaps extra abilities. For this reason, in the extended version of ELMS, it is possible to define an agent as a *norm supervisor*, which will enable it to receive information about the relevant normative information as well as about the actions being done by other agents at a given normative place.

The agents in charge of norm supervision may be system agents, designed to check agents' compliance to norms or may be common agents whose interests require that certain agents follow certain norms. As the norm and the possible violations are contextualised in a specific normative place, it is much easier to define the possible violations of those norms. Through the use of simple rules, a norm supervisor can check the compliance of agents to norms, and then according to the capabilities given to it, it may interrupt the course of action of another agent, issue penalties or appropriate "punishment", or simply report the breaching of the norm to some centralised agency or the user.

It is important to note that norm supervisors are not meant only to try and stop rule breaking by other agents. Norm supervisors are agents that have access to extra information in order to be able to check the compliance to norms. The simulation designer may enable such capacity in a agent just to help it achieving its goal, to use such information to monitor the simulation, or as an input to a reputation system, among other things.

For instance, according to [5], an agent may be motivated to verify the compliance to norms by other agents in order to assure that the costs of norm adherence is being paid by the other agents too. A norm abiding agent will want that all the others addressees of the norms follow it too, otherwise the norm adhering behaviour may become some sort of competitive disadvantage. In [5], the authors refer to agents with such behaviour as *norm defenders*.

4.5   Environment-Agent Cycle

In this section, we present, in general terms, how the environment is simulated. Figure 1 shows some activity states for the environment simulation on the left-hand side, a

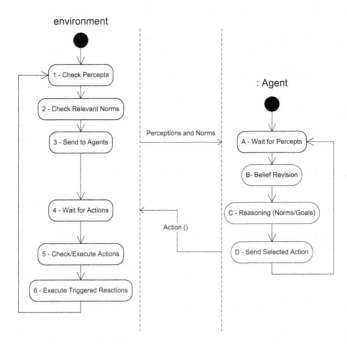

Fig. 1. Environment-Agent Cycle

simplified model of an agent's activity states on the right-hand side, and the main communication between them at the centre. The environment states are described bellow:

1. For each agent, the environment simulation controller process checks the class of the agent and which perception levels are enabled for it. Then, it checks which perception levels fulfil the conditions specified in the ELMS perception specification and gathers the appropriate environment properties to be sent to the agent.
2. The normative objects that are in the same normative place as the agent are checked in order to decide if they contain normative information relevant to the agent. If the conditions are fulfilled the norms are also gathered to be sent to the agent.
3. The environment sends the specific percepts and normative information to each agent.
4. The environment waits for the action selected by each agent.
5. The environment checks if the selected action is enabled for the agent that requested it and whether it fulfils the conditions specified on the ELMS action definition. If so, environment properties are changed as specified in the action definition.
6. The environment checks which reactions of the objects were triggered by the current state of environment properties. The triggered reactions are executed, changing the environment state. Then the cycle starts over again, going back to Step 1.

A general outline of a *protocol* that agents should follow is described bellow:

A. The agent waits until it receives percepts and normative information from the environment.

B. The agent could then compare the perceptions received with its own world representation in order to detect changes which may be relevant for its choice of action.
C. The agent will select an action to execute, based on its own goals and the perceived norms. Such decision involves a balance between a wide range of factors, of which we mention just a few:
   – beliefs about the environment;
   – goals, i.e., states-of-world that the agent wants to bring about;
   – selection of which goal to achieve;
   – selection of which norms to follow or not;
   – solve conflicts between goals and norms;
D. The agent sends the selected action to the environment simulation.

If the agent is a norm supervisor, the main difference is that it will be enabled to receive normative information that may or may not be relevant for itself and extra information about the behaviour of other agents. Using such information the norm supervisor agent may verify the compliance to norms. Then, in case of non-compliance, the norm supervisor may reason about the breaching of norms and take an action according to the capacities made available to it by the system designer, which may include the power to interrupt a course of action, issue penalties/sanctions/punishments, report the norm breach, or simply keep a record of the episode.

5   Modelling Environments Using ELMS

As the MAS-SOC platform does not enforce a particular agent-oriented software engineering methodology, designers can use the one they prefer. It is possible to model a multi-agent system that will have an ELMS environment using any approach: starting from the system organisation (top-down), or starting from the agents and their interactions (bottom-up).

In both approaches, the modelling of the organisational structures and the agents' reasoning need fine tuning to achieve the desired results. To have a stable point on which to base the fine tuning of the agents' reasoning or the organisational model, we suggest the use of an explicitly defined environment description written in the ELMS language and the notions presented in the Section 3. The environment is an important part of a multi-agent system, and although it can be very dynamic, in regards to design it is usually the most "stable" part of the system.

Even when the environment of the multi-agent system is the "real world" and the agent is a robot with sensors and effectors, the environment model should play a significant role in the design of the system. Any robot should have a set of sensors that give a predefined set of percepts that the robot will acquire when sensing the environment. Also, it should have a set of effectors that allow a restricted set of (parameterisable) actions. Thus, the possible sensor inputs and effectors output should be modelled first to facilitate the development of the software for the robot.

Based on these observations, we suggest that the multi-agent system design should start with the environment definition, followed by the definition of the normative places. The environment modelling should proceed as follows:

1. Definition of which kinds of action each type of agent is able to perform in the environment. Actions typically produce effects on objects of the environment or other agents.
2. Based on the changes that the agents' effective capabilities are able to make in the environment and the objectives of the simulation, the size and granularity of the grid can be determined. For example, how many cells an agent can move within one action or simulation cycle, and in how many simulation cycles the agent would be able to traverse the simulated space.
3. Based on the granularity and size of the spatial environment, the sensorial capabilities of the agents can be modelled, determining for example in which range an agent can detect other agents and objects.
4. Based on an agent's sensorial capabilities and on its typical activities, it should be possible to define which attributes of that agent is important to declare as accessible to other agents. For example, if agents identify each other's role by the colour of their uniform, the "agent body" should have an attribute that represent the colour of the agent's uniform.
5. The types of objects or resources present in the environment should also be modelled based on which attributes will be perceptible by the agents and which actions can affect them.
6. Finally, instances of the agent and object classes should be placed in the environment, determining its initial state.

The definition of the environment should be followed by the definition of normative places, followed then by the definition of the spatially distributed normative objects, as follows:

1. As the resource and agent instances are placed in the environment, the activities for each spatial place can be defined.
2. By grouping the neighbouring cells where similar activities are done, the normative places and its extensions can be defined.
3. By instantiating normative places into sets of cells, the *normative places* are created.
4. Then, based on the set of activities that can possibly be performed in each type of normative place, the norms that are relevant to that type of place can be defined.
5. Finally, the types of *normative objects* can be defined and instantiated in the normative places, defining the locations where situated norms can be perceived.

Using the environment as the basis, i.e., using the information contained in the environment model, the agents' reasoning capabilities can then be defined so as to help agents achieve their goals as well as those of the groups to which they belong. Also, the detailed definitions of possible organisational structures can be fine tuned, in order to allow the overall system to achieve its (social) goals. In MAS-SOC, we use AgentSpeak to define the practical reasoning for each agent; in particular, we use the extended version of AgentSpeak as interpreted by *Jason*; for details, see [2].

6 Example

Below we give an example showing how normative objects are defined using our approach. It is based on the scenario presented in [3], a scenario in which the agents are placed in an environment where they can eat the food they find, attack another agent to take its food, or move in search of food.

In this scenario, an agent owns any (free) food item that is near to itself (at a distance of up to 2 cells). The agents can "see" food and other agents in a radius of 1 cell, but can sense food in a radius of 2 cells. The physical space is represented by a grid of 10×10 cells.

The norms used in that scenario essentially concern the respect for the ownership of a food item, which means they prescribe non-aggressive behaviour. In the original scenario, the norms were valid throughout the grid (that is, the whole environment was treated as just one single normative place), but in the following example we use normative objects and establish smaller normative places within the environment.

A shortened version of the physical environment description is given below. The actual environment description of environments in ELMS is stored in XML format (with the help of a GUI), but in order to save space and improve readability, we have adopted a pseudocode representation, just to show the main points of the environment model in ELMS.

```
environment.name:="FOOD-CHASERS";
environment.grid.dim(10,10);

food = Resource{
    owner: string ("none")
    id: integer}

agent = Agent_body{
    id: integer(SELF);
    power: integer(50);
    vision: PERCEPTION;
    sense_food: PERCEPTION;
    walk: ACTION;
    attack: ACTION;
    eat: ACTION;
    SUPERVISION:=ENABLED;
    ENFORCING:=NONE;
}

vision = PERCEPTION{
    cell[+0][+0].contents;  cell[+0][+1].food.owner;
    cell[+0][-1].contents;  cell[+1][+0].food.owner;
    cell[-1][+0].contents;
    cell[+0][+0].food.owner; cell[+0][+1].food.owner;
    cell[+0][-1].food.owner; cell[+1][+0].food.owner;
    cell[-1][+0].food.owner;
}

sense_food = PERCEPTION{
    cell[+1][+1].food.id;  cell[-1][-1].food.id;
    cell[-1][+1].food.id;  cell[+1][-1].food.id;
    cell[+0][-2].food.id;  cell[+0][+2].food.id;
    cell[-2][+0].food.id;  cell[+2][+0].food.id;
}

eat = ACTION(FOOD_ID:integer){....}
walk = ACTION{....}
attack = ACTION{...}
```

In the code excerpt above, the grid size is defined, then `food` is defined as a generic type of environment resource, then a generic type of agent body is defined. The agent body is defined as being capable of two types of perception — vision and food sensing – and being able to perform three types of actions: walk, attack, and eat. The `vision` perception type allows the agent to perceive the contents of the current cell and the 4 neighbouring cells, while `sense_food` allows it to perceive food within a 2-cell radius. The agent also have the `SUPERVISION` property enabled, which means that the agents will perceive normative information contained in its current location which may not be relevant to itself. Also the agent will be able to receive information about the actions performed by agents that are in the same normative space. The `ENFORCING` parameter has `NONE` as value, meaning that the agent has no group or institutional power to enforce the norms. However, the agent may keep the record of norm breaching for its future reference; the kept record can also be used for an eventual retaliation or to be shared with other agents.

For this example, the grid is partitioned in four normative places of equal sizes, and normative objects are defined and placed in three of the four quadrants, as shown in the code excerpt below:

```
upper-left = PLACE{
type = "food-protected"
environment.grid[0..4][0..4];
}

upper-right = PLACE{
    type = "food-protected"
    environment.grid[5..9][0..4];
}

lower-left = PLACE{
type = "food-protected"
environment.grid[0..4][5..9];
}

norm-obj1 = NORM_OBJ{
    type := "prohibition";
    place:= "upper-left"
    norm := "prohibited(true,attack(SELF,AGENT))";
}

norm-obj2 = NORM_OBJ{
    type := "prohibited";
    place:= "upper-right"
    norm := "prohibited(not(in-possession(SELF,FOOD)),eat(SELF,FOOD))";
}

norm-obj3 = NORM_OBJ{
    type := "prohibition";
    place:= "lower-left"
    norm := "prohibited(true,attack(SELF,AGENT))";
}

norm-obj4 = NORM_OBJ{
    type := "prohibited";
    place:= "lower-left"
    norm := "prohibited(not(in-possession(SELF,FOOD)),eat(SELF,FOOD))";
}
```

The normative objects in the above example are very simple, and are given simply to illustrate how they can be modelled in our approach. For instance, `norm-obj1` and norm-obj3 say that an agent ought not to attack (steal food from) another agent, while norm-obj2 and norm-obj4 say that the agent ought not to eat a food item which is not in possession of the agent itself.

Clearly, the agents' behaviour will be different in the four quadrants of the environment:

- in the upper-left quadrant, agents are advised against eating food that is in the possession of another agent, since the situated norm states that agents are prohibited from stealing food;
- in the upper-right quadrant, agents are apparently prohibited from doing that, but not effectively, since the situated norm only prohibits the eating of food that is not currently in the possession of the agent itself (rather than the stealing of food); so, an agent can eat food that previously was in the possession of another agent if it first manages to steal the food;
- in the lower-left quadrant, both restrictions are in place; we note that this situation can be seen as redundant, if one understands that the second norm is implied by the first one;
- the remaining quadrant (lower-right) is a lawless area, where agents are completely free to attack each other and to eat anyone else's food.

Notice that prohibited is used as a conditional deontic operator, with two arguments: the first argument is a condition to be tested, the second argument is the action that is prohibited. In the modelled scenario, agents are not forced to follow the rules, but they may use the normative information to monitor each other, being able to use it, for example, as input to a reputation system.

7   Related Work

The notion of artifacts [17] and coordination artifacts [13] resembles, in some aspects, our notion of *normative objects*. As defined in [13], coordination artifacts are abstractions meant to improve the automation of coordination activities, being the building blocks to create effective shared collaborative working environments. They are defined as runtime abstractions that encapsulate and provide a coordination service to the agents. Artifacts [17] were presented as a generalisation of coordination artifacts. Artifacts are an abstraction to represent tools, services, objects, and entities in a multi-agent environment.

As building blocks for environment modelling, artifacts encapsulate the features of the environment as services to be used by the agents. The main objective of a coordination artifacts is to be used as an abstraction of an environmental coordination service provided to the agents. However, coordination artifacts express normative rules only implicitly, through their practical effects on the actions of the agents, and so their normative impact does not require any normative reasoning from the part of the agents. In our work, rather than having a general notion of objects that by their (physical) properties facilitate coordination, *normative objects* are used specifically to store *symbolic* information that can be interpreted by agents, so that they can become aware of norms that should be followed within a well-defined location.

Our choice in regards to normative objects has the advantage of keeping open the possibility of agent autonomy, as suggested in [4]. Agents are, in principle, able to decide whether to follow the norms or not when trying to be effective in the pursuit of their goals. This is something that is not possible if an agent's action can only happen if it is in accordance implicit norms enforced by coordination mechanisms.

Another important difference is that *normative objects* are spatially distributed over a physical environment, with a spatial scope where they apply, and closely tied to the part of the organisation that is physically located in that space. While the objective of the notion of coordination artifacts is to remove the burden of coordination from the agents, our work tries to simplify the way designers can guide the behaviour of each individual agent as they move around an environment where organisations are spatially located; this allows agents to adapt the way they behave in different social contexts.

In [8], the authors present the AGRE model, an extension to the previous AGR model. Those latest extensions allow the definition of structures that represents the physical space. The approach defines organisational structures (i.e., groups) and the physical structures (i.e., areas) as "specialisations" of a generic space. We find, however, that in their approach, the social structures are not contextualised in the space as they are in our work, leaving the social and physical structures rather unrelated.

In ELMS, however, it is not possible to explicitly define social structures, even though it would be possible to implicitly define them through the norms. This is because our aim in the present ELMS extension is to allow for environmental infrastructures to be compatible with existing approaches to organisational modelling, not for the modelling of organisations as such; the combination of ELMS with existing approaches to modelling organisations is the first item in our current research agenda.

Another important series of related work is that on Electronic Institutions [9]. The internal working of an electronic institutions is given (in rough terms) as a state-machine where each state is called a "scene". Each scene specifies the set of roles that agents may perform in it, and a "conversation protocol" that the agents should follow when interacting in the scene. To traverse the series of scenes that constitute the operation of the electronic institution, agents must do a sequence of actions in each scene, and also to commit to certain actions in certain scenes, as the result of their having performed certain other actions in certain other scenes. Our notion of normative space was inspired by such notion of scene, in giving it a physical, spatial reference where norms apply.

Similar to the electronic institutions approach, there is work on *computational institutions* [15], which are defined as virtual organisations ruled by constitutive norms and regulative norms. In computational institutions, organisational modelling uses the abstraction of coordination artifacts as building blocks, in a way that is very similar to our use of normative objects in spatially distributed organisations, but still keeping implicit in coordination artifacts the normative content imposed on the agents.

8 Conclusions

In this paper, we extended the ELMS language for describing environments with the means to define normative structures that make part of an environment representation. There are currently various approaches to designing and implementing multi-agent systems: some are top-down approaches with focus on the organisations, while bottom-up approaches focus on the agents. We believe that including environment modelling at the initial stages of both approaches would help the modelling and implementation of multi-agent systems. To help such modelling, we have proposed an approach with an explicit environment description which now also includes the notions of *situated norms*, *normative places*, and (spatially distributed) *normative objects*.

It is important to note that our work is not an approach for modelling the organisational dimension of a multi-agent system. With the definition of *normative places*, where group structures would be situated, we intend to fill a conceptual gap between the usual ways in which organisations and physical environments are modelled. In future work, with the integration of existing approaches to defining organisational structures into ELMS, and thus the possibility of associating them to normative places, we hope to contribute to a more integrated approach to designing and implementing the various aspects of multi-agent systems: concentrating on one particular organisation section at a time, specially if it is an organisation section attached to a spatial location, make it easier for designers to define the groups, roles and agent behaviour that should operate in that particular organisation section.

We believe that an explicit environment description is an important part of a multi-agent system because it is a stable point from where the agent reasoning and the organisational structures can be fine-tuned so as to facilitate the development of agents and organisations that can achieve their goals. We believe that the notion of *spatially distributed normative objects* that we have introduced in our work is a suitable approach to connecting definitions of organisations and definitions of environments. Additionally, distributing the organisational/normative information can facilitate the modelling of large organisations.

We plan to make possible such association for existing approaches to modelling agent organisations, such as $\mathcal{M}\textsc{oise}^+$ [10], OperA/OMNI [16], GAIA [19], and approaches based on electronic institutions [6,7]. However, the recursive nature of normative places may not be compatible with some of such approaches to organisations, where the (possibly implicit) system of normative rules has no provision for a recursive structure in its operation.

By distributing the normative information in the environment, it is possible to partition the environment in a functional way, thus helping the structured definition of large simulations, norms being associated only with the places where they are meant to be followed. It is also more efficient (by taking advantage of the natural distribution of certain environments) to have norms spread in an environment than having them in a centralised repository made available to the whole society, as it is usually the case. Another advantage of having the information distributed is the possibility of the *precompilation* of the norms with the spatial context information, which we call *situated norms*. This makes it much easier to make norms operational, both for following norms and checking norm compliance. Using the resulting information of the norm compliance checking as input, e.g., for a reputation system, given that different places can have different norms, it may turn out that, despite exhibiting exactly the same behaviour at different places, an agent will have different reputations at different places, leading to the notion of *locality of reputation*; this is another interesting subject for future work.

It is interesting to note that, being conditioned on the possibility of checking the existence of a normative object, the normative reasoning required from agents that deal with normative objects is necessarily of a non-monotonic nature; the experience of programming such reasoning in AgentSpeak is something we also plan to do in the future.

Acknowledgements

This work was partially supported by CNPq and FAPERGS.

References

1. R. H. Bordini, A. C. d. R. Costa, J. F. Hübner, A. F. Moreira, F. Y. Okuyama, and R. Vieira. MAS-SOC: a social simulation platform based on agent-oriented programming. *Journal of Artificial Societies and Social Simulation*, 8(3), 2005.
2. R. H. Bordini, J. F. Hübner, and R. Vieira. *Jason* and the Golden Fleece of agent-oriented programming. In R. H. Bordini, M. Dastani, J. Dix, and A. El Fallah Seghrouchni, editors, *Multi-Agent Programming: Languages, Platforms and Applications*, chapter 1. Springer-Verlag, 2005.
3. C. Castelfranchi, R. Conte, and M. Paolucci. Normative reputation and the costs of compliance. *Journal of Artificial Societies and Social Simulation*, 1(3), 1998. <http://www.soc.surrey.ac.uk/JASSS/1/3/3.html>.
4. C. Castelfranchi, F. Dignum, C. M. Jonker, and J. Treur. Deliberative normative agents: Principles and architecture. In *6th International Workshop on Intelligent Agents VI, Agent Theories, Architectures, and Languages (ATAL)*, Lecture Notes In Computer Science, Vol. 1757, pages 364–378, Londo, 1999. Springer-Verlag.
5. R. Conte and C. Castelfranchi. *Cognitive and Social Action*. UCL Press, London, 1995.
6. M. Esteva, D. de la Cruz, and C. Sierra. Islander: an electronic institutions editor. In *AAMAS*, pages 1045–1052. ACM, 2002.
7. M. Esteva, B. Rosell, J. A. Rodríguez-Aguilar, and J. L. Arcos. Ameli: An agent-based middleware for electronic institutions. In *AAMAS*, pages 236–243. IEEE Computer Society, 2004.
8. J. Ferber, F. Michel, and J.-A. Báez-Barranco. Agre: Integrating environments with organizations. In *E4MAS*, pages 48–56, 2004.
9. A. Garcia-Camino, P. Noriega, and J. A. Rodríguez-Aguilar. Implementing norms in electronic institutions. In F. Dignum, V. Dignum, S. Koenig, S. Kraus, M. P. Singh, and M. Wooldridge, editors, *AAMAS*, pages 667–673. ACM, 2005.
10. J. F. Hübner, J. S. Sichman, and O. Boissier. $\mathcal{M}OISE^+$: Towards a structural, functional, and deontic model for MAS organization. In *Proceedings of the First International Joint Conference on Autonomous Agents and Multi-Agent Systems (AAMAS'2002), Bologna, Italy*, 2002.
11. F. Y. Okuyama, R. H. Bordini, and A. C. da Rocha Costa. Spatially Distributed Normative Objects. In G. Boella *et al.*, editors, *Proceedings of the International Workshop on Coordination, Organization, Institutions and Norms in Agent Systems (COIN)*, held with ECAI, Riva del Garda, Italy, 28 August 2006.
12. F. Y. Okuyama, R. H. Bordini, and A. C. da Rocha Costa. ELMS: An environment description language for multi-agent simulations. In D. Weyns, H. van Dyke Parunak, and F. Michel, editors, *Proceedings of the First International Workshop on Environments for Multiagent Systems (E4MAS), held with AAMAS-04, 19th of July*, number 3374 in Lecture Notes In Artificial Intelligence, pages 91–108, Berlin, 2005. Springer-Verlag.

13. A. Omicini, A. Ricci, M. Viroli, C. Castelfranchi, and L. Tummolini. Coordination artifacts: Environment-based coordination for intelligent agents. In *AAMAS'04*, 2004.
14. A. S. Rao. AgentSpeak(L): BDI agents speak out in a logical computable language. In W. Van de Velde and J. Perram, editors, *Proceedings of the Seventh Workshop on Modelling Autonomous Agents in a Multi-Agent World (MAAMAW'96), 22–25 January, Eindhoven, The Netherlands*, number 1038 in Lecture Notes in Artificial Intelligence, pages 42–55, London, 1996. Springer-Verlag.
15. R. Rubino, A. Omicini, and E. Denti. Computational institutions for modelling norm-regulated MAS: An approach based on coordination artifacts. In G. Lindemann, S. Ossowski, J. Padget, and J. Vazquez-Salceda, editors, *1st International Workshop "Agents, Norms and Institutions for Regulated Multi-Agent Systems" (ANI@REM 2005)*, AAMAS 2005, Utrecht, The Netherlands, 25 July 2005.
16. J. Vázquez-Salceda, V. Dignum, and F. Dignum. Organizing multiagent systems. *Autonomous Agents and Multi-Agent Systems*, 11(3):307–360, 2005.
17. M. Viroli, A. Omicini, and A. Ricci. Engineering MAS environment with artifacts. In D. Weyns, H. V. D. Parunak, and F. Michel, editors, *2nd International Workshop "Environments for Multi-Agent Systems" (E4MAS 2005)*, pages 62–77, AAMAS 2005, Utrecht, The Netherlands, 26 July 2005.
18. D. Weyns, H. V. D. Parunak, F. Michel, T. Holvoet, and J. Ferber. Environment for multiagent systems: State-of-art and research challenges. In D. Weyns, H. van Dyke Parunak, and F. Michel, editors, *Proceedings of the First International Workshop on Environments for Multiagent Systems (E4MAS), held with AAMAS-04, 19th of July*, number 3374 in Lecture Notes In Artificial Intelligence, Berlin, 2005. Springer-Verlag.
19. M. Wooldridge, N. R. Jennings, and D. Kinny. The GAIA methodology for agent-oriented analysis and design. *Autonomous Agents and Multi-Agent Systems*, 3(3):285–312, 2000.

Enhancing the Environment with a Law-Governed Service for Monitoring and Enforcing Behavior in Open Multi-Agent Systems

Rodrigo Paes[1], Gustavo Carvalho[1], Maíra Gatti[1],
Carlos Lucena[1], Jean-Pierre Briot[1,2], and Ricardo Choren[3]

[1] PUC-Rio, Rua M de S Vicente 225, Gávea
22453-900, Rio de Janeiro, Brazil
{rbp, guga, mgati, lucena}@inf.puc-rio.br
[2] LIP6, 4, place Jussieu
75005 Paris, France
jean-pierre.briot@lip6.fr
[3] IME, Pça General Tibúrcio 80, Praia Vermelha
22290-270, Rio de Janeiro, Brazil
choren@de9.ime.eb.br

Abstract. Environment is an essential part of any multi-agent system (MAS), since it provides the surrounding conditions for agents to exist. For some sort of systems, the environment can be viewed as providing a set of services, in which some of them, such as directory facilities, are used explicitly by the agents to perform their tasks, and other such as monitoring, behavioral enforcement and security can be done transparently by the environment. We join the idea that the specification of environments of open multi-agent systems should include laws that define what and when something can happen in an open system. Laws are restrictions imposed by the environment to tame uncertainty and to promote open system dependability. This paper proposes a design approach and application of a middleware based on laws in multi-agent systems. The approach can be viewed as a set of services provided by the environment.

1 Introduction

The agent development paradigm has posed many challenges to software engineering researchers. This is particularly true when the systems are distributed and inherently open to accept new modules that may have been independently developed by third parties. Such systems are characterized by having little or no control over the actions that agents can perform. The greater the dependence of our society on open distributed applications, the greater will be the demand for dependable applications.

Environment is an essential part of any multi-agent system (MAS), since it provides the surrounding conditions for agents to exist [25]. Several aspects of MAS that are vital for agents do not belong to agents themselves but are part of the environment [5]. We believe that the specification of environments of open

D. Weyns, H.V.D. Parunak, and F. Michel (Eds.): E4MAS 2006, LNAI 4389, pp. 221–238, 2007.
© Springer-Verlag Berlin Heidelberg 2007

multi-agent systems (MAS) should include laws that define what and when something can happen in an open system [4][5]. Laws are restrictions imposed by the environment to tame uncertainty and to promote open system dependability [15][17]. In this sense, the environment performs an active role monitoring and verifying if behavior of agents are in conformance with the laws. This kind of environment is composed of a governance mechanism, which is the mediator that enforces the law specification. Examples of governance mechanisms are LGI [15], Islander [7] and MLaw [18].

Governance for open multi-agent systems can be defined as the set of approaches that aims to establish and enforce some structure, set of norms or conventions to articulate or restrain interactions in order to make agents more effective in attaining their goals or more predictable [14].

Despite the growing interest in the area, mature governance approaches will only be achieved through the use of Software Engineering techniques and tools that support the development of more predictable and better quality software systems. There has been advance in this area through well founded engineering tools for governed interaction such as the work of LGI [15], Islander [7] and Rubino [21]. This paper deals with the above mentioned problem through a design approach and application of a middleware for governance in multi-agent systems. Notably, we propose the modeling of laws for governance, based on XML. This includes norms but also other abstractions such as protocols, scenes, constraints and clocks, in order to achieve a good expressivity. In another paper, we also addressed the issue of specialization of governance specifications using abstractions for extension [4]. The middleware can be used in conjunction with a specific agent platform (such as JADE [2]), and it permits configuration of interaction rules, monitoring of agent interaction and verification of the conformity between the interaction specification and the actual interaction. We have already used the middleware in a variety of different situations, such as monitoring criticality of agents [11], tests [20] and mediation of inter-bank operations.

This paper is organized as follows. Section 2 introduces the relationship between the environment and the interaction Laws. Section 3 introduces the main Governance concepts used in this paper. Section 4 presents the middleware for governance used in this work. Section 5 shows how the framework can be effectively used to enhance the notion of environment and presents an experiment that was performed using the middleware. Section 6 presents some related work and details on where this paper gives the contribution. Finally, Section 7 presents some discussion and conclusions about this work.

2   Environment and Interaction Laws

The precise definition of environment is still under the core of the discussions among the research community [26]. One of the reasons that definitions of environment have proliferated is that MAS have been applied to a wide range of different application domains [24]. For example, it is natural for designers of a business-to-business application to associate the environment with the existent infrastructure of hardware and software on which the agents will have to execute. In another domain, such as an agent-based simulation of an ecosystem, the environment as well as the agents will be custom built for the application [24].

A very common distinction for environments is between physical and virtual environment. In the physical environment there are the physical constraints of the existent entities. An example is that in an agent system that controls robots in which two robots are not allowed to occupy the same place at the same time. The virtual environment provides the principles and processes that govern and support the exchange of ideas, knowledge and information [24].

A very deep discussion on environments can be found in [26]. They define an environment as a first-class abstraction that provides the surrounding conditions for agents to exist and that mediates both the interaction among agents and the access to resources.

An environment provides the conditions under which an entity exists [16]. Multi-agent environments are typically open and have no single centralized designer, they contain agents that are autonomous, distributed and may be self-interested or cooperative. Furthermore, environments provide a computational infrastructure that enables agents to communicate with one another [13].

It is the responsibility of the environment to define the rules for, and enforce the effects of, the agents' actions. An appealing way to exert the necessary level of control over an agent in an open system is through an adequate MAS infrastructure [23], which can be viewed as part of the environment. The type of services provided by the infra-structure, and the way in which these services are enacted, limit the set of possible actions [23]. For that, a MAS designer can use a governing infrastructure to structure and shape the space of action within MAS in an open environment. This governing perspective allows managing agent interactions form an external and global point-of-view.

In this sense, the environment is viewed as an active entity that also contains the set of behavioral (social) laws, which is constantly monitoring and reacting to agents' actions. It is very important for the agents to be able to perceive the environment. Agents can use the percepts to update their knowledge about the environment or use it for decision making [24]. In this sense, a virtual environment should provide explicit data structures for notify changing on the environment state.

We have used the reference model of the environment (Figure 1) proposed in [26] to show how the environment can be viewed. It shows that the environment provides a set of services, in which some of them, such as directory facilities, are used explicitly by the agents to perform their tasks, and other such as monitoring, behavioral enforcement and security can be done transparently by the environment[1]. The list of services shown in Figure 1 shows an environment as the basic infrastructure for supporting agents' activities in a more dependable manner. In this paper we focus on the governance services (the law box in the figure), which are used to monitor and enforce the behavior of agents.

---

[1] In fact, it may be discussed if social laws (regulating interactions between agents) and social entities (like organizations) are, conceptually and architecturally speaking, part of the environment of a MAS or if they have a distinct existence (see, e.g., [9]). In this paper, we describe governance (of social laws) as part of the services offered by a MAS environment.

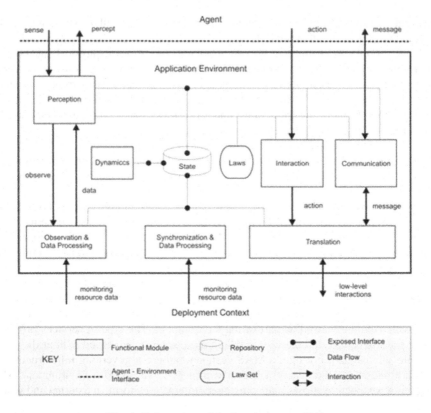

Fig. 1. Reference model of environments [26]

3   Governing Interactions

Law-governed architectures are designed to guarantee that the specifications of open systems will be obeyed. The core of a law-governed approach is the mechanism used by the mediators to monitor the conversations between components. We have developed a software support [18] that, whenever necessary, permits extending this mechanism to fulfill open system requirements or interoperability concerns. In this architecture, a communication component is provided to agent developers.

M-Law works by intercepting messages exchanged between agents, verifying the compliance of the messages with the laws and subsequently redirecting the message to the real addressee, if the laws allow it. If the message is not compliant, then the mediator blocks the message and applies the consequences specified in the law (Figure 2). This architecture is based on a pool of mediators that intercept messages and interpret the previously described laws. A more detailed explanation about how this architecture was in fact implemented can be found in [19]. As more clients are added to the system, additional mediators' instances can be added to improve throughput. In relation with the list of services shown in Figure 1, M-Law implements the monitoring and enforcing of agents' behavior.

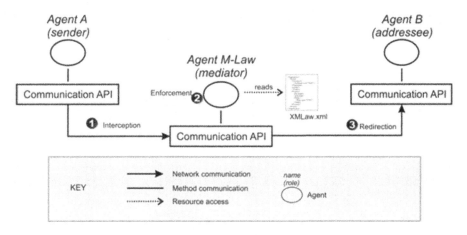

Fig. 2. M-Law architecture

M-Law was built to support law specification using XMLaw [17][3]. XMLaw is used to represent the interaction rules of an open system specification. As mentioned before, XMLaw is the description language used to configure the M-Law. These rules are interpreted by M-Law that analyzes the compliance of software agents with interaction laws at runtime. XMLaw represents the structure and the relationships between important law elements (Figure 3). A more detailed definition of the conceptual model can be found in [3] and [17]. A law is a description composed of law elements, such as e.g., protocols, norms, and scenes, as described in the next paragraphs.

Norms can be used to enhance scene and transition definitions; constraints in norms and transitions can act as filters of events; and actions can be used as an adaptation mechanism to support an active behavior of the environment in an open system. We selected some elements from XMLaw conceptual model to illustrate our proposal. Below, we will discuss XMLaw structure using the specification of laws for the TAC SCM example to facilitate its understanding.

The conceptual model uses the abstraction of Scenes to help to organize interactions. The idea of scenes is similar to theater plays, where actors play according to well defined scripts, and the whole play is composed of many scenes sequentially connected. Scenes are composed of Protocols, Constraints, Clocks, and Norms. It means that these four elements share a common interaction context through the scenes. Because protocols define the interaction among the agents, different protocols should be specified in different scenes. Scenes also specify which agent role has permission to create scene instances.

Statically, an interaction protocol defines the set of states and transitions (activated by messages or any other kind of event) allowed for agents in an open system. Norms are jointly used with the protocol specification, constraints, actions and also temporal elements, to provide a dynamic configuration for the allowed behavior of components in an open system. The mediator keeps information about the set of activated elements to verify the compliance of software agents, the set of deactivated elements and any other data regarding system execution.

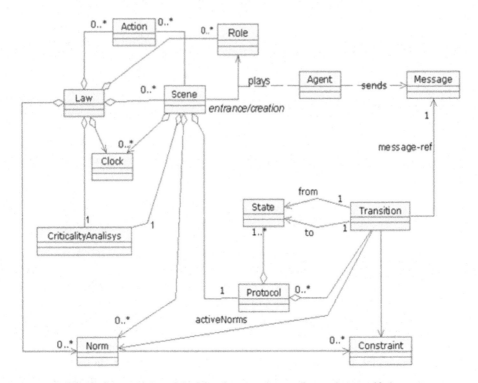

Fig. 3. Conceptual model of the elements that can be used to specify laws

Laws may be time sensitive, e.g., although an element maybe active at time t1, it might not be active at time t2 (t1 < t2). XMLaw provides the Clock element to take care of the timing aspect. Temporal clocks represent time restrictions or controls and they can be used to activate other law elements. Clocks indicate that a certain period has elapsed producing clock-tick events. Once activated, a clock can generate clock-tick events. Clocks are activated and deactivated by law elements. Both are referenced to other law elements. Below, we detail the structure of the elements that will be exemplified in this paper.

3.1 Simple Scenario

The example that will guide our explanation is the Trading Agent Competition - Supply Chain Management (TAC SCM). The TAC SCM [22][1][6] editions provide some evidence that the interaction specification evolves over time and so an extension support can reduce maintenance efforts.

The TAC SCM has been designed with a simple set of rules to capture the complexity of a dynamic supply chain. SCM applications are extremely dynamic and involve an important number of products, information and resources among their different stages. In our case study, we mapped the requirements of TAC SCM into interaction laws and agents are implemented with JADE [2].

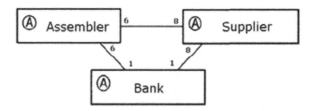

Fig. 4. Roles, relationships and cardinalities of TAC SCM

In TAC SCM, we chose the scenario of negotiation between the suppliers and assemblers to explain how interaction laws are used (Figure 1). According to [1], the negotiation process involves an assembler agent that buys components from suppliers. A bank agent also participates in this negotiation because an assembler must pay the components for the supplier. In this scenario, an assembler may send RFQs to each supplier every day to order components offered by the supplier. Each RFQ represents a request for a specified quantity of a particular component type to be delivered on a specific date in the future. The supplier collects all RFQs received during the "day" and processes them. On the following "day", the supplier sends back to each agent an offer for each RFQ, containing the price, adjusted quantity, and due date. If the agent wishes to accept an offer, it must confirm it by issuing an order to the supplier.

3.2 Norms

There are three types of norms in XMLaw: obligations, permissions and prohibitions. The obligation norm defines a commitment that software agents acquire while interacting with other entities. For instance, the winner of an auction is obligated to pay the committed value and this commitment might contain some penalties to avoid breaking this rule. The permission norm defines the rights of a software agent at a given moment, e.g. the winner of an auction has permission to interact with a bank provider through a payment protocol. Finally, the prohibition norm defines forbidden actions of a software agent at a given moment; for instance, if an agent does not pay its debts, it will not be allowed future participation in a scene.

In TAC SCM, one permission norm was created about the maximum number of requests for quotation that an assembler can submit to a supplier. According to the TAC SCM specification, each day each agent may send up to a maximum number of RFQs. Besides this permission, the constraint on the acceptable due date of an RFQ regulates the same interaction, the request for quote message.

The structure of the Permission (Code Fragment 1), Obligation and Prohibition elements are equal. Each type of norm contains activation and deactivation conditions. In the example, an assembler will receive the permission upon logging in to the scene (scene activation event) and will lose the permission after issuing an order (event orderTransition). Furthermore, norms define the agent role that owns it through the attribute Owner. In that case, the assembler agent will receive the permission. Norms also have constraints and actions associated with them, but these elements will be explained later. Norms also generate activation and deactivation events. For instance, as a consequence of the relationship between norms and transitions, it is possible to specify which norms must be made active or deactivated for firing a transition. In this sense, a transition could only fire if the sender agent has a specific norm.

```
<Norm type="permission" id="AssemblerPermissionRFQ">
 <Assignee role-ref="assembler"
           role-instance="$assembler.instance"/>
  <Activations>
   <Element ref="negotiation"
            event-type="scene_creation"/>
  </Activations>
  <Deactivations>
   <Element ref="orderTransition"
            event-type="transition_activation"/>
  </Deactivations>
  <Constraints>
   <Constraint id="checkCounter" class="CounterLimit"/>
  </Constraints>
  <Actions>
   <Action id="permissionRenew" class="ZeroCounter">
    <Element ref="nextDay" event-type="clock_tick"/>
   </Action>
   <Action id="orderID" class="RFQCounter"/>
    <Element ref="rfqTransition"
             event-type="transition_activation"/>
   </Action>
  </Actions>
 </Norm>
```

Code 1. Permission structure

3.3 Constraints

Constraints are restrictions over norms or transitions and generally specify filters for events, constraining the allowed values for a specific attribute of an event. For instance, messages carry information that is enforced in various ways. A message pattern enforces the message structure fields [17]. A message pattern does not describe what the allowed values for specific attributes are, but constraints can be used for this purpose. In this way, developers are free to build as complex constraints as needed for their applications.

Constraints are defined inside the Transition (Code Fragment 2) or Norm (Code Fragment 1) elements Constraints are implemented using Java code. The Constraint element defines the class attribute that indicates the java class that implements the filter. The use of Java code allows for the specification of complex user defined filter implementation. This class is called when a transition or a norm is supposed to fire, and basically the constraint analyzes if the message values or any other events' attributes are valid. In Code Fragment 2, a constraint will verify if the date expressed in the message is valid according to TAC rules; if it is not, the message will be blocked. In Code Fragment 1, a constraint is used to verify the number of messages that the agent has sent until now; if it has been exceeded, the permission is no longer valid.

```
<Transition id="rfqTransition" from="as1" to="as2"
            message-ref="rfq>
 <Constraints>
  <Constraint id="checkDueDate" class="ValidDate"/>
 </Constraints>
 ...
</Transition>
```

Code 2. Constraint in transition tags

3.4 Actions

Environment actions, or just actions, are domain-specific Java codes that run integrated with XMLaw specifications. Actions can be used to plug services in an environment. For instance, an environment can call a debit service from a bank agent to automatically charge the purchase of an item during a negotiation. In this case, we specify in the XMLaw that there is a class that is able to perform the debit.

Since actions are also XMLaw elements, they can be activated by any event such as transition activation, norm activation and even action activation. The action structure is showed in the example of Code Fragment 1. The class attribute of an Action specifies the java class in charge of the functionality implementation. The Element tag references the events that activate this action, and as many Element tags as needed can be defined to trigger an action. In this example, the action is used to update the context of the norm, counting the number of submitted messages.

An action can be defined in three different scopes: Organization, Scene and Norms. An action defined in a Norm is only visible at this level. This means that any element in this scope can reference events issued by this action and that this action can get and update information at this level and upper levels. Actions defined in the scene scope can be referenced by any element at this level. And actions defined in the organization scope are visible to all elements at this level.

4 M-Law

Agent technology advances rely on the development of models, mechanisms and tools to build high quality systems. The design and implementation of such systems is still expensive and error prone. Software frameworks deal with this complexity by reifying proven software designs and implementations in order to reduce the cost and improve the quality of software. In this way, an object-oriented framework is a reusable, semi-complete application that can be specialized to produce custom applications [8].

M-Law was designed as an object-oriented framework, and its hotspots make possible to plug-in existing agent infrastructures, change the communication mechanism used by the agents, and plug-in new functionalities through the component module (to be detailed further in this section).

M-Law middleware has to provide the means to effectively support XMLaw and its evolutions. M-Law is composed of four modules: agent module, communication module, a mediator agent and an event module. The agent module contains classes that agent developers may use to develop agents. This module provides a set of facilities to interact with both the mediator and other agents through methods for receiving and sending messages. The Agent module uses a Communication module to send and receive messages. In fact, the Communication module contains a set of abstract classes and interfaces that have to be extended in order to provide real functionality. We have made some experiments using JADE Agent Framework to implement this module. In addition to Jade, we have also implemented a communication module using pure socket communication. This flexibility provides the means to build agents using different existing agent frameworks.

On the side of the mediator agent, which is in charge of monitoring and enforcing agent interaction, there are three main modules: Event, Component and Communication. Those modules are not visible to agent developers but they were used to build the mediator agent and they can be extended to support new functionalities. Agent criticality analysis presented in [11] is an example of the component module extension.

The event module implements event notification and propagation. It is basically an implementation of the observer design pattern [10] allowing elements for listening and receiving events. The communication module has a similar implementation as the communication module on the client side.

The elements such as scenes, clocks and norms, are implemented to be plugged into the component module. The component module defines a set of concrete and abstract classes and interfaces that allows new functionality to be inserted.

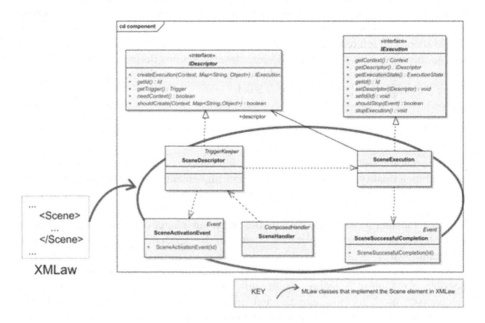

Fig. 5. Scene component

Components are the set of classes placed in the mediator that implements the behavior of the XMLaw language elements; for example, Figure 5 shows the scene element in XMLaw and its set of classes that implements its behavior. In Figure 5, the scene Element in XMLaw (therefore an XML element) is mapped to a descriptor (IDescriptor) and execution (IExecution) hierarchies in the internal implementation of the MLaw. Those hierarchies are hotspots of the component module, and they are used to plug in new elements in the law definition, allowing, for example, to change the XMLaw conceptual model.

As shown in Figure 5, the core classes and interfaces of the component module that provide the hotspots that have to be extended by concrete elements are:

- Handlers: SimpleHandler and ComposedHandler – The component module has a default XML parser that reads a law specification in XML and delegates the treatment of each XML tag to a specific handler. The handler is in charge of receiving the tokens provided by the parser and building the descriptor of the element.

- IDescriptor – It represents the object model of the XML tag. For example, in Figure 6, the scene tag in XML is represented by the SceneDescriptor class. Its main responsibility is creating execution instances of the descriptor.

- IExecution – An object that implements the IExecution interface is an instance of an element represented by an IDescriptor object. For example, a scene may be instantiated many times and even various scenes may be running at the same time (various auctions running in parallel, for instance). Each instance (IExecution) has to keep its instance attributes and control its lifecycle. The IExecution interface defines all the callback operations needed by the component module to control instances.

As an example of how M-Law works in a practical scenario, suppose an agent playing the role of an employer asks for increasing its own salary to other agent playing the role of accountant. However, there is a norm specified in XMLaw stating that employers are prohibited from asking for salary increase. Despite the simplicity of this scenario, the example is useful to illustrate the basic flow of events inside the M-Law. Then, M-Law works in the following way:

1. Mediator agent reads the XMLaw specification and starts the component module;
2. Employer agent calls its communication module and sends the request message asking for salary increase;
3. The communication module redirects the message to the mediator;
4. Mediator receives the message through its communication module;
5. Mediator fires an event of message arrival through event module;
6. Event module notifies the component module;
7. Norm element, which is part of the component module, receives the event, verifies that the message is not allowed and fires a message not compliant event;
8. The mediator receives the message not compliant event and as a consequence, does not redirect the message to the accountant agent.

The main design objectives of M-Law were simplicity, flexibility and reuse. That is why the elements were implemented as components. In this way, some architectural decisions made have direct impact over scalability in the current version of M-Law. The following items discuss in more details some architectural and design aspects of M-Law:

- Scalability – M-Law is implemented as a centralized mediator. In this way, it may become a bottleneck for very large systems. In fact, the design of XMLaw aimed primarily at expressivity (using abstractions such as constraints, scenes, etc.) and at flexibility (specialization of laws [4]). Also, although a centralized solution poses scalability questions, it allows the easy specification of global laws with no need for state synchronization. Furthermore, temporal problems are also avoided, once there is just one host controlling clocks. We are currently working on alternative, more decentralized, solutions to this problem. We are performing experiments on both a network of decentralized mediators, such as LGI [15], and hierarchal organized mediators, such as Internet DNS.
- Expressivity – M-Law provides full support for XMLaw, which means it is possible to specify non-deterministic state-based machines, notions of commitments through norms, time sensitive laws, and execution of java code.
- Flexibility – The use of indirect communication through events in combination with the component-based module makes it possible to add new functionality with little difficulty. However, it is known that event-based communication may lead to software that is harder to understand and debug due to the implicit nature of communication. We have tried to deal with this drawback by systematically building test cases, performing code inspections and writing exhaustive documentation.

5 Using the Middleware

To use the middleware it is necessary perform at least four tasks. First, one must write the interaction laws using XMLaw language. Second, the mediator has to be started by execution of the script files provided with M-Law. Then, one has to inform the mediator about the existence of the new Law (XMLaw file). Finally, the application agents may be started. The idea is to use the middleware as an environmental service. In other words, the middleware should be available for the agent developers once they have their agents running on the environment.

Regarding the development of the application agents, agent developers may want to extend the agent class provided by the client API of M-Law. This class provides methods for sending and receiving of messages and methods for direct communication with the mediator, once the mediator can provide useful information about the current status of interaction, such as which scenes are running and how many agents are interacting. In fact, the class LawFacade provides methods for direct communication with the mediator, and agent class provides methods for sending and receiving messages. Figure 6 shows the details of those classes.

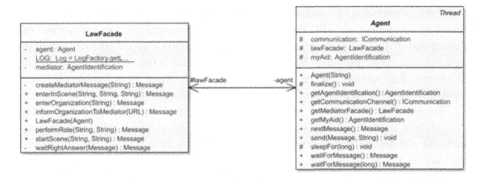

Fig. 6. Client API: LawFacade and Agent classes

We encourage agent developers to use the agent class either by inheritance or delegation. Yet, developers are free to build their agents using any architecture or technology. The only requirement is that the agent should know both how to "speak" FIPA-Agent Communication Language[2] and which messages the mediator expects.

5.1 Case Study (CB)

The Central Bank of Brazil regulates and supervises the national financial system. This experiment is running based on the SELIC system requirements. SELIC is the central depository of securities issued by the National Treasury and the Central Bank of Brazil. It also settles outright and rep transactions with these securities. Besides the National Treasury and the Central Bank of Brazil, commercial banks, investment banks, savings banks, dealers and brokers, clearing operators, mutual investment funds and many other institutions that integrate the financial system participate in SELIC as holders of custody accounts. In December 2004, the system was composed of 4,900 participants (or agents).

SELIC system is clearly a system that has a central entity (Central Bank) that mediates and controls the interaction among the other entities. We have, then, specified the laws that the institutions must follow using XMLaw, and we have used M-Law as a mediator that control the interactions. We have implemented a prototype of a subset of the actual SELIC system for doing this experiment. The experiment was performed with 10 agents representing different financial institutions and 1 mediator agent (the MLaw).

There are several requirements that influence the interaction of financial institutions in a committed operation, as the several types of messages that could be sent and the several behaviors that should be implemented according to the messages specified, including norms and constraints. Below (Figure 7), an interaction scenario is taken from SELIC. This interaction scenario contains three entities: two financial institutions and the SELIC.

---

[2] FIPA is the organization that establishes specifications for agents. http://www.fipa.org/

In this scenario, a financial institution A (FI A) needs to sell bonds to the financial institution B (FI B). Below (Code Fragment 3), we illustrate the description of this basic negotiation protocol in XMLaw. We called it Negotiation. The specification provides the details regarding the expected attributes of the messages. Furthermore, there in the transition st1 there is a verification step implemented within a constraint.

This example shows how the laws can be specified and then provided to the environment through the M-Law in order to effectively monitor and enforce agents' behavior. On the side of the developers of the domain agents, it is necessary to extend the class Agent provided with the client API (Figure 6) and then use its methods to communicate.

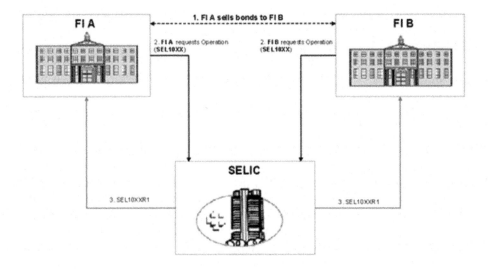

Fig. 7. SELIC example

The preliminary results have shown that M-Law and XMLaw have brought some consequences such as:

- Transparency of the process – Before using our governance solution, the system had all the laws hard-coded into the source code. With XMLaw the laws are specified in a purpose specific language which brings the specification to a higher level of abstraction and then decreases the distance between the requirements and the implementation. M-Law has a crucial role in this scenario, since it monitors and interprets the laws.
- Better support for rules customization/configuration – Changing a law with XMLaw and M-Law is a matter of changing the XMLaw specification, i.e., there is no need to go into source code of the application.

```
<Scene id="Negotiation" time-to-live="infinity">
 <Protocol id="negotiation-protocol">
  <Messages>
   <Message id="startMsg">...</Message>
   <Message id="request">
    <Content>
     <Entry key="CodMsg" value="SEL1054"/>
     <Entry key="TpCompr" value="02" />
     <Entry key="NOPRET"/>
    </Content>
   <Message id="inform">
    <Content>
     <Entry key="CodMsg" value="SEL1054"/>
     <Entry key="TpCompr" value="04" />
     <Entry key="NOPRET"/>
    </Content>
   </Message>
  </Messages>
  <States>
   <State id="s1" type="initial"/>
   <State id="s2" type="execution"/>
   <State id="s3" type="execution"/>
   <State id="s4" type="success"/>
  </States>
  <Transitions>
   <Transition id="start" from="s1" to="s2"
       ref="startMsg" event-type="message_arrival" />
   <Transition id="st1" from="s2" to="s3" ref="request"
       event-type="message_arrival"
    <Constraint
      class="selic.constraint.ConditionNOPRET"
      semantics="NOPRETEmpty" />
   </Transition>
   <Transition id="st2" from="s3" to="s4" ref="inform"
       event-type="message_arrival"/>
  </Transitions>
 </Protocol> ...
</Scene>
```

Code 3. Negotiation structure definition

6 Related Work

It is possible to cite at least two important research projects in which the goals are in some sense similar to the goals of the work presented here. The first approach is proposed by Esteva [7]. He uses a set of concepts that have points of intersection with those used in XMLaw, in fact XMLaw has borrowed some of the ideas of Esteva and proposed new ideas. For example, both Esteva scenes and protocol elements specify the interaction protocol using a global view of the interaction. The time aspect is represented in the Esteva approach as timeouts. Timeouts allow activating transitions after a given number of time units passed since a state was reached. On the other hand, due to our event model, the clock element proposed in XMLaw can both activate and deactivate not only transitions, but also other clocks and norms. Connecting clocks to norms allows a more expressive normative behavior; norms become time sensitive elements.

Furthermore, XMLaw also includes the concept of actions, which allows execution of java code in response to some interaction situation. From the implementation point of view, Esteva does not provide the internal details of its framework (ISLANDER); but the general architecture proposes to use a set of mediators instead of using only one mediator. One consequence of this solution is that once a law is specified as a global view, all the mediators must constantly synchronize their internal states to keep them consistent. It means that for every message sent by an application agent, messages are broadcast among the mediators to synchronize the state.

From the point of view of integration with other existent solutions, Islander allows the use of JADE as communication layer; but only Jade is allowed and there is no support for extension on this point. Furthermore, there is no indication about the possibility of integration between Islander and different approaches, such as integration tests and criticality analysis.

Minsky [15] proposes a coordination and control mechanism called law governed interaction (LGI). This mechanism is based in two basic principles: the local nature of the LGI laws and the decentralization of law enforcement. The local nature of LGI laws means that a law can regulate explicitly only local events at individual home agents, where home agent is the agent being regulated by the laws; the ruling for an event e can depend only on e itself, and on the local home agent's context; and the ruling for an event can mandate only local operations to be carried out at the home agent. On the other hand, the decentralization of law enforcement is an architectural decision argued as necessary for achieving scalability.

However, when it is necessary to have a global view of the interactions, the decentralized enforcement demands state consistency protocols, which may not be scalable. Furthermore, it provides a language to specify laws and it is concerned with architectural decisions to achieve a high degree of robustness. In contrast, M-Law uses XMLaw, which provides an explicit conceptual model and focuses on different concepts, such as Scenes, Norms and Clocks. In other words, in our opinion, LGI design aimed primarily at decentralization and XMLaw design aimed primarily at expressivity and at possibilities for specialization [4]. A current limitation of XMLaw is the centralization of the mediator.

A promising direction is to investigate how XMLaw specification could be compiled into decentralized LGI mediators. In this way, LGI could be viewed by having the basic foundation to build higher level elements, such the ones in XMLaw. Moreover, by using M-Law, it is possible to extend the framework hotspots and introduce new components, which represent concepts in the conceptual model; and change the communication mechanism.

7   Conclusions

Governance is required in open MAS Environments. A trustable Environment should offer a service to guarantee that the rules of interaction are obeyed. In this paper, we proposed to include a governance service within any open MAS Environment. This paper has presented some of the main ideas behind research into governance of agent systems. Then, from a Software Engineering perspective, we have proposed a middleware that allows the development of law-regulated systems. We have presented the main design goals of the middleware, such as flexibility and integration with other platforms. We believe that this middleware is an enhancement of the current state-of-the-art of Software Engineering for Governance in the sense that it supports a language that expresses the main concepts of governance with a good level of expressivity, and also due to its design concerns, which make use of techniques such as frameworks and components. Current implementation relies on a centralized mediator, which is a limitation on scalability. We are currently studying the design of a future distributed version, inspired from LGI decentralized mediators.

We have shown the use of the middleware on an example inspired from a real application of the central bank of Brazil. We hope that this example could illustrate some benefits brought by the use of M-Law, and more generally speaking, the merits of MAS governance for future applications.

Acknowledgments. This work was partially funded by CNPq through the ESSMA Project (552068/2002-0) and through individual grants. The work was also supported by CAPES, in the CAPES/Cofecub International Cooperation Program, through the EMACA Project (0981-04-4).

References

1. Arunachalam, R., Sadeh, N., Eriksson, J., Finne, N., Janson, S.: The Supply Chain Management Game for the Trading Agent Competition 2004. CMU-CS-04-107, (2004)
2. Bellifemine, F., Poggi, A., Rimassa G.: JADE: a FIPA2000 Compliant Agent Development Environment. In: Fifth International Conference on Autonomous Agents (2001)
3. Carvalho, G., Brandão, A., Paes, R., Lucena, C.: Interaction Laws Verification Using Knowledge-based Reasoning. In: Workshop on Agent-Oriented Information Systems (AOIS-2006) at AAMAS 2006.
4. Carvalho, G., Lucena, C., Paes, R., Briot, J.: Refinement operators to facilitate the reuse of interaction laws in open multi-agent systems. In Proceedings of the 2006 International Workshop on Software Engineering For Large-Scale Multi-Agent Systems (2006)
5. Carvalho G., Almeida H., Gatti, M., Vinicius, G., Paes, R., Perkusich, A., Lucena, C.: Dynamic Law Evolution in Governance Mechanisms for Open Multi-Agent Systems. Second Workshop on Software Engineering for Agent-oriented Systems (2006)
6. Collins, J., Arunachala, R., Sadeh, N., Eriksson, J., Finne, N., Janson, S.: The Supply Chain Management Game for the 2005 Trading Agent Competition. CMU-ISRI-04-139. http://www.sics.se/tac/tac05scmspec_v157.pdf (2005)
7. Esteva, M.: Electronic institutions: from specification to development, Ph.D. thesis, Institut d'Investigació en Intelligència Artificial, Catalonia - Spain. (2003)
8. Fayad, M., Schmidt, D., Johnson, R.E.: Building application frameworks: object-oriented foundations of framework design. John Wiley & Sons (1999)
9. Ferber, J., Gutknecht, O., Michel, F. From Agents to Organizations: an Organizational View of Multi-Agent Systems. In Agent-Oriented Software Engineering (AOSE) IV, P. Giorgini, Jörg Müller, James Odell, eds, Melbourne, July 2003, LNCS 2935, pp. 214-230 (2004)

10. Gamma, E., Johnson, R., Helm, R., Vlissides, J.: Design Patterns: Elements of Reusable Object-Oriented Software. Addison Wesley, (1995)
11. Gatti M., Lucena C., Briot J.P.: On Fault Tolerance in Law-Governed Multi-Agent Systems. 5th International Workshop on Software Engineering for Large-scale Multi-Agent Systems (SELMAS) at ICSE (2006)
12. Guessoum, Z., Faci, N., Briot, J-P.: Adaptive Replication of Large-Scale Multi-Agent Systems - Towards a Fault-Tolerant Multi-Agent Platform. In: International Workshop on Software Engineering for Large-scale Multi-Agent Systems - SELMAS at ICSE (2005)
13. Huhns, M.N., Stephens, L.M.: Multi-agent Systems and Societies of Agents. G. Weiss (ed.), Multi-agent Systems, ISBN 0-262-23203-0, MIT press (1999)
14. Lindermann, G., Ossowski, S., Padget, J., Vázquez Salceda, J.: International Workshop on Agents, Norms and Institutions for Regulated Multiagent Systems (ANIREM 2005), http://platon.escet.urjc.es/ANIREM2005/ accessed in December, 2006.
15. Minsky, N.H., Ungureanu V.: Law-governed interaction: a coordination and control mechanism for heterogeneous distributed systems, ACMTrans. Software Engineering Methodology 9(3) 273–305. (2000)
16. Odell, J., Parunak, H.V.D., Fleischer, M., Breuckner, S.: Modeling Agents and their Environment. Agent-Oriented Software Engineering III, Giunchiglia, F., Odell, J., Weiss, G. (eds.) Lecture Notes in Computer Science, Vol. 2585. Spriner-Verlag, Berlin Heidelberg New York (2002)
17. Paes, R.B., Carvalho G.R., Lucena, C.J.P., Alencar, P.S.C., Almeida H.O., Silva, V.T.: Specifying Laws in Open Multi-Agent Systems. In: Agents, Norms and Institutions for Regulated Multi-agent Systems (ANIREM), AAMAS2005. (2005)
18. Paes, R.B, Lucena, C.J.P, Alencar, P.S.C.: A Mechanism for Governing Agent Interaction in Open Multi-Agent Systems. http://wiki.les.inf.puc-rio.br/index.php/Publications (2005)
19. Paes, R.B., Gatti, M.A.C., Carvalho, G.R., Rodrigues, L.F.C., Lucena, C.J.P.: A Middleware for Governance in Open Multi-Agent Systems. Technical Report 33/06, PUC-Rio, 14 p. (2006)
20. Rodrigues, L., Carvalho, G., Paes, R., Lucena, C.: Towards an Integration Test Architecture for Open MAS. In: Software Engineering for Agent-oriented Systems - SEAS05 , (2005)
21. Rubino, R., Omicini, A., Denti, E.: Computational Institutions for Modeling Norm-Regulated {MAS}: An Approach Based on Coordination Artifacts. In: Coordination, Organizations, Institutions, and Norms in Multi-Agent Systems, Springer, vol. 3913, 127—141 (2006)
22. Sadeh, N., Arunachalam, R., Eriksson, J., Finne, N., Janson, S.: TAC-03: a supply-chain trading competition, AI Mag. 24 (1) 92–94 (2003)
23. Schumacher, M., Ossowski, S.: The Governing Environment, E4MAS (2005)
24. Weyns, D., Parunak, H.V.D., Michel, F., Holvoet, T., Ferber, J.: Environments for Multiagent Systems: State-of-the-Art and Research Challenges. Lecture Notes in Computer Science Vol. 3374, Springer (2004)
25. Weyns, D., Michel, F., Parunak, H.V.D.: The Third International Workshop on Environments for Multi-Agent Systems - http://www.cs.kuleuven.ac.be/~distrinet/events/e4mas/2006/print.php - accessed in October (2006)
26. Weyns, D., Omicini, A., Odell, J.: Environment as a first class abstraction in multiagent systems. In: Autonomous Agents and Multi-Agent Systems 14(1), 5-30 (2007)

Urban Traffic Control with Co-Fields

Marco Camurri, Marco Mamei, and Franco Zambonelli

Dipartimento di Scienze e Metodi dell'Ingegneria,
University of Modena and Reggio Emilia
Via Allegri 13, 42100 Reggio Emilia, Italy
{camurri.marco.31767, mamei.marco, franco.zambonelli}@unimore.it

Abstract. Traffic control can be regarded as a multiagent application
in which car-agents and traffic-light-agents need to coordinate with each
other to optimize the traffic flow and avoid congestions. Environment abstractions naturally suit this scenario in that agents actions are mainly
driven by traffic-related information that are distributed across the environment both at a practical and conceptual level. In this context we
present traffic-control mechanisms on the basis of our Co-Fields model
and discuss some experimental results we obtained in simulations that
validate our proposal.

1 Introduction

Traffic management is a very complex problem. Millions of people every day
suffer from congestion in urban road networks. This has led researchers to wonder
whether is possible to regulate traffic flow in order to reduce the congestion (i.e.,
to reduce the average time that a car takes to reach its destination) [1,2,3,4,5].
Apart from long-term structural solutions (i.e., building new roads), it is possible
in principle to control the urban traffic flow either acting on the individual cars
(that could try to move avoiding traffic jams) or acting on the traffic-lights (that
could try to dynamically optimize the overall throughput).

Both these candidate approaches naturally suit the agent paradigm and it is
rather easy to conceive such a scenario in terms of car-agents and traffic-light-
agents coordinating their actions to improve the traffic flow. It is also rather easy
to understand that these kind of applications (where the agents' goal is inherently
related to their motion in an environment) are killer-applications with regard to
the environment-in-multi-agent-system idea. In this context, in fact, environment
abstractions are natural and their power in decoupling agents' actions and in
providing context-awareness is undisputable [6,7].

The main contribution of this paper is to illustrate how the Co-Fields [8]
model can be fruitfully applied to this application scenario, and to present some
experimental results we obtained (in simulations) adopting it.

The Co-Fields model is based on distributed data structures spread across an
environment implementing digital mockups of physical fields (such as the gravitational one). Such distributed data structures mediate and rule the coordination
activities among agents that act on the the basis of the perceived local field configuration [8]. In our case study, a *traffic* field will be used to convey aggregated

D. Weyns, H.V.D. Parunak, and F. Michel (Eds.): E4MAS 2006, LNAI 4389, pp. 239–253, 2007.
© Springer-Verlag Berlin Heidelberg 2007

information about the current traffic conditions. In each area, this field will have a magnitude proportional to the amount of traffic in there. Car-agents can use such information (which is actually an environment abstraction) to coordinate their motion avoiding traffic jams. In a similar way, traffic-light-agents can tune their green-light policy according to the perceived value of the *traffic* field.

The rest of this paper is organized as follows. Section 2 presents some backgrounds. In particular, it briefly illustrates the Co-Fields model and describes the GLD (Greed Light District) simulation platform where we run our experiments. Section 3 presents our proposal to control traffic on the basis of Co-Fields. Section 4 shows and discusses experimental results. Finally, Section 6 concludes and sketches future works.

2   Backgrounds

In this section we will briefly review the coordination model Co-Fields [8] that is at the heart of our proposal, and we present the Green Light District [9] platform used to perform simulations and experiments on realistic traffic situations.

2.1   Co-Fields

Co-Fields is a coordination model for multiagent systems in which environment abstractions have a central role. The main idea in Co-Fields is to provide agents with an effective and easy-to-use representation of their operational environment. To this end, Co-Fields delegates to the infrastructure the task of constructing and automatically updating an essential distributed "view" of the system situation - possibly tailored to application-specific coordination problems - that "tells" agents what to do (i.e., how to act to implement a specific coordination patterns). Agents are simply let with the decision of whether to follow such a suggestion or not.

To achieve this goal, we take inspiration from the physical world, i.e., from the way particles in our universe move and globally self-organize accordingly to that contextual information which is represented by potential fields. In particular, in our approach, contextual information is expressed in the form of distributed computational fields (Co-Fields). A computational field is a distributed data structure characterized by a unique identifier, a location-dependent numeric value, and a propagation rule identifying how the field should distribute across the environment and how its value should change during the distribution. Fields are locally accessible by agents depending on their location, providing them a local perspective of the global situation of the system. Each agent of the system can propagate specific fields across the environment, conveying application-specific information about the local environment and/or about itself. Agents can locally perceive these fields and act accordingly, e.g. following the fields' gradients. The result is a globally coordinated behavior, achieved with very little efforts by agents.

More in detail, the Co-Fields approach is centered on few key concepts:

1. Contextual information is represented by "computational fields", spread by agents and/or by the infrastructure, diffused across the environment, and locally sensed by agents;
2. A coordination policy is realized by letting the agents act on the basis of the local field configuration, the same as a physical mass moves in accord to the locally sensed gravitational field.
3. Both environment dynamics and agents' actions may induce changes in the fields' surface, automatically propagated by the infrastructure, thus inducing a feedback cycle (point 2) that can be exploited to globally achieve a global and adaptive coordination pattern.

In the next section we will present how this model can be easily applied to the traffic control problem.

2.2   Green Light District

GLD (Green Light District) is a program that performs discrete simulations of road networks. The full application consists of two parts: an Editor and a Simulator. The Editor enables the user to create an infrastructure (a road map) and save it to disk. The Simulator can then load the map and run a simulation based on that map. Before starting a simulation, the user can choose which traffic light controller and which driving policy will be used during the simulation. A **traffic light controller** (or simply TL-Controller) is an algorithm that specifies the way traffic lights are set during the simulation (i.e., it specifies traffic-lights green-red policy). A **driving policy** specifies which are the paths followed by cars to reach their destinations. Since GLD is open source, it can be easily extended in order to add new algorithms for TL-Controllers and for driving policies. This is exactly what we did to test our algorithms. In order to get a more realistic simulation, two values can be adjusted for each edge node in the map (i.e., for each node that can put cars into the map):

Spawn frequency: is the frequency (or probability) at which a node spawns new road users. Its values range between 0 and 1. For example, a spawn frequency of 0.5 for a node means that the node will spawn one car every other time step (or cycle).

Destination frequency: a random destination point is assigned to every car entering the map. With this parameter it is possible to specify the probability distribution from which the destinations are drawn. This allows to create crowded destinations and a not-uniform traffic-flow.

While running a simulation (see Fig. 1), GLD can track different types of statistics such as the number of road users that reached their destination, the average junction waiting time or the average trip waiting time. The data collected from the simulation can be displayed in a window, or exported in text format for further analysis.

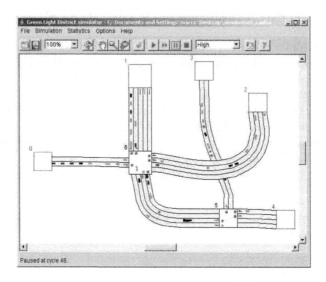

Fig. 1. The GLD traffic simulator

3   Traffic Control

In this section, we describe the Co-Fields policies we realized to implement traffic control. We realized both mechanisms to control cars and traffic-lights. The effectiveness of these policies will be tested with the aid of a simulation tool.

The most direct approach to try to manage traffic is to improve the traffic light control algorithms (i.e., the way traffic lights are switched to regulate the flow of cars). So far traditional methods have tried to optimize the flow of vehicles for a given car density by setting appropriate phases and periods of traffic lights [4]. However, the use of static timing patterns does not take into account the actual state of traffic (for instance, the current speed of cars might be greater than the expected one). In other words, traditional traffic lights controller cannot adapt to the current car density, and thus they cannot manage correctly unusual and extraordinary situations (for instance, a stream of cars leaving a stadium or a big concert) [10,11].

As an alternative to the previous approach, we can imagine a network of "intelligent" traffic lights that can perceive the current state of traffic and dynamically self-organize their timings, without the need of any complex central controller. The core idea of our approach is to induce a cooperative behavior between traffic lights, by means of simple, field-mediated interactions.

Improving traffic lights control algorithms is not the only way to make traffic management more efficient. Thanks to the wide diffusion of low-cost wireless communication devices, new approaches to the problem are becoming feasible. It is not difficult to imagine that, in few years, each car will be equipped with a mobile computer capable of communicating with a computer network embedded in the city streets and junctions. In this way, a car could get useful information about traffic jam or queues, and suggest alternative paths to its driver. In this scenario, both traffic lights and cars can be seen as simple software agents able to interact with each other in order to improve traffic conditions [12,13,14].

3.1   Co-Fields Cars

The aim of our Co-Fields driving policy is to guide the cars toward their destinations avoiding the most crowded areas. With reference to Fig. 2: let us suppose that five cars are leaving node A to reach node H. If a shortest-path driving policy is used, all the cars will follow the path ACFH. If our Co-Fields driving policy is used, the last two cars will follow an alternative (possibly longer) path, because the shortest one is too crowded.

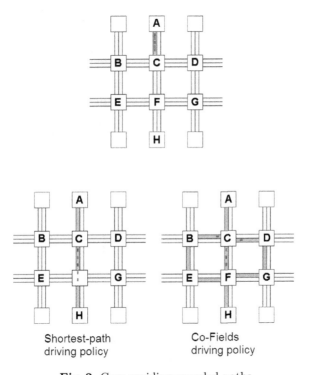

Shortest-path
driving policy

Co-Fields
driving policy

Fig. 2. Cars avoiding crowded paths

I order to obtain such policy using the Co-Field model, we need the cars to perceive two kind of fields: a distance field and a traffic field.

Distance Field

This field is generated by each node of the map, and its values does not change over time. It has value 0 in the node that generates it. In a generic node N it has a value equal to the length of the shortest path between N and the node from which the field generates. If DF_H is the distance field generated by node

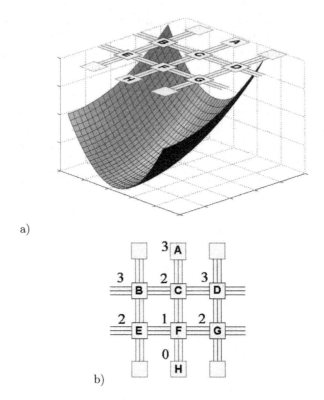

a)

b)

Fig. 3. (a) Distance field generated by node H. (b) Values of the distance field generated by node H.

H, then on each node a car can perceive the fields DF_1, DF_2, ... , DF_N, where N is the number of nodes in the map.

Traffic field

The traffic field (TRF) represents the intensity of traffic in a given point of the map. In each lane, it has a value equals to the number of cars on the lane, divided by the length of the lane. The traffic field is dynamic and its values change over time depending on the car's movements.

A car heading to node H evaluates a combined field (CF) [1] as the linear combination between the distance field (DF) generated by node H and the perceived traffic field (TRF):

$$CF = DF_H + \alpha \cdot TRF$$

The first term of the coordination field is a field that has its minimum point in correspondence of the destination node H. Because of the shape of this field, then, cars following downhill this field are guided towards theirs destinations.

---

[1] This is actually the Coordination Field described in [8].

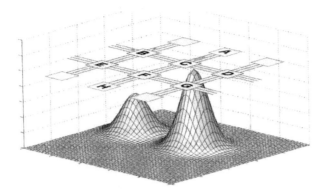

Fig. 4. Traffic field

The second term takes into account traffic. Having its maximum points where the car density is high, the field TRF (with $\alpha > 0$) tends to repulse cars from these points. For this reason, α can be regarded as the weight assigned to traffic information in the choice of the path. If α is very small, cars will follow their shortest path without considering traffic conditions. If α is very high, cars will prefer a possibly longer path whenever the shortest one is a bit crowded (see Fig. 5). From the above description is should be clear that α should be set to the correct value not to underestimate or overestimate the traffic situation. For example, cars in Fig. 2 clearly overestimate the traffic condition (α is too high)[2].

3.2   Co-Fields Traffic Lights

The key idea in our Co-Fields TL-Controller is to propagate a computational field throughout the map, that helps traffic lights to coordinate with their immediate neighbors.

Each traffic light evaluates the local value of a specific *Green Field* (GF) as the sum between the number of cars waiting in its queue and the number of cars waiting in the queues of those traffic lights that can send cars toward it. If $N(s_0)$ is the number of cars waiting for traffic light s_0, and s_1, s_2, ... s_n are the traffic lights that can send cars to s_0, then s_0 evaluates its green field as follows:

$$GF(S_0) = \frac{N(s_0)}{l_0} + \gamma \cdot \left(\frac{N(s_1)}{l_1} + \frac{N(s_2)}{l_2} + ... + \frac{N(s_n)}{l_n} \right)$$

where l_i is the length of the lane regulated by s_i. Fig. 6 shows how $GF(s_0)$ is computed. In the previous formula, γ measures the importance given to the traffic conditions of neighboring traffic lights. If $\gamma = 0$ there is no coordination between neighboring traffic lights: each one takes its own decision simply looking at the number of cars on its lane.

---

[2] This misconfiguration was actually made on purpose to emphasize and illustrate the Co-Fields driving policy.

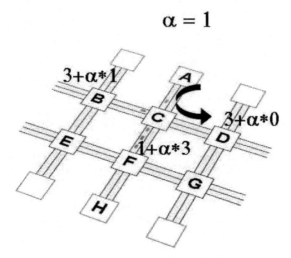

Fig. 5. A car following downhill the combined field. For example in the road between C and F there are 3 cars. The field value there is $1 + \alpha \cdot 3$.

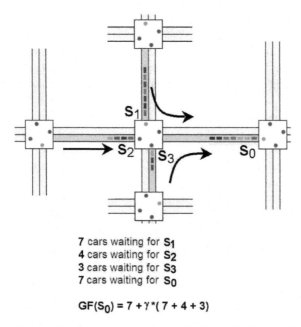

7 cars waiting for S_1
4 cars waiting for S_2
3 cars waiting for S_3
7 cars waiting for S_0

$$GF(S_0) = 7 + \gamma * (7 + 4 + 3)$$

Fig. 6. Example of calculus of GF for traffic lights S0

We can regard the intensity of the Green Field as a measure of the advantage that can be obtained if the underling traffic light is set to green. At every step of the simulation and for every junction, the traffic lights having the highest value of green field are set to "green", while the others are set to "red". Serious problems arise when the green field changes its values too rapidly over time, because in this case traffic lights switches from "red" to "green" very frequently, and cars spend too much time waiting for the "yellow" light to become "green". For this reason we limited the maximum rapidity of variation of GF by adding a new parameter, T_{min}, which represents the minimum time between two consecutive variations of GF.

It is worth noting that this approach is particulary interesting in that – in contrast with the vast majority of field-based applications [15] – it involves a coordination task that is not related to motion coordination.

4 Experiments

In this section we want to test that the coordination policies presented in the previous section for cars and traffic lights can improve traffic management by avoiding or reducing traffic congestion. Road networks congestion happens when the rate at which new cars enter the map is greater than the rate at which they exit. Looking at the chart that plot the number of arrived road users over time, road-net congestion appears as a flattening of the curve (it means that no new cars get to their destination).

4.1 Simulation Set-Up

For our experiments, we decided to use a map like the one in Fig. 7, which consists in a square 8x8 grid of junctions. All the roads have exactly 2 lanes -one for each direction- and a length of 50 blocks. Each car has a length of 2 blocks and a speed of 2 blocks per time step. Cars enter the map from 32 edge nodes placed along the perimeter. Destination for cars spawned by north nodes is randomly chosen from south nodes; destination for cars spawned by west nodes is chosen from east nodes, and so on. This is necessary if we want the traffic to be evenly spread throughout the map.

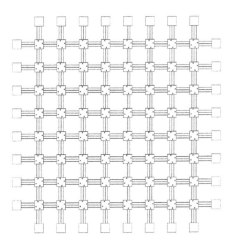

Fig. 7. Map used in the experiments

4.2   Results of the Experiments

Co-Fields traffic lights controller. In order to test the performance of our Co-Fields TL-Controller, we compared it with a standard TL-Controller that simply switches lights according to a pre-determined cycle. Thus, if the standard TL-Controller is used, traffic lights remain green for T cycles of simulation, switch to red for the next T cycles, and then become green again, and so on. Parameter T is said to be the period of the standard TL-controller. Graphs in Fig. 8 show the results of simulations on the map presented at the beginning of this section. A spawn frequency of 0.2 cars/cycle was set for every edge node. It can be seen that the Co-Fields method performs better than the standard method. To make sure that the advantage is not due to the particular choice of T and T_{min}, we set the same value for T and T_{min} (results for T = T_{min} = 4 are shown in plots B and C). Then we repeated the experiment with different values of T and T_{min} (results for T = T_{min} = 10 are shown in plots D and E). In all tests, standard TL-Controllers reach deadlock after about 2500 simulation cycles, while Co-Fields TL-Controllers manage to avoid it. The A line shows the performance of a random TL-Controller which randomly switches lights at every cycle.

Co-Fields driving policy. Before comparing the performance of our Co-Fields driving policy with a standard shortest-path driving policy, we performed some simulations to find the optimal value for parameter α . During all tests, a standard

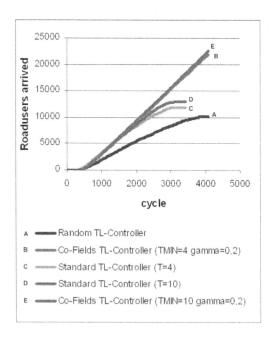

Fig. 8. Performance of various traffic light controllers

TL-Controller was used (with period T = 10 cycles) and a spawn frequency of 0.2 was set for each edge node. Results obtained for various values of α (see Fig. 9) indicate that the algorithm has best performance when α ranges between 2 and 7.

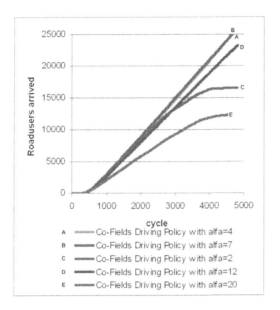

Fig. 9. Performance of Co-Fields driving policies varying α

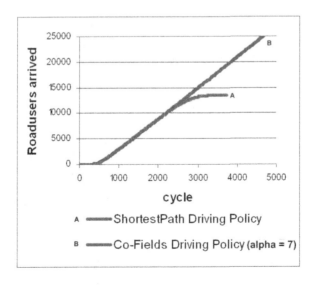

Fig. 10. Comparison between shortest path and Co-Fields driving policies

Then we compared our Co-Fields driving policy (with $\alpha = 7$) with the shortest path driving policy (i.e., a driving policy that makes cars strictly follow the shortest path towards their destinations without avoiding crowded areas). Results displayed in Fig. 10 shows that the shortest path driving policy lead to deadlock after about 2500 cycles, while our driving policy avoids it.

Comparison between Co-Fields cars and Co-Fields traffic lights. We conclude this section with a comparison between the two presented approaches. In order to understand the interaction between the two methods, we set a very high traffic level in the map (0.3 cars/cycle for each edge node) so that both methods, separately, do not manage to avoid net congestion. Then we applied them simultaneously. Results are shown in Fig. 11. The worst performance (A) is obtained when traditional methods are used both for traffic lights control and for driving policy (i.e. standard TL-Controller and shortest path driving policy). This lead to deadlock after about 1500 cycles. Better results are obtained if the Co-Fields TL-Controller or the Co-Fields driving policy are used. In these cases (B and C lines) net congestion is clearly delayed. Concurrent use of both approaches (E) yields the best performance, and manage to avoid congestion. The following parameters were used during simulations:

- Standard TL-Controller with T = 10
- Co-Fields TL-Controller with $\gamma = 0, 2$ and $T_{min} = 10$
- Co-Fields driving policy with $\alpha = 4$

Apart from these promising experimental results and the Co-Fields strengths in managing agents' coordination activities, a correct evaluation of the Co-Fields model cannot overlook the following drawbacks:

1. Co-Fields and the strictly local perspective in which agents act promote a strictly greedy approach in their coordinated actions. In fact, agents act on the basis of their local viewpoint only, disregarding that a small sacrifice now can possibly lead to greater advantages in the future. With regard to traffic, this implies, for example, that cars would be better queue for a short-time other than looking for uncrowded path that can be longer or also (more) crowded in other areas.

2. The Co-Fields model is not supported by a well-specified engineering methodology. In other words, we still have not identified a principled way to help us identify, given a specific coordination pattern to be enforced, which fields have to be defined, how they should be propagated, and how they should be combined by the recipient agents. For example, although the presented coordination tasks are rather natural and easy to be identified, the coefficients specifying how the different fields have to be combined have to be hand-tuned.

3. From an implementation point of view, the Co-Fields approach requires a distributed computer infrastructure to store the distributed data structures representing the fields. In the presented approach, all the possible destinations have to propagate a field across this infrastructure and this of course

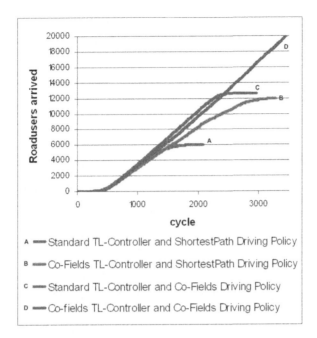

Fig. 11. Comparison between Co-Fields driving policy and Co-Fields TL-Controller

might create scalability concerns. However, it is rather easy to extend the current model to aggregate fields and save resources. For example, the fields associated to close destinations could be merged together to save bandwidth and storage, once a suitable distance from their sources have been reached. Such an extension, is in our future work.

5   Conclusion and Future Work

In this paper we presented a field-based approach to traffic control. Both mechanisms to control cars and traffic-lights have been presented.

While the reported tests are encouraging, a more thorough evaluation is required to better assess real world potential. In particular, we think that the following points are critical to better assess our model:

1. One obvious and important step is to use a more sophisticated simulator e.g., CORSIM [16], TRANSYT7F [17], or SimTraffic [18] that better approximates realistic traffic behavior. With a more sophisticated simulator, we could also test real intersection configurations and historical traffic patterns, which would allow a more objective assessment of the results.
2. It would be also important to measure other parameters in order to better understand the pros and cons of our proposal. Parameters such as: the average journey time, the waiting time, the number of detours cars have to take are important aspects to assess the model.

3. In addition, it would be interesting to compare our approach with more advanced and sophisticated control mechanisms both in terms of cars and traffic-lights.

Finally, a more pragmatic but nonetheless critical followup to this research would be an assessment of the costs and additional factors necessary to deploy a system like ours in an actual urban environment.

Acknowledgments

Work supported by the project CASCADAS (IST-027807) funded by the FET Program of the European Commission.

References

1. Fehon, K., Chong, R., Black, J.: Adaptive traffic signal system for cupertino california. In: Asia-Pacific Transportation Development Conference, San Francisco (CA), USA (2003)
2. Ferreira, E., Subrahmanian, E., Manstetten, D.: Intelligent agents in decentralized traffic control. In: IEEE Intelligent Transportation Systems. IEEE CS PRess (2001)
3. Gershenson, C.: Self-organizing traffic lights. Complex Systems **16** (2005) 29 – 53
4. Wiering, M.: Intelligent traffic light control. ERCIM News, European Research Consortium for Informatics and Mathematics **53** (2003) 40 – 41
5. Bazzan, A., Chaib-draa, B., Kluegl, F., Ossowski, S.: Workshop on agents in traffic and transportation. In: Workshop in conjunction with the Conference on Autonomous Agents and Multiagent Systems, Hakodate, JP (2006)
6. Weyns, D., Parunak, V., Michel, F., Holvoet, T., Ferber, J.: Environments for Multiagent Systems, State-of-the-art and Research Challenges. Springer Verlag - LNAI 3374 (2005)
7. Weyns, D., Parunak, V., Michel, F., Holvoet, T., Ferber, J.: Environments for Multiagent Systems II. Springer Verlag - LNCS 3830 (2006)
8. Mamei, M., Zambonelli, F., Leonardi, L.: Co-fields: A physically inspired approach to distributed motion coordination. IEEE Pervasive Computing **3** (2004) 52 – 61
9. (Green-Light-District) http://www.students.cs.uu.nl/swp/2001/isg/.
10. Dresner, K., Stone, P.: Multiagent traffic management: a reservation-based intersection control mechanism. In: International Joint Conference on Autonomous Agents and Multiagent Systems. ACM Press, Melbourne, Australia (2004)
11. Nigarnjanagool, S.: Development and evaluation of an agentbased adaptive traffic signal control system. In: Conference of Australian Institutes of Transport Research. (2003)
12. Bandini, S., Bogni, D., Manzoni, S., Mosca, A.: St-modal logic to correlate traffic alarms on italian highways: Project overview and example installations. In: International Conference on Industrial and Engineering Applications of Artificial Intelligence and Expert Systems. Volume 3533 of Lecture Notes in Computer Science. Springer (2005)
13. Kroon, R.: (Dynamic vehicle routing using ant based control) Masters thesis, Delft University of Technology, 2002.

14. Marco Mamei, Franco Zambonelli, L.L.: Distributed motion coordination with co-fields: A case study in urban traffic management. In: IEEE Symposium on Autonomous Decentralized Systems. IEEE CS Press, Pisa, Italy (2003)
15. Mamei, M., Zambonelli, F.: Field-based Coordination for Pervasive Multiagent Systems. Springer Verlag (2005)
16. (Federal-Highway-Administration-CORSIM) fhwatsis.com/corsim page.htm.
17. (TRANSYT-7F) mctrans.ce.ufl.edu/featured/TRANSYT-7F.
18. (Trafficware-SimTraffic) trafficware.com/simtraffic.htm.

Designing Self-organising MAS Environments: The Collective Sort Case

Luca Gardelli, Mirko Viroli, Matteo Casadei, and Andrea Omicini

Alma Mater Studiorum—Università di Bologna
via Venezia 52, 47023 Cesena, Italy
{luca.gardelli, mirko.viroli, m.casadei, andrea.omicini}@unibo.it

Abstract. Self-organisation is being recognised as an effective conceptual framework to deal with the complexity inherent to modern artificial
systems. In this article, we explore the applicability of self-organisation
principles to the development of multi-agent system (MAS) environments. First, we discuss a methodological approach for the engineering
of complex systems, which features emergent properties: this is based on
formal modelling and stochastic simulation, used to analyse global system dynamics and tune system parameters at the early stages of design.
Then, as a suitable target for this approach, we describe an architecture
for self-organising environments featuring artifacts and environmental
agents as fundamental entities.

As an example, we analyse a MAS distributed environment made of
tuple spaces, where environmental agents are assigned the task of moving
tuples across tuples spaces in background and according to local criteria,
making complete clustering an emergent property achieved through self-
organisation.

1 Introduction

The typical MAS scenario involves a set of autonomous situated entities interacting with each other and exploiting resources in the environment to achieve
a common goal [1,2]. When designing the MAS environment, other than functional properties concerning the available services offered to agents, one has also
to consider non-functional properties. First, it is crucial to balance the computational power devoted to the provision of such services: several maintenance
activities must be performed on-line and in background to guarantee a certain
level of quality of service at low computational cost. Moreover, the design of
environment should feature the emergence of quality properties: since the dynamics of interactions with agents cannot be fully predicted, several unexpected
situations have to be handled automatically and effectively.

As standard optimisation techniques (e.g. in resource allocation) are offline
and possibly computationally expensive, we need to rely on different approaches.
Self-organisation theory is a rich source of inspiration for sub-optimal strategies
that can be performed on-line, like every natural system does, and that require

D. Weyns, H.V.D. Parunak, and F. Michel (Eds.): E4MAS 2006, LNAI 4389, pp. 254–271, 2007.

little computational power, e.g. because of local communications. For these reasons, we look for a methodological approach for the development of MAS environments that can systematically adopt self-organisation principles, as a means to more effectively and efficiently provide agents with useful services.

We consider the A&A (agents & artifacts) meta-model as our reference model for MAS [3,4]. *Artifacts* are environment abstractions encapsulating resources and services provided by the environment to agents: agents exploit artifacts in order to achieve individual as well as social goals. Following some early exploration of self-organising systems [5,6], we see the environment as a set of artifacts, exploited by *user agents* and managed by *environmental agents*, the latter having the responsibility of regulating artifact behaviour and state, and making interesting quality properties emerge whenever needed. This vision is of course shared by the Autonomic Computing initiative [7]: in particular Autonomic Computing emphasises the need for artificial systems to self-configure, self-protect, automatically recovers from errors (self-healing) and self-optimise.

In order to focus on the the application of self-organisation principles to the engineering of MAS environment, we devise a methodological approach based on formal modelling and stochastic simulations. In spite of the difficulty of designing "emergence", this approach allows us to preview global system dynamics and tune the system model until possibly converging to a system design matching the expected requirements.

As a case study we discuss an application called *collective sort*, which is a generalisation of the brood sorting problem of swarm intelligence [8] to a distributed tuple space scenario [9]. User agents interact with each other by putting and retrieving information on the environment in the form of tuples: the distributed environment consists of a set of artifacts resembling tuple spaces, which are kept ordered by environmental agents exploiting self-organising techniques. The objective is to devise a fully-distributed, swarm-like strategy for clustering tuples according to their type (as a tuple template), so that tuples with same type are aggregated into the same, unique tuple space. In this case, it is the agent-environment coupling that creates the feedback loop supporting emergence of ordering, by balancing between positive and negative feedback [10]. We provide an architecture and simulation results for this problem, showing the effectiveness of the strategy proposed.

This paper is structured as follows: in Section 2 we discuss our methodological approach for engineering self-organising systems, and its application to our basic architecture for MAS environments. We then apply the methodology—which is based on the three steps of *modelling*, *simulation*, and *tuning*—to the collective sort scenario. Specifically, in Section 3 we devise a model for a self-organising environment, in Section 4 we show simulation results from the system model in order to investigate global dynamics, and then in Section 5 we tune the strategy for achieving better performance, relying on load-balancing techniques. In Section 6 we discuss some related work, and finally in Section 7 we conclude by pointing at some possible future developments.

2   A Design Approach for Self-organising MAS Environments

In the MAS community, several engineering methodologies have been developed [11,12,13], but they typically do not face some of the most important issues in self-organisation: Given a problem, (how) can we design the individual agent's behaviour in order to let the desired property emerge? Once a candidate behaviour is specified, (how) can we guarantee that the specific emergent property will appear?

We recognise in general two approaches to tackle the above issues: (i) analysing the problem and designing by decomposition an *ad-hoc* strategy that will solve it; (ii) observing a system that solves a similar problem, and trying to reverse-engineer the strategy. The former approach is applicable only to a limited set of simple scenarios, since the non-linearity in the rules makes the results quite difficult to predict—indeed, it hardly scales with the complexity of a problem [14]. A self-organisation viewpoint suggests that the latter approach might be more fruitful: indeed, several tasks accomplished by social systems have their counterpart in computer science algorithms and architectures [8,15]. Unfortunately, strategies for specific problems are often unknown, so they are inferred by modifying the original models: but then, how can we guarantee that such modifications would not produce side-effects, namely, behaviours that significantly differ from the expected one?

In general, ensuring that a design leads to the desired dynamics is still an open issue. Although it is possible to verify properties of a deterministic model via automated tools and techniques—e.g. with model checking—, as soon as stochastic aspects enter the picture, verification becomes more difficult—existing works in this context appear to be somehow immature. Hence, although applying model checking techniques is part of our medium-term research objectives—see a discussion in Section 7—it is necessary to resort to a different methodology for analysing the behaviour and qualities of a design.

Then, in the remainder of this section, we describe our methodological approach and, next, how concepts from the methodology map onto design abstractions.

2.1   A Methodological Approach Based on Formal Modelling and Stochastic Simulations

Our approach starts from the deliverable of analysis, and has the goal of devising out an *early design* of the system, to be later detailed and implemented. However, we do not aim at devising a complete methodology: instead of covering the complete development process and tackling all functional and non-functional aspects, we rather intend to use it in combination with other existing AOSE methodologies. So, working at the early design phase, in our approach we aim at evaluating several strategies and their crucial parameters, with the goal of discovering the one that could provide the quality attributes required for the application at hand.

In particular, our approach is articulated around three activities:

Modelling — to develop an abstract formal specification of the system;
Simulation — to qualitatively investigating the dynamics of the system;
Tuning — to change model parameters to adjust system behaviour.

In the *modelling* activity, we formulate a few strategies that seemingly fit the behaviour to be implemented: as far as self-organisation is concerned, natural models are an obvious source of inspiration. Such strategies should form an abstract model of the system for possible architectural solutions. Specifically, in the case of self-organising systems where complex patterns arise from low-level interaction, selective models can make us focus on the properties of interest. To enable further automatic elaborations—such as simulation and automatic verification of properties—these descriptions should be provided in a formal language, which promotes unambiguity and precise selection of the features to be modelled and those to be abstracted away. Although we do not endorse any particular language, given the nature of the target systems we prefer languages that easily and concisely express notions such as distribution, concurrency, communication and compositionality [5]. Moreover, they must be able to deal with stochastic aspects, which are required in order to properly abstract over unpredictability of certain behaviours and events.

The deliverable of the modelling phase is then a formal specification. In the subsequent activity, this specification is used in combination with simulation tools in order to generate *simulation* traces. Simulation is a very useful tool able to provide a first feedback about the suitability of a solution: for this purpose, tools like SPiM [16] for the stochastic π-calculus have been proved to be quite useful [5,6]. Tools that do not directly support simulation features could be extended by using e.g. the Gillespie algorithm [17], as done for the SPiM simulator [18]. Some general-purpose engine can also be developed to this end, like e.g. the MAUDE term rewriting system module described in [9].

Since self-organising systems tend to display different qualitative dynamics depending on initial conditions, it may happen that simulations of the current design do not exhibit interesting behaviours: the model is then to be tuned until the desired qualitative dynamics is reached. Thus, the parameters employed works as a coarse set of parameters for implementation, while fine tuning is delayed until the actual implementation has been developed. The tuning process may end up with unrealistic values for parameters, or simply may not converge to the required behaviour, meaning that the chosen model cannot be implemented in a real scenario: in this case another approach should be tested, going back to the modelling activity.

2.2   A Basic Architecture for Self-organising Environments

The multi-agent paradigm is a natural choice for modelling natural systems and developing nature-inspired, artificial ones. In particular, in this paper we adopt

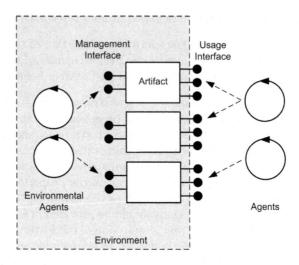

Fig. 1. Basic architecture for a MAS featuring environmental agents as artifacts administrators

the agents & artifacts meta-model (A&A) for MAS, where MAS are modelled and engineered based on two fundamental abstractions: *agents* and *artifacts* [3,19]. Agents are the (pro-)active entities encapsulating control: they are in charge of the goals/tasks that altogether build up the whole MAS behaviour. Artifacts are instead the passive, reactive entities in charge of the services and functions that make individual agents work together in a MAS, and which shape agent environment according to the MAS needs. Other than being an interpretation means for a number of existing concepts in MAS—coordination media, e-institutions, stigmergic fields, web services [3]—this meta-model has also an impact on practise: it is e.g. the basis of the CArtAgO project for developing a general-purpose infrastructure for MAS environments [4].

Based on this meta-model, we focus on the development of environments featuring self-organisation properties, accordingly propose an architectural solution, and then discuss the impact on methodological issues. From the viewpoint of *(user) agents*, that exploit the services provided by artifacts, we see the environment as composed by a set of *environmental agents*, other than the artifacts themselves. As depicted in Figure 1, artifacts exhibit a usage interface which is accessible to user agents, and which provides the artifact services, while the management interface is accessible only to environmental agents, and provides features related to controllability and malleability of artifacts. Environmental agents are in charge of managing resources—say, in an Autonomic Computing style—by adjusting artifact behaviour and status, and by performing periodic administration tasks, possibly taking part in the self-organisation process that the environment should globally exhibit. In particular, this architecture supports the positive/negative feedback loop together with agents: since self-organisation is an active process, it is often the case that artifacts alone cannot close the feedback loop because of the lack of pro-activity, which is instead featured by environmental agents.[1]

2.3   Relating the Methodology to the Architecture

Modelling. When modelling an environment according to our architecture, we have to consider three elements: *(i)* the user agents requesting services, *(ii)* the artifacts providing the interface to the services, and *(iii)* the environmental agents administering the artifacts and driving the self-organisation process (when needed).

Starting from user agents, we observe that they cannot be modelled as fully predictable entities because of their autonomy, and because their behaviour is mostly unknown to the environment designer: abstraction is a necessary process here to cope with the peculiarities of agents to come. Hence, stochastic models are to be used in order to abstract away from agent internal behaviour, simply exposing timing and probability aspects—such as e.g. at which rate they interact with artifacts.

On the other hand, the behaviour of artifacts is predictable by definition, for artifacts automatise the service: hence, in the modelling stage it is typically possible to precisely model their internal state and describe their step-by-step behaviour.

Finally, environmental agents lie somehow in the middle: because they are strongly coupled with artifacts, they are typically designed along with them. Hence, in spite of their autonomy, we can make quite reliable predictions about the behaviour of environmental agents, though stochastic aspects can be anyway useful to model their effect on artifacts.

If the system is designed to exhibit emergent properties, then user and environmental agents are necessarily functionally coupled: such a coupling is required for the positive/negative feedback loop, in that the result of actions performed by user agents eventually triggers a response by environmental agents. Hence, some assumptions about the nature of feedback have to be made: however, these assumptions are not too restrictive, since the set of services offered by the environment is limited.

Simulating. When it comes to simulating, it is necessary to provide a set of operating parameters for the system modelled. It is worth noting that, for the simulation to be meaningful, parameters should represent actual values, otherwise it is not possible to decide about the feasibility of the solution: hence, devising such parameters is probably the most crucial aspect in the simulation

---

[1] It is worth noting that our view of MAS environment should not be considered as a departure from the original idea of the A&A model, where the environment is made by artifacts alone. Indeed, drawing the boundary of the environment is a subjective task: as far as we call "environment" what is outside a particular subset of agents, it could be naturally seen as made of artifacts and by the remaining agents. So, our architecture here is to be considered as a possible specialisation of the A&A meta-model to the case of self-organising environments.

stage. It is then possible to investigate the system global dynamics before actually implement it. In order to preview certain behaviours, it is necessary to sweep through unbounded parameters: tweaking parameters is almost unavoidable since—working with complex systems—small modifications likely lead to qualitatively very different results.

While it is possible to precisely characterise the behaviour of artifacts and environmental agents, we cannot foretell user agents behaviour: then, stochastic and probabilistic models can abstract from those details, though introducing simplifying assumptions that should be later validated. What we actually need is to devise likely scenarios—completeness is typically unfeasible—each of which characterised by a statistical description of user agents' interaction with artifacts. For example, if system behaviour depends on the distribution in time of service requests, it is necessary to investigate several scenario, e.g. even, random, burst distribution and the like. The goal of each simulation is then to understand whether the behaviour of environmental agents is suitable to achieve the properties required.

Tuning. While parameters for artifacts and user agents likely reflect an actual implementation, environmental agents are the real place where tuning occurs: working parameters of environmental agents are to be adjusted, keeping them within the range of physical feasibility, until the system exhibits the desired behaviour. If the required behaviour is not reached with a valid set of parameters, it is then necessary to *tune the model* until such a behaviour is displayed. Modifications usually involve aspects linked to locality and computational cost, that is, in order to make the system converge to the desired state it might be necessary to extended the locality boundaries to let an environmental agent gather further information, or to adopt more sophisticated strategies. However, it is worth noting that pursuing that line too forward moves us away from what is the *self-organisation philosophy* towards the more traditional approach of devising optimal solutions—which typically require too much computational price, and are therefore unsuitable e.g. for on-line tasks.

In the end, it may happen that, despite these modifications, the desired behaviour is not met: then, we have to look for different models and strategies, going back to the modelling stage.

3   Step 1: Modelling the Collective Sort Strategy

In the rest of the article, we apply our methodology to a case we name *collective sort* [9]:

1. we start by defining the problem and identifying key aspects of a possible solution;
2. the strategy is translated into a suitable formalism, enabling the execution of stochastic simulations and analysis of results;
3. variations on the strategy can be evaluated by tuning system model so as to increase the expected performance.

3.1 Motivation and Problem Description

We aim at developing an environment that keeps similar tuples—i.e. having the same template—clustered in the same tuple space, uniformly distributing the load across the nodes where tuple spaces reside. In several scenarios, sorting tuples may increase the overall system performance. For instance, it can make it easier for an agent to find an information of interest based on its previous experience: the probability of finding an information where a related one was previously found is high. Moreover, when tuple spaces contain tuples of one kind only, it is possible to apply aggregation techniques to improve performance, and it is generally easier to manage and achieve load-balancing.

Increasing system order however comes at a computational price. Since we want the sorting process to take place on-line and in background, we look for suboptimal algorithms, which are able to guarantee a certain degree of ordering in time without requiring too much computational power. To this purpose, we look at existing self-organising systems to find one that exhibits this capability of sorting items: in particular, we identify a suitable solution in the *brood sorting* problem of swarm intelligence [8]. In brood sorting, ants cluster broods that were initially dispersed in the environment: although the actual behaviour of ants is still not fully understood, there are several models that are able to mimic the dynamics of the system. Ants behaviour is modelled by two probabilities [8], respectively, the probability to pick up P_p and drop P_d an item

$$P_p = \left(\frac{k_1}{k_1 + f} \right)^2, \quad P_d = \left(\frac{f}{k_2 + f} \right)^2, \tag{1}$$

where k_1 and k_2 are constant parameters, and f is the number of items perceived by an ant in its neighbourhood and may be evaluated with respect to the recently encountered items. To evaluate the system dynamics, it could be useful to provide a metric for system order: such an estimation can be obtained by measuring the spatial entropy, as done e.g. in [20]. Basically, the environment is subdivided into nodes, and P_i is the fraction of items within a node, hence the local entropy is $H_i = -P_i \log P_i$. The sum of H_i having $P_i > 0$ gives an estimation of the order of the entire system, which is supposed to decrease in time, hopefully reaching zero (complete clustering).

We aim at generalising this approach for an arbitrary number of item kinds, and we call it *collective sort*. We conceive this environment itself as a MAS, i.e. made of artifacts and environmental agents: the goal of these agents is to collect and move tuples across the environment so as to order them according to an arbitrary shared criterion. We consider the case of a fixed number of tuple spaces hosting tuples of a known set of tuple types: the goal of agents is to move tuples from one tuple space to another until the tuples are clustered within different tuple spaces according to their tuple type.

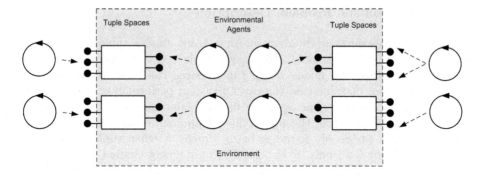

Fig. 2. The basic architecture consists in a set of environmental agents moving tuples across tuple spaces

3.2   A Solution to the Collective Sort Problem

The basic bricks are user agents and tuple spaces (realised through artifacts): user agents are allowed to read, insert and remove tuples in the tuple spaces. Transparently to user agents, the environment provides a sorting service in order to maintain a certain degree of ordering of tuples in tuple spaces. This functionality is realised by a class of environmental agents that is responsible for the sorting task. Hence, each tuple space is associated with one or more environmental agents—see Figure 2—whose task is to compare the content of the local tuple space against the content of another tuple space in the environment, and possibly move some tuple. Since we want to perform this task on-line and in background we cannot compute the probabilities in Equation 1 to decide whether to move or not a tuple: the approach would not be scalable since it requires to count all the tuples for each tuple space, which might not be practical.

Hence, we devise a strategy based on tuple sampling, and suppose that tuple spaces provide for a reading primitive we call **urd**, *uniform read*. This is a variant of the standard **rd** primitive that takes a tuple template and yields any tuple matching the template: primitive **urd** instead chooses the tuple in a probabilistic way among all the tuples that could be returned. For instance, if a tuple space has 10 copies of tuple $t(1)$ and 20 copies of tuple $t(2)$ then the probability that operation $urd(t(X))$ returns $t(2)$ is twice as much as $t(1)$'s. As standard Linda-like tuple spaces typically do not implement this variant, it can e.g. be supported by some more expressive model like ReSpecT tuple centres [21]. When deciding to move a tuple, an agent working on the tuple space TS_S follows this agenda:

1. it draws a destination tuple space TS_D different from the source one TS_S;
2. it draws a kind k of tuple;
3. it (uniformly) reads a tuple T_1 from TS_S;
4. it (uniformly) reads a tuple T_2 from TS_D;
5. if the kind of T_2 is k and it differs from the kind of T_1, then it moves a tuple of the kind k from TS_S to TS_D.

The point of last task is that if those conditions hold, then the number of tuples k in TS_D is more likely to be higher than in TS_S, therefore a tuple could/should be moved. It is important that all choices are performed according to a uniform probability distribution: while in the steps 1 and 2 this guarantees fairness, in steps 3 and 4 it guarantees that the obtained ordering is appropriate.

It is worth noting that the success of this distributed algorithm is an emergent property, affected by both probability and timing aspects. Will complete ordering be reached starting from a completely chaotic situation? Will complete ordering be reached starting from the case where all tuples occur in just one tuple space? And if ordering is reached, how many moving attempts are globally necessary? These are the sort of questions that could be addressed at the early stages of design, thanks to a simulation tool.

4   Step 2: Simulating the Collective Sort Strategy

In this section we briefly describe simulation results obtained by using the MAUDE tool. MAUDE is a high-performance reflective language supporting both equational and rewriting logic specifications, for specifying a wide range of applications [22]. Since MAUDE does not directly provide any facility for simulation purposes, we developed a general simulation framework for stochastic systems: the idea of this tool is to model a stochastic system by a labelled transition system where transitions are of the kind $S \xrightarrow{r:a} S'$, meaning that the system in state S can move to state S' by action a, where r is the *(global) rate* of action a in state S—that is, its occurring frequency. We do not describe here the simulation framework since that would requires a separate treatment: interested readers can refer to [9] for more details about MAUDE and a comprehensive description of our framework.

Given the strategy described in Section 3.2, we translated it into the MAUDE syntax. Our reference case sticks to the case where four tuple spaces exist, and four tuple kinds are subject to ordering: we represent the distributed state of a system in MAUDE using a syntax of the kind:

```
< 0 @ ('a[100])|('b[100])|('c[10])|('d[10]) > |
< 1 @ ('a[0])   |('b[100])|('c[10])|('d[10]) > |
< 2 @ ('a[10])  |('b[50]) |('c[50])|('d[10]) > |
< 3 @ ('a[50])  |('b[10]) |('c[10])|('d[50]) >
```

It expresses the fact that we work with the tuple kinds 'a, 'b, 'c, and 'd, and with the tuple spaces identifiers 0, 1, 2, and 3. The content of a tuple space 0 is expressed as < 0 @ ('a[100])|('b[100])|('c[10])|('d[10]) >, meaning that we have 100 tuples of kind 'a, 100 of kind 'b, 10 of 'c, and 10 of 'd. The formal definition of agents agenda is defined in terms of simple transition rules. The chart in Figure 3 reports the dynamics of the winning tuple in each tuple space, showing e.g. that complete sorting is reached at different times in each space. The chart in Figure 4 displays instead the evolution of the tuple space 0: notice that only the tuple kind 'a aggregates here despite its initial concentration was the same of tuple kind 'b.

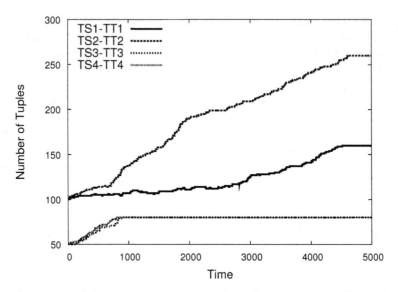

Fig. 3. Dynamics of the winning tuple in each tuple space: notice that each tuple aggregates in a different tuples space

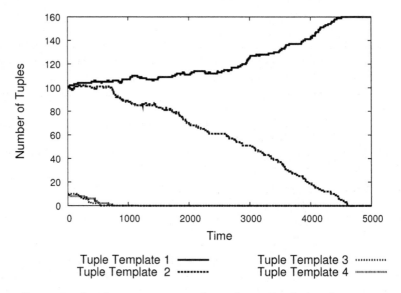

Fig. 4. Dynamic of tuple space 0: notice that only one kind of tuple aggregates here

Although it would be possible to make some prediction, we do not know in general which tuple space will host a specific tuple kind at the end of sorting: this is an emergent property of the system and is the very result of the *interaction* of environmental agents through the tuple spaces. It is interesting to analyse the trend of the entropy of each tuple space as a way to estimate the degree of order

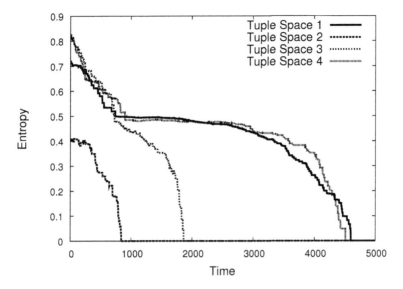

Fig. 5. Entropy of tuple spaces in the constant rate case: they all eventually reach 0, that is, complete ordering

in the system through a single value: since the strategy we simulate is trying to increase the inner order of the system we expect the entropy to decrease, as it actually happens as shown in Figure 5.

5   Step 3: Tuning the Collective Sort Strategy

Such a strategy based on constant rates is not very efficient, since agents are assigned to a certain tuple space and keep working also if the tuple space is already ordered. We may exploit this otherwise wasted computational power by assigning idle agents to unordered tuple spaces, or rather, by dynamically adapting the working rates of agents. This alternative therefore looks suited to realise a strategy to more quickly reach the complete ordering of tuple spaces.

   In order to adapt the agents rate, we adopted spatial entropy as a measure of system order. If we denote with q_{ij} the amount of tuples of the kind i within the tuple space j, n_j the total number of tuples within the tuple space j, and k the number of tuple kinds, then, the entropy associated with the tuple kind i within the tuple space j is

$$H_{ij} = \frac{q_{ij}}{n_j} \log_2 \frac{n_j}{q_{ij}} \tag{2}$$

and it is easy to notice that $0 \leq H_{ij} \leq \frac{1}{k} \log_2 k$. We want to express now the entropy associated with a single tuple space

$$H_j = \frac{\sum_{i=1}^{k} H_{ij}}{\log_2 k} \tag{3}$$

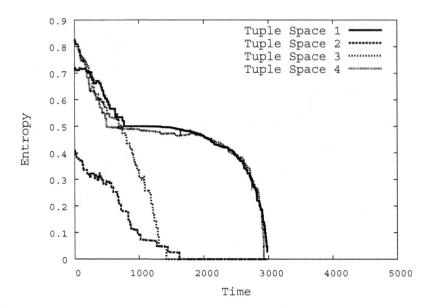

Fig. 6. Entropy of tuple spaces in the variable rate case: the system reaches the complete ordering since step 3000

where the division by $\log_2 k$ is introduced in order to obtain $0 \leq H_j \leq 1$. If we have t tuple spaces then the entropy of the system is

$$H = \frac{1}{t} \sum_{j=1}^{t} H_j \qquad (4)$$

where the division by t is used to normalise H, so that $0 \leq H \leq 1$. Being t the number of tuple spaces then it also represents the number of agents: let each agent work at rate $H_j r$, and tr be the maximum rate allocated to the sorting task. If we want to adapt the working rates of agents we have to scale their rate by the total system entropy, since we have that

$$\gamma \sum_{j=1}^{t} r H_j = tr \Rightarrow \gamma = \frac{t}{\sum_{j=1}^{t} H_j} = \frac{1}{H} \qquad (5)$$

then each agent will work at rate $\frac{r H_j}{H}$ where H_j and H are computed periodically.

Using *load balancing* we introduced *dynamism* in our model: indeed in each simulation step the activity rate associated with a tuple space—i.e. the probability at a given step that an agent of the tuple space is working—is no longer fixed, but it depends on the entropy of the tuple space itself. Hence, as explained above, agents belonging to completely ordered tuple spaces can consider their goal as being achieved, and hence they no longer execute tasks. Moreover, this strategy guarantees a better efficiency in load balancing: agents working on tuple

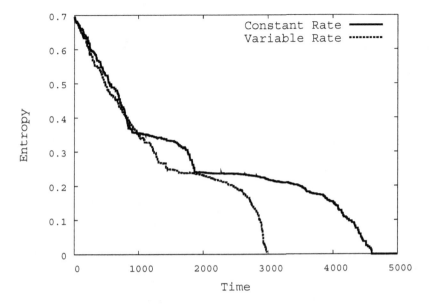

Fig. 7. Comparison of global entropy in the case of constant and variable rate: the latter reaches the complete ordering quicker

spaces with higher entropy, have a greater activity rate than others working on more ordered tuple spaces.

Using the collective sort specification with variable rates, we ran a simulation having the same initial state of the one in Section 4: the chart of Figure 6 shows the trend of the entropy of each tuple space. Comparing the chart with the one in Figure 5, we can observe that the entropies reach 0 faster than the case with constant rates: in fact, at step 3000 every entropy within the chart in Figure 6 is 0, while with constant rates the same result is reached only after 4600 steps in Figure 5. The chart in Figure 7 compares the evolution of global entropy (see Equation 5) in the case of constant and variable rates: the trend of the two entropies represents a further proof that variable rates guarantee a faster stabilisation of the system, i.e. its complete ordering.

6   Related Works

Since the environment plays a crucial role in MASs, existing methodologies are incorporating guidelines for environment design. Furthermore, there exist a few methodologies also considering issues related to self-organization: we will briefly describe some of these methodologies and design practices.

In [14] it is recognised that traditional methodologies cannot help complex systems engineers: indeed, the required coordination between components is incompatible with the decomposition approach. We agree with that consideration and do not follow the decomposition approach, rather look for suitable solutions among the catalogue of known self-organising systems. Furthermore, in [14] some useful guidelines are provided for the engineering process, although they are not organised in an actual methodology.

In [23] an architecture for MAS-based manufacturing control application is described. In particular, they describe an architecture and a case study which initial solution is inspired by stigmergy in ant colonies: although, they do not provide any hints on how to apply their approach to other domains or problems.

A more general approach is presented in [24] and focuses on reactive MAS for collective problem solving. A problem model is specified in the environment and constraints are assimilated to environment perturbations: agents collectively solve the problem by regulating environment perturbations. Hence, the MAS as a whole acts as a regulation process, in a way similar to automatic control. The methodology proposed is articulated in four steps, namely (i) defining the problem model, (ii) defining agent perceptions, (iii) defining agent interaction mechanisms and (iv) measuring the result as an emergent structure [24]. Although, methodology mainly focuses on problem solving suggesting that it is not well suited for environments as service providers. Instead, the main focus of our contribution is on developing a methodology for environments offering services with self-* capabilities, where environment is conceived as a run-time entity.

A more comprehensive methodology explicitly tailored for self-organising systems is ADELFE [13] which covers all the steps involved in adaptive systems engineering. Nonetheless, the authors overlooked the two most important issues in self-organization, that is (i) a general approach for devising a solution by emergence and (ii) metrics and performance assessment of the solution provided. Our approach, compared to ADELFE, is less comprehensive: composing them would however be an interesting future work.

7   Conclusion and Future Work

In this article we discuss an approach to the design of self-organising MAS environments: as far as methodological aspects are concerned, the approach relies on formal methods and tools for modelling and performing stochastic simulations. We briefly describe our A&A meta-model for MAS based on agents and artifacts, and discuss a basic architecture for self-organising environments: this solution features environmental agents as artifacts managers for the self-organisation process.

To better clarify our approach, we consider the case of a self-organising environment featuring automatic clustering of tuples of the same kind. The solution to this problem, that we call *collective sort*, has been derived from the swarm intelligence problem known as *brood sorting*, which we consider as a paradigmatic application of emergent coordination through the environment. Then, we elaborate on the idea of collective sort by evaluating entropy as a possible metric to drive the self-organisation process, showing its effectiveness.

Currently, we are working to refine the simulation framework developed on top of MAUDE, and to implement the collective sort application in TuCSoN. Future works include

- deeper testing of the convergence properties of the strategy;
- applying advancements in the field of formal methods, for the analysis of system specifications;
- identifying applicable patterns from self-organisation theory to the engineering of MAS environments.

References

1. Weyns, D., Omicini, A., Odell, J.: Environment as a first-class abstraction in multi-agent systems. Autonomous Agents and Multi-Agent Systems **14**(1) (2007) 5–30 Special Issue on Environments for Multi-agent Systems.
2. Viroli, M., Holvoet, T., Ricci, A., Shelfthout, K., Zambonelli, F.: Infrastructures for the environment of multiagent systems. Autonomous Agents and Multi-Agent Systems **14**(1) (2007) 49–60 Special Issue on Environments for Multi-agent Systems.
3. Omicini, A., Ricci, A., Viroli, M.: *Agens Faber*: Toward a theory of artefacts for MAS. Electronic Notes in Theoretical Computer Sciences **150**(3) (2006) 21–36 1st International Workshop "Coordination and Organization" (CoOrg 2005), COORDINATION 2005, Namur, Belgium, 22 April 2005. Proceedings.
4. Ricci, A., Viroli, M., Omicini, A.: *Construenda est* CArtAgO: Toward an infrastructure for artifacts in MAS. In Trappl, R., ed.: Cybernetics and Systems 2006. Volume 2., Vienna, Austria, Austrian Society for Cybernetic Studies (2006) 569–574 18th European Meeting on Cybernetics and Systems Research (EMCSR 2006), 5th International Symposium "From Agent Theory to Theory Implementation" (AT2AI-5). Proceedings.
5. Gardelli, L., Viroli, M., Omicini, A.: On the role of simulations in engineering self-organising MAS: The case of an intrusion detection system in TuCSoN. In Brueckner, S.A., Di Marzo Serugendo, G., Hales, D., Zambonelli, F., eds.: Engineering Self-Organising Systems. Volume 3910 of LNAI. Springer (2006) 153–168 3rd International Workshop (ESOA 2005), Utrecht, The Netherlands, 26 July 2005. Revised Selected Papers.
6. Gardelli, L., Viroli, M., Omicini, A.: Exploring the dynamics of self-organising systems with stochastic π-calculus: Detecting abnormal behaviour in MAS. In Trappl, R., ed.: Cybernetics and Systems 2006. Volume 2., Vienna, Austria, Austrian Society for Cybernetic Studies (2006) 539–544 18th European Meeting on Cybernetics and Systems Research (EMCSR 2006), 5th International Symposium "From Agent Theory to Theory Implementation" (AT2AI-5). Proceedings.
7. Kephart, J.O., Chess, D.M.: The vision of autonomic computing. Computer **36**(1) (2003) 41–50
8. Bonabeau, E., Dorigo, M., Theraulaz, G.: Swarm Intelligence: From Natural to Artificial Systems. Santa Fe Institute Studies in the Sciences of Complexity. Oxford University Press (1999)

9. Casadei, M., Gardelli, L., Viroli, M.: Simulating emergent properties of coordination in Maude: the collective sorting case. In Canal, C., Viroli, M., eds.: 5th International Workshop on Foundations of Coordination Languages and Software Architectures (FOCLASA'06), CONCUR 2006, Bonn, Germany, University of Málaga, Spain (2006) Proceedings.

10. Camazine, S., Deneubourg, J.L., Franks, N.R., Sneyd, J., Theraulaz, G., Bonabeau, E.: Self-Organization in Biological Systems. Princeton Studies in Complexity. Princeton University Press (2001)

11. Zambonelli, F., Jennings, N.R., Wooldridge, M.J.: Developing multiagent systems: The Gaia methodology. ACM Transactions on Software Engineering and Methodology (TOSEM) **12**(3) (2003) 317–370

12. Molesini, A., Omicini, A., Denti, E., Ricci, A.: SODA: A roadmap to artefacts. In Dikenelli, O., Gleizes, M.P., Ricci, A., eds.: Engineering Societies in the Agents World VI. Volume 3963 of LNAI. Springer (2006) 49–62 6th International Workshop (ESAW 2005), Kuşadası, Aydın, Turkey, 26–28 October 2005. Revised, Selected & Invited Papers.

13. Bernon, C., Gleizes, M.P., Peyruqueou, S., Picard, G.: ADELFE: A methodology for adaptive multi-agent systems engineering. In Petta, P., Tolksdorf, R., Zambonelli, F., eds.: Engineering Societies in the Agents World III. Volume 2577 of LNAI. Springer (2003) 156–169 3rd International Workshop (ESAW 2002), Madrid, Spain, 16–17September2002. Revised Papers.

14. Bar-Yam, Y.: About engineering complex systems: Multiscale analysis and evolutionary engineering. In Brueckner, S.A., Serugendo, G.D.M., Karageorgos, A., Nagpal, R., eds.: Engineering Self-Organising Systems: Methodologies and Applications. Volume 3464 of LNCS. Springer (2005) 16–31 The Second International Workshop on Engineering Self-Organising Applications, ESOA'04, New York, USA, July 20, 2004, Selected Revised and Invited Papers.

15. Mamei, M., Menezes, R., Tolksdorf, R., Zambonelli, F.: Case studies for self-organization in computer science. Journal of Systems Architecture **52**(8–9) (2006) 443–460 Special Issue on Nature-Inspired Applications and Systems.

16. Phillips, A.: The Stochastic Pi Machine (SPiM) (2006) Version 0.042 available online at http://www.doc.ic.ac.uk/~anp/spim/.

17. Gillespie, D.T.: Exact stochastic simulation of coupled chemical reactions. The Journal of Physical Chemistry **81**(25) (1977) 2340–2361

18. Phillips, A., Cardelli, L.: A correct abstract machine for the stochastic Pi-calculus. In Ingolfsdottir, A., Nielson, H.R., eds.: Workshop on Concurrent Models in Molecular Biology (BioConcur 2004), CONCUR 2004, London, UK (2004)

19. Ricci, A., Viroli, M., Omicini, A.: Programming MAS with artifacts. In Bordini, R.P., Dastani, M., Dix, J., El Fallah Seghrouchni, A., eds.: Programming Multi-Agent Systems. Volume 3862 of LNAI. Springer (2006) 206–221 3rd International Workshop (PROMAS 2005), AAMAS 2005, Utrecht, The Netherlands, 26 July 2005. Revised and Invited Papers.

20. Gutowitz, H.: Complexity-seeking ants. In Deneubourg, J.L., Goss, S., Nicolis, G., eds.: 2nd European Conference on Artificial Life (ECAL'93), Brussels, Belgium (1993) 429–439

21. Omicini, A., Denti, E.: From tuple spaces to tuple centres. Science of Computer Programming **41**(3) (2001) 277–294

22. Clavel, M., Duràn, F., Eker, S., Lincoln, P., Martí-Oliet, N., Meseguer, J., Talcott, C.: Maude Manual. Department of Computer Science University of Illinois at Urbana-Champaign. (2005) Version 2.2.

23. Valckenaers, P., Holvoet, T.: The environment: An essential absraction for managing complexity in mas-based manufacturing control. In Weyns, D., Parunak, H.V., Michel, F., eds.: Environments for Multi-Agent Systems II. Volume 3830 of LNCS. Springer (2006) 205–217 Second International Workshop, E4MAS 2005, Utrecht, The Netherlands, July 25, 2005, Selected Revised and Invited Papers.
24. Simonin, O., Gechter, F.: An environment-based methodology to design reactive multi-agent systems for problem solving. In Weyns, D., Parunak, H.V., Michel, F., eds.: Environments for Multi-Agent Systems II. Volume 3830 of LNCS. Springer (2006) 32–49 Second International Workshop, E4MAS 2005, Utrecht, The Netherlands, July 25, 2005, Selected Revised and Invited Papers.

Author Index

Lecture Notes in Artificial Intelligence (LNAI)

Vol. 4198: O. Nasraoui, O. Zaïane, M. Spiliopoulou, B. Mobasher, B. Masand, P.S. Yu (Eds.), Advances in Web Mining and Web Usage Analysis. IX, 177 pages. 2006.

Vol. 4196: K. Fischer, I.J. Timm, E. André, N. Zhong (Eds.), Multiagent System Technologies. X, 185 pages. 2006.

Vol. 4188: P. Sojka, I. Kopeček, K. Pala (Eds.), Text, Speech and Dialogue. XV, 721 pages. 2006.

Vol. 4183: J. Euzenat, J. Domingue (Eds.), Artificial Intelligence: Methodology, Systems, and Applications. XIII, 291 pages. 2006.

Vol. 4180: M. Kohlhase, OMDoc – An Open Markup Format for Mathematical Documents [version 1.2]. XIX, 428 pages. 2006.

Vol. 4177: R. Marín, E. Onaindía, A. Bugarín, J. Santos (Eds.), Current Topics in Artificial Intelligence. XV, 482 pages. 2006.

Vol. 4160: M. Fisher, W. van der Hoek, B. Konev, A. Lisitsa (Eds.), Logics in Artificial Intelligence. XII, 516 pages. 2006.

Vol. 4155: O. Stock, M. Schaerf (Eds.), Reasoning, Action and Interaction in AI Theories and Systems. XVIII, 343 pages. 2006.

Vol. 4149: M. Klusch, M. Rovatsos, T.R. Payne (Eds.), Cooperative Information Agents X. XII, 477 pages. 2006.

Vol. 4140: J.S. Sichman, H. Coelho, S.O. Rezende (Eds.), Advances in Artificial Intelligence - IBERAMIA-SBIA 2006. XXIII, 635 pages. 2006.

Vol. 4139: T. Salakoski, F. Ginter, S. Pyysalo, T. Pahikkala (Eds.), Advances in Natural Language Processing. XVI, 771 pages. 2006.

Vol. 4133: J. Gratch, M. Young, R. Aylett, D. Ballin, P. Olivier (Eds.), Intelligent Virtual Agents. XIV, 472 pages. 2006.

Vol. 4130: U. Furbach, N. Shankar (Eds.), Automated Reasoning. XV, 680 pages. 2006.

Vol. 4120: J. Calmet, T. Ida, D. Wang (Eds.), Artificial Intelligence and Symbolic Computation. XIII, 269 pages. 2006.

Vol. 4118: Z. Despotovic, S. Joseph, C. Sartori (Eds.), Agents and Peer-to-Peer Computing. XIV, 173 pages. 2006.

Vol. 4114: D.-S. Huang, K. Li, G.W. Irwin (Eds.), Computational Intelligence, Part II. XXVII, 1337 pages. 2006.

Vol. 4108: J.M. Borwein, W.M. Farmer (Eds.), Mathematical Knowledge Management. VIII, 295 pages. 2006.

Vol. 4106: T.R. Roth-Berghofer, M.H. Göker, H.A. Güvenir (Eds.), Advances in Case-Based Reasoning. XIV, 566 pages. 2006.

Vol. 4099: Q. Yang, G. Webb (Eds.), PRICAI 2006: Trends in Artificial Intelligence. XXVIII, 1263 pages. 2006.

Vol. 4095: S. Nolfi, G. Baldassarre, R. Calabretta, J.C.T. Hallam, D. Marocco, J.-A. Meyer, O. Miglino, D. Parisi (Eds.), From Animals to Animats 9. XV, 869 pages. 2006.

Vol. 4093: X. Li, O.R. Zaïane, Z. Li (Eds.), Advanced Data Mining and Applications. XXI, 1110 pages. 2006.

Vol. 4092: J. Lang, F. Lin, J. Wang (Eds.), Knowledge Science, Engineering and Management. XV, 664 pages. 2006.

Vol. 4088: Z.-Z. Shi, R. Sadananda (Eds.), Agent Computing and Multi-Agent Systems. XVII, 827 pages. 2006.

Vol. 4087: F. Schwenker, S. Marinai (Eds.), Artificial Neural Networks in Pattern Recognition. IX, 299 pages. 2006.

Vol. 4068: H. Schärfe, P. Hitzler, P. Øhrstrøm (Eds.), Conceptual Structures: Inspiration and Application. XI, 455 pages. 2006.

Vol. 4065: P. Perner (Ed.), Advances in Data Mining. XI, 592 pages. 2006.

Vol. 4062: G.-Y. Wang, J.F. Peters, A. Skowron, Y. Yao (Eds.), Rough Sets and Knowledge Technology. XX, 810 pages. 2006.

Vol. 4049: S. Parsons, N. Maudet, P. Moraitis, I. Rahwan (Eds.), Argumentation in Multi-Agent Systems. XIV, 313 pages. 2006.

Vol. 4048: L. Goble, J.-J.C.. Meyer (Eds.), Deontic Logic and Artificial Normative Systems. X, 273 pages. 2006.

Vol. 4045: D. Barker-Plummer, R. Cox, N. Swoboda (Eds.), Diagrammatic Representation and Inference. XII, 301 pages. 2006.

Vol. 4031: M. Ali, R. Dapoigny (Eds.), Advances in Applied Artificial Intelligence. XXIII, 1353 pages. 2006.

Vol. 4029: L. Rutkowski, R. Tadeusiewicz, L.A. Zadeh, J.M. Zurada (Eds.), Artificial Intelligence and Soft Computing – ICAISC 2006. XXI, 1235 pages. 2006.

Vol. 4027: H.L. Larsen, G. Pasi, D. Ortiz-Arroyo, T. Andreasen, H. Christiansen (Eds.), Flexible Query Answering Systems. XVIII, 714 pages. 2006.

Vol. 4021: E. André, L. Dybkjær, W. Minker, H. Neumann, M. Weber (Eds.), Perception and Interactive Technologies. XI, 217 pages. 2006.

Vol. 4020: A. Bredenfeld, A. Jacoff, I. Noda, Y. Takahashi (Eds.), RoboCup 2005: Robot Soccer World Cup IX. XVII, 727 pages. 2006.

Vol. 4013: L. Lamontagne, M. Marchand (Eds.), Advances in Artificial Intelligence. XIII, 564 pages. 2006.

Vol. 4012: T. Washio, A. Sakurai, K. Nakajima, H. Takeda, S. Tojo, M. Yokoo (Eds.), New Frontiers in Artificial Intelligence. XIII, 484 pages. 2006.

Vol. 4008: J.C. Augusto, C.D. Nugent (Eds.), Designing Smart Homes. XI, 183 pages. 2006.

Vol. 4005: G. Lugosi, H.U. Simon (Eds.), Learning Theory. XI, 656 pages. 2006.

Vol. 4002: A. Yli-Jyrä, L. Karttunen, J. Karhumäki (Eds.), Finite-State Methods and Natural Language Processing. XIV, 312 pages. 2006.

Vol. 3978: B. Hnich, M. Carlsson, F. Fages, F. Rossi (Eds.), Recent Advances in Constraints. VIII, 179 pages. 2006.

Vol. 3963: O. Dikenelli, M.-P. Gleizes, A. Ricci (Eds.), Engineering Societies in the Agents World VI. XII, 303 pages. 2006.